# WOMEN ICONS OF POPULAR MUSIC

**Recent Titles in**
**Greenwood Icons**

Icons of Business: An Encyclopedia of Mavericks, Movers, and Shakers
*Edited by Kateri Drexler*

Icons of Hip Hop: An Encyclopedia of the Movement, Music, and Culture
*Edited by Mickey Hess*

Icons of Evolution: An Encyclopedia of People, Evidence, and Controversies
*Edited by Brian Regal*

Icons of Rock: An Encyclopedia of the Legends Who Changed Music
Forever
*Scott Schinder and Andy Schwartz*

Icons of R&B and Soul: An Encyclopedia of the Artists Who
Revolutionized Rhythm
*Bob Gulla*

African American Icons of Sport: Triumph, Courage, and Excellence
*Matthew C. Whitaker*

Icons of the American West: From Cowgirls to Silicon Valley
*Edited by Gordon Morris Bakken*

Icons of Latino America: Latino Contributions to American Culture
*Roger Bruns*

Icons of Crime Fighting: Relentless Pursuers of Justice
*Edited by Jeffrey Bumgarner*

Icons of Unbelief: Atheists, Agnostics, and Secularists
*Edited by S.T. Joshi*

# WOMEN ICONS OF POPULAR MUSIC

## The Rebels, Rockers, and Renegades

## VOLUME 1

## Carrie Havranek

Greenwood Icons

Greenwood Icons

**Institute** of Production & Recording

GREENWOOD PRESS
Westport, Connecticut · London

Library of Congress Cataloging-in-Publication Data

Havranek, Carrie, 1974–
Women icons of popular music : the rebels, rockers, and renegades / Carrie Havranek.
   v. cm. — (Greenwood icons)
  Includes bibliographicval references, discographies, and index.
  Contents: Vol. 1. Tori Amos; Joan Baez; Mary J. Blige; Patsy Cline; Ani DiFranco;
Missy Elliott; Aretha Franklin; Emmylou Harris; Debbie Harry; Chrissie Hynde; The Indigo
Girls; Janis Joplin — Vol. 2. Carole King; Madonna; Sarah McLachlan; Joni Mitchell;
Dolly Parton; Liz Phair; Bonnie Raitt; Linda Ronstadt; Diana Ross; Patti Smith; Tina Turner;
Suzanne Vega.
  ISBN 978-0-313-34083-3 ((set) : alk. paper) — ISBN 978-0-313-34084-0
((vol. 1) : alk. paper) — ISBN 978-0-313-34085-7 ((vol. 2) : alk. paper)
  1. Women singers.  2. Women rock musicians.  I. Title.
ML82.H39 2009
782.42164092′273—dc22
[B]                    2008027475

British Library Cataloguing in Publication Data is available.

Library of Congress Catalog Card Number: 2008027475

ISBN: 978–0–313–34083–3 (set)
     978–0–313–34084–0 (Volume 1)
     978–0–313–34085–7 (Volume 2)

First published in 2009

Greenwood Press, 88 Post Road West, Westport, CT 06881
An imprint of Greenwood Publishing Group, Inc.
www.greenwood.com

Printed in the United States of America

The paper used in this book complies with the
Permanent Paper Standard issued by the National
Information Standards Organization (Z39.48-1984).

10 9 8 7 6 5 4 3 2 1

# Contents

## Volume Two

# List of Photos

Tori Amos (page 1) performs on *Last Call with Carson Daly* (NBC), 2005. Courtesy of Photofest.

Joan Baez (page 23). Courtesy of Photofest.

Mary Blige (page 45) performs at NBC's *Radio Awards*, 2005. Courtesy of Photofest.

Patsy Cline (page 65), circa 1950s. Courtesy of Photofest.

Ani DiFranco (page 85) poses for a portrait at her home in New Orleans, Dec. 30, 2003. AP/Wide World Photos.

Missy Elliott (page 105), circa early 2001. Courtesy of Photofest.

Aretha Franklin (page 121) plays and sings during a recording session for Columbia Records in New York, 1961. Frank Driggs Collection/Getty Images.

Emmylou Harris (page 141) performs on *Good Morning America* (ABC) on June 28, 2002. Courtesy of Photofest.

Debbie Harry (page 161), circa 1970s. Courtesy of Photofest.

Chrissie Hynde (page 179) of the Pretenders. Courtesy of Sire/Photofest.

Indigo Girls Amy Ray and Emily Saliers (page 195), 2004. Courtesy of Photofest.

Janis Joplin (page 213), circa 1969. Courtesy of Photofest.

Carole King (page 233), during the 1970s. Courtesy of Photofest.

Madonna (page 253) performs at New York's Madison Square Garden during her Reinvention Tour, 2004. AP/Wide World Photos.

Sarah McLachlan (page 273) performs in her hometown of Halifax on Wednesday, June 1, 2005. AP/Wide World Photos.

Joni Mitchell (page 293), outside The Revolution Club in London, 1968. © Central Press/Getty Images.

Dolly Parton (page 315), circa 1990s. Courtesy of Photofest.

Liz Phair (page 335) lays down some guitar licks, 1994. © Tom Maday/Time Life Pictures/Getty Images.

Bonnie Raitt (page 353), 1995. Courtesy of Photofest.

Linda Ronstadt (page 375), circa mid-1970s. Courtesy of Photofest.

Diana Ross (page 397) performs in the rain at New York City's Central Park, 1983. AP/Wide World Photos.

Patti Smith (page 419), as photographed by Robert Mapplethorpe, circa 1975, for her album *Horses*. Courtesy of Photofest.

Tina Turner (page 439) launches her *Break Every Rule* tour in Munich, Germany, in 1987. AP/Wide World Photos.

Suzanne Vega (page 459) performs at the Palace of Arts in Budapest, Hungary, 2006. AP/Wide World Photos.

# Series Foreword

Worshipped and cursed. Loved and loathed. Obsessed about the world over. What does it take to become an icon? Regardless of subject, culture, or era, the requisite qualifications are the same: (1) challenge the status quo, (2) influence millions, and (3) impact history.

Using these criteria, Greenwood Press introduces a new reference format and approach to popular culture. Spanning a wide range of subjects, volumes in the Greenwood Icons series provide students and general readers a port of entry into the most fascinating and influential topics of the day. Every title offers an in-depth look at approximately twenty-four iconic figures, each of which captures the essence of a broad subject. These icons typically embody a group of values, elicit strong reactions, reflect the essence of a particular time and place, and link different traditions and periods. Among those featured are artists and activists, superheroes and spies, inventors and athletes, the legends and mythmakers of entire generations. Yet icons can also come from unexpected places: as the heroine who transcends the pages of a novel or as the revolutionary idea that shatters our previously held beliefs. Whether people, places, or things, such icons serve as a bridge between the past and the present, the canonical and the contemporary. By focusing on icons central to popular culture, this series encourages students to appreciate cultural diversity and critically analyze issues of enduring significance.

Most important, these books are as entertaining as they are provocative. Is Disneyland a more influential icon of the American West than Las Vegas? How do ghosts and ghouls reflect our collective psyche? Is Barry Bonds an inspiring or deplorable icon of baseball?

Designed to foster debate, the series serves as a unique resource that is ideal for paper writing or report purposes. Insightful, in-depth entries provide far more information than conventional reference articles but are less intimidating and more accessible than a book-length biography. The most revered and reviled icons of American and world history are brought to life with related sidebars, timelines, fact boxes, and quotations. Authoritative entries are accompanied by bibliographies, making these titles an ideal starting point for further research. Spanning a wide range of popular topics, including business, literature, civil rights, politics, music, and more, books in the series provide fresh insights for the student and popular reader into the power and influence of icons, a topic of as vital interest today as in any previous era.

# Acknowledgments

This project would not have been possible without the literal, spiritual, and metaphorical help of many people. First and immediately, I need to thank my editors at Greenwood, Lindsay Claire and Kristi Ward, for whom no question was too small and for their editorial guidance and sharp insights. Fellow Greenwood author Chris Smith deserves thanks for recommending me for this project. An extension of gratitude goes to Christine Marra, whose keen eye and close attention to detail polished this manuscript to a spit-shine through its final stages. Alexis Walker assisted early on with some sidebar research and writing. Abra Berkowitz, who worked with me as an independent study, needs special mention for her boundless enthusiasm, the old articles she excavated, her passionate questions and exclamatory notes in the margins, the YouTube videos of Joan Baez, and her attention and interest in this project long past the confines of receiving a grade. Her ability to relate to these women, many of whom are exponentially older than her own nineteen years, demonstrates that the appeal of these artists extends far beyond arbitrary designations like age. The interlibrary loan, circulation, and reference staffs of Skillman Library at Lafayette College worked tirelessly to track down obscure pieces of data and procure the many materials necessary to undertake a task of this scope. To them I say: Thank you, thank you, thank you.

I have to thank my parents, Chuck and Susan, who immersed us in a disparate musical environment—Lambert Hendricks and Ross, Barbra Streisand, The Beatles, Cal Tjader, Crosby, Stills, and Nash, and the entire American songbook—which encouraged my curious approach to music and, later, cultural forms in general. My sister Christy offered levity just by being herself; I relied on her entertaining and reassuring responses to my Instant Messenger questions seeking gut-check reactions to a-ha insights throughout my writing. On a professional note, the work of Ellen Willis was an early and significant influence on my thinking (and writing) about feminism, politics, and popular culture. I was blessed to have the opportunity to study with her as a graduate student at New York University, an experience that offered solace that I could possibly make a living writing about music and popular culture. She, along with Susie Linfield, helped me through what then felt like somewhat inchoate responses to the cultural landscape. And the writing of Ann Powers illustrated continuity and gave me hope that women of another generation were still finding much to say—and doing so in artful, provocative ways—about women, music, pop culture, politics, and everything in between.

Finally and most important, none of this would be possible or worthwhile without my husband John, the original, irreplaceable music maker in my life. Thank you, in this case, is an understatement.

# Introduction

What is an icon? What is popular music? What constitutes a female icon in popular music? These are loaded questions, brimming with complicated, discussion-inducing answers. When compiling the list for the twenty-four icons in this book, it was useful to start off by consulting the dictionary. But that move initially made things trickier, as the first definition of the word indicates a pictorial representation, and the second definition involves the creation of a religious image used for devotional purposes. Although some of the icons in this book boast fans who are ardent and dedicated, that connotation does not satisfy, either. The third definition, "an object of uncritical devotion: idol," brings us closer. This definition, though, seems to negate our ability to be discerning and discourages the use of subjectivity, which is delightfully, frustratingly, at the core of listening to and talking about music. Finally, the fourth definition, "emblem, symbol," seems more open-ended and suitable to a wider range of musicians. Regardless of their differences (which we embrace), the women in this two-volume set symbolize a particular moment, aspect, quality, genre, emotion, or memory in the relatively short but extraordinarily diverse twentieth-century convention known as popular music.

In the process of selecting candidates for this book, I discussed with my editors whether or not the artist in question has, during the course of her career, produced compelling material and demonstrated an essential star, or iconic, quality. Furthermore, we also looked at whether she exemplifies an outstanding level of artistic and/or commercial achievement. Artists such as Madonna, Dolly Parton, Diana Ross, and Tina Turner came to mind quickly—women whose grit and determination and pronounced, early ambition set them apart from their peers and catapulted them to international fame and multiplatinum sales. But beyond this stellar success, these women are true trailblazers who influenced many artists who followed—and in some cases also creatively deviated—from their footsteps. Reading the remarkable stories of others—such as Patsy Cline and Janis Joplin—that are comprised of much personal struggle highlighted the inevitability of their success and underscored the sadness of their tragic, early passing. Cline and Joplin have become icons of country-pop crossover and blues-rock, respectively, and their discovery by younger generations of fans and artists via greatest hits collections and boxed sets attests to their powerful legacies.

Admittedly, some of the artists we chose for this volume have not reached multiplatinum commercial sales—at least not yet. But that is not, nor should it be, a determining factor for inclusion; neither is it solely a marker of one's relevance or importance. Such a fact, however, ought not discredit the impact and reach of those whose work means something very specific or captures the zeitgeist in some way. We simply cannot compare the monumental, unprecedented success of Dolly Parton or Madonna—who boast millions of albums sold worldwide—to that of Suzanne Vega, Liz Phair, or Patti Smith, for example. The music world would not be the same without the spare, sensitive, and socially conscious imagery in Suzanne Vega's songwriting. Nor would the landscape of pop music in the late 1990s and onward be the same without risk-takers such as Liz Phair, who boldly tackled the male rock canon of the Rolling Stones on her debut *Exile in Guyville*. Nor would punk-pop be the same without Patti Smith, an unapologetic icon-worshipper herself, and her approach to music as performance art. Ironically, she is iconic herself, embodying a particular downtown–New York aesthetic sensibility. Vega showed other female artists that it was possible to combine the impulses of folk music and reach the masses. Phair's work brought out the latent anger in her female listeners and suggested that it was perfectly justifiable for women to use bluntly honest sexual references and, when necessary, curse words in songwriting. And Smith, an androgynous artist with a capital A, infiltrated the world of Baudelaire and punk rock. Her path created a trajectory for those artists—male and female alike—who felt restricted by what they felt were arbitrary designations, such as gender, even as such artists remain cognizant to the ways in which it informs their process. Idiosyncratic artists such as these (and others found in these two volumes such as Joni Mitchell and Tori Amos) give us permission to have a larger—and necessary—conversation about art, feminism, politics, performance, image, and songwriting.

We also took into consideration the formative impact these female performers had on other artists, whether that meant contemporaries or future generations. Many of the sidebars to the entries are devoted to some of those deserving female artists whose careers could not be overlooked because they showed a lineage to the women in this set. For example, the sidebar in the entry on Patsy Cline, a firecracker of a woman with a big, confident voice, focuses on the Dixie Chicks, whose crossover success in the pop world from country music and outspoken ways illustrate a direct link to Cline.

The sidebars also enable an exploration of trends and moments in popular music as they pertain to these women. We are able to explore in detail, for example, Lilith Fair, a traveling concert full of female artists organized by

Sarah McLachlan during three summers in the late 1990s. Its sellout success forced the music business to acknowledge not only the very real artistic power of these women but the very real and heretofore largely untapped commercial power of female audiences. Including Ani DiFranco in this set, an artist whose career trajectory was sharply rising during the 1990s, allowed us to explore and focus further on her staunchly independent ethos and her label, Righteous Babe Records. And at times, the subject matter of these sidebars dovetails across musical genres. Looking at Madonna in the context of the dawn of music videos reveals her shrewd understanding (and successful control) of her image as an early and enthusiastic adopter of MTV. Fifteen years later, Missy Elliott does something similar with image making in the context of hip-hop, by surprising and shocking fans and the hip-hop community through her own fearless fashion sense and creative restlessness that compels her to never create the same video—or costume—twice.

Thus, by asking who we consider to be icons, we found ourselves thinking in adjectives rather than genres: creative, exemplary, intriguing, controversial, groundbreaking, singular, iconoclastic, savvy, feisty, and innovative. Ultimately, when considering these women, their decisions, their achievements, and, most important, their music had to feel necessary to the concept of popular music. Consequently, if they were essential to the evolution of popular music, they must have a home in these two volumes. In discussions with my editor Kristi Ward and editorial consultant Chris Smith, we tried to create a list of women who felt absolutely essential to our understanding of popular music. Because our approach permitted a generous definition, it logically followed that the conversation could include the early crossover success of country-pop singer Patsy Cline as much it included the multiplatinum R&B artist Mary J. Blige or the eccentric but engaging Tori Amos. This more encompassing approach was also something my editors felt was largely absent among shorter, less in-depth women in rock books. Invariably, some readers may disagree with our choices or wonder why certain artists were omitted. As a two-volume set that is geared toward use by high school and college students, along with general readers and fans who are seeking a deeper perspective on what constitutes a female pop music icon, such conversation is welcome. Music critics have been constructively arguing about such ideas for years.

Although not every reader may sit down and read the text from start to finish, those who do and those who read through a few chapters will likely encounter some thematic elements that unite these women. Furthermore, as I researched and read about these women, I began to uncover similarities, some of which were surprising, in their struggles, trajectories, backgrounds, or ideals. When examining the early years of artists such as Diana Ross, Dolly Parton, and Madonna, for example, it becomes clear that all three women possessed an unwavering ambition and unassailable sense of their own fame and musical destiny. Many share an initial early interest in other art forms like painting or dance, such as Joni Mitchell, Madonna, Ani DiFranco, Liz Phair, and Suzanne Vega. Others, like Tina Turner and Emmylou Harris, discovered some of their hidden talents late in their careers; Turner found her voice when she became liberated from her difficult marriage to Ike, and Harris, who has been a much sought-after guest vocalist, found her own voice by writing much more of her own material. Joplin, Turner, and Blige are united by the personal pain that has galvanized their music and performance, which then gave them a reason for triumph. Joni Mitchell and Carole King share the odd distinction of marriages that shaped their work, albeit in different ways. Despite her short marriage to Chuck Mitchell, Joni Mitchell retained his surname as she made a name for herself, and King gained early success with her husband, Gerry Goffin, during the songwriting heyday of the early 1960s before striking out on her own later in the decade.

For many of these women the 1960s was formative—either as immediate cultural participants (such as Joan Baez, Joni Mitchell, or Janis Joplin, whose work broadened the possibilities for female singers and songwriters) or for those whose work bears the influence of the decade's ideals. For example, many of these women have used their celebrity as a consciousness raiser in some way, shape, or form. Joan Baez made a career out of strongly weaving her beliefs into her songwriting and fighting for causes she believed in and influenced generations of women; she calls the folk-rock duo the Indigo Girls her "young whipper-snappers" due to their shared impulses to make the world a better place through activism and the belief that folk music in particular is best suited for conveying socially conscious messages. Bonnie Raitt, a long-suffering artist whose heady, gutsy mix of blues, rock, and roots music took nearly twenty years to catch on with audiences, is a veteran supporter of nuclear disarmament and established the benefit concerts called No Nukes to rally concern and cash for her ideals. Years later, this impulse was present when Chrissie Hynde, a vegetarian, found herself getting arrested at PETA demonstrations and Tori Amos created RAINN, an organization geared toward providing for women who have been victims of abuse. Through her music and her record label, Ani DiFranco embodies many of the 1960s ideals about making the world a better place, but she also infuses it with a punk rock, do-it-yourself impulse and blends in her own feminism and self-determinism to become the ultimate independent artist.

Finally, a woman in the music business is situated in a traditionally male-dominated industry, which can mean she is one woman fighting against a larger system that often leaves her subjected to a process of decision making, image making, and money making that may be beyond her control. Refusing to be victim to what feminist film theorist Laura Mulvey termed "the male gaze," many of the icons here took the reins of their careers, called the shots, and tried to create their own paths on their own terms. Many of them played with, manipulated, and/or subverted the idea of what it meant to be a sex symbol. We see this with Debbie Harry, who gave her band the name Blondie as a tongue-in-cheek reference to the catcalls she would receive on the streets of New York. She deliberately subverted the ideas of movie star glamour before Madonna had even moved to New York. Madonna made image reinvention her mission throughout her career. Liz Phair still shows a flirtation with these ideas and expectations about female behavior even as her material reinvented itself for a larger, younger audience that was unburdened by her previous devil-may-care indie rock persona. Others show different approaches to this idea and have created new paradigms. The tough-and-tender Chrissie Hynde is essentially the Pretenders, but she feels most comfortable as front woman leading a group of men. With her flaming red mane and scorching guitar skills, Bonnie Raitt often appears to be one of the guys, joking and getting along in a historically male-dominated field—blues. And Joni Mitchell just did what she wanted, the way she wanted—confessional songwriting— but never stopped there. Throughout her career she has followed her own muse (much like Patti Smith) and always emerges as someone who anticipates a trend or explores a sound well in advance of the rest of mainstream American popular music.

The number twenty-four initially seemed limiting, but it forced all of us involved to shape the content in a compelling, unique way. If the careers of these women are, to borrow a phrase from Tori Amos, "little earthquakes," the women they've influenced are the aftershocks. Through these twenty-four icons we are permitted a glimpse at what came before them and what has followed. Based on what we've uncovered, we can speculate about what is yet to come for women in popular music. But because of the depth and breadth of biography and criticism these chapters encompass, we can now have a conversation that deepens their reach, makes plain their roots, and leaves us all rocking in their wake.

# Timeline

| | |
|---|---|
| 1954 | Patsy Cline signs with Four-Star/Decca. |
| 1955 | Patsy Cline sings on the Grand Ole Opry at age twenty-two. Anna Mae Bullock (Tina Turner) meets Ike Turner. |
| 1956 | At age fourteen Aretha Franklin makes her recording debut on a gospel album for Chess Records. |
| 1957 | "Walkin' After Midnight" by Patsy Cline becomes a number two country hit and a number twelve pop singles hit. |
| 1958 | Carole King and Gerry Goffin start working at Aldon Music, across the street from the Brill Building in New York City. At Aldon, they compose "Will You Love Me Tomorrow?," "Take Good Care of My Baby," and the number one hit "The Loco-Motion." Anna Mae Bulock is renamed "Tina Turner" by Ike Turner, with whom she had been performing as part of his Rhythm Kings. |
| 1959 | Joan Baez makes her public debut at the Newport Folk Festival. Dolly Parton makes her first appearance at the Grand Ole Opry at the age of thirteen. A year later, she receives her first recording contract for the song "Puppy Love" with Mercury Records. |
| 1960 | Patsy Cline becomes a member of the Grand Ole Opry. Carole King marries songwriting partner Gerry Goffin; she is just eighteen years old. |
| 1961 | Cline suffers a severe auto accident and almost dies; "I Fall to Pieces" goes to number one on the country chart. The Supremes sign to Tamla, a subsidiary of Motown. Aretha Franklin releases *Aretha*, her major label recording debut on Columbia Records. "It's Gonna Work Out Fine," a song by Ike and Tina Turner, hits number fourteen on the pop charts and number two on the R&B charts on the heels of 1960's hit "A Fool In Love," which |

went to number three on the R&B chart and twenty-seven on pop charts.

1962    Cline reports premonitions of her death to friends June Carter, Loretta Lynn, and Dottie West.

Joan Baez sees three of her albums hit the Top 20—*Joan Baez in Concert, Joan Baez, Volume 2,* and *Joan Baez* hit number ten, thirteen, and fifteen, respectively on the pop albums chart.

1963    Patsy Cline dies in March in a plane crash at age thirty.

Joan Baez meets relatively unknown folk singer Bob Dylan. By the following year they are performing together and become the "It" couple of protest folk music.

1964    The Supremes have their first smash number one hit with "Where Did Our Love Go?"

Linda Ronstadt drops out of college and moves to California to pursue music fulltime. Shortly thereafter, she joins the band the Stone Poneys, but the band breaks up in early 1968. She begins her solo recording, which results in her 1969 debut *Hand Sown . . . Home Grown.*

1965    Roberta Joan Anderson marries songwriter Chuck Mitchell and officially becomes Joni Mitchell. The marriage doesn't last, but the name sticks. Three years later she releases her debut *Song to a Seagull.*

1966    Aretha Franklin signs with Atlantic Records; a year later, her breakthrough smash album *I Never Loved a Man the Way I Love You* is released. The single "Respect" is certified gold; several months later "Baby I Love You" also receives gold certification as a single. "Respect" earns her two Grammy Awards.

Janis Joplin moves back to San Francisco and auditions for the band Big Brother and the Holding Company. The following summer she takes the crowd by storm at Monterey International Pop Music Festival, regarded by many as a precursor to Woodstock.

Tina Turner records the *River Deep, Mountain High* record with producer Phil Spector. Ike and Tina tour with the Rolling Stones, and Tina teaches Mick Jagger how to dance.

1967    *Patsy Cline's Greatest Hits*, a collection of her twelve most successful singles, including seven of her eight Top 10 country hits, is released.

1968    After personnel issues illustrate that Janis Joplin is destined for bigger things, she leaves Big Brother and the Holding Company in the fall. The following spring, she suffers a serious drug overdose but still manages to release her first solo album, *I Got Dem Ol' Kozmic Blues Again Mama!*

Carole King and Gerry Goffin split up as a married couple but continue working as songwriting partners.

1969    Woodstock, the three-day festival of music, takes place in the summer on a farm in upstate New York. Joan Baez is a featured performer, along with Janis Joplin. Joni Mitchell is slated to perform but does not; her song "Woodstock," however, is later recorded by Crosby, Stills, Nash, and Young, which performs at the festival along with Jimi Hendrix, the Band, Grateful Dead, and other contemporary acts.

At age twenty, Bonnie Raitt appears with Buddy Guy and Junior Wells as part of their opening act for the Rolling Stones. Two years later her self-titled debut is released.

1970    Janis Joplin dies of a drug overdose before the release of her second album, *Pearl*.

Diana Ross plays her final concert with the Supremes and releases her first single, "Reach Out and Touch (Somebody's Hand)," in the spring.

1971    Joan Baez has a number three pop singles hit and a number one adult contemporary hit with her spirited cover of the Robbie Robertson–penned song "The Night They Drove Old Dixie Down."

"Joshua" becomes Dolly Parton's first number one country hit. Three years later, her signature song "Jolene" becomes her second number one country hit.

Carole King releases her breakthrough solo record *Tapestry*, which contains the number one hits "I Feel the Earth Move" and "It's Too Late." The record also nabs her four Grammy Awards in one year: She becomes the first woman to do so.

Joni Mitchell releases her landmark album *Blue*, and the dawn of the confessional singer/songwriter movement arrives.

Patti Smith reads her poetry at St. Mark's Poetry Project in New York City for the first time; in the spring of the following year, her first volume of poetry, *Seventh Heaven*, is published.

The Ike and Tina Turner song "Proud Mary" hits number four on the pop singles charts.

1972    Linda Ronstadt's self-titled album peaks at thirty-five on the country album charts and also squeaks into the pop albums chart at 163, marking the first time she hits both the country and pop charts for the same record.

Diana Ross's album *Lady Sings the Blues*, released as the soundtrack to the film in which she plays Billie Holiday, becomes a number one hit. Ross is nominated for an Oscar and receives a Golden Globe Award.

| 1973 | Patsy Cline becomes the first solo female artist to be inducted into the Country Music Hall of Fame. |
|------|-----------------------------------------------------------------------------------------------------|
| 1973 | Emily Saliers and Amy Ray meet in grammar school in Decatur, Georgia. |
| 1974 | Debbie Harry and Chris Stein form the punk-pop band Blondie in New York City. |
|      | *Heart Like a Wheel* becomes Linda Ronstadt's breakthrough crossover hit, peaking in top slots on both country and pop charts. |
| 1975 | Emmylou Harris's album *Pieces of the Sky*, her first for a major label, hits number seven on the country chart, and "Too Far Gone" becomes a number thirteen hit on the country singles chart. One year later, *Elite Hotel* becomes her first number one country record; yields two number one country singles, "Sweet Dreams," and "Together Again"; and leads to her first Grammy Award for Best Female Country Vocal Performance. |
|      | Bonnie Raitt, who was an early favorite by critics but not yet a commercial success, appears on the cover of *Rolling Stone* magazine for the first time. |
|      | Clive Davis signs Patti Smith to a seven-album deal with the label Arista for $750,000. Later that year, her critically and commercially acclaimed record *Horses* is released. |
| 1976 | Linda Ronstadt nearly repeats her 1975 success with the record *Hasten Down the Wind*, which peaks at number one on the country album chart and number three on the pop albums chart. |
|      | Patti Smith and her band make their television debut as the musical guests of *Saturday Night Live*. |
|      | Tina Turner breaks away from Ike Turner and becomes a Buddhist, which empowers her to finally leave him for good. |
|      | Suzanne Vega lands her first gig in a church basement near 81st Street and West End Avenue in New York, at the age of sixteen. |
| 1977 | Blondie signs to Chrysalis Records and releases *Plastic Letters*, tours with Iggy Pop, and breaks through in the United Kingdom with the song "Denis." |
| 1978 | Dolly Parton wins her first Grammy Award. The album *Here You Come Again* nabs a statue for Best Female Country Vocal Performance and was a number one country album hit the previous year. |
|      | Madonna drops out of college and moves to New York to pursue her dance career. |
|      | Chrissie Hynde forms the Pretenders, whose members eventually include James Honeyman-Scott, Pete Farndon, and Martin Chambers. Within four years, however, Honeyman-Scott and Farndon die of drug-related causes, beginning a series of personnel shifts through the course of the band's career. |

Patti Smith has a productive year: Her fourth volume of poetry, *Babel*, is published, along with her third album, *Easter*. She also appears on the cover of *Rolling Stone*.

1979    At the age of nine, Ani DiFranco gets her first guitar and soon thereafter plays her first public gig.

Blondie's album *Parallel Lines* becomes a number six pop albums hit, aided by the number one smash single "Heart of Glass" and the strength of two other singles, "One Way or Another" and "Hanging on the Telephone."

*Mingus*, Joni Mitchell's foray into jazz, is released and is mostly misunderstood and unappreciated, but it shows how far ahead of the curve the artist is in predicting musical currents.

1980    Aretha Franklin changes labels to Arista Records. Two years later, *Jump To It* goes gold. Three years after that, her career is completely rejuvenated with the multiplatinum success of the record *Who's Zoomin' Who?*

Fueled by Chrissie Hynde's sassy, no-nonsense delivery, the Pretenders song "Brass in Pocket" becomes a number fourteen hit in the United States, propelling the band's self-titled album, also released that year, into the Top 10.

Bonnie Raitt performs at the historic No Nukes benefit concert at Madison Square Garden and co-founds Muse (Musicians for Safe Energy).

Linda Ronstadt appears in New York Shakespeare Festival's presentation of *The Pirates of Penzance*.

1981    Amy Ray and Emily Saliers make a basement recording called *Tuesday's Children*.

Diana Ross sings a duet with Lionel Richie, "Endless Love," used in the film of the same name. It spent nine weeks at number one.

1982    Madonna meets John "Jellybean" Benitez, a producer with whom she will have a relationship both personal and professional. He becomes involved in her hit "Holiday," which became her first Top 40 hit.

Two members of the Pretenders, Pete Farndon and James Honeyman-Scott, die within weeks of each other due to drug-related causes. Two years later, a reformulated line-up has success with the release *Learning to Crawl*.

1983    Madonna releases her self-titled debut on Sire Records, and by a little more than a year after its release, in December 1984, it has sold 2 million copies.

Linda Ronstadt records *What's New?*, an album of standards with arrangements by Nelson Riddle, and it becomes a triple-platinum success very quickly. It's followed by similar-themed projects, *Lush Life* (1984) and *For Sentimental Reasons* (1986), also with Riddle.

Suzanne Vega signs a record deal with A&M.

Diana Ross, Cindy Birdsong, and Mary Wilson briefly reunite for the television special *Motown 25: Yesterday, Today, Forever.*

1984    Tina Turner's debut solo record *Private Dancer*, released at the age of forty-five, launches her comeback status and becomes a top five hit and a number one R&B hit. Turner also wins four Grammys for the record, including Record of the Year and Song of the Year for "What's Love Got to Do With It?"

1985    Amy Ray and Emily Saliers call themselves the Indigo Girls. Three years later Epic Records signs the group, and in 1989, their self-titled second album comes out and receives gold certification, buoyed by the Top 40 hit "Closer to Fine."

1986    Madonna begins collaborating with songwriter and producer Patrick Leonard. The partnership will yield some of her biggest hits of the decade, including "Live to Tell," "La Isla Bonita," "Cherish," and "Like a Prayer." They work together periodically, most notably up through her 1998 album *Ray of Light.*

Tina Turner's tell-all autobiography, *I, Tina*, written with Kurt Loder is published and sets the record straight on her tumultuous relationship with Ike.

1987    Tori Amos is signed to Atlantic Records. One year later she and her band release the forgettable self-titled record *Y Kant Tori Read.*

Canadian singer/songwriter Sarah McLachlan writes her first song and signs with Nettwerk, a small Canadian label, but it's not until her 1994 album *Fumbling Towards Ecstasy* that McLachlan becomes a household word.

In the second year of its induction process, Aretha Franklin becomes the first woman to be inducted into the Rock and Roll Hall of Fame, alongside B.B. King, Bill Haley, Bo Diddley, Marvin Gaye, Smokey Robinson, and Muddy Waters.

Linda Ronstadt, Dolly Parton, and Emmylou Harris release their joint effort *Trio* after a decade in the making. It nabs them a Grammy Award for Best Recording.

Suzanne Vega's second record, *Solitude Standing*, is released, and the single "Luka," about child abuse, goes to number three on both the *Billboard* Hot 100 and Adult Contemporary charts.

1988    After a hiatus from recording through much of the earlier part of the decade, Patti Smith releases the record *Dream of Life.*

1989    Rap is added as a new category to the *Billboard* charts and Mary J. Blige is signed to Uptown Records.

Robert Mapplethorpe, Patti Smith's longtime friend and creative guru, dies of complications from HIV-AIDS.

Ani DiFranco moves to New York City and releases her first album, by herself, on cassette. One year later, she forms her very own Righteous Babe Records.

Bonnie Raitt finally breaks through and receives commercial acclaim, two years after becoming clean and sober, with her first release for Capitol Records, the aptly-titled and Grammy Award-winning *Nick of Time*.

1990     Amy Ray forms the independent, not-for-profit label Daemon Records in Decatur, Georgia. Some of its artists include Rose Polenzani, Danielle Howle, and the group Magnapop.

Carole King and Gerry Goffin are inducted into the Rock and Roll Hall of Fame.

1991     Mary J. Blige meets hip-hop producer and budding mogul Sean "Puffy" Combs.

Ike and Tina Turner are inducted into the Rock and Roll Hall of Fame.

1992     Missy Elliott's first all-girl group Sista meets DeVante Swing, who signs them to his label.

Liz Phair is signed to Matador Records and starts writing and recording what will become her ambitious 1993 debut record *Exile in Guyville*, designed as a song-by-song response to the Rolling Stones record *Exile on Main Street*.

Madonna forms her own music and publishing company, Maverick, with Time Warner and releases the expensive coffee table erotica photography book *Sex*, which sells a million copies within a week.

Suzanne Vega gets some production assistance from Mitchell Froom on the experimental *99.9 F*. The pair marry in 1995 and divorce in 1998.

1993     Liz Phair's record *Exile in Guyville* tops many best-of lists, including *The Village Voice* and *Spin* magazine.

The film adaptation of Turner's autobiography, *What's Love Got To Do With It?*, is released; she appears in the final sequence of the film; the soundtrack is also released.

1994     Tori Amos co-founds the organization RAINN for women who have been victims of abuse. Her second album, *Under the Pink*, receives platinum status by the year's end.

Aretha Franklin receives a Kennedy Center honor and a Grammy Award for lifetime achievement.

Patti Smith's husband Fred Smith passes away, followed one month later by the death of her brother Tony. Her 1996 record *Gone Again* eulogizes their passing. One year later, poets

|      | William S. Burroughs and Allen Ginsberg also die, inspiring her record *Peace and Noise*. |
|------|------|
| 1995 | *Wrecking Ball*, with its eerie sounds and textures, becomes Emmylou Harris's comeback record, exposing her to a younger generation of listeners. |
| 1996 | Missy Elliott works with childhood friend and producer Timbaland on songs for R&B singer Aaliyah's second album *One in a Million*. Its success leads her to leverage a deal with Elektra to launch her own imprint, Gold Mind. |
|      | Ani DiFranco's album *Dilate* debuts at number eighty-seven on the *Billboard* 200 album chart, a milestone for an independent release. |
|      | Madonna appears in the starring role of the film *Evita*, playing Evita Perón, garnering arguably her best reviews to date for a film role and winning her a Golden Globe for Best Actress Musical or Comedy. |
| 1997 | Missy Elliott's first solo album *Supa Dupa Fly* debuts at number three on the *Billboard* pop albums chart and goes platinum within three months of its release. It also becomes a number one hit on the R&B/hip-hop album chart. |
|      | Joni Mitchell is inducted into the Rock and Roll Hall of Fame, along with contemporaries Crosby, Stills, and Nash. |
|      | Sarah McLachlan founds the all-female touring summer music festival Lilith Fair, which runs through the next two years. Indigo Girls, the Pretenders, Liz Phair, Emmylou Harris, and Suzanne Vega are among those who perform. The festival draws more than 2 million people and raises more than $7 million for charities and nonprofit organizations benefiting women and humanitarian causes. |
| 1998 | Blondie reunites and plans an album, *No Exit*, and accompanying tour for the following year. |
| 1999 | Patsy Cline receives a star on the Hollywood Walk of Fame; Dolly Parton is inducted into the Country Music Hall of Fame. The music downloading software Napster is born and enables users to illegally download music for free. Its popularity signals a huge shift in the music business. Its success—and ultimately its court-ordered shuttering—helps give rise to Apple computer's iTunes, which launches an online music store in 2003 and within five years, becomes the number one retailer of music in the United States with more than 4 billion songs sold. |
|      | *Billboard* names Emmylou Harris as the recipient of the Century Award, its highest honor. She was only the eighth recipient at the time, in the same company as James Taylor, Joni Mitchell, Buddy Guy, and George Harrison. |

| | |
|---|---|
| 2000 | Emmylou Harris's record *Red Dirt Girl* is a signature effort of mostly her own songwriting, the first of its ilk since her 1985 quasi-autobiographical record *The Ballad of Sally Rose*. During this year she also appears in the award-winning soundtrack to the film *O Brother, Where Art Thou?* Bonnie Raitt is inducted into the Rock and Roll Hall of Fame in the same year as James Taylor and Eric Clapton. |
| 2001 | Missy Elliott wins her first Grammy Award for Best Rap Solo Performance for the hit song "Get Ur Freak On." Suzanne Vega organizes *Vigil: N.Y. Songs Since 9/11*, a record designed to benefit widows and family members of those who lost loved ones in the terrorist attacks on September 11, 2001. Proceeds went to the Windows of Hope Family Relief Fund. |
| 2002 | Missy Elliott's song "Work It" becomes a top five hit across six different *Billboard* charts, hitting number one on three of them. Gibson names a line of guitars, the Emmylou Harris L-200, in honor of the artist. Joni Mitchell, appearing increasingly cranky and discontent in the few interviews she grants to journalists, announces she is retiring from the music business. Mary J. Blige receives her first Grammy Award as a solo artist for the song "He Thinks I Don't Know," in the category of Best Female R&B Vocal Performance. In 1995, she had won a Grammy as part of a duet she performed with Method Man called "I'll Be There For You/You're All I Need To Get By." |
| 2003 | Tori Amos founds the Bridge Entertainment Group with long-time tour managers Chelsea Laird and John Witherspoon for artists who are in transition between projects, labels, or ideas. After a five-year absence from the record stores, the self-titled, aggressively produced *Liz Phair* is released to much ballyhoo. Old fans criticize its commercial pop sound and call her a sellout, but the song "Why Can't I?" becomes a big hit and receives gold certification. Madonna publishes her first children's book, *The English Rose*. It sells well and is followed quickly by three more children's books within the next year. |
| 2004 | Respect M.E., Missy Elliott's line of clothing, is launched in conjunction with Adidas. Verve Records releases Linda Ronstadt's first jazz record in nearly twenty years, *Hummin' to Myself*. |
| 2005 | Carole King's career receives a big boost after launching a small-scale tour called *The Living Room Tour*, which results in a two-CD set and DVD of the live performance. |

2006            Legendary New York music club CBGB closes its doors after
                extensive protests, some of them from Debbie Harry and Patti
                Smith, among others.
                Blondie is inducted into the Rock and Roll Hall of Fame.
2007            Joan Baez receives a lifetime achievement Grammy Award—it is
                her sole award from the National Academy of Recording Arts
                and Sciences.
                Suzanne Vega's *Beauty & Crime* is released on Blue Note
                Records; many of its songs are love letters to her native New
                York City.
                Patti Smith is inducted into the Rock and Roll Hall of Fame, an
                honor that she felt uneasy about—so much so that she wrote an
                editorial about it for the *New York Times*.
                Joni Mitchell releases the acclaimed record *Shine*; and jazz
                musician Herbie Hancock's album of interpretations of her
                songs, *River: The Joni Letters*, is released and wins the coveted
                Album of the Year Award at the Grammys.
2008            Madonna is inducted into the Rock and Roll Hall of Fame and
                several months later releases *Hard Candy*, her last contractually
                obligated album for Warner Brothers. The record climbs to
                the top of the Canadian, Internet, and *Billboard* 200 charts
                simultaneously.
                At the age of sixty-eight, Tina Turner announces that she is
                returning to the concert circuit in the United States for the first
                time in seven years.
                ATO Records, the label founded by musician Dave Matthews,
                announces it will release a fifteenth anniversary edition of Liz
                Phair's debut *Exile in Guyville*, along with B-sides and a special
                DVD. She also announces that ATO will release her new album
                in the fall.

Courtesy of Photofest

# Tori Amos

## OVERVIEW

Tori Amos is one of the most unusual success stories to emerge from the world of popular music in the 1990s. Melding her classical piano training, her curiosity about human nature, and an unconventional and occasionally arresting approach to songwriting and performance, Amos's musical lineage traces itself to England's Kate Bush for her otherworldly approach and Joni Mitchell because of the confessional nature of her lyrics. Much of Amos's material is grounded in an examination of feminism and womanhood. Idiosyncratic, fearless, smart, and warm, Amos has an intensely loyal fan base and is surprisingly accessible to her fans. She is also well known for (and sometimes chided by critics because of) her exuberant, sensual approach to playing the piano. Fans were initially surprised by her early concerts, during which she frequently would be writhing, wriggling, and pounding away on the piano—redefining the way in which women relate to musical instruments and reclaiming a little piece of pop music for herself. Known for her vivid imagination, a keen grasp of metaphor, and a tendency toward personification—she refers to her songs as "my girls"—Amos constantly pushes, plays, and pokes at the boundaries we inhabit within ourselves, in our relationships to others, and in our world. Some have called her "perversely cryptic," but Amos believes each song has its own life force, its own agenda, and its own mission. If you listen to her music long enough, you start to grasp the intricate inner logic at work.

Almost every single one of Amos's albums has at least gone gold except for three: a cover album, *Strange Little Girls* (2001); *The Beekeeper* (2005); and *American Doll Posse* (2007). *Little Earthquakes* (1992), *Under the Pink* (1994), *Boys for Pele* (1996), *From the Choirgirl Hotel* (1998), and *To Venus and Back* (1999) have all been certified platinum at least once. Additionally, three video collections, *Little Earthquakes, The Complete Videos 1992–1998,* and *Welcome to Sunny Florida*, are all certified gold. Amos has seen her albums achieve spots on a handful of different charts, including a number one slot for *Little Earthquakes* on the Heatseekers chart and a number one slot for *To Venus and Back* for Top Internet Albums. Nearly every other release placed in the *Billboard* 200; the thorny *Boys for Pele* even peaked at number two, and *From the Choirgirl Hotel*, number five. Her songs have made thirty appearances to date on various *Billboard* singles charts, from adult Top 40 to the Hot 100 to modern rock tracks to hot dance music/club play, which says as much about her wide appeal as it does the increasingly fragmented, diversified nature of the music culture of the 1990s.

Amos has earned eight Grammy Award nominations for not only her music but also for the packaging of one release: a limited edition of *Scarlet's Walk*. *Strange Little Girls* received a nomination for Best Female Rock Performance for "Strange Little Girl" and a nomination for Best Alternative Music Performance. *Boys for Pele* also gained her a nomination for Best Alternative Music

Performance. In 1999, *From the Choirgirl Hotel* earned her a nomination for Best Alternative Music Performance and Best Female Rock Vocal Performance for the song "Raspberry Swirl." *To Venus and Back* also earned two nominations in 2000: one for Best Female Rock Vocal Performance for "Bliss" and one for Best Alternative Music Performance. Despite these accolades, she has yet to win a Grammy.

One of Amos's most striking characteristics is her extreme approachability and warmth. She takes seriously her relationship to her audience and her fans and attempts to encourage them to find their own creative calling (Amos and Powers 2005, 8). Many fans, taking solace from the difficult stories her songs have told—especially the a capella "Me and a Gun," told from the perspective of a woman being raped—have written her letters and have visited her backstage, seeking counsel and telling her how much her music has been a comfort.

In fact, one such conversation was with a fourteen-year-old girl who came backstage after a concert to have a cup of tea with Amos. The girl begged her to take her on tour with her, and Amos asked why. The girl revealed, "when I get home I will be raped by my stepfather like I was last night and will be tomorrow. I have been raped for seven years" (Bell 1999). In June 1994 Amos co-founded the Rape, Abuse, and Incest National Network (RAINN). The network is comprised of a toll-free phone number that connects callers with their local rape crisis center. Since its inception, the nonprofit organization, which is the largest anti–sexual assault organization in the United States, has assisted more than 900,000 people. Its mission is to assist victims of sexual assault and ensure that rapists are brought to justice. The organization has forged many relationships with community outreach organizations and entertainers to spread its message at concerts, on college campuses, and in communities.

The commercial and critical success of Tori Amos is no small matter; it has paved the way for and inspired a whole generation of female singer/songwriters, granting them the right to work out their own demons and thoughts on the piano. Many of these women share Amos's penchants for thorny, introspective, surprising material. Most notably, Amos has influenced and made possible the work of Fiona Apple, Paula Cole, Nellie McKay, Regina Spektor, Leona Naess, Kate Earl, Sonya Kitchell, and to some degree Norah Jones (see sidebar).

By the time *Scarlet's Walk* was released in 2002, Amos's commercial popularity had started to fade slightly, although she currently enjoys a loyal cult following around the world and her tours regularly sell out. Her concerts are legendary, intense affairs, noted for their constantly changing set lists, thus inspiring already devoted fans to attend multiple performances. Amos believes that each city, each new location, has its own energy; this helps keep her live performances fresh and unique. She feels moved to respond to many different factors, from mundane items such as the news of the day in a particular city and the time of year to musical considerations such as creating seamless transitions, allowing for different instrumentation (organ, Rhodes, and the piano, for example), and establishing an emotional momentum for the audience.

## A Legion of (Occasionally) Long-Haired Females Takes Its Place at the Piano

Tori Amos has become known for her eccentricities, her classical training, and her intensely personal and imaginative songwriting. She has inspired a diverse generation of piano-playing, introspective female songwriters: the classically trained Russian émigré Regina Spektor; the wounded, engaging Fiona Apple; the ethereal Leona Naess; the folky-electronica Beth Orton; and even R&B pianist sensation Alicia Keys.

Apple shares with Amos the sultry, sullen aspects of performance. Her multi-platinum 1996 debut *Tidal* created several successful singles: The knowing "Shadowboxer" and the bluesy "Criminal," which starts with the lyric, "I've been a bad bad girl/I've been careless with a delicate man." Like Amos's *Little Earthquakes*, *Tidal* took critics by storm for its emotional depth and Apple's virtuoso playing. *Tidal* and her 1999 follow-up *When the Pawn . . .* feature heavy contributions by the unconventional producer Jon Brion, known for lurching, nearly kaleidoscopic arrangements. In three albums over nine years, Apple has demonstrated a storyteller's eye for detail and metaphor. Her songwriting has become more surprising and textured, especially on 2005's *Extraordinary Machine*.

Although Spektor has released only two albums via major labels—2004's *Soviet Kitsch* and 2006's *Begin to Hope*—she is also a critical favorite. Spektor shares with Amos a classical background, a lively percussive approach, and an elastic vocal style. Artsy like Amos, Spektor's compositions often are sprawling numbers filled with her singing world-weary lyrics in a combination of English, French, and Russian. On *Begin to Hope*, Spektor added electric guitars and a drum kit and used her voice for percussive flourishes, especially on the engaging ode to relationship foolishness "Fidelity." *Begin to Hope* poises her for a breakthrough; it has sold nearly 750,000 copies worldwide and spent five straight weeks at number one on the *Billboard* New Artist chart.

## EARLY YEARS

Tori Amos was born in Newton, North Carolina, in 1963 as Myra Ellen Amos, daughter of Edison Amos, a Methodist minister, and Mary Ellen Amos, a schoolteacher. Her family moved to Baltimore when she was two, and as a child, Amos was intellectually and musically precocious, always asking questions of her elders. She recalls her earliest musical memory as trying to get herself up on the piano stool at the age of about two and a half. By the age of four, she was playing piano and singing in the church choir; her father served as the pastor of a large church in Baltimore. Her parents, especially her father, encouraged this budding talent, and Amos started taking piano lessons on a scholarship at Baltimore's Peabody Conservatory at Johns Hopkins University from 1968 to 1974. During her time at Peabody it eventually became apparent that she could play well by ear but that reading music was much more difficult for her.

The childhood she describes in her autobiography seems characterized by open intellectual discussion and debate at the dinner table regarding religion, politics, and other topics. Her parents, both educators by training though her mother stopped working to raise Amos and her older siblings Michael and Marie, created an environment where intelligent inquisition could flourish. Both of her parents had an equal, albeit different, influence on her as an artist, a person, and a feminist. As an adult, Amos reports being impressed by her father's humanitarian bent and his ability to minister to people in their time of need; it can be argued that much of what Amos does with her music is similar, because her songwriting often tackles difficult material and crosses social taboos. He came from a Scots-Irish background. However, her mother's side of the family—the Cherokee side—really impacted her life and her imagination.

Amos was extremely close with her maternal grandfather, Calvin Clinton Copeland, whom she called Poppa and who passed away when she was nine and a half. In the summertime she would spend time at his home in North Carolina, where he would regale her with stories of her ancestors. His Southern colloquialisms, his Eastern Cherokee heritage, his gift for speaking in quaint metaphors, and his belief that all living things contained some special, intrinsic knowledge made an indelible impression on her during her formative years. He would also urge her to pay attention to the powerful stories of her ancestors. She learned, for instance, the Native American story of the Corn Mother and her reverence for what the Earth can provide. Amos remembers being impressed, too, with her Poppa's perfect pitch; she recalls in her co-authored biography *Piece by Piece* many days when his rich tenor voice sang her to sleep. He told her stories of her ancestors, in particular the grandmother who raised him, Margaret Little, and whom he described as a fierce, shrewd woman who survived the Trail of Tears by carefully wrapping and burying dry goods, food, and necessities in a white Christian graveyard. This strategy enabled her to evade the ransacking and pillaging of "the Bluecoats" because she knew that they, Christians themselves, would not attack a Christian burial ground.

Amos's paternal grandmother also held an important role in her life but not because the two got along well. Instead, she served as a catalyst for Amos to scrutinize her own beliefs more closely. An ordained Christian minister, missionary, and teacher, Addie Allen Amos (called Grandma) possessed a strict, unwavering interpretation of the Bible and was steadfast in her approach to serving as Amos's grandmother and moral-checker. Amos refers to her as a "shame inducer" and was constantly falling out of favor and made to feel guilty for asking questions and playing music.

Amos recalls an occasion where her Grandma punished her by "trying to pray the fear of Jesus into me" because she "talked out of line." Amos felt she needed to try to understand why her grandmother seemed so destructive (Amos and Powers 2005, 36). In *Piece by Piece* she notes that her ancestors from her father's Irish side had been weavers, and Amos took this as her first entry point to try to understand the woman's control issues and how fear can force people to believe something. Amos says she decided she would "weave" herself into her grandmother's mindset to understand her and ultimately show mercy on her (Amos and Powers 2005, 36).

Perhaps what was most disappointing to Amos was the fact that her grandmother had received a college education in the 1920s, something unusual for a young woman at that time. "She was masquerading as a feminist while jailing the Feminine," she says. Encountering such hypocrisy—or seeming contradiction—made a lasting impression on Amos. Still, she sagely reflects on her Grandma's ways, saying that she recognized that Amos was different, which enabled her to understand herself as a child (Amos and Powers 2005, 36–37). Irrespective of her Grandma's branding of her, Amos certainly was aware from a very young age that she was different. Not only her talent marked her, but her sensibility did too. She writes, "I was born a feminist. And then, at age five, when my strict Christian grandmother punished me, I realized, I'm not penetrating here. I'm just pissing people off. So I had to find another way to penetrate" (12).

But like almost every experience, Amos was able to learn something important from these negative encounters, and put those revelations to constructive creative and personal use. And as any budding songwriter would agree, music became an escape, a safe haven, and a wellspring of good energy. As a result of her grandmother's influence, Amos realized something important. "I never would let anyone have power . . . that's when I started writing songs that other people couldn't walk into, and I discovered my creative spark" (Amos and Powers 2005, 41). Indeed, her family unknowingly helped lay the groundwork to create a complex, thoughtful, spiritual tapestry that is, admittedly, often oblique. This revelation from Amos sheds light on her songwriting and explains why her music often sounds to listeners like something more than a sophisticated metaphor: a puzzle, a secret language, an enigma. Her songs retain that quality to this day.

The way in which Amos would explore her ideas was made more complicated, and arguably more interesting, by her burgeoning sense of inquisitiveness about patriarchy, religion, and personal sacrifices. Of particular interest was her mother, whom Amos says played the part of the perfect wife at church functions (41). Growing up, Amos had trouble reconciling this smart, progressive woman in private with the public submissive, docile persona. As Amos got older and was able to converse with her mother about this, she began to understand how women can contain multitudes. And this, naturally, filtered into her music.

Despite any perceived failings, Amos's mother was still a strong role model. She would read to her daughter nearly every day, starting, of course, with children's books but quickly moving on to more challenging texts. Her mother would read some of her own favorite poems and short stories from writers such as Robert Browning, Edgar Allen Poe, and William Faulkner. Mary Ellen Amos was a major in literature in college, which she attended for two years before she left school and married Edison. Amos describes her father as particularly encouraging of her career and as someone who believed in and supported civil rights and the idea that women should be educated. Additionally, Amos credits her mother's extensive record collection and her older brother Michael's music as early influences; he brought home the Beatles' album *Sgt. Pepper's Lonely Hearts Club Band* when she was a child.

Growing up surrounded by both the written and oral traditions of extended family, Amos says simply, "My mother gave me the text and my father gave me theology" (Amos and Powers 2005, 3). Her parents have remained important throughout her career. Despite the at times shockingly frank nature of her songs and their potential to offend, she and her parents have conversations about her music. In 1994, Edison Amos told a reporter for *Washington Magazine*, "We love her songs. We don't always agree with everything she writes and says. But when she writes about God, she writes about how images of God are so extreme, and that males made the rules of religion and left women out" (Dalphonse 1994).

Around age eleven or twelve, Amos had started asking teachers at the Peabody Conservatory—who were training her classically—about John Lennon and Paul McCartney. She was already interested in crossing boundaries, mixing genres, and creating something new with music. She wanted to know why the students were not permitted to learn and practice the music of these artists and why there was a separation between classical and popular music. Amos became particularly enamored with Robert Plant of Led Zeppelin and Elton John. She recalls her father coming home from meetings with Christian fathers, remarking that no one knew what to do about Led Zeppelin; no Christian father wanted the band's records in the house. Because she had difficulty reading music and instead played by ear, she was reportedly kicked out of Peabody at age eleven.

Undeterred, Amos continued her musical education in other venues. By the time she was fourteen, her father got her gigs playing standards several nights a week at hotels and Georgetown piano bars, including Mr. Henry's, which had a primarily gay clientele. Although some family friends raised an eyebrow at a minister's daughter playing at a gay bar, her father, ever tolerant and wise, knew that she would be left alone there. Performing cover tunes gave her experience and an opportunity to learn something new.

*Over a lifetime of learning to compose, Tori Amos has perfected her own methods for transforming raw creative material into art. Her process takes her from preliminary, inspirational wanderings throughout the world and within her well-stocked library to the calm space of her workroom and then into the recording studio, where she leads her small crew of collaborators in realizing her compositions.*

—Ann Powers, music journalist and biographer

Amos used her middle name, Ellen, growing up, but spent much time while performing trying out other names for herself. The process of naming herself was an empowering step toward independence, especially because she shares elements of her name with her mother (Mary Ellen) and sister (Marie Allen). Because the name was prescribed to her, it did not feel unique; she felt limited. Finally, at age seventeen, the boyfriend of a friend of hers suggested the name Tori (Amos and Powers 2005, 53). It seemed to fit: She liked its cadence and liked that it was part of other words—conservatory, victory, and many others. Thus, a new name gave her new potential, new opportunities, and the promise of personal growth and reinvention, as well as a reintegration of the various selves that were fighting—and would continue to do so—to gain a voice and power, in her music.

## CAREER PATH

Though her relationship with her parents—especially her father—was close, like any rebellious teenager who wanted to make music, Amos knew that she had to find her own voice and forge her own path. Despite the fact that she was earning her own money playing and singing she was still living at home, which meant she had to live with her father's watchful eyes and strict curfews. Amos left Baltimore for Los Angeles in 1984 at the age of twenty-one, prompted by a friend (Stephen Himmelfarb), who left Washington, DC, for North Hollywood to become a sound engineer.

For Amos, the departure amounted to something much more than just a stereotypical coming-of-age story. She had grown up with numerous stories of her ancestors and experienced the judgment of her strictly religious grandmother, so for her it was more a matter of finding her place in this family long history. The stories that had inhabited her were slowly beginning to itch to be told. Ironically, religion served as a wellspring of inspiration as Amos tried to reconcile dogma with reality and feminism with religion's historic subjugation of women.

After she moved to Los Angeles, where she lived in an apartment behind a Methodist church, Amos began to meet with A&R executives who kept telling her that "this piano girl thing is dead." They did not think that her particular talents would appeal to listeners and that she might be too much of a retread of successful artists who had become prominent in the 1970s such as Joni Mitchell and Kate Bush, to whom Amos, ironically, would ultimately be compared. However, Amos managed to sign a six-record deal with Atlantic Records in 1987. Although she felt that what she was doing was not working—the executives did not have faith in her style—she swallowed her pride and did as instructed. The end result was an album (and band) called *Y Kant Tori Read,* released in 1988. The album was a cross between pop and metal, with Amos depicted on the cover wearing black, wielding a sword, with her scarlet hair teased out wildly. Titled as a self-deprecating nod to her inability to read music, this first effort was a dismal failure—it sold very few copies and gained little airplay on radio. She recalls in her autobiography that at that time in the music business in California, either the rock chick or the folk poet worked. Clearly, the "Record Company Cheeses" (as she refers to them) felt that rock chick would work better.

Somehow, the label did not drop her despite this initial misstep even though Amos had had a hand in writing nearly all of the sixteen tracks on the album. *Y Kant Tori Read* is regarded by fans who have rediscovered it as somewhat cheesy, corporate, and shallow—in other words, the antithesis of a Tori Amos album.

Although hindsight can provide much insight and perspective about one's life, Amos is especially philosophical about this time period. She told *Billboard* magazine in 1992, "Every place you land in life has a reason and lesson . . . I think that period of time was partially a means of dealing with sexual repression I experienced when I was growing up" (Flick 1992). Additionally, Amos says that it "took a while to recover and reintegrate" not only after the failure of *Y Kant Tori Read* but also the experience of producing a result other people wanted rather than something in which she deeply believed herself. In her autobiography, she writes, "By the time I finally got to make *Little Earthquakes*, I made a conscious decision not to be objectified here. My material had to be about the content . . . they couldn't come between me and my piano" (Amos and Powers 2005, 74). And so, by 1990 she had started writing her haunting, confessional story-songs, visceral in their imagery and marked by the myths, stories, and legends inspired by her own family's method of storytelling.

### Breaking Through: The First Few Albums

The four years between the releases of *Y Kant Tori Read* and *Little Earthquakes* were well spent but difficult. Amos recorded a batch of songs designed to be released following the commercial failure of *Y Kant Tori Read*, but those did not see the light of day—at least not in that incarnation. She went back into the studio and this time recorded with producer Eric Rosse and reworked the material. Despite the fact that her label, Atlantic, had misgivings about releasing an album of a woman playing the piano, Doug Morris, CEO of Atlantic, stuck by her and encouraged her to be herself, essentially, in her songwriting.

Limited by the perspective and tired of the vibe of Los Angeles, Amos decided she needed a change of scenery. Knowing that breaking through in America would be tricky because of the large, diverse market and because her music was eclectic, Morris ingeniously decided to send Amos to England to work on the songs and perform in London in the clubs and for music critics.

*I just find different things
every time we play a song. She
likes that, which is great for
us. She reacts to the rhythmic
choices I make as if it were a
jazz gig . . . I feel completely
satisfied at the end of a gig. I
feel I've played some music.*
—drummer Matt Chamberlain

It was a successful move by all accounts, and her album gained raves from top British music publications, including *Q*.

The nineteenth-century feminist writer Virginia Woolf wrote about the need for women to find their own space for creativity and thinking in her groundbreaking book *A Room of One's Own. Little Earthquakes*, released in 1992, advocates a similar philosophy. The twelve songs are a collective clarion call for women to heal themselves, live for themselves, claim their rights to create, and find their own voices. But the songs are not all introspective and quiet—instead, Amos charts anger, disappointment, frustration, shame, and naked aggression with a full range of instruments at her disposal, from her signature Bösendorfer piano to electric guitars, cello, haunting vocal tracks floating behind her own, and even the suggestive crack of a whip. Some of the tracks were co-written with producer (and then-boyfriend) Eric Rosse.

In "Crucify," which leads off the album, Amos uses the chorus to suggest the idea of crucifixion as a means by which women defeat their own best interests and must push past self-doubt to find strength. "Crucify" was only the beginning of religious themes that would naturally surface in her songwriting.

In the chorus of the cello-tinged "Girl," Amos sings "she's been everybody else's girl/Maybe one day she'll be her own." No song suggests this better than "Silent All These Years," which was one of the album's two official singles. In the course of five minutes, Amos creates an evocative portrait of a narrator seeking to find herself, find love, and literally find her voice: "sometimes I hear my voice and it's been here/silent all these years."

The penultimate song, "Me and a Gun," tells the story of rape from the point of view of a woman experiencing it. It is perhaps one of her more controversial songs, difficult to listen to because of its bracing honesty and descriptive details, as the narrator invokes a prayer as her body is violated. As a flash point for conversation, the song garnered much attention, possibly more than any of her other songs to date, because it was instrumental in providing an immediate emotional connection with fans who had experienced the same thing. In short, Amos gave voice to sexual assault, which enabled others to find their own voice and speak of similar experiences. "I got a lot of letters and heard so many, many stories from fans who were going through situations of rape and abuse; everything from they were at a party and someone raped them to people being abused by someone in their home," Amos told *Billboard* (1999). The experience led her to found RAINN.

When it was released, the aptly named *Little Earthquakes* sent shockwaves throughout the music industry and garnered critical acclaim. Her success made it more likely for deejays to play two female artists in a row, a practice that before her success was more or less unheard of on commercial radio stations. Amos told *Billboard* magazine after the release of *Little Earthquakes* she considers it a "moment in time when I looked at things I hadn't ever before. That record was like a first kiss. It started a discovery process that never stops" (Flick 1992).

From a marketing point of view, Amos boggled the minds of the industry because her music did not neatly fit into one category or another. Initially Amos garnered comparisons to predecessors such as Laura Nyro, Joni Mitchell, and Kate Bush. However, her reach was more diverse because her work was so different and her success on various *Billboard* types of charts throughout her career exemplifies this point. *Little Earthquakes* barely scratched the surface of Amos's ultimate capability as a songwriter, but it provided good clues: simple, piano-driven songs alternating with complex, dramatic, orchestrated songs. Doug Morris told the *Washington Post*, "We're stretching boundaries with her. . . . These songs are very provocative. She's on her journey" (Harrington 1992).

When it came time to promote her second album *Under the Pink* in 1994, label executives sent the single "God" to alternative, college, and album alternative radio format stations. The album, on the whole, is not as immediately startling as its predecessor, but it is a logical progression wherein Amos begins to dig more deeply beyond the surface of what she had begun to uncover in *Little Earthquakes*. The album was recorded in a hacienda in New Mexico with co-producer Eric Rosse. Still, despite its deeper digging, Amos wrote that she was still very much a fragmented woman who had not yet found a way to integrate those separated selves. She said the tour was long and "the compartmentalization process within me had gotten worse and worse" (Amos and Powers 2005, 78). She acknowledged that the fact that she was compartmentalizing herself was useful and served a purpose, to perhaps allow a singular focus on the road, but she observed it could also be destructive. Amos realized that she needed to acknowledge all the seemingly disparate parts of her personality (78). The fragmentation stemmed literally from the events in her life—the relationship between Amos and producer Eric Rosse broke up during the tour.

The album's first single, "God," humorously but effectively imagines the narrator as what Amos describes in *Piece by Piece* as "Ms. God" or "God's lover." With a screechy guitar, a synthetic drum beat, and other rhythmic flourishes, the song possesses that telltale rolling, rhythmic structure that can be found in many of her later songs, anchored by her soulful playing. In the song, Amos asks in the verse "God sometimes you just don't come through/Do you need a woman to look after you?" Again, the structure is atypical—Amos does not save the name of the song for the refrain—she gets right down to business from the first word of the song in a direct address.

The metaphors she was creating on *Under the Pink* started to become more involved, but somehow Amos was still accessible. One might consider the philosophical "Pretty Good Year" a paean to the success of her solo debut. The contemplative "Baker Baker" uses tropes of a nursery rhyme to liken a relationship's process to making a cake. The oddly titled "Cornflake Girl," Amos has said, was inspired by an Alice Walker novel about female circumcision called *Possessing the Secret of Joy*. Angered by the ways in which women betray each other, she wrote the song and set up two camps— cornflake girl (which could be read as white) and raisin (African American) girls. In "The Waitress," which starts off quietly but tensely, the narrator states that she wants to "kill this waitress," only to crescendo in the chorus, with Amos practically shrieking "but I believe in peace, bitch." Amos's ability to quickly convey complexity—often a duality—of thought, in this case female jealousy, consistently surprises. Amos tackled another taboo, masturbation, in the tinkling, piano-based "Icicle" and linked it with religion in one swift line: "And when they say take of his body/I think I'll take of mine instead."

*Under the Pink* explored what was beyond the surface, lurking underneath the exterior of things, the pinkness, the newness, and the vulnerability of the top layer of skin, for example. In its first two weeks of release, it sold 113,000 copies; in contrast, *Little Earthquakes* sold 2200 copies in that same time frame, according to SoundScan. Furthermore, Amos had built a momentum with her first record and the success of *Under the Pink*, which received platinum status in November 1994, undoubtedly helped *Little Earthquakes*'s sales, which received platinum status just two months later.

Amos's third album, *Boys for Pele*, feels the most impenetrable of all her releases to date; the songs are dark and often move in unexpected directions. Named for the Hawaiian fire goddess (for whom a volcano is named in Hawaii), the album's eighteen tracks comprise some of Amos's more elaborately abstract and largely piano-based compositions. Few artists would be so bold as to put a six-minute song first to lead off an album, but Amos did so with the spare and haunting "Horses." She calls *Boys for Pele* "a woman's journey into the hidden parts of the feminine unconscious" (Reece 1996). Fittingly, given her preoccupations and background, it was recorded in a church in Ireland.

In the eyes of some critics, however, *Boys for Pele* further cemented her image as a strange, unpredictable musician, especially because of the artwork and photography that accompanied the release: Amos is sitting and staring straight at the camera as a pig suckles her breast. The album, regardless of its perceived impenetrability, remains a fan favorite, but it polarized critics. *Boys* lacks the immediacy and intimacy of her first two releases in exchange for a more difficult engagement with the issues of darkness, light, and anger she was wrestling with during the album's creation.

Adding to *Boys for Pele*'s thorniness, the songs take unexpected leaps and moves in subject matter, instrumentation, and the use of her voice. The percussion-heavy "Professional Widow" uses harpsichord, and the middle section suddenly stops and veers into some light, deft piano playing before returning to heaviness. In this song, Amos sings about death—the woman in the song wants to convince her man to kill himself so she does not leave any trace of guilt. Amos also began to really use her own voice as an instrument of its own merit—especially in the album's single "Caught A Lite Sneeze," in which she wraps her voice around syllables and a melody in the most surprising way, just a few hairs short of the tempo of the song, but never completely at odds with its rhythm. "Hey Jupiter," situated in the middle of the album, marks a turning point for the narrator of the songs. "She knows the way she has looked at relationships with men and put them on a pedestal is over. There's a sense of incredible loss because I knew that I would never be able to see the same way again. It's freeing, and [yet] there's a sense of grieving with that" (Cohen 1996).

What's interesting to note, however, is that despite any perceived impenetrability or difficult or odd nature of some of the songs, the record sales did not initially indicate any dismissal by fans. In fact, *Boys for Pele* sold 170,000 copies in its opening week. "I didn't change what I do. I actually took it further, and people are opening up to it," she told *Billboard* after its release. The record went platinum by late August 1996, indicating that her fans were indeed open to her creative whims.

### Responding to Tragedy, Both Personal and Political

By the time her fourth album *From the Choirgirl Hotel* came out in the spring of 1998, many fans probably knew that Amos was fond of calling her songs "my girls" as if they were her daughters. But there was something behind what may have appeared simply as a silly, whimsical classification: Amos had suffered a miscarriage before she started work on this album, and most certainly felt the child was a girl. Music helped her work through her grief and pain; she says at one point in *Pieces* that she wanted to bring the child back. Instead, she realized she had to make the songs of *Choirgirl* her own; that they were her own sonic creations.

It makes sense, then, that *Choirgirl* represented a true turning point for her as a songwriter. Amos started to tackle bigger themes because her life was presenting her with bigger challenges. Consequently, the album took on a fuller sound that was more like that of a modern rock band. The addition of drum loops and other electronic embellishments added a heaviness and new sonic textures, as did multiple and at times overlapping vocal tracks. However, singles such as "Spark," the album's first track, still exude a feel that can be found in all of her successful singles—a loping, looping, rollicking sensibility and a chorus that ambles and climbs with acrobatic vocals, all of which resolves itself by the song's end.

The intimate, difficult nature of some of the content of the songs, though, did yield some accessible emotional entry points for listeners. Additionally, they were more tuneful than the classically oriented compositions from *Boys*. On *Choirgirl*, too, her biting, wicked sense of humor started to emerge.

For example, she told *Rolling Stone* magazine, "Songs started to come, and they showed me different ways of feeling and expressing, ways that surprised me. 'Playboy Mommy' dealt with my feelings of rejection—'Wasn't I enough to be your mother, didn't you want me? Well, don't come, then. Go choose some little right-wing Christian for your mother.' It's a human response" (Daly 1998).

Unfortunately, Amos would suffer through two more miscarriages in the next two years by the time she was touring in support of *To Venus and Back*, a double album released in September 1999. The title pays homage to Venus, the goddess of love, but (according to Amos) in a more compassionate way, as Amos says most women perceive Venus as permission to be narcissistic. Amos sought the more benevolent, healing aspects of the planet Venus's mythical influence, responding to events in her personal life and in the music business where there was too much aggression—which she likens astrologically to Mars—especially in rap music.

Despite the hardship and emotional upheaval wrought by the miscarriages, Amos said that when she was working on *Choirgirl* and also *Venus*, "I was home." Her selves were more integrated. "If your human woman doesn't catch up with what's happening in the song world, then you can't imprint this knowledge and thread it into your living tapestry" (Amos and Powers 2005, 119). With *Venus*, that tapestry was even more deeply embedded in electronica with some otherworldly influences, as heard in the single "Bliss," with its rambling chorus, and the mid-tempo, keyboard-heavy song "Concertina." However, there are moments of straightforward, piano-based narratives, such as the single "1000 Oceans." The first album, which she dubbed "Venus orbiting" is comprised of eleven new songs and the second, "Still orbiting," takes its material from live performances recorded in 1998. *All Music Guide* called the album "her most cohesive work since *Under the Pink*." Although the album eventually went platinum along with the three tracks that sold as singles, it became her first album to not debut in the Top 10 UK chart—a significant lapse, considering her longstanding success in that market. The single "Bliss" also garnered considerably less radio play than her previous albums and peaked at ninety-one on the *Billboard* Hot 100.

Amos finally became pregnant successfully and decided to listen to her body and take some time off while she was pregnant with her daughter Natashya. Because she only had one album left to satisfy her contract with Atlantic, she decided to release a collection of covers of songs by male songwriters and singers, rendered from a female perspective. She called the album *Strange Little Girls*. It was another way she could pay homage to Venus. Notable covers included songs by Slayer, Tom Waits, The Beatles, Neil Young, Depeche Mode, and Eminem.

She did not work, per se, during her pregnancy and she did not tour, but the songs she wrote for what would become 2002's *Scarlet's Walk* began to take root as she spent time in her beach house in Florida. As her first release for Epic

Records in 2002, the album's eighteen songs explored Native American history and Amos's own Eastern Cherokee roots. Amos cast herself as Scarlet, who journeys through the album's stops, turns, and moments toward becoming, for all intents and purposes, a middle-aged woman. Scarlet's "walk" is situated against a meandering map of America included in the album art. The songs "A Sorta Fairytale," "Crazy," "Your Cloud," "Indian Summer," and "Wampum Prayer" all concern the reverence for the earth that she was taught as a child. "I wanted to communicate that your relationship to your nation, and to the earth, is very personal," and that this relationship is something that people must claim for themselves. "The land has a spirit and she is alive," said Amos (Amos and Powers 2005, 218).

Something oddly prescient happened during the writing of this particular album. Although Amos wrote the song "I Can't See New York" in May 2001, by the time the album was released in 2002 in the aftermath of the terrorist attacks in New York City on September 11, 2001, most listeners couldn't help but imbue it with a different meaning. The album also felt more political than previous material, as Amos was responding to America's military involvement in Afghanistan and the second Gulf War. In "Amber Waves," inspired by the name of actress Julianne Moore's character in the film *Boogie Nights*, Amos visits a friend who is an aging, fading porn star by the same name. But Amos also acknowledges that America, as an idea, has been "pimped out," bought and sold and marketed as a commodity. In some ways, the album can be read as a gentle critique, an affectionate warning, to Americans: If we do not preserve and revere our own land, it will be taken away from us.

Although some critics thought *Scarlet's Walk* was an all-too-easy rock formula—the concept album—many agreed that it marked a strong return to her previous form. The album, as a whole, for all its extensive metaphorical underpinnings, showed a warmth, cohesion, and groundedness that many fans welcomed. It peaked at number seven on the *Billboard* Top 200 Album chart, and the same position for *Billboard*'s Top Internet albums; it also is the only of her albums, thus far, that has stalled before reaching gold status.

While writing the songs for 2005's *The Beekeeper*, Amos kept in mind ideas of pollination, of the various sides and components that create the shape and substance of a honeycomb. "I've been walking through many different types of gardens. The songs were trying to show me they formed a shape and were independent but connected to each other, no different from the structure of hexagonal cells that make up the beehive," she wrote (Amos and Powers 2005, 78).

*She's a really, really strong player. She has a really wide depth of range, just dynamically, and she knows the instrument really well. . . with Tori, it's as if she's made for the instrument in a certain sort of way. There's some sort of spatial relationship between her brain and her body and the piano—everything's always right there. She rarely makes a mistake, even when she's doing something that's not rehearsed or if she's improvising.*

—Jon Evans, bassist

Much as Amos was able to use this metaphor to unite and celebrate the various components—or sides—of her own persona, the album also deals with loss—specifically, the loss of her brother in a tragic car accident prior to its release. The title track addresses it. "It was originally written about my mother—she was critical, and she flat-lined and came back. That's the last time I saw my brother," she told *Rolling Stone* in an online exclusive story. The album's sad and poignant capper, "Toast," was written on the airplane on the way home from her brother's funeral. Overall, like *Scarlet's Walk*, *The Beekeeper* was another overly long (nineteen tracks), loosely autobiographical song-cycle, situated this time in different gardens all tended to by the album's beekeeper protagonist. Musically *The Beekeeper* introduces the Hammond B3 and other organs, which allowed Amos to further expand her songwriting capabilities and imbue her music with a newfound soulfulness and at times, a bit of funkiness. The album debuted on the *Billboard* chart at number five, selling 83,000 units in the first week. *Billboard* called it "some of the most accessible music of her career, coupled with beautifully obscure lyrics" (2005). At press time, however, the album had not yet reached Recording Industry Association of America (RIAA) certification; it has sold about 350,000 copies in the United States.

The album is not completely about loss. Although admittedly inspired by her new B3 organ (she calls it "Big Momma") and her relationship with another B3 that she views as a male organ, she wrote "Sweet the Sting" to some degree about "the marriage of the sacred and the profane" and the balancing of the masculine and feminine elements in her own songwriting. This merging of sacred and profane, however, is Amos's lifelong mission as a songwriter: to unite sexuality and spirituality and fight the dichotomy that American popular culture establishes for young women. On her 2007 release *American Doll Posse*, Amos took the idea of image formation even further. Over the course of twenty-three songs, she sings from the perspective of women whose personalities relate somehow to Greek and Roman female archetypes. As a concept, it's probably the most risky, intellectual, and "out there" album she has yet to release. In 2007, Jenny Eliscu in *Rolling Stone* paid Amos a bit of a left-handed compliment and said that "there's way too much conceptual malarkey surrounding the songs, but if you can ignore her fake posse, you'll find this is Amos's best album in many years." Nevertheless, fans are still with her: It became a number five seller on the *Billboard* 200 album charts and fared the same for the Internet album charts.

## MISSION, MOTIVATION, PROCESS

From the very start of her songwriting career, Amos, like many artists, wrestled with the demons, unanswered questions, and inconsistencies she experienced growing up. When she does not know the answer to something, Amos is likely to turn to books for the answer. Amos travels with a library on the tour bus, an extensive collection of books, newspapers, magazines—anything that shows potential to become fodder for songwriting or general contemplation. When Amos released her first greatest hits album, it was not too surprising that she called it *Tales of a Librarian*.

As for cataloging her songwriting process, inspiration, and ideas, Amos keeps a file—literally or figuratively—of what she calls her "song motifs," which consist of anything from a line or a lyric to a full-fledged melody. She is painstaking but somewhat disorganized about it and keeps a recorder next to her Bösendorfer piano at her home. She keeps tapes stacked up but not in any particular order—she knows where to find what she needs.

When she sits down to write, she has already gathered hundreds of notes, snatches of conversations, ideas, words, and phrases. Amos can sit for hours doing this sort of work, but it's no guarantee that the result is useful. Still, she has faith that although a good idea will stick with her, it may not always reemerge when she's seeking it. She admitted that sometimes songs do just come through but also ". . . if I don't go through this painstaking cataloging process, then these pieces of music are just ideas that never become tangible" (Amos and Powers 2005, 110). Sometimes a motif will emerge. Her husband Mark Hawley said that he has seen her write songs in a few minutes, such as "Marianne" from *Boys for Pele*, but it is not the usual procedure. He says that Amos works painstakingly hard on all aspects of her songwriting, regardless of whether it is one lyric line or an entire section of a song.

Inspiration can strike at any moment, and she believes "verses are setups; choruses are payoffs. They need to be. Music and words often come together when a song Being initially shows herself to me. I don't always get the full story" (115). Showing her keen grasp of and love for metaphor, Amos likened the structure of a song to the structure of a house. "Sometimes you want the chorus to be the kitchen in a song. Sometimes you want the chorus to be the shower, very cleansing. Sometimes it is in the bedroom" (106–107).

Regarding the songwriting process, she said, "I believe that the songs choose you, but you have to be willing to develop and stretch as a player, or your repertoire is only going to be of a certain type." Certainly this is something she has managed to steer clear of: learning to play various types of the organ has expanded her songwriting and essentially changed her music. But she returns to the metaphor of architecture—of a blueprint, of a building. "Imagine that you have been able to let yourself into this fascinating architectural space but you are in only one room and you do not know how to get to the other rooms because as of now there are no doorways. It becomes like a sonic puzzle" (117).

### Themes: Goddesses, Myths, Archetypes, and Religion

Traveling with the extensive library allows Amos to dip into various subjects and areas of interest, whether it's Jungian archetypes, religious figures, feminism, or mythology. Most of what she writes is filtered through this self-conscious reservoir of information, and she believes she is "in service" to these myths and ideas. This deep understanding of myths and archetypes allows Amos to explore how they surface in her own life and in her songwriting.

One of Amos's longstanding archetypes of exploration is Mary Magdalene. She tells of a formative experience that occurred when she was just eight years old, sitting at the Sunday dinner table with her family and some bishops from the Methodist church. The bishops were using a metaphor to describe Jesus's relationship to the church and its followers. The bishop likened Jesus to a bridegroom and the Christian church to his bride. Bravely, but politely, Amos asked about Mary Magdalene. The question raised a few eyebrows and prompted a discussion at the table among the bishops and her father about how Mary Magdalene was a fallen woman whom Jesus saved and blessed. Amos realized that organized religion had downplayed Mary Magdalene's role.

The conversation stayed with her, and as she began to play music and develop into a songwriter, more scholarly and literary works were published that explored the controversial idea (among religious scholars and believers) that Jesus and Mary Magdalene were married. It is also debated that she is an uncredited apostle whose teachings and writings were suppressed and subsequently forgotten during the choosing of the gospels—and for much of recent history. But that is not entirely the point—it is not important that Amos believes in what some might consider an historical footnote at best. She was able to see a parallel between the way in which Mary Magdalene had not only been ostracized and eliminated from history by the church, but the way in which women in general—and specifically in Amos's own line of work—were silenced and marginalized. She began to see the inflexible thinking that is common in established institutions—religion and capitalism specifically—and started to explore the idea of how a woman could be both sensual and spiritual. These questions stay with her and form much of the impetus of her songwriting. How can a woman be whole if she does not and cannot acknowledge both of these sides of her humanity? Amos believes that the piano enables her to resolve and unite those issues.

From the beginning of her solo career, Amos started exploring what she calls the archetypes of the two Marys—Mary, the virgin mother of Jesus, and Mary Magdalene. Feminist scholars refer to this dichotomy of culturally constructed roles for women as the virgin/whore complex—a woman is exclusively one or the other and cannot contain elements of both. Amos also refers to this process as integrating the sacred and profane. She describes the song "God" as a turning point, because it enabled her to unite those seemingly disparate parts of her being. Other songs later in her career, such as "Marys of the Sea," reprise this attempt for reconciliation as well. In the aforementioned song "Amber Waves" from *Scarlet's Walk*, the narrator watches Amber retain her dignity and sense of self in the midst of her own demise. As Amos has commented, "the Magdalene and America are really good synonyms because they've both been pimped out, though they always resurface" (Amos and Powers 2005, 99).

By the time she was set to write *Boys for Pele*, Amos was in the thick of researching archetypes. The self-fragmentation process she describes coming out of *Under the Pink* was fully explored when she went to Hawaii and took a spiritual journey with a female guru who was able to break a person down into his or her very essence. Amos needed to come to terms with her own anger—her own darkness, so to speak—and so she set out exploring the Dark Prince archetype, the one who can bring light in the darkness. Consequently, *Boys* is probably her darkest, most difficult listen.

What is perhaps most controversial—or intriguing, depending on your perspective—is how all this research inspires and surfaces in her songwriting. With such heady, obscure references and metaphorically heavy songs, it is understandable that she would be misunderstood at times. Although Amos does not let anyone else dictate what she should do with her songwriting and her career, she does want to be understood. She has even joked about this, saying "I know I sound like *The Little Mermaid* on acid. People have had a really hard time, because they think you cannot be a really strong woman and sound like I do. I just refuse to buy anybody's projections of what my instruments are, what the sound of my voice is, what my songs are" (Reece 1996). Of course, people will make snap judgments, but her fans (and most thoughtful music journalists) have enough working knowledge of how her songs are put together that there is an implicit understanding; fans are willing to go on the ride that each Tori Amos song provides.

## LEGACY AND OTHER INTERESTS

By the late 1990s, many of the major labels had merged and consolidated, leaving many critically acclaimed but underselling artists homeless. Although Amos generally enjoyed an amicable relationship with Atlantic until the end of her run with them, the music business is a fickle beast. After the departure of executive Polly Anthony from Epic Records in September 2003, Amos left the label and formed a partnership with industry veterans John Witherspoon, who has worked with Amos for over a decade, and Chelsea Laird, who had served as tour manager for a few years, to launch the Bridge Entertainment Group. Their mission was to aid artists who were in transition—between labels or management companies or who were putting their efforts toward touring and reaching the media. With this focus on aiding artists who were without management, Amos was the new venture's first client. According to Bridge's Web site, Amos cites the "shocking" exit of Epic Records president Polly Anthony as the catalyst for starting the new company. "Polly was one of the main reasons why I signed with the label," Amos said in a Web posting. But the music business was changing; labels were "letting a lot of ideas people go, and for a lot of artists that are dependent on these people, they don't know where to turn," Amos told *Billboard*. That's how Bridge was born. Bridge Entertainment Group's first release was Amos's greatest hits collection *Tales of a Librarian*.

To say that the Internet has simply changed the way musicians can market and distribute their materials—and connect with fans—would be an understatement. With the advent of the iTunes software in early 2001, which enables users to download music either by the album or by the song, Amos, like many artists with a backlog of interesting material, released an iTunes-exclusive mini-album called *Tori Amos Live Session* in 2005, with four songs. The Internet has also made it much easier to find singles, which were often packed with special bonus material. It has served as a way for the prolific Amos to share music that might not otherwise get released—such as the haunting cover of Nirvana's "Smells Like Teen Spirit"—and give the fans something special. These EP-like singles have become collector's items, the songs (such as "Take to the Sky," which initially appeared on *Y Kant Tori Read*) now part of her regular touring repertoire.

Additionally, in 2005, Sony released a handful of live albums, available individually through iTunes or as a set through retail outlets. Each album was recorded in one city, such as Boston, Chicago, Denver, and Los Angeles in the United States and Manchester and London in England. Fans rejoiced and hailed it as a long overdue move by her record label.

Amos's legacy as an unconventional artist has shown that it is possible to be thoughtful and complex and still reach a broad and engaged audience that remains devoted and curious as to what she might come up with next. Her strength and uncompromising approach to songwriting inspired untold numbers of women to find their own voices, too. In establishing the organization RAINN, Amos parlayed her experiences and her own growing musical profile to provide women in difficult times of abuse with resources they need. She has spoken from both her imagination and her life in her songwriting, which has cemented her status as an icon.

## SELECTED DISCOGRAPHY

*Little Earthquakes*. Atlantic, 1992
*Under the Pink*. Atlantic, 1994
*Boys for Pele*. Atlantic, 1996
*From the Choirgirl Hotel*. Atlantic, 1998

## FURTHER READING

Amos, Tori, and Ann Powers. *Tori Amos: Piece By Piece: A Portrait of the Artist, Her Thoughts, Her Conversations*. New York: Broadway Books, 2005.

Bell, Carrie. "Artist-Founded Agency Offers Support to Rape Victims." *Billboard* (August 14, 1999).

*Billboard.* "Album Reviews." (February 22, 2005).

Bridge Entertainment Group. See www.tbentgroup.com.

Cohen, Howard. "Tori-Speak Makes Sense, If You Listen Awhile." *Miami Herald* (April 12, 1996).

Dalphonse, Sherri. "The Virtues of Tori Amos." *Washington Magazine* (February 1994).

Daly, Steven. "Her Secret Garden." *Rolling Stone* 789 (June 25, 1998).

Eliscu, Jenny. "American Doll Posse." *Rolling Stone* online (May 3, 2007). Available online at www.rollingstone.com/reviews/album/14300667/review/14459317/american_doll_posse.

Flick, Larry. "Tori Amos Shares Life Lessons." *Billboard* (March 28, 1992).

Flick, Larry. "Label Tickled 'Pink' Over New Tori Amos Set." *Billboard* (December 4, 1993).

Harrington, Richard. "Finally, a Prodigy Finds Her Song: Tori Amos, Back Home With a Haunting Album." *Washington Post* (March 22, 1992).

Harrington, Richard. "Tori Amos, In the Pink: Singer Moves Beyond the Horrors of Her Past to Stardom." *Washington Post* (June 20, 1994).

Morris, Chris. "'O'-for-1: Omarion Along at Top." *Hollywood Reporter* (March 3, 2005).

Newman, Melinda. "The Beat: Amos Builds a Bridge for Artists." *Billboard* (October 25, 2003).

Reece, Douglas. "International Fan Base Propelling Tori Amos' Atlantic Set." *Billboard* (February 17, 1996).

Robertson, Jessica. "Q&A: Tori Amos Talks in Tongues." *Rolling Stone* online (March 30, 2006). Available online at www.rollingstone.com/artists/toriamos/articles/story/9549653/qa_tori_amos_talks_in_tongues.

Courtesy of Photofest

# Joan Baez

## OVERVIEW

It is not easy to categorize Joan Baez as just a singer/songwriter or an inter-preter, because she has done both throughout her nearly fifty-year career. She is well known outside the music industry for many things—her activism, her relationship with Bob Dylan in the 1960s, and her beautiful voice. To some extent, Joan Baez is perhaps better known for her political activism and ef-forts to raise awareness on a number of issues from immigration to human rights and, most notably, the peace movement; Baez has advocated for nonviolent resolution to political and social problems.

Baez's career has ebbed and flowed over the years. Marked by a strong debut at the dawn of the 1960s and a period of intense activity during the ensuing two decades, Baez's career slipped into relative obscurity in the 1980s as the tenor of the music business shifted and artists with personal and politi-cal messages fell out of favor. However, that would change somewhat in the early 1990s when the singer/songwriter movement emerged. Artists such as Sinead O'Connor, Tracy Chapman, Michelle Shocked, and Suzanne Vega and the band 10,000 Maniacs brought social, humanitarian, and political con-cerns into their songwriting and gained fans and critical acclaim doing so. These artists owed no small debt to Baez. Unlike many of those folksingers, however, Baez started out interpreting the classic works of others, so much so that *All Music Guide* calls her "the most accomplished interpretive folksinger of the 1960s." Music journalist Kurt Loder said "Baez explicitly combined the qualities of folkie purism and social virtuousness. She was an inspiration to a generation of young women who grew their hair long and free and parted it in the middle" (Holt 1989, 83).

Baez's career has also been inextricably linked with that of folk-rock musi-cian Bob Dylan, whose iconic, long-term success and relevance some might argue surpasses her own. However, she was an early supporter of his then-unique folk-rock style. Together, the two have collaborated on projects and extensively performed and written songs. Their difficult relationship and intriguing dynamic is most vividly captured on the D.A. Pennebaker docu-mentary film *Don't Look Back* (1967) and in her own music on the 1975 album *Diamonds & Rust*.

During the 1960s through the mid-1970s, Baez was arguably at her most prolific and produced her most noteworthy albums; from 1959 until 1979, Baez released nearly an album a year and made appearances on numerous others. She has appeared on more than two dozen recordings with or by other artists, most consistently those of Bob Dylan. Her material in the mid-1980s through the mid-1990s is not nearly as critically well regarded as her earlier work, partially due to a change in her voice—it got lower. Perhaps more important, the musical climate during the late 1980s and early to mid-1990s, despite the success of artists such as Tracy Chapman and Suzanne Vega, did not overwhelmingly embrace female artists who wrote didactic, politically charged songs. Consequently, Baez did not sell records in significant numbers through this transitional period. Her *Billboard* charting history illustrates this: From 1962 through 1979, Baez's albums appeared almost annually on the *Billboard* top albums charts (the chart system then was not nearly as complex and fractionalized as it is now). Despite her output through the 1980s, after 1979's *Honest Lullaby*, Baez experienced a nearly twenty-five-year absence on the *Billboard* charts. Her work did not appear there again until 2003's *Dark Chords on a Big Guitar*, which peaked at thirty-nine on the *Billboard* Top Independent Albums chart.

With over several dozen records released to date, starting from her self-titled debut in 1960 through 2005's *Bowery Songs* (live), Baez's albums, surprisingly, have never reached platinum status. A mere seven of them have achieved gold status, including *Joan Baez, Volume 2, Joan Baez in Concert, Joan Baez, Blessed Are . . . , Any Day Now, Diamonds & Rust*, and the single "The Night They Drove Old Dixie Down." In 2007, she received a Lifetime Achievement Award from the National Association of Recording Arts and Sciences, the organization that awards the Grammys. Baez never received a Grammy Award for a specific recording despite the nearly fifty years that she has been active in the music business.

Baez's trajectory as an artist is typical of many from her generation who came of age and started writing music during the politically tumultuous 1960s. Like an artist who starts as a voice for the counterculture and then gradually reaches a wider mass audience, Baez experienced some growing pains and critical resistance. Through the years, critics noted that Baez's voice was starting to sound different—her range had decreased—a fact that may explain some but not all of her audience erosion. Still, for someone who makes a living using her voice it is not unusual to have to adjust one's material accordingly. Baez calls her singing voice her "greatest gift," and that voice shaped her life.

## EARLY YEARS

Baez is the product of middle-class Quaker upbringing. Her physicist father, Alberto Vinicio Baez, also worked as a UNESCO consultant and is author of a textbook called *The Spiral Approach to Physics*. Born in Staten Island, New York, Baez is the second of three daughters, in between older sister Pauline and younger sister (and longtime activist) Mimi. Although her father was certainly skilled and talented enough to work for the government, he instead went into higher education. The family traveled a lot because of his work, and as a child Baez spent time in Paris, Baghdad, Bangkok, and Switzerland. When she was in fifth grade the family moved to southern California. Baez is named after her mother, Joan Bridge Baez, who was born in Scotland and moved to the United States when she was just two years old. Bridge Baez's own mother died when she was three.

One formative experience Baez describes, acknowledging her mother's intelligence at raising girls in foreign places, took place when they were living in Baghdad, Iraq. The Baez sisters were getting into a lot of trouble, Joan especially, and for about a year her mother kept her out of school. She learned and explored on her own, made cakes, dug around and looked for ants and watched their behavior. Baez realized that that year of freedom contributed to her creativity and acknowledged her mother for giving that chance to her. By Joan's accounts, their relationship was close, supportive, and warm. Later, her mother even went to jail with Joan for civil disobedience.

In a Quaker house, silence, meditation, and introspection are all essential components of the religion. By the time Baez had reached junior high, she had grown accustomed to being teased for her dark skin and her Mexican background (on her father's side). The experience of living with her own ethnic difference undoubtedly gave her sympathy and compassion for others who were different or somehow socially awkward. In her 1968 memoir *Daybreak*, she reflects on her upbringing and her time spent in foreign countries and tells stories of looking after neighborhood animals that had been neglected, injured, or abused. As a child, she describes herself as sad and skinny and eager for friends. Around eighth grade, she was so depressed that she related an occasion where she had not eaten anything for three days and expressed self-consciousness about the dark rings under her eyes, her skinniness, and her pimples. She went to see the Baez family doctor, who told her she was beautiful and gave her a milkshake and a hamburger. At this point, the Baez family was back in southern California. This undercurrent of sadness and melancholy would remain with her in varying degrees throughout her life, although somehow it never interfered with or detracted from her idealism and activism.

Her Quaker background helped develop her steadfast dedication to pacifism and nonviolence. By the time Baez was a teenager in high school, she had already become influenced by the writing of Mahatma Gandhi. Baez started practicing civil disobedience as a teenager, so by the time she became a recorded musician it was a natural activity. For instance, when she was in high school in Palo Alto, California (the family had moved again), she protested an air raid drill the school had scheduled after she had done some reading in her father's books that basically proved that there was not enough time to walk home and go into the cellar—a common activity during an air raid drill. Instead, she stayed in her seat (Ingram 1991, 55).

In the 1950s, the Baez family moved to Boston so Alberto could teach at MIT, and Baez enrolled at Boston University to study theater. "I don't know why I went in the theater school, because I hated every second of it. After a while, I just dropped out, flunked everything." However, the time in Boston was well spent, because the scene there exposed her to the possibilities and provided her with a place to play. "I was really drawn into the whole scene of coffee shops and singing and the early English folk songs" and said she was "very stuffy" about her choice of music (Holt 1989, 86). Around this time she was listening to Odetta, Harry Belafonte, and other lesser-known folk artists such as Joe Mapes, Cynthia Gooding, and John Jacob Niles. Inspired by a visit to one of these coffee shops, Tulla's Coffee Grinder, with her father, Baez started playing guitar. Another establishment in town, Club 47, was primarily a jazz joint but Tuesdays were free, so the women who ran it offered Baez the opportunity to play for ten dollars (Holt 1989, 86). She says there were fewer than ten people there, but word of mouth was good. Despite the fact that Baez forgot the words in the middle of a song, a crowd began to form week after week to hear her play.

Baez made her noteworthy public debut at the first Newport Folk Festival in 1959, which was created as an offshoot of the then six-year-old Newport Jazz Festival, held in Newport, Rhode Island every summer. Also appearing at the folk festival were Pete Seeger, Odetta, the New Lost City Ramblers, Kingston Trio, Bob Gibson, and Earl Scruggs. Writing in the *New York Times* about her performance, Robert Shelton said her "fervid, lush soprano voice was impressive" (Shelton 1959). Gibson personally invited her to Newport to perform "Virgin Mary Had One Son" and "Jordan River" with him because she was not well known enough to have merited an invitation under her own steam.

When she started making subsequent public appearances, writers such as Shelton called her a "folk revivalist," in reference to earlier protest songwriters such as Woody Guthrie and Pete Seeger. He wrote of a performance of hers at the 92nd Street YMCA in New York City that illustrated the contrast between Baez and many other folk singers of the day—she possessed a cool stage manner and delivery that permitted her poetic lyrics and pretty melodies to stand out, and he continued to predict that she faced a bright future (Shelton 1960).

She appeared at the 1960 Newport Folk Festival, and at that point she had been signed by Vanguard Records. She recorded her first album in four nights in a stinky hotel ballroom on Broadway, with just two microphones: one for the voice and one for the guitar. At the time, it was common to record quickly and efficiently and live, without too much fuss. The sonic trappings of a recording studio would not make much sense on the debut record of a folk artist.

More accolades came on the release of her self-titled debut *Joan Baez* in 1960, when she was just twenty years old. The *New York Times* loved her, with critic Robert Shelton commending her tone as especially noteworthy because she had not had any vocal training, but he said that it was a "clear-as-glass sound, sometime shimmering with a glint of reflected sunlight, then darkening a bit with a passing lowering cloud" (Shelton 1961). She had indeed made her mark on folk music, but she had yet to really establish herself among a field of other female folk artists such as Odetta, Mary O'Hara, Jeannie Robertson, Judy Collins, and Isla Cameron. He did offer some critique for her stage presence, saying that she seemed to slip away from her audience and into something resembling a trance with her music. Periodically, this criticism would surface throughout her career, but as she got older she turned to storytelling in between songs and that would bring the audience back.

But early success took its toll, like it often does on younger artists. Somehow, she was compared to the image of the Virgin Mary. "I thought that was a terrific idea. In fact, I was sure I was, and I felt very benign and wonderful. Because up until then, the only image I had of myself was of a dumb Mexican" (Holt 1989, 87). The political consciousness would come slowly, through the years. At the time, though, it is fair to say that Baez knew there was something she wanted to say, but she was not quite sure yet what it was. "I hadn't really emerged. I think I was probably known for some civil rights work at the time, but it wasn't clear to anybody—and it wasn't clear to me—what I was doing" (Holt 1989, 87).

## CAREER PATH

### *Political Consciousness and the Folksinger: The 1960s*

The tumultuous 1960s were really Baez's formative years. One might argue that if she had not come of age during this time period, she may never have recorded music quite in the same way she did, which just happened to be a way that made her famous. And one might argue that if she had never met Bob Dylan, she would not be nearly as well known for politically active songwriting and nonviolent activism as she currently is. Indeed, some twenty years after her arrival on the scene it is said that one of her most important contributions to the "folk" public included making accessible the traditional English ballads and the difficult early ballads of the unknown Bob Dylan.

After her debut album, which was made up of thirteen traditional songs, some of them children's ballads, she did not waste much time putting together live albums and studio releases. Shortly after *Joan Baez*, which sold modestly, *Joan Baez, Volume 2* came out in September 1961, which helped sell even more copies of her debut. This was followed by *Joan Baez in Concert* in September 1962. Although it is not easy to find response to Baez's work from that time—the convention of music criticism would not fully emerge until later in that decade with the launch of *Rolling Stone* magazine—commercial response does indicate some degree of cultural resonance, as all three of these albums went gold and remained on the charts for more than two years (Eder). *Time* magazine described her in a June 1962 article called "The Folk Girls" as possessing "an impeccable sense of dynamics and phrasing, and an uncanny ability to dream her way into the emotional heart of a song." *Time* reported that Baez was committed to the cause of folk music despite her growing, early success, saying, "she turned down $100,000 worth of concert dates in a single year." At the time, she was only touring on college campuses and for only a few months per year, but she also played at Carnegie Hall at the tender age of twenty-three.

In 1963, at the age of twenty-two, Baez met then-unknown folk singer Bob Dylan and began having an affair with him. She brought him onstage with her, and by 1964 the pair were performing together. She credits his song "The Death of Emmitt Till" as the catalyst that turned her into a political folk singer (Perry 2002). In retrospect, their relationship seems natural, inevitable even, given their interests and abilities. Their process felt symbiotic. Baez said that in the summer of 1962 "[h]e was turning out songs like ticker tape and I was stealing them as fast as he wrote them" (Goldsmith 1982).

> *Folk music depends on intent. If someone desires to make money, I don't call it folk music.*

There is much debate among critics about the degree to which Dylan was genuinely motivated and engaged with the antiwar protest and how "political" his songs really are. Furthermore, many feminist music critics contend that Baez opened his eyes to nonviolence and humanitarian issues. Starting in 1963, Baez refused to pay sixty percent of her income taxes to the government, claiming that it would have gone to "armaments" for the Vietnam War. Although the IRS ultimately got the money it was owed by putting a lien on her house, her car, and her land, she continued to do this for several years in the 1960s while the war was still going on.

Regardless of what was happening with her personal life, however, the song and the movement were inextricable and no one could deny her passion and commitment. In an article in the *New York Times* in 1980, Neil Alan Marks wrote an assessment of folk music, claiming that there was a resurgence. The article highlighted many important musical contributors to this genre and suggested that Baez's approach was "the acting out of folksong. One sensed her becoming the characters she sang about. As she presented a sensual (and much imitated) physical image, she also possessed what was, for the genre, a flawless soprano." Marks went on to declare that her self-titled debut held up through the years—he said it was "still lovely" and that her *Joan Baez in Concert* (1962) and *Farewell Angelina* (1965) releases were evidence that she had "reached artistic peaks." Critics agreed, saying that the latter release showed she was starting to beef up her mostly acoustic approach by adding other instruments and her voice, no doubt an influence of her relationship with Bob Dylan—who by 1965 had started to show signs of turning into the folk-rock artist he would ultimately become. Much of *Angelina* features songs he wrote, such as the title track (which he himself never officially recorded) along with "A Hard Rain's a-Gonna Fall" and "It's All Over Now Baby Blue."

As the 1960s progressed, Dylan became less of a factor in her songwriting and her music, and they gradually grew apart. She released a Christmas album called *Noel* in 1966 with Peter Schickele as arranger/conductor, and in 1967 worked with him again on an ornate album simply titled *Joan*, that was trying to come to terms with the change in the music world by integrating pop, rock, and folk. *All Music Guide*'s Bruce Eder calls it "the most self-consciously beautiful record Baez ever cut," most likely because Schickele added some lovely but sedate orchestral arrangements on ten of the album's twelve songs.

*This country has gone mad.*
*But I will not go mad with it.*
*I will not pay for organized*
*murder. I will not pay for the*
*war in Vietnam.*

Baez pulled from John Lennon and Paul McCartney but also Paul Simon, Jacques Brel, and her late brother-in-law Richard Farina. Two of her own compositions include "North" and "Saigon Bride," the latter of which is, unsurprisingly, an anti–Vietnam War song. Like many musicians of the 1960s, opposition to the Vietnam War gave her a cause to rally against, but for Baez it was pivotal, turning her toward the nonviolence movement so singularly that it would define the rest of her activism throughout her life.

By 1967, Baez was picketing outside draft boards in San Francisco, an act that got her arrested and charged with disturbing the peace, failure to disperse, and trespassing. Her future husband, David Harris, spoke at the event; he was identified as the former head of the Stanford University student body and a leader of the group called "The Resistance" (Turner 1967). During her ten-day sentence in jail she met Harris and they fell in love.

### The 1970s: Marriage, Protest, and Experimenting with New Sounds

Her marriage to antiwar protest leader David Harris in 1968 resulted in a few albums that were tinged with country sounds (Harris was a fan of country music) such as *David's Album* in 1969 and *One Day at a Time* in 1970. Cementing her position as a skilled interpreter of other people's music, the double album *Blessed Are . . .* went gold and featured a Top 10 hit, a cover of The Band's classic "The Night They Drove Old Dixie Down."

James Coyne made a documentary film in black and white about Baez and her husband Harris called *Carry It On*. Baez released an album by the same name as a soundtrack to the film (Eder). The marriage did not last long, however. In December 1969 Baez gave birth to a son, Gabriel. Starting in mid-1969, Harris served a jail sentence for draft dodging and was released in 1971; she wrote "A Song for David," and "Fifteen Months," among others, during his incarceration. By January 1972 the pair had separated, and as of August of 1973 they officially divorced after five years of marriage. At the time, Harris explained to his friends (as told by *Time* magazine), "Living together is getting in the way of our relationship." And Baez agreed. "We're continuing to work together, and our son Gabriel is thriving, and that's all that matters anyway" (*Time* 1972). Later, in his autobiography, Harris suggested that the marriage was a product of the times. Baez has remained a single parent since then, and in 1973 she told the press she was bisexual.

She switched labels to A&M Records for the 1972 album *Come From the Shadows*, which bore more of a pop music influence than folk music. By the turn of the decade, starting with the 1970 release of *One Day at a Time*, rather than strictly working as an interpreter and collaborator Baez started to write her own material. The best example of those efforts is her landmark album *Diamonds & Rust* (1975), which also marked her best chart position, just missing the Top 10 and peaking at number eleven in 1975. The album also achieved gold selling status. Although it had covers of songs written by Stevie Wonder, John Prine, Jackson Browne, and the Allman Brothers Band, the album also featured many of tracks written by Baez herself.

In *Rolling Stone*, Kurt Loder calls *Diamonds & Rust* "the celebrated ode to Bobby," meaning her defunct relationship with Bob Dylan. Much of her songwriting bears the influence of her time with him, both musically and lyrically, but none more so than the title track, "Diamonds & Rust," which has a meandering, repetitive melody with verses that merely mention the title of the song and that does not have a clear-cut chorus. The song reveals pieces of a relationship vis-à-vis a phone call. In the opening line, she sings, "Well I'll be damned/Here comes your ghost again." She continues the straightforward reminiscence with affection and leads up to what should be the payoff of the chorus but instead, a solemn revelation: "We both know what memories can bring/They bring diamonds and rust." Later in the album, Baez covers The Band's song "The Night They Drove Old Dixie Down." Baez sings of herself in third person in "Winds of the Old Days," and she forgives Dylan for abandoning the protest movement and says goodbye, at least in song, to the days of the 1960s.

The success of that album was followed an album full of all-Baez compositions, *Gulf Winds* (1976). The ensuing years were marked by label changes; *Blowin' Away* was released by CBS Records' Portrait Label in June 1977, as was *Honest Lullaby* (1979). She left CBS and released *European Tour* (1980) in Europe on the Portrait label but not in the United States. Although during 1979 Baez toured in support of *Honest Lullaby* in twenty-two cities, her activist efforts were starting to occupy more of her time than her songwriting. But with such shuffling around from label to label, it was not clear what kind of audience was still left for aging folksingers who were trying to find their place in a post–Vietnam War era.

The *Washington Post* called *Honest Lullaby* "disturbingly ambivalent, torn between the artist's personal past and her political present. . . The arrangements are simple, clean and clearly tailored to serve as a backdrop" (Joyce 1979). Baez took part in writing four of the ten tracks, and Joyce says that her "congested wordplay" is on display on the title track and on "Michael," but he credits her own composition "For Sasha" and her take on the reggae classic "No Woman, No Cry." In general, however, he argued that the release showed that Baez felt safe drawing from the "wellspring of traditional ballads and spirituals" (Joyce 1979).

The late 1970s were not an easy time for Baez, personally or professionally, but they were only a warning of the transition she would find herself facing in the ensuing years, in the wake of the Vietnam War, the dissolution of her marriage, the splintering of the antiwar movement, and a sense of homelessness in terms of her musical career, as she moved from label to label (Darling 1969).

*Action is the antidote to despair.*

Despite the unsettled nature of her personal life and her musical career and her disappointment that the movement's efforts that the end of the Vietnam War did not mean the end of violence, Baez continued her activism. She told the *Washington Post* in mid-1979, "I wasn't disillusioned. I've always saved disillusionment and depression for my personal life" (Darling 1979).

In 1979, Baez's attention turned more consistently to nonviolence and forming her own organization, called Humanitas International. Baez started Humanitas, along with six activist women friends, not only as a way to address human rights issues around the world that other organizations could not handle but also because she was motivated to do her own thing. "Instead of helping other people out with theirs, I wanted to be able to define what I did." The work comes at the expense of any political orientation. "[O]ur whole emphasis at Humanitas is to drop ideology and learn to see repression for what it is. A rubber-hose beating is a rubber-hose beating, whether it's administered in South Africa or Latin America or Siberia" (Holt 1989, 88).

By mid-1979, Baez had her issue—the Vietnamese government's oppressive and cruel treatment of its own political prisoners. Certainly Baez had not remained silent on the issue of the Vietnam War and visited Hanoi in the early 1970s, but her position surprised many in the antiwar movement for its bold attack on a Communist government. She wrote an open letter to Vietnam's leaders, which was published in a handful of newspapers and signed by Lily Tomlin, Norman Lear, James Michener, Cesar Chavez, and Nat Hentoff—none of them strangers to protest movements of the 1960s and 1970s (Graustark 1979). This act alienated her from other activists regarding the Vietnam War, including Jane Fonda, Daniel Ellsberg, Tom Hayden, and others (Graustark 1979). Baez was beginning to carve out her own niche and display that she said what she meant and she meant what she said, that torture is torture regardless of ideology. Her efforts did not always make her popular. On tour in support of *Honest Lullaby* in Seattle, for example, she was taunted by crowds with chants of "The CIA Loves Joan Baez" and "Don't Swallow Joanie's Baloney" (Beck, Reese, and Kasindorf 1979). Alternately, Baez spent time touring Southeast Asia's refugee camps, singing at fundraisers in Washington, DC, and appearing before the Senate Judiciary Committee, describing the poverty and homelessness of the refugees (Beck, Reese, and Kasindorf 1979). By the end of the 1970s, Baez's voice had reached many new audiences, more loudly and clearly than ever before.

### Staying Vital in Music's Changing Climate: The Reagan Years

Whereas Baez may have become more solidly committed to her beliefs than ever before throughout the 1970s, cementing her position in American music and culture, she was experiencing, for the first time, the limitations of her voice and the ravages of time and touring. She started taking voice lessons for the first time and said, "[T]he upper range is dulling in my old age. A little training and I can stretch my voice another five, ten years" (Beck, Reese, and Kasindorf 1979). Although political matters gave her a different voice and stretched her in new directions in the 1980s, the music business was less kind to her.

*I'm not a utopian fool. I see the world full of conflicts.*

After the release of *Honest Lullaby*, it took another seven years for Baez to find an American record label that was willing to work with her. Her politics had complicated matters, but she still had plenty of material for an album. The early part of the 1980s continued much in the same vein as did the late 1970s—with Baez lending her support and her efforts to causes worldwide, such as the Catholic Church's human rights and workers' committees efforts and anti–nuclear war efforts in Brazil (*New York Times* 1981), and she gave a free concert in Chile in support of a human rights group. She was prohibited from performing in commercial venues in Brazil and Chile because they thought her music was too threatening, so she sang wherever she could—in churches, people's homes, and anywhere else people gathered (McCarthy 1981). During these tours she sang her own material, native folk songs in Spanish and Portuguese, and covered John Lennon's ode to peace "Imagine" and Dylan's 1960s classic "Blowin' in the Wind."

Still, when she performed Baez could still captivate a crowd even with an evening of protest songs. In a concert review in 1981, Paul Hume of the *Washington Post* wrote that she "held forth with the high quivering luscious vocals that have marked her as one of the more distinctive song stylists of her generation. As usual, her voice was both an amazing and saving grace that somehow managed to override the soppier sentiments" (Hume 1981). The *New York Times* waxed similarly poetic, saying "her chest tones are, if anything, richer and darker than a decade ago, while her upper register remains remarkably clear and limber. Her voice is a truly oracular folk-pop instrument" (Holden 1982). If technically she was still proficient, critic Stephen Holden was less kind about her songwriting, saying that the likes of "Warriors of the Sun" and "Happy Birthday, Leonid Brezhnev," both original songs, were examples of the didactic excesses of folk music and "should be shelved."

In an interview with Kurt Loder of *Rolling Stone* in 1983, Baez said she had offers from European labels while she was working on material for a new album. It made sense, as Baez has consistently been popular with European audiences and spent much of the early 1980s touring Europe (Lacey 1982). The touring experience was fodder for songs that stemmed from her observations of the young adults in her audience who were trying to understand her message and reconcile it with their own apathy or cynicism; Baez was tentatively calling the album *Children of the Eighties*. About this growing collection of songs, she said that it needed other people's material and that for the first time, she really felt that she had to think carefully about her career, especially if she wanted to sell records in the United States. She recorded her demo tape with Mickey Hart of the Grateful Dead but it did not work out in the end—Baez said that she was "an intrusion" and there was "too much dope intake for me to break through" (Holt 1989, 85). But it was also difficult for her to make headway with American labels; she wasn't sure if they thought she was too old or that most young people were listening to and interested in something else.

Baez went with Gold Castle for *Recently* (1987), which was followed by the live album *Diamonds & Rust in the Bullring* (1989) and the studio release *Speaking of Dreams* (1989). Ingram writes that all these albums "continue to reflect her commitment to social issues" (Ingram 1991, 60). Three years later Virgin records released *Play Me Backwards*. Writing about this time period, Kurt Loder assessed that "when she had to choose between pursuing her political goals and maintaining a viable recording career, it was the beliefs that she stuck with" (Holt 1989, 83). At the time of the interview with *Rolling Stone*, Baez was forty-eight, still dedicating much of her time to humanitarian causes and only singing when the occasion called for it.

Along with all of these activist and musical projects, Baez wrote her second autobiography called *And A Voice To Sing With* (1987). Reviewing the book in the *New York Times*, Barbara Goldsmith summed up Baez's state of affairs succinctly, saying that Baez had "spent the last five years abroad, has not had a hit record in a decade and has no recording contract" and that in our "instant gratification, celebrity worshipping society, Joan Baez appears anachronistic and trails a weary wisdom" (1987). Baez herself writes of her struggle to make sense of the 1980s, "I am a stranger in my own land, always looking to feel comfortable without selling my soul" (Goldsmith 1987). Baez's book goes a long way to shed light on the psychological aspect of her experience—to quote Bob Dylan, the times, they were a-changing.

### The Resurgence of the Singer/Songwriter: 1990s and Beyond

Lucky for Baez, history—predictably—often repeats itself. In the mid 1990s, singer/songwriters, male and female alike, began to become popular once again. The resurgence was most likely a direct response to the rough, electric guitar–centric, masculine rock genre known as grunge, which became popular in the early 1990s with the likes of Nirvana, Pearl Jam, and Soundgarden, among others. Fans and music business moguls were looking for something different, although those different things were not the same thing. Fans were looking for something less masculine, less rough; music business honchos were looking for the next great musical trend they could market and make a profit from. But overall, the shift in the climate was beneficial for Baez. "I don't think anybody can pretend that folk music is coming back, but there seems to be an appetite for music you have to listen to with a more careful ear," she told the *New York Times* (Gavin 1992). The activities of the decade would prove her comment an understatement.

When she signed with Virgin Records in 1990, Baez knew that she needed something new so as to not sound like a relic of the 1960s (Gavin 1992). And different they are, as the songs for *Play Me Backwards* show Latin and African influences along with the steel slide guitar. The album was her twenty-eighth release and her first recording for a major music label since 1979. Baez wrote some of her own material, from "I'm With You," dedicated to her son Gabe, to the father-daughter reflection of "Edge of Glory," "all shining with autumnal wisdom," according to James Gavin of the *New York Times*. She brings her own beautiful touch to Mary Chapin Carpenter's classic "Stones in the Road," Janis Ian's "Amsterdam," and John Hiatt's "Through Your Hands." "Stones in the Road" even became Baez's first music video (Gavin 1992).

*Ring Them Bells* is a live album that features Baez and other artists whose material owes a great deal to her—Mary Chapin Carpenter, the Indigo Girls, and Mary Black. The album was released in 1995 and was recorded at the then-longstanding folk music club in New York called The Bottom Line. Although many of the tracks are her classics such as "Diamonds and Rust" and "The Night They Drove Old Dixie Down," there is something compelling about hearing Baez backed by female artists who have come into their own because of her pioneering work (Bessman 2003). In 1997 she released her first studio album in five years on Capitol called *Gone From Danger*. The material suggested that she had indeed been reinvigorated by working with many artists whom she had inspired: The album featured just one song written by Baez and the rest of the tracks are material from Sinéad Lohan, Dar Williams, Richard Shindell, and Betty Elders. In 1998, in support of the release, Baez benefited from touring with the younger, witty, literate songwriter Dar Williams and other similar artists, which enabled her to reach a whole new generation of music fans. Her appearance at the Newport Folk festival in summer 1997 helped to reinvigorate her career as much as it was a testament to her longevity. The largesse of spirit is indicative of the folk music community. In a review of the festival in the *Boston Globe*, Steve Morse said that artists such as Gillian Welch and Dar Williams sang with her on stage "like awestruck disciples," and that Baez "still infused the songs with that beautiful, if weathered soprano dating to 1959, when she first played Newport" (Morse 1997).

In the late 1990s, the folk-based singer/songwriter renewal was still going strong, and Baez spent much time touring—more time touring, in fact, than in the studio. Along with Ellis Paul, Patty Larkin, and the Nields, Baez helmed a fortieth anniversary celebration of the folk music mainstay Club Passim in Cambridge, Massachusetts, in 1999. Writing in the *Boston Globe*, Joan Anderman proclaimed that Baez "was, in a word, radiant. Time has softened her demeanor . . . and her voice, which is as powerful as when she cut her teeth at Club 47 in the late 50s, yet less stern and shrill" (Anderman 1999).

Yet another long span of time passed—six years—before *Dark Chords on a Big Guitar* was released in 2003. In the wake of the tragic attacks on the United States in September 2001, many people turned to the simple power of music for comfort, and musicians of all kinds responded with albums that addressed the nation's fragility as well as more overtly political issues such as calling the government to task for spearheading a war in Iraq. Proving that folk music can sustain itself and that she is still a relevant player in the pantheon, the record features songs by contemporary and at times edgier songwriters such as Ryan Adams, Steve Earle, Joe Henry, Natalie Merchant, Josh Ritter, and Gillian Welch and David Rawlings. The producer, Mark Spector, found the songs for the album, which she emphasized had to be "in the countercultural vein—a derivate of folk music of some kind" (Bessman 2003). The material, although not overtly political, does conjure up some latent activist suggestions. The song "Christmas in Washington," by Steve Earle, himself a roots rock songwriter who is not afraid to speak his mind, was a great fit for the album because it seeks the return of Woody Guthrie in an era that's driven by politicians and programmers. The song "In My Time of Need," by the prolific and versatile songwriter Ryan Adams, speaks from the point of view of a farmer who reflects on hard times.

In the interview with _Billboard_ to promote _Dark Chords on a Big Guitar_, Baez was alternately honest and humorous. She said that the situation of working with younger artists needs to be mutually beneficial and hoped that the experience would inspire other songwriters to write material expressly for her. "Working with younger songwriters gives the illusion that I'm younger than I am," she told _Billboard_. (At the time of the release she was sixty-two years old.) "But nobody in the world is as old as I am—except maybe Kris Kristofferson!" Baez, though, remains sanguine about the process and seems to feel inspired by what the younger folk musicians were putting together (Bessman 2003).

A year later, in 2004, a live recording was made of a concert in New York, and in 2005 it was released as _Bowery Songs_. The advent of digital media and the increasing number of niche-like opportunities for music distribution enabled Baez to reach a whole new generation of music lovers. From the Internet to digital radio, iTunes, and other pay-for-play download services, Baez was enabled to stay active in new ways. XM Radio invited artists from many different genres to come into the studio and revisit some of their most classic songs. She appeared on the satellite radio company's first volume alongside artists such as Bonnie Raitt, Tracy Chapman, Roseanne Cash, Bruce Hornsby, and Willie Nelson. XM's _Artist Confidential_ was distributed at Starbucks locations across the country and released in 2006. She's even appeared on stage in impromptu settings, such as at a Bruce Springsteen and the Seeger Sessions Band's concert in Concord, California, in June 2006 for a version of "Pay Me My Money Down" (Joan Baez official Web site).

## MISSION, MOTIVATION, PROCESS

As a singer who came into her fame at the dawn of the 1960s through her clear soprano voice, skills as an interpreter, and a burgeoning interest in nonviolent politics, Baez seems like the ideal candidate to embody the voice of the 1960s. As the decade progressed, Baez became more politically aware and emerged as a vocal critic of many issues.

Perhaps there was no better songwriting material for her interpretative talent than the songwriting of Bob Dylan. Their first encounter was in 1961 at Gerde's Folk City in New York's Greenwich Village, where, despite Bob's shaggy haircut and tattered jacket, Baez knew that she was in the presence of a future star (Baez 1989, 84). At the time, Dylan had barely made a name for himself on the New York coffeehouse circuit. Sensing his potential, Baez invited him to join her on her August 1963 tour, but when he strummed alongside her at the August freedom march on Washington, DC, he was all but forgotten by the press (Hajdu 2001, 182). During their budding romance and Joan's rapidly blossoming fame, Dylan found himself starstruck. As Dylan admitted in *Positively 4th Street*, "I lived with her, and I loved the place. And, like, I lived with her. Hey, I lived with Joan Baez" (Hajdu 2001, 184). In letters to her mother during the summer of 1964, Baez gushed that she had "gotten very close to Bobby in the last month. We have such FUN! . . . I really love him" (Baez 1989, 86–87). Their relationship seems inevitable, symbiotic; a product of its time.

*I love singing with him. He isn't in tune, the phrasing is nuts, and he always wants to do a song I've never heard before . . . It's always an interesting happening when Bob appears.*

*—about Bob Dylan*

While Dylan was being criticized for what the *New York Times* called "the lack of control over his stage manner and his raucously grating singing" (Shelton 1964), Baez was picking up the praise for his compositions. Yet with the release of *The Freewheelin' Bob Dylan*, he began to gain attention and steal the spotlight from a jealous Baez. When D.A. Pennebaker's *Don't Look Back* was filmed spring 1965, Baez, who had trekked to England to be with her floppy-haired disciple, did not receive a single invitation to join him onstage and for the first time in her career found herself slipping into the background. In a scene of Pennebaker's documentary, Baez is approached by a reporter who asks her, after taking a few pictures, what her name is, completely unaware of her status as a countercultural icon. He proceeds to spell her name wrong and realizes later who she is. In her autobiography, she comments on that period, "For the first time in my short but monumentally successful career someone had stolen all my thunder from under my nose" (Baez 1989, 96).

Still, throughout those few years they spent an enormous amount of time together, and many of her thoughtful interpretations of his songs heavily populated several of her albums, starting with "With God On Our Side" and "Don't Think Twice, It's All Right" on *Joan Baez in Concert, Part 2*. Dylan's songs also make appearances on *Joan Baez/5*, including "It Ain't Me Babe," and on *Farewell Angelina*, on which four out of the album's eleven tracks are Dylan takes, from the title cut to "It's All Over Now, Baby Blue" and "A Hard Rain's Gonna Fall." Her interpretations of his songs were so popular and beloved by fans that in 1968 Vanguard released *Any Day Now*, an album of sixteen Dylan covers, including "Love is Just a Four-Letter Word." Additionally, *Don't Look Back* also reveals some footage of Baez performing "Love is Just a Four-Letter Word" in her own kitchen.

One might think that a pair of such prolific artists would have appeared on each other's albums numerous times, but Baez and Dylan were both staunchly independent. They only appear on two albums together. On *The Bootleg Series Volume 5: Bob Dylan Live 1975, The Rolling Thunder Revue*, they sing "Blowin' in the Wind," "Mama, You Been On my Mind," "I Shall Be Released," and "The Water is Wide"; and on *The Bootleg Series, Volume 6: Bob Dylan Live 1964—Concert at Philharmonic Hall*, they sing "Silver Dagger," "With God On Our Side," and "It Ain't Me, Babe." A search for footage of Baez and Dylan, either performing together or her singing his songs on YouTube, the popular video-sharing Web site, reveals a large number of videos available for viewing. They range from them singing "Deportees" in 1976 to "Blowin' In the Wind" to an early performance of them in 1963 singing "When the Ships Come In" at the civil rights march in Washington, DC, at the dawn of his career. It is worth seeking out these scratchy videos. Baez discusses how they performed together in front of a crowd; in those early years she got incredibly nervous before going onstage. "We had to look straight at each other when we were singing. It was just too moving to look out at the sea of faces. We never sang that way, staring straight into each other's eyes. We gave each other strength, and it was very intimate and the most public thing we ever did," said Baez (Hajdu 2001, 183).

The relationship was truly symbiotic, and in a 1983 interview much later, with Kurt Loder of *Rolling Stone*, Baez explained Dylan: "He didn't *do* what he wrote about—I did what he wrote about, in a sense. I *was* politically active. But to have it in song was what was so miraculous to me, because I didn't write then. And I've never written that well anyway" (Holt 1989, 87). Finally and perhaps most eloquently, in his book *Positively 4th Street*, David Hajdu wrote about Dylan and Baez's performances together, saying "Their voices were odd together, a mismatch—salt pork and meringue; but the tension between their styles made their presence together all the more compelling" (Hajdu 2001, 152).

Despite Baez's self-criticism about her songwriting abilities, she did start writing songs, starting with the 1967 album *Joan*. Perhaps her sensitivity to her own shortcomings can be traced to the fact that she has a history of stealing from other musicians, starting with her college friend Debbie Green. "It's true. When I first started, I used a lot from Debbie's act, but the alternative would have been codependent silliness . . . She was modestly talented but not ambitious. I was going someplace, she wasn't. I didn't hurt her. I only helped myself" (Hajdu 2001, 18). Many critics contend that her real skills were as an interpreter of others' material. Perhaps sensitive to that observation and self-conscious about her strengths and weaknesses, in many live performances Baez would preface a song by saying something self-deprecating about her own material.

Because much of Baez's career has been inextricably linked with activism and protest, her songwriting has been influenced by her involvement in causes ranging from the Vietnam War to gun control, to political prisoners, to the draft, to immigration, to civil rights, and to refugees. For example, her song "Children of the Eighties" was inspired by an odd concert in which she was sandwiched on a bill between Frank Zappa and Genesis in Germany. Baez described the crowd of 50,000 or so revelers as "very happy, doped-out kids" with whom she struggled to connect. But connect she did, once she started talking about war, human rights, and peace. "I meant something to them—I represented the Sixties, that was clear" (Holt 1989, 85).

In the early 1960s, you could find Baez marching with Dr. Martin Luther King in Mississippi, singing "We Shall Overcome" to a crowd of 250,000 (Ingram 1990, 58). Baez has spent time with civil rights workers in Montgomery and Birmingham, Alabama, and has served time in jail for peaceful demonstrations. Baez has even spoken out against the more radical approaches of the Black Panthers and the Chicago Seven (Beck, Reese, and Kasindorf 1979). Throughout, she has often been misunderstood by the media, her peers in activism, and the music industry in general. "In the beginning, there were the hippies, the freaks, the pinkos and I was called all of those things. Now, I'm accused of working for the CIA," she sighed. "There has been no change [on my part] whatsoever," she told *Newsweek* (Beck, Reese, and Kasindorf 1979).

In 1972, Baez visited Hanoi as a guest of the North Vietnamese during nearly two weeks of the infamous Christmas bombings. Her experience there, huddled in shelters night after night, inspired the material for her album *Where Are You Now My Son?* According to Caroline Ingram, it is the album "of which Joan Baez is most proud. The effects of her time in a war have stayed with her. To this day, she sometimes jolts out of deep sleep when she hears a plane overhead" (Ingram 1990, 59). As a result of being so active in numerous humanitarian causes all over the world, from Latin America to Africa to Russia, Czech Republic, Afghanistan, Turkey, Israel, and Lebanon, it is crucial that Baez finds some peaceful time for reflection. "I find I need quiet time. Silence has been enormously important to me in whatever I'm doing because it keeps me from doing too much. It keeps things somehow calmed down" (Ingram 1990, 65). Baez has spent years in therapy and used self-help tapes and other materials to keep herself grounded.

## LEGACY AND OTHER INTERESTS

Baez has been a supporter of nearly every nonprofit humanitarian organization one might think of, from Amnesty International to Humanitas, to serving as the opening performer to the 1984 Live Aid—Artists United Against Hunger concert (Ingram 1990, 59).

*I think rap is very important—whether we like it or not. It speaks most clearly about the sector of this country that needs to be heard—and [rappers are] so desperate to be heard that the words often come out the way they do.*

Baez's legacy is that of an activist musician—her career is a quintessential textbook example of how an artist can use her art as a platform to raise awareness about issues that are important to her. In her early years, her activism made its way directly into her music and other creative efforts. As she has gotten older, it is fair to say that her activist efforts have taken more of her time than her music. Although she continues to tour the United States, Europe, and other parts of the world, she is not recording new material as frequently as she did during the heyday of her career, from 1959 through the late 1970s. By the 1990s, though, Baez had set aside activism thanks to a younger generation of musicians with a renewed interest in her (see sidebar).

### Joan Baez and the New Folk Movement

Joan Baez epitomizes a counterculture icon who has left her mark on more than a generation of performers, in the growing folk-pop genre that includes Dar Williams, the Indigo Girls, Laura Cantrell, Erin McKeown, Richard Shindell, and Catie Curtis. Many of Baez's disciples even emerged from the same Cambridge, Massachusetts, venues where she started out.

The new folk movement that started in the middle to late 1990s relies on innovation and genre blending, but all show a strong debt to Baez. Dar Williams and Catie Curtis are folk-pop pioneers with roots in Massachusetts who possess vocal talent and songwriting abilities reminiscent of Baez's highly personal songs. Curtis's intensely self-reflective lyrics chronicle lesbianism, motherhood, and adoption to great critical acclaim. Reminders of Baez's darkly literate hit "Diamonds & Rust" can be found throughout Williams's ballads "If I Wrote You" and "February." Baez even covers those two selections on her 1997 album of cover songs. Both Williams and Baez have a silvery, delicate soprano and a knack for phrasing. In fact, the complex narratives in "If I Wrote You" and "February" are a page out of the Baez heartbreak canon, using nature, written communication, and metaphor.

The Indigo Girls, frequent collaborators of Baez's, have built a lasting career with progressive folk rock; their song "Welcome Me" was covered by Baez in her 1995 album of covers *Ring Them Bells*. Baez explained of the Indigo Girls, "They call me their matriarch, and I call them my whipper-snappers" (Bessman 2003). Baez stressed that she learns from the process and knows it ensures her legacy. She said, "People say to me, 'How nice you're introducing these artists.' What, are you kidding? These artists are literally giving me back my career" (Bessman 2003).

Baez continues to inspire collaborations and work by other artists and continues to participate in new and compelling artistic projects. She herself has created some wall paintings in locations such as Paris, France and Brusson, Italy. Baez has appeared with the Teatro ZinZanni in San Francisco a number of times—the organization puts on a European-style cabaret show with vaudeville, sketches, and circus acts, done in the form of dinner theater. In October 2003, classical guitarist Sharon Isbin debuted the composition "Joan Baez Suite, Opus 144." John Duarte wrote the piece for Isbin, which was commissioned by the Augustine Foundation. The opus features some work from the early part of Baez's career.

Much of Baez's time is wrapped up in activism efforts, many of them sharing a central tenet against violence, government intrusion, antiwar, and anti-efforts that destroy or threaten the environment, the Earth, and local communities. Living in California has kept her busy; in recent years, for example, she has lent her voice to farmland preservation. In May 2006, she joined other activists, artists, and actors such as Julia Butterfly Hill, Daryl Hannah, John Quigley, Ben Harper, and Leonardo diCaprio in supporting the South Central Farm in Los Angeles, which is believed to be the largest urban garden/community farm in the United States. Part of her protest involved setting up camp in a tree in the garden overnight with fellow activists Hill and Quigley. The farm's future is threatened by development (Joan Baez official Web site).

Baez has written extensively about her experiences in two autobiographical books, and she has been the subject of numerous critical essays. It took her nearly forty years, but she seems finally able to impart some wisdom and maturity about her affiliation with Dylan. "It's a wonderful thing to be linked forever with Bob Dylan. Now that I'm over whatever emotional stuff I had to leave behind, it's an honor. . . because he created the best music we had in the '60s" (CBS News 2004).

It is probably not too much of a stretch to argue that any female artist who has written a protest song in the past thirty years owes a musical debt to Joan Baez. She is a woman whose career consistently shows the ability to be a respected musician yet still retain one's conscience and remain steadfast in one's beliefs. Her Quaker roots taught her an unfailing sense that it was important to tell the truth, and Baez has indeed remained true to herself throughout her career, inspiring legions of artists to do the same.

## SELECTED DISCOGRAPHY

*Joan Baez*. Vanguard, 1960
*Joan Baez, Volume 2*. Vanguard, 1961
*Joan Baez in Concert*. Vanguard, 1963
*Farewell Angelina*. Vanguard, 1965

*Noel.* Vanguard, 1966
*Any Day Now.* Vanguard, 1968
*Blessed Are . . .* Vanguard, 1971
*Diamonds & Rust.* A&M, 1975
*Gone from Danger.* Capitol, 1997
*Dark Chords on a Big Guitar.* Koch, 2003
*Bowery Songs.* Proper, 2003


## FURTHER READING

Anderman, Joan. "Night of Gratitude, Talent at Passim." *Boston Globe* (January 18, 1999).

Baez, Joan. *Daybreak.* New York: Dial Press, 1968.

Baez, Joan. *And A Voice To Sing With: A Memoir.* Book Sales, 1989.

Baez, Joan. Official artist Web site: www.joanbaez.com.

Beck, Melinda, with Michael Reese and Martin Kasindorf. "The Voice of Joan Baez." *Newsweek* (August 13, 1979).

Bessman, Jim. "Baez Turns to New Generation for Latest Songs." *Billboard* (September 13, 2003).

CBS News. "Joan Baez: The Good Life, Folk Singer is Happy to Sing Tunes from the Past." (March 21, 2004). Available online at www.cbsnews.com/stories/2004/03/18/sunday/main607215.shtml.

Connolly, Patrick. "Joan Baez Reaches the Awkward Age." *Globe and Mail*, Toronto, Canada (June 7, 1982).

Darling, Lynn. "Joan Baez at 38: New Anthems for the Eternal Crusader." *Washington Post* (June 29, 1979).

Eder, Bruce. Joan. *All Music Guide.* Available online at www.allmusic.com/cg/amg.dll?p=amg&sql=10:ajfpxqr5ldte.

Gavin, James. "Joan Baez: the First Lady of Folk." *New York Times* (November 29, 1992).

Goldsmith, Barbara. "Life on Struggle Mountain." *New York Times* (June 21, 1987).

Graustark, Barbara. "Newsmakers." *Newsweek* (June 11, 1979).

Hajdu, David. *Positively 4th Street: The Lives and Times of Joan Baez, Bob Dylan, Mimi Baez Farina and Richard Farina.* New York: Farrar, Straus, & Giroux, 2001.

Hall, Carla. "The Timeless Ballad of Joan Baez: Doing Donahue, Singing of Ladi Di and Working the Washington Scene." *Washington Post* (October 10, 1981).

Holden, Stephen. "Joan Baez's Voice." *New York Times* (July 4, 1982).

Holt, Sid, (ed.), and the editors of *Rolling Stone.* *The Rolling Stone Interviews: The 1980s.* New York: St. Martin's Press, 1989.

Hume, Paul. "Joan Baez." *Washington Post* (October 12, 1981).

Ingram, Catherine. *In the Footsteps of Gandhi: Conversations with Spiritual Social Activists.* Berkeley, CA: Parallax Press, 1990.

Joyce, Mike. "Baez's 'Lullaby,' Muldaur's 'Eyes.'" *Washington Post* (August 26, 1979).

Lacey, Liam. "Baez Makes Listener Rejoice." *Globe and Mail*, Toronto, Canada (March 1, 1982).

McCarthy, Colman. "A Rolling Stone Carries No Message." *Washington Post* (December 12, 1981).

Morse, Steve. "Newport Mingles Past, Future." *Boston Globe* (August 11, 1997).

*New York Times*. "Joan Baez Again Refuses to Pay Part of Income Taxes." (April 16, 1965).

*New York Times*. "Two Baez Concerts Banned in Brazilian Cities." (May 26, 1981).

Perry, Joellen. "In Diamonds and In Rust: Social Beliefs and Influence of Folk Singer Joan Baez." *U.S. News and World Report* (July 8, 2002).

Ruhlmann, William. "Joan Baez biography." *All Music Guide.* Available online at www.allmusic.com/cg/amg.dll?p=amg&token=&sql=11:0ifqxql5ldte.

Shelton, Robert. "Folk Joins Jazz at Newport." *New York Times* (July 19, 1959).

Shelton, Robert. "Joan Baez, 19, Offers Folk-Song Program." *New York Times* (November 7, 1960).

Shelton, Robert. "Bridging the Gap." *New York Times* (April 16, 1961).

Shelton, Robert. "Joan Baez Sings at Forest Hills." *New York Times* (August 10, 1964).

*Time*. "The Folk Girls." (June 1, 1962).

*Time*. "People." (January 31, 1972).

Turner, Wallace. "Antiwar Demonstrations Held Outside Draft Boards Across U.S." *New York Times* (October 16, 1967).

Courtesy of Photofest

# Mary J. Blige

**OVERVIEW**

*She is Aretha to the rap
generation. She embodies the
hip-hop woman in her dress
and mannerisms. She has
attitude and she can sing.
Every hip-hop fan loves her.*
—Chris Wilder, *The Source*

In just a little more than a dozen years, Mary J. Blige has proven that it is possible, although not always easy, to be a successful, strong, independent black woman in the music business. Initially, she was proclaimed to be either the new Aretha Franklin or Chaka Khan, but she shares little with her predecessors other than the milieu of rhythm and blues and a strong, beautiful voice. Her success was something new within the then-burgeoning world of rap and hip-hop. There was not, before the ascension of Mary J. Blige, a paradigm for a smart, successful, strong African American singer whose music melded the smooth soulfulness of rhythm and blues with the attitude, delivery, and collaborative approach that customarily characterizes the hip-hop and rap worlds. With her trademark (often) blonde hair, oversize sunglasses, and super-fly outfits, Blige set the fashion standard for the female hip-hop songstress; even when she was just wearing chunky white sneakers and jeans, her self-described "yo girl" look, she always looked carefully put together, a woman aware of her image.

From the beginning of her career, Blige's songs made an impact on a number of different types of audiences, thanks to the fact that her unique musical style would later inspire the successful, uncompromising careers of female African American artists such as Missy Elliott, Lil' Kim, Lauryn Hill (both on her own and as part of the Fugees), Alicia Keys, Destiny's Child, Ashanti, and Aaliyah, among others (see sidebar). *Rolling Stone* even went so far as to say she "pioneered the movement that would become neo-soul" (George-Warren, Romanowski, and Pareles 2001), which includes the likes of Alicia Keys along with Lizz Wright, Erykah Badu, Jill Scott, Macy Gray, Vivian Green, and other gospel and rhythm and blues–influenced African American singers and songwriters. Blige herself cites gospel music and the music of Aretha Franklin, the Staple Singers, Otis Redding, Gladys Knight, and Sam Cooke as influences. Her voice is not technically proficient, but it is imbued with passion, pain, and determination. Indeed, the imagery of Blige throughout her career has from the very start reinforced those ideas, as her album covers often feature a close-up of her face with her name scrawled across them, reminiscent of either her signature or urban graffiti.

Remarkably, every single one of her albums has placed well, usually fairly high, on myriad *Billboard* charts—some even in Canada—dating all the way back to her debut record *What's the 411?*, recorded in 1992. Each of her albums, with the exception of 2002's *Dance for Me*, has reached a number one slot on a number of different charts, including Top R&B/Hip-Hop Albums, Top Internet Albums, or the *Billboard* 200. The Recording Industry Association of America's inventory of gold and platinum recordings, including singles and albums, lists Blige no fewer than thirty-two times. Every one

## Say It Loud: I'm Black and I'm Proud and I'm Female

Mary J. Blige's career took a turn toward the personal with her 1994 album *My Life*, which consisted of songs she had written herself. The record was a watershed moment, introducing a sense of fierce honesty and pride into R&B. The autobiographical elements present through the album's songs gave other strong female singers in R&B license to give voice to their own pain, suffering, and accomplishments. The diverse group of soul, R&B, and hip-hop artists—especially Erykah Badu, MeShell Ndegéocello, Lauryn Hill, Jill Scott, Destiny's Child, Lizz Wright, and Alicia Keys—owe something to Blige's trailblazing self-righteousness and classy example.

Badu emerged in 1997 with the jazzy, meditative single "On and On," from her number two charting debut *Baduizm*. The record gave her the tag of "neo soul" and earned her comparisons to Billie Holiday as well as earning her the first of four Grammy Awards.

When songwriter and singer Lauryn Hill broke away from the men of the Fugees and released her solo record *The Miseducation of Lauryn Hill* in 1998, it effortlessly combined rap, reggae, soul, and R&B, and she came across as a wise, literate sister who could offer advice and empower the listener. In 1999, Hill won five of the eleven Grammys for which she was nominated.

Three years later, in 2000, Jill Scott, who used to perform with The Roots, released her debut *Who Is Jill Scott? Words and Sounds Volume 1*. At the Essence Music Festival in 2006, the two-time Grammy-winning Scott urged listeners, particularly females, to demand better from rap and hip-hop, which often portrays women of color in a negative manner. The poet-singer peppers her albums with spoken words and collaborated with Badu to write the song "You Got Me," recorded by The Roots in 1999.

of her albums has achieved at least gold and/or multiplatinum status except for 2002's *Dance for Me*. Several of her singles, from 1992's "You Remind Me" to "Real Love" and "Not Goin' Cry," have also achieved at least gold status. Videos such as the single video for "Not Today" and the long form video for *Live From Los Angeles* have reached platinum and gold status, respectively. However, it was not until the release of the aptly named *The Breakthrough* that her fan base expanded beyond hip-hop kids, and "urban/Latino chicks, and some Japanese." She told *Rolling Stone* in 2006 that "now we're getting fifty-year-old white men with gray hair. It's amazing" (Edwards 2006).

Commercial acclaim tells only part of an artist's story; the rest is revealed by the esteem of critics and musical peers. Blige's albums are especially noteworthy because they inspire agreement from both critics and consumers. Her work is always deemed worthy of interest by music writers and critics, yet it consistently reaches a broad commercial audience. Blige also continually wins the regard of her colleagues within her own musical community, inspiring collaboration with a wide range of artists including Sean Combs, George Michael, Sting, and U2. Blige offered her searing, passionate vocals to the U2 song "One" and turned it into a duet with Bono; it appears on her 2006 album *The Breakthrough*.

She has received three Grammy Awards and been nominated numerous times. In 1995 she won the award, along with Method Man, for Best Rap Performance by a Duo or Group for the Ashford and Simpson tune "I'll Be There for You/You're All I Need to Get By." Two more followed: Best Female R&B Vocal Performance in 2002 for the song "He Think I Don't Know" and Best Pop Collaboration With Vocals in 2003 for "Whenever I Say Your Name," a song she recorded with Sting for his album *Sacred Love*. In 2006 she was nominated for an unprecedented number of Grammys—eight—with the song "Be Without You," nominated for both record and song of the year. She walked away with three Grammys: *The Breakthrough* garnered her one apiece for Best R&B Album and Best Female Vocal Performance, and "Be Without You" nabbed her and her three co-writers a Grammy for Best R&B Song.

Throughout her career, Blige has battled the triple threats of drugs, depression, and alcohol, which have been a result of low self-esteem, anger, and unresolved issues from her childhood. This caused her to earn a reputation in the earlier years of her career as a difficult diva. But although substances complicate how an artist may be perceived by those who work with her on a daily basis and by her fans, her own uncompromising personality and razor-sharp focus on what she wants could also earn an artist the label "difficult." It is worth speculating, however, that if a man were exhibiting these characteristics, such pejorative terms would not be entertained.


## EARLY YEARS

It is not always clear how much of what consumers experience and understand about the personae of beloved rap and hip-hop stars is posturing and how much of it really stems from that artist's life experiences. It is safe to ascribe Mary J. Blige to the category of the latter, for she grew up a difficult environment, and whereas her songwriting comes from that rough place it also offers her an opportunity for transcendence.

Blige was born in the Bronx as the youngest of Cora and Thomas Blige's two daughters. Her dad was a jazz musician who left the family before Blige turned four. Her mother took her and her older sister, La Tonya, to their grandmother's house in Savannah, Georgia (Brown 2007, 10). During that time she was exposed to gospel music in her grandmother's Pentecostal church in Savannah, which, over the years, helped break her out of her shyness. "I used to be scared. I'm shy now but I was terribly shy then. But everyone would push me," she told *USA Today* (Jones 1992). They spent a little over a year there and returned to the Bronx before Mary turned five. After another couple of years the family moved to the Schlobam housing projects in Yonkers, a crime-ridden neighborhood. Blige spent her time evading both the local hoodlum "Juice" and girls who were jealous of her because she was dating the hottest guy on the block, who also happened to be a drug dealer (Jones 1992).

> *Be careful what you ask for, because real love is not people yes ma'aming you to death. Real love is painful, in a good way, because real love is finding out who you are.*

She described her years there, saying that she would get into fights and that she constantly had to prove herself to protect herself from harm. About her experience, she said, "Growing up in the projects is like living in a barrel of crabs. If you try to get out, one of the other crabs tries to pull you down" (Brown 2007, 10). Years later on *The Oprah Winfrey Show* she would reveal that she was sexually assaulted during those years.

Thankfully, music was always a part of her life, and it was her solace. Blige spent her youth singing in church choirs and entering talent shows (McAdams 1992) and winning a contest when she was seven by singing "Respect" by Aretha Franklin (Brown 2007, 11). The roots of her sound were informed by what she heard, especially the classics. She said, "All my life, old music has been the best music to me. I have more old records than new stuff. I have an old soul" (Jones 1992). In addition to being an old soul, living in the projects forced Mary and her sister to grow up much more quickly than normal. Although their mother, a nurse, kept the family together and stayed strong, the Blige women had some difficult times.

With a foundation in soul, gospel, and rhythm and blues, Blige found her genre as a teenager when she became obsessed with hip-hop. Block parties would take place in the streets of the neighborhood, and the deejays would bring their records. People would try to rap, and she credits those block parties for inspiration for her own beats (Jones 1992). Blige dropped out of high school during her junior year, and when she was seventeen, she made a demo of herself at a mall in nearby White Plains. Her song of choice was Anita Baker's "Caught up in the Rapture," her favorite at the time. The tape got passed through the hands of her stepfather, who worked with a singer who then gave it to his manager. Somehow it got to Jeff Redd, an A&R representative for Uptown Records, and then into the hands of Uptown Records's CEO Andre Harrell. The process took four years for her to get signed, but apparently her Mount Vernon neighborhood had been a mining ground for other Uptown talent such as Heavy D, Al B. Sure!, and Kyle West (McAdams 1992). Harrell signed in her in 1989 and she became the label's youngest and first female artist (Brown 2007, 21). As so many female rhythm and blues singers have historically done, Blige got her break singing backup; in her case, on albums for local artists such as Father MC. Even greater exposure came through her song "You Remind Me," which appeared on the soundtrack to the film

*Strictly Business.* "I didn't think it was going to be that big. It's all been a big surprise," she said (McIver 1992).

Blige met Sean "Puffy" Combs, who at the time was serving as the senior director of A&R for Uptown, in 1991. Combs treated her as his protégé and took her under his wing. (Later on, Combs would be given his own label with Uptown Records.) At the time she recorded that infamous tape at the mall, Blige said she was not looking for a music career. "I wasn't looking for a deal, I wasn't looking for anything! I was just playing around. But I thank God for it," she told *Billboard* (McAdams 1992).

With her debut *What's the 411?*, released in July 1992 on MCA Records, Blige became the "reigning queen of her own hybrid category: hip-hop soul," according to Stanton Swihart of *All Music Guide*. Prior to the release, label honcho Harrell had predicted just that when he told *Billboard* magazine, "Mary is going to bet the new queen of hip-hop soul," a moniker that was emblazoned on T-shirts during the release of her record (McAdams 1992). The album itself, comprised of twelve tracks written by various artists, includes songs that she herself did not write along with sonic embellishments such as answering machine snippets. Critics were able to frame her music in a larger context, and certainly tracks such as "Real Love" and Chaka Kahn's "Sweet Thing" sound like timeless classics, partially because they call to mind the best of Khan and Franklin. Other tracks do not hold up quite as well and feel more dated, such as "Reminisce" and "Love No Limit," which are primarily driven by synthesizers. Standout songs include "You Remind Me" and the duet "I Don't Want To Do Anything," a duet with Jodeci's K-Ci.

Critical response, for the most part, was favorable. *Billboard* called her "young, sassy and streetwise, with a hard-hitting, raised-in-church voice" and described the songs as both "hip-hop soul and ghetto avant-garde," and calls the debut "vastly appealing" and Blige "an artist to watch" (*Billboard* 1992). *Billboard* mentioned her style and voice, saying that Blige managed to meld the nuances and delivery of gospel with hip-hop style; the material was strengthened by the fact that the backing vocals were multi-tracked (McAdams 1992). Although many critics could agree that Blige had promise and that her voice was smooth, strong, and beautiful, the quality of her songs was a matter of debate. In *Rolling Stone*, her biography asserts that "even the sweet songs" on her debut were noteworthy because they offered a bit of hard-won realism that had been missing from many of the popular love songs on the charts at the time.

Blige made an impact that resonated throughout other genres and styles of music. *USA Today* declared her the "first woman to break into the male-dominated world of new jack swing" (Jones 1992). Blige disagreed with that terminology, preferring the term hip-hop soul, which has stuck with her through her career. "There's a difference. It's more street. We use old James Brown beats. This is a time where people want to hear more old than new," she explained. Rapper Grand Puba, who featured her on his album *Reel to Reel* and who sang a duet with her on her debut's title cut, said that "she's dope because she blends hip-hop beats with R&B flavors, and keeps her music raw, not overproduced." Blige emphasized to *USA Today* that she intended that specific feel—"only the necessary instruments were used. We were trying for a whole different sound. Everything is laid back—even the dancing tunes" (Jones 1992).

*At the end of the day, hip-hop is the foundation of Mary J. Blige. Hip-hop is the reason my music even exists. I wouldn't have a bed of music [without it] . . . I'm never going to resent or disrespect it. When I rise, it rises. . . . It's part of Mary J. Blige.*

The album appealed to a broad audience, thus indeed making her an artist worth watching. Chart positions reinforced that promise, such as number one on the Top R&B/Hip-Hop Albums as well as number six on the *Billboard* 200, along with six songs that placed on a number of singles charts. Her songs have found listeners in a variety of categories, from "Real Love" in 1992 peaking at number one on the Hot R&B/Hip-Hop Singles & Tracks chart to another number one peak for "You Remind Me" on the same track to appearances on Top 40 mainstream, Hot Dance Music, Rhythmic Top 40, and *Billboard* Hot 100. The album had a two-year staying power, since the song "My Love" climbed to number twenty-three in 1994 on the Hot R&B/Hip-Hop Singles & Tracks chart. Additionally, the album is remarkable because it went gold within two months of its release (by September 1992), reached platinum status by October 1992, and went multiplatinum, reaching sales of 2 million copies, by the following February.

Although Blige had created that tape at the mall on a lark, by the time it got into the hands of Combs, he had other thoughts—he saw the potential audience. He told *Billboard* in 1992 that he was looking to create a female artist that young hip-hop kids would like and that young black females did not have many artists to look up to. When he met Blige and they started working together, things changed. "Then the whole concept developed into ghetto avant-garde, a combination of hip hop beats with jazz and soul undertones. As we progressed with the album, her voice started progressing, started reminding people of a Chaka or Anita or Sade mixture" (McAdams 1992). With *What's the 411?*, the queen of hip-hop soul had arrived.

## CAREER PATH

More singles from the album were released in 1993, including "Love No Limit," "Reminisce," and the cover of Chaka Khan's "Sweet Thing." By the end of that year, *411* had sold 3 million copies. The success inspired a remix album, which was released in December 1993. Those versions crept into radio and took up residence through part of 1994—a great place to be if you're an artist who is working on the next project.

Looking back at the immediate success of *What's the 411?*, it is not easy to determine how much of that album is a genuine reflection of Blige's talent because much it was written with collaborators. Consequently, it is hard to say how much of its success can be attributed to her, and how much to the hip-hop mastermind Sean Puffy Combs, who oversaw its production, the producers Dave Hall and DeVante Swing, and/or other players such as Tony Dofat and rapper Grand Puba. Their artistic touch, however, helped Blige make her mark. And through the years Blige, like many other female music icons, has done much to subtly redefine herself, tweak her image, and battle the kind of personal demons that often stereotypically accompany those who are famous, rich, or otherwise in the limelight. Around this time she was in a long-term relationship with musician K-Ci Hailey, a member of the group and label mate Jodeci (Brown 2007, 20).

While working on the next album, Combs helped Blige develop her voice and become more conscious of her image. At this point he had left Uptown to create his own label, Bad Boy Entertainment, but he served as the executive producer of her subsequent release, *My Life*, in 1995 (Brown 2007, 22). Although it was yet another project created with the heavy influence of Sean Combs, the epic feel of *My Life* strayed a bit from its roots. What it lost in "street cred" it more than made up for in personal truths. The record gave voice to her own personal pain, which is plainly clear throughout and engages the listener. Never one to view her world with rose-colored glasses, Blige's seventeen songs strongly suggest that sadness and happiness can and often do coexist. Sometimes, those seemingly contradictory emotions can work together beautifully. In the case of Blige's *My Life*, they express her own heartfelt truths, which helped fans understand a bit more about where she was coming from.

At times, some critics have noted, the music verges on becoming over-wrought. This album is perhaps the first time we see Mary J. Blige come through personally in her work; she had a hand in writing or co-writing nearly every track, with the exception of three. Her songs chronicle the "bitter pain and dark depression she had experienced in her life," according to Terrell Brown (Brown 2007, 22). Overall, though, the decision to be honest capti-vated her fans and their reaction surprised her. Biographer Terrell Brown wrote that her "brutal honesty" distinguished her from the sea of singers and musicians, regardless of the fact that some critics did not think her voice itself was remarkable (Brown 2007, 22).

The response to *My Life* inspired her to get her life in order. She says that many people wrote to her about her music and explained how they could relate to her pain. "I didn't want them to go through those suicidal pains, so I wanted to get myself together so that we could all get ourselves together. I can't force things down people's throats but what I can do is try to fix Mary" (Brown 2007, 22–23). Without irony and in all earnestness, the album's first single, a groovy funk song, was titled "Be Happy." It peaked at twenty-nine on the *Billboard* Hot 100, and then landed at number six on the R&B Singles chart. Blige told *Rolling Stone* "my girlfriend Arlene helped me write that song.

We were in these terrible relationships and we just wanted to be happy, so we were smoking cigarettes" (Edwards 2006). She said, looking back on the song, "When I perform it, everybody always sings it. When I wrote those lyrics, I was going through so much. I really wanted to be happy. What I found is that I have to love myself in order to be happy" (Herndon 2007).

The album had great success with radio; several more songs were released as singles, such as a cover of the Rose Royce song "I'm Goin' Down" along with "You Bring Me Joy" and "I Love You." The songs are unfettered and uncorrupted by excessive collaborators or producers and are aided through the smart, unobtrusive use of samples. The album's cover art establishes a fierce, uncompromising impression on the unsuspecting casual consumer, with a photograph of Blige wearing a black leather cap pulled low, her eyes just about obscured and her hair dyed blonde and plaited into two braids on either side of her head.

Subsequent to the success of *My Life*, Blige experienced some difficulties with personal relationships. Stardom had brought the issues of her youth and teen years to a head—the anger and struggle now had to compete with success and fame. Blige, unprepared for the fame she was experiencing, was suffering from low-self esteem after being told all her life by her "mean aunts" that she would never amount to anything worthwhile (Brown 2007, 11). She was battling drug addictions, alcoholism, and depression. To further complicate matters, her relationship with K-Ci Hailey had turned abusive. Reflecting back on this period to *Rolling Stone*, she said, "It seems like I've always been in a situation where a man is jealous of me" (Edwards 2006). She said that in soul music, in particular in its relation to *My Life* and her personal relationships, the pain was so heavy she was not sure how else to handle it (Edwards 2006). After its release, she decided to gain better control of her work. Blige cut her artistic ties with Combs, who had begun focusing on the burgeoning career of The Notorious B.I.G. and Uptown Records, whose had lost Harrell to Motown (Brown 2007, 26). She signed with MCA Records and hired Death Row Records label honcho Marion "Suge" Knight as her financial advisor.

The success of her two previous albums enabled her to start making decisions on her own for the third. For *Share My World*, released in 1997, Blige hired many hands to help her out, including Babyface, Rodney Jerkins, R. Kelly, and the duo of Terry Lewis and Jimmy Jam, who are creative minds who had done much great work with Janet Jackson. *Share My World* debuted at number one on the *Billboard* charts and spawned four number one singles, including "Love is All We Need" (featuring Nas), "I Can Love You" (with Lil' Kim), "Everything," and "Seven Days." The album went triple platinum and sold 5 million copies worldwide—no small feat. By the beginning of 1998, the album nabbed for her an American Music Award for Favorite Album—Soul/Rhythm & Blues. She toured in support of *Share My World*, and the fruits of those labors resulted in the live album called *The Tour*, which eventually went gold (Brown 2007, 27–29).

## *Turning a Musical Corner and Digging Into Her Soul*

Nevertheless, *Share My World*'s success continued to pave the way for *Mary*, whose songs are packed with more celebrity-musician appearances than any of her releases to date. It includes the memorable duet with Lauryn Hill "All That I Can Say." She also judiciously used samples as well as performance contributions from some heavy hitters from other genres such as Eric Clapton, Stevie Wonder, Elton John, and Bernie Taupin. For instance, "Deep Inside" snatches parts of Elton John's "Bennie and the Jets," while another track, "Time," takes bits from Stevie Wonder's "Pastime Paradise" and Al Green's "I'm Glad You're Mine." The album showed a continued embrace of her own emotional power, although some of the grittier, more confrontational elements had disappeared. Blige was starting to forge her own path, growing as an artist. She was unafraid to get a helping hand and collaborate with another artist while maintaining her strong presence throughout the album so that the listener does not feel, as with her earlier albums, that her music jumps genres.

The rock critic who goes solely by the name Toure observed a subtle psychological shift in Blige's songwriting, describing it in *Rolling Stone* as "Blige seems to have moved from the Terry McMillan once-again-he's-breaking-my-heart mantra to, perhaps, an Oprah love-your-spirit ethos" (Touré 1999). In juxtaposing two prominent African American women—McMillan, a novelist whose books *How Stella Got Her Groove Back* and *Waiting to Exhale* are about strong women who've been done wrong, and Oprah Winfrey, the queen of motivational, self-affirming, you-go-girl-ism on daytime television, in magazines, and in other media—an attempt was made to place Blige within a context of other African American women with much national, cultural influence. In other words, Blige's songwriting is less about victimhood that comes with songs about love gone wrong and more about a woman finding her independence and struggling to take responsibility for herself and her life (Touré 1999). In "All That I Can Say," produced by Lauryn Hill, Blige declares "loving you is wonderful/Something like a miracle."

A few songs later, in "Beautiful Ones," her lyrics directly answer or counter what Touré calls her "classic theme song," "Everyday it Rains." He observed that Blige was "moving away from the hip-hop tinged interpolation-heavy sound of her earlier albums" (1999). Working with a live band, or singing with Eric Clapton's guitar or Elton John's piano pointed toward a more soulful, organic sound—an evolution. Blige ends the album with a sassy take on the disco classic "Let No Man Put Asunder," which finds her trying to hang onto a "love too good to throw away." Ending on that feel-good vibe somewhat reprises the sentiments she expressed in *My Life*, "All I want is to be happy." The quest for something expressed so simply, however, is far more complex than that.

At the end of 1999, the album was released as a double disc set containing videos for the singles "All That I Can Say" and "Deep Inside," and two bonus tracks including "Confrontation" and "Sincerity," which featured Nas and DMX. The album was critically acclaimed and went double platinum. Around this time, Blige and her label MCA decided it would be a good idea to dip into the club music market, so they issued danceable remixes of the singles from *Mary*, which were met with success.

## Mid-Career Crisis: Battling Personal Demons

At this point in her career, although her sound—and her style—had solidified, her personal life was suffering. Blige had earned a reputation, particularly in the media, for being unreliable, moody, and difficult to work with (Brown 2007, 33). During this difficult period leading up to *No More Drama*, Blige got involved in a car accident and she was frequently too high or drunk to be of much use during photo shoots and other media-related events (34).

Ironically, her pain gave her much fame, which made the cycle difficult to break. "I had no idea that my personal pain would create such a big fan base. Everything that was bringing me down was everything that rose me up from a business standpoint that is . . . All the money and fame in the world couldn't change what was going on in my heart. That's how messed up I was, and how depressed I was" (34). It was time for change; regardless of her fan base, her personal life was starting to make a consistently negative impact on her business. Years later she recalled the experience to *Essence* magazine, highlighting how in some ways she felt powerless despite the fact that her albums were regularly selling in the millions. "Everyone was making decisions about me and what I should be doing, but I didn't necessarily agree with everything, so I wouldn't do things." She also noted that the whole business was not as glamorous as it seemed. The harsher realities of fame had kicked in. She broke up with K-Ci finally and started to try to put things behind her. Her battle with and subsequent freedom from addictions to drugs and alcohol informed her strong fifth release *No More Drama*.

There were a couple of things that changed her significantly in 2001. First, the death of hip-hop singer Aaliyah in a plane crash. The two did not know each other well, but it seemed to Blige like some kind of warning. The other event that impacted her came from her new record executive boyfriend Kendu Isaacs, whom she met through singer and actress Queen Latifah. He told her she had to stop drinking. She said she tried to switch to wine, but "not just glasses of wine, bottles of wine" (Edwards 2006). That was not so effective, but returning to the Bible on an everyday basis helped her immensely. She now reads a chapter of Proverbs daily, per the day of the month. She said that when she was trying to get sober, there were a few that stood out, especially the thirty-seventh Psalm: "Fret not thyself because of evildoers, neither be envious against the workers of iniquity." The message—do not fear or worry if other people try to hurt you, because they will—is one that she has taken to heart.

*My God is a God who wants me to have things. He wants me to bling. He wants me to be the hottest thing on the block.*

Ultimately, her relationship with Isaacs helped her bury her personal demons and stop drinking and using drugs. She told *Parade* magazine that Isaacs "was the first person to ever challenge what I did: 'Why are you drinking? Why do you hate yourself? You don't need to be around people who tear you down. You're beautiful, Mary.' He was the first man to ever tell me that" (2007). Around this time, she turned to food instead and gained some weight—which critics, of course, were quick to point out—but she took charge of herself, started exercising, and lost it. She credited Isaacs with saving her life, telling her that she was "scarred inside." She said she remembers the night that changed everything and the impetus their relationship had on her decision. "I decided to stop drinking that night and forgive all the people who had hurt me and to forgive and love myself, because I loved him and I wanted to be true" (*Parade* 2007).

More perhaps than any of her previous albums, *No More Drama* is marked most by her own songwriting, although the trademark emotional expressiveness of earlier releases remained intact. Blige says when she sings the declaration "No More Drama," she means it. "I was in a relationship where I had a gun pulled on me and a dude tried to kill me. And in the midst of this abuse, I'd have to go and do some coke. 'No More Drama' is for real," she told *Rolling Stone* (Edwards 2006).

Sarah Rodman of the *Boston Herald* remarked that "Mary J. Blige may have resolved some problems in her personal life, but *No More Drama* is definitely misnamed. Thank goodness—because Mary without drama is like the beach without sand" (Rodman 2001). Noteworthy tracks include the lead-off "Love" and its over-the-top kiss-off and duet "Where I've Been" with rapper Eve. There's even a funny, honest ode to hormones called "PMS." Writing for the *Village Voice*, Barry Walters said that Blige embodied more than the pain and pleasure her songs often convey. He eloquently described her work as "riddled with luscious imperfections, her cry doesn't fall from a pristine heaven. Instead, this grounded black angel brings home the pain of ascending a broken earth" (Walters 2001).

Overall, *No More Drama*'s joyous moments, characterized by tracks such as the opener "Love" and the somehow hopeful autobiographical "Where I've Been," showed that Blige was starting to turn away from her personal demons and to celebrate her life. Blige directly and indirectly engaged with some of the slings and arrows she suffered both at her own hands and the hands of the media throughout the album's seventeen tracks. Throughout *No More Drama*, Blige thoroughly mined the experiences that brought her to that very moment of self-recognition and, ultimately, reconciliation. The title track, along with honest girl talk of "PMS," brought Blige into what one might call Oprah Winfrey territory—sentimental, confrontationally female, yet strong and unapologetic. The title track, produced by Jimmy Jam and Terry Lewis, sampled the piano riff from the theme to the soap opera *The Young and the Restless*. Although the song starts off quietly, the stark beauty of the opening introduces a first line declared in a tired voice, "So tired, tired of all this drama," which leads to a verse packed with shifting rhythms as the piano sample continues its sad undercurrent and a drum machine kicks in. An anthemic chorus that bears the power of gospel comes alive, with Blige singing, "No one's gonna make me hurt again." As the song progresses, new sounds, blips, and textures are added, immediately complicating the production and adding a layer of near cacophony that mirrors life's own obstacles and noisy interruptions.

Commercially, *No More Drama* fared well quickly, selling over a quarter million copies in its first week of release and coming in second place for sales behind the release of young R&B singer Aaliyah's debut album not quite two weeks after her tragic death (Conniff 2001). The release of *No More Drama* also coincided with the terrorist attacks in New York City; Washington, DC; and Pennsylvania in September 2001, and some critics were quick to make connections, however accidental they might be. The connotation of her album title in the larger world context inspired Neva Chonin to write in the *San Francisco Chronicle* that the idea of banishing drama—personal, political, or global—is not a bad one. "A little peace would go down well these days, not only in the political and social spheres but in the commercial rap world, too" (Chonin 2001).

## A New Mary for the New Millennium

Oddly, although *No More Drama*'s singles did well, MCA wanted bigger sales, so the label repackaged and re-released it in early 2002, causing *No More Drama* to become a double platinum album and sell 4 million copies worldwide. Blige won her second Grammy for the song "He Think I Don't Know." In 2003, she followed that up with *Love & Life*—that album marked a reunion with P. Diddy (as Sean Combs was known at that point), with whom she collaborated on producing (and writing) a number of the album's tracks. The songs often juxtapose the ups and downs of romance and sex—the tracks with 50 Cent and Method Man cameos are particularly well-produced, said Tom Moon in *Rolling Stone*. Blige quickly realized that she had relied too heavily on Diddy's opinion that her fans did not want to hear anything depressing after the heaviness of *No More Drama*, and so she wrote to suit him. It did not feel honest, and fans knew it. The disagreements led Blige and Combs to part ways artistically yet again.

Perhaps it is not surprising that, given the content and even *Love & Life*'s title, Blige married Isaacs in December 2003 and became stepmother to his three children. They live in a quiet part of New Jersey, where Blige spends whatever downtime she has reading self-help books and exploring her renewed spirituality (Edwards 2006).

Getting her next album, *The Breakthrough*, to break through took a bit of work. She told *Rolling Stone* that the album was finished in August 2004, a

*The best advice was from Chaka Khan, someone I truly love, when she told me to get out of my own way. She said that to me the first time I ever met her. I guess she'd been watching me. I didn't understand it then, but I love her to this day for it. She was right.*

year prior to its actual release date in 2005. This is contrary to circulating rumors that the album was finished just in time. For some reason, she said that those at Geffen (which had absorbed the label MCA) were more focused on her greatest hits collection, which they wanted to release first. However, she got lucky when label head Jimmy Iovine heard her record and changed the plans. It was a smart move—the album hit number one and has helped to broaden her fan base considerably (Edwards 2006).

The songs of *The Breakthrough* are like a manifesto from a woman who has fought, survived, and made a success of herself. Tracks like "Good Woman Down," in which she says in the chorus, "You can't hold a good woman down/You can't hold me" testify to her strength. Indeed the humorously titled, infectious track "MJB Da MVP" is an autobiographical celebration of her trials and struggles and a biographical narration of her career, with the refrain: "I'm the soul hip-hop queen and I ain't goin' nowhere/but you already know me." She thanks TV, radio, friends, family, and "most of all I wanna thank my fans, who hang through the bad times." The pleasant, four-minute song features a guest appearance by rapper 50 Cent. She told Canada's *City News*, "*The Breakthrough* is about triumph, about not being a victim, but being a victor. It's about loving yourself" (*City News* 2006).

Developments in her personal life, too, have helped ground her and give her perspective. In an interview in March 2006 with *Rolling Stone*, Blige told reporter Gavin Edwards about how she had changed since the earlier days of her career. He wrote, " 'For the first time in my life, I'm proud of myself. I'm not an ignorant idiot jerk that don't want to learn no more.' She lets that sentence hang in the air, gathering the weight of all the bad decisions she has ever made, and then she laughs. 'But I must admit—I still have my ignorant moments.' "

When *Reflections: A Retrospective* was put out in December 2006, *The Breakthrough*'s lead single "Be Without You" was still on the R&B chart and had remained there for nearly a year, and *Breakthrough*'s fifth single, "Take Me As I Am," had stunningly taken up residence on the same chart for over four months. Throughout, *Retrospective* includes her big hits, her signature songs—the ones that are likely to resonate most strongly with her fans. At the same time, though, the album boasts a few previously unreleased tracks, such as "We Ride (I See The Future)," in which Blige sings "Mary ain't mad no more," a declaration that can easily be interpreted as the mantra for the new Mary. In "Reflection (I Remember)" she looks "back when pain was I all had to give" and notes her relative ignorance when she started out, "signing the contract/no guidelines." She even reflects on her diva reputation, "I used to throw a fit." She told *Performing Songwriter* that interviewers ask her, "Remember when you were this difficult person, and you were angry?" And she would respond with a laugh, "Yeah! How many years are we gonna talk about this? Haven't you guys discovered I'm a new person?" (Neal 2007). If it seems repetitive that she needs to keep reminding people, it is only because these types of labels have followed, haunted, and limited her throughout her career. And certainly the topic persists because she keeps the conversation alive with lyrics that acknowledge that as part of her past.

Although *Reflections* features some of her greatest songs, it omits many. Some fans criticized it for being a lean collection when many of her works, specifically songs that appeared in films and well-loved collaborations with other artists, are absent from this seventeen-track compilation. Considering the fact that she has had nine number one singles over the course of her career thus far, it is a fair critique. But then again, the term "greatest hits" or "best of" is often subjective, and sometimes artists do not always have complete control over the selections.

Still, some of her best and most signature songs are included; "Be Happy," "No More Drama," "Not Goin' Cry," and "Real Love," which might resemble a song by Anita Baker if the production did not emphasize rhythmic complexity. Also on the album is her classic "Family Affair," along with revisions of older songs, such as the reflective "My Life '06" that has a vibe recalling the best of 1970s soul music, complete with the warm tones of a Fender Rhodes piano and lyrics that give thanks to the "man above." Deciding which songs to put on the album was not easy, she admitted. Still, she said, "I knew that what I put on there would be the songs that have been a big part of people's lives" (Neal 2007). She said she received a letter from a young girl who was bitten on her face by a dog and that the song "No More Drama" got her through the harrowing ordeal. Similarly, the triumph-through-adversity theme surfaced as a reason to include "Not Goin' Cry." Blige said women tell her, "Mary this song got me out of an abusive relationship." But for every song about personal pain, there are songs such as "You're All I Need to Get By," which Blige said "was a great hip-hop record, but a love song at the same time" (Neal 2007).

## MISSION, MOTIVATION, PROCESS

Blige started from a place of relative inexperience as a singer, songwriter, and performer, and she has learned much along the way, often at considerable emotional, personal, and financial cost. In some ways, Blige's career is an example of a woman who has battled the visions of what other people—namely men—have wanted for her career versus what she herself might have wanted. In the early part of her career, her path—financial or otherwise—was somewhat laid out and defined by the interests of her label. Over the course of her career, Blige has taken control over her image, slowly but surely, and remained a respected, strong, smart artist throughout her endeavors. Although she has relied on the opinions of others, most consistently and notably Sean Combs, especially in the beginning years, in the end she learned how to make her own decisions and trusted her own instincts.

Much of hip-hop is defined by collaboration. Because Blige is identified primarily with that musical genre, collaboration has been key to her early and continued success. Interestingly, her partners have often come from the most unlikely places, from fellow hip-hop stars Wyclef Jean, Will.I.Am, Sean Combs, Timbaland, and Dr. Dre, to legacy artists such as Sting, U2, Eric Clapton, and George Michael, and even soulful crooners such as up-and-coming Kanye West protégé John Legend. These artists have all sung her praises, and Blige chalks up their common bond as "passion."

Of course, for her first album, she left much of the work to her producers and trusted those around her would take care of her. At the time, she said, "I let everybody around me do everything. I just loved to sing, it was the only thing that freed me" (Neal 2007). By the time *My Life* came around, she had started writing and collaborating on songs but did not receive much of the credit. Back then, she was comfortable letting those in power make the decisions and handle her publishing until she figured out for herself how important publishing is. When she was structuring *My Life*, she was worried, because it was the first time she was doing the writing herself. Her process of writing songs was mostly self-taught and can be described best as intuitive. She told *Performing Songwriter*, "It wasn't something I learned. I was going through hell and just said, 'You know what? I'm going put it on paper.' I was in so much pain, I didn't know what to do with everything that was coming out of me. As I wrote songs like 'My Life' I was crying" (Neal 2007). She was concerned because Sean Combs was the A&R man for her record, and her new compilation was filled with intensely personal and difficult music compared to the party vibe of her first album, but she said that "when Puff approved what I had done, it made me feel good because at the time, he was the only person I depended on as far as his ears were concerned" (Neal 2007).

Usually, she writes with whoever is producing a particular track or album, and it typically takes place right in the studio as they're recording. About the process, she said, "It has to be with someone I've got total chemistry with, who understands where I'm coming from, where I've been and what I'm doing. It has to be a person willing to have an open mind for my ideas." She said when she wrote "Enough Cryin'" with Sean Garrett, for example, from 2005's *The Breakthrough*, she had to explain her story and then he made his touches on it and added to it. "It's not a hard thing to do, especially when it comes from a place that's honest" (Neal 2007).

She has learned the hard way, however, that fans can tell when the music is honest and when it is not. After *No More Drama*, which had its emotional ups and downs, she released *Love & Life* in 2003. When creating the album she listened to Combs, who told her that people did not want to hear any more depressing songs. "So I began to write what he said people wanted to hear—but I couldn't, because I couldn't relate to it. When it came out, people were like, 'we don't believe this shit' [laughs]" (Neal 2007). Blige didn't either.

Often, songs reflect an artist's place in her life, and with Blige that is no exception. Throughout her career she has struggled with the demons of drugs, alcohol, and depression. In an interview with *Rolling Stone* in early 2006, she told reporter Gavin Edwards that the album *No More Drama* declares just that. In some ways, a psychologist might say that the violence and abuse from men in her life established a pattern very early in her life—by the time she was five her father had deserted the family and she had been molested by a man whom she has not named. Drinking and using drugs were taking a toll on her physically as well as emotionally. She recalled her 1999 tour, which was sponsored by Seagram's. She explained that every time she came offstage she drank a plastic cup full of gin and grapefruit juice. "And I would guzzle that, go to the club and have wine and whatever every single night after the show and then wonder why I couldn't sing." Looking back, she is almost sad. She told *Rolling Stone*, "I wasn't able to give people what they needed vocally. I listen back to some of that stuff and I think, 'What do people like about Mary J. Blige?'" These days, she likes herself and has found some peace, and she can appreciate even the minor flaws (Edwards 2006). Sadly, it has taken her nearly fifteen years in the music business, quitting drugs and alcohol, finding God, and finding love, for Blige to reach that level of self-acceptance.

In many ways, *No More Drama* is an album that defined a turning point in her writing career. The album's best-known single, "Family Affair," was, like so many of her other songs, a collaborative effort. The song spent six weeks on the *Billboard* Hot 100 chart at number one. It began, as she told *Performing Songwriter* magazine, with "just a skeleton of a track" from producer Dr. Dre. While on vacation in Aruba, her brother, Bruce Miller, wrote some lyrics for it. It had a party-going vibe, which made sense for her at the time. She was clubbing a lot then. So she sang the lyrics over the track and returned it to Dr. Dre, who gave it a thumbs-up but said that it needed a bridge. Blige took a crack at it herself, and the rest, as they say, is history. "That gave the song a little meat and potatoes. It was just celery and peanut better before I got my hands on it," she said with a laugh. "The bridge took it to the next level, and it became a monster." She said the song "made the entire world party and feel good" (Neal 2007). With its insinuating beat, and her coaxing the listener, "come on everybody get on up . . . come on baby just party with me/let loose and set your body free." She goes on to preach love and tolerance, and declares "cause we celebrating No More Drama in our life."

Blige has collaborated with many artists, but her duet with Bono of U2 of the Irish rock band's song "One" at the 2006 Grammys put her in front of a different audience—a broader one—as a performer, since she really accentuated the song's inherent gospel and spiritual qualities. Collaborating across musical styles sent a larger philosophical message, too, especially in the wake of tragedies. She said, "Bono wrote an incredible record . . . After 9/11, and the tsunami, and Katrina, we bond together. And then we separate once we think it's ok. We need to remember that all races, all levels of life, gay, straight, mental, sane, we're all one and we help each other. We're like a chain. It's hard when you live in a separated, selfish world" (Powers 2006). Her collaborations have not only given her street cred among the hip-hop and rap community, but they have also done much to bolster her critical acclaim, broaden her audience, and show that she is a legitimate artist in her own right who has survived and remained committed to her craft and to challenging herself artistically. As for who is next on her horizon? She is vocal about wanting to work with hip-hop superstar and master producer Kanye West; he is outspoken, uncompromising, and has helped the careers of many up-and-coming singers and rappers, so her desire is unsurprising. "I just think the guy is really talented and I feel everything he does. What I love about Kanye is that he doesn't care what people think about him. You have to respect that" (Powers 2006).

## LEGACY AND OTHER INTERESTS

Even in the beginning of her career, Blige participated in events that raised her profile professionally, artistically, and as a humanitarian. Blige also has had her fair share of scrapes with organizations such as PETA, which has taken her to task for wearing fur.

She was a participant in Charity Rap Fest in August 1992, as one of fifty-two acts. The concert was declared the biggest benefit of its kind to feature groups such as TLC, Arrested Development, and DJ Quik, among others. In 1995, fresh off the success of her first two albums, Blige worked on other projects in addition to her own music. She recorded a cover of Aretha Franklin's classic "(You Make Me Feel Like A) Natural Woman," which was used on the soundtrack to the Fox network show *New York Undercover*. For the film *The Show*, she contributed "Everyday It Rains." Shortly after that, she recorded the emotional ballad "Not Goin' Cry," which appeared on the soundtrack to the popular film based on the Terry McMillan novel *Waiting to Exhale*, with the sassy and memorable lyric "I shoulda left yo' ass a long time ago." Written and produced by Babyface, the song shared company on the soundtrack with Toni Braxton and Whitney Houston (who appeared in the movie), which significantly raised her profile and widened her audience.

In 2001, the MAC Cosmetics company announced that Blige, Elton John, and singer Shirley Manson would be the new spokespeople for the VIVA Glam lipstick line and MAC AIDS Fund. The Viva Glam lipstick is a fundraiser that started in 1994 and at the time of Blige's appointment had raised more than $7 million for the cosmetics company's AIDS fund. She had previously worked with the MAC AIDS Fund and was proud to assist in raising awareness and funds for the disease. Blige has also participated in other concerts that raise funds for AIDS research; she has given her time toward benefit events that fund music education in public schools and has performed in concerts that benefit NetAid, which seeks to "educate young people about global poverty and provide opportunities for them to take concrete actions that will make a difference in the lives of the world's poor." She has also participated in Rap the Vote 2000, an offshoot of the Rock the Vote program in which musicians band together to increase political awareness among unregistered voters (Brown 2007, 53).

Blige has also had some experience with acting during her career. She appeared as a preacher's daughter on the *Jamie Foxx Show*, and in 2001 played a role in the independent film *Prison Song*, which stars rapper Q-Tip. She also had the experience of acting off-Broadway in 2004, when she portrayed a woman named Sunny Jacobs in the acclaimed play *The Exonerated*, which tells the stories of real-life death row inmates. In December 2005, news came out that Blige had been tapped to star in the MTV film on Nina Simone in the lead role, thanks to the film's screenwriter Cynthia Mort, who believed that Blige was the best woman for the part. Although some people—fans of Blige as well as fans of Simone—believed it was an insult or found her ill-suited to play the "High Priestess of Soul," the two artists do share similarities; both are outspoken, often misunderstood, deeply soulful, and introspective. In some ways, one might argue that Blige comes from Simone's lineage, despite the fact that the latter's songs spanned blues, jazz, gospel, and African music and Blige is the "Queen of Hip-Hop Soul."

In the course of ten albums in fifteen years, Mary J. Blige has established herself as a multiplatinum-selling artist whose music has reached across genres. In 2007, she released a number one album titled *Growing Pains*, a sentiment that arguably could apply to much of her career. But Blige is more than just a commercially successful artist; she has overcome poverty, crime, addictions, troubled relationships, and a broken home to become an indomitable hip-hop soul icon of female power and self-healing.

## SELECTED DISCOGRAPHY

*What's the 411?* MCA, 1992
*My Life.* MCA, 1992
*Mary.* MCA, 1999
*No More Drama.* MCA, 2001
*The Breakthrough.* Geffen, 2005

## FURTHER READING

*Billboard.* Album Reviews (August 7, 1992).
Brown, Terrell. *Hip-Hop: Mary J. Blige.* Broomall, PA: Mason Crest Publishers, 2007.

Chonin, Neva. "Rap Needs to Lend Some Drama to Rock." *San Francisco Chronicle* (December 20, 2001).

*City News* Canada. "Mary J. Blige Garners Most Grammy Noms With 8." (December 7, 2006). Available online at www.citynews.ca/news/news_5940.aspx.

Conniff, Tamara. "Fans' Tribute to Late Singer: Aaliyah No. 1." *Hollywood Reporter* (September 6, 2001).

Edwards, Gavin. "The Continuing Drama of Mary J. Blige." *Rolling Stone* online (March 10, 2006). Available online at www.rollingstone.com/artists/maryjblige/articles/story/9447919/the_continuing_drama_of_mary_j_blige.

George-Warren, Holly, Patricia Romanowski, and Jon Pareles (eds.). "Mary J. Blige Biography." *Rolling Stone Encyclopedia of Rock and Roll*. New York: Simon and Schuster, 2001. Available online at www.rollingstone.com/artists/maryjblige/biography.

Herndon, Jessica. "Mary J. Blige Looks Back." *People Weekly* (January 8, 2007).

Jones IV, James T. "Mary J. Blige, Streetwise to New Jack Swing." *USA Today* (November 13, 1992).

McAdams, Janine. "Dynamic Diva: Buzz Builds on Mary Blige; Uptown Artist Turning Heads with 'Strictly' Track." *Billboard* (July 11, 1992).

McIver, Denise L. "Music News: Blige Strikes Right Chord With Gospel Background." *Daily Variety* (October 26, 1992).

Neal, Chris. "Mary J. Blige: Soul Survivor." *Performing Songwriter* (January/February 2007).

*Parade.* "Mary J. Blige: You Can Find a Way to Heal." (February 4, 2007). Available online at www.parade.com/articles/editions/2007/edition_02-04-2007/Mary_J._Blige.

Powers, Ann. "Dear Superstar: Mary J. Blige." *Blender* (May 2006).

Rodman, Sarah. "Mary J. Blige: No More Drama. Review." *Boston Herald* (September 16, 2001).

Swihart, Stewart. "What's the 411?" *All Music Guide.* Available online at www.allmusic.com/cg/amg.dll?p=amg&token=ADFEAEE47817D849AA7E20C79A3E52DBB57DF702FE5AFB86112F0456D3B82D4BBD0E4FE06BC2AB81B5E577B066ADFF2EAC160DD9CBEF5CFEDF765D40&sql=10:wcftxqu5ld6e.

Touré. "Mary. Review." *Rolling Stone* online (September 2, 1999). Available online at www.rollingstone.com/artists/maryjblige/albums/album/257650/review/6210379/mary.

Walters, Barry. "Marked Woman." *Village Voice* (September 11, 2001).

Courtesy of Photofest

# Patsy Cline

## OVERVIEW

Patsy Cline is hailed as one of the most significant female singers in country music, responsible for making possible the careers of so many other women in the music industry. Cline battled the male-dominated, good-old-boy network of the Nashville music scene in the 1950s when she started to gain attention for her singing. Noteworthy as a crossover artist for making country popular with a larger audience, Cline's career was short but has had a tremendous impact even after her death. It can be perceived in two stages: The first one took place while she was alive, and the second came as interest in her surged when MCA Records released a Patsy Cline box set in 1991. With the reprint of *Honky Tonk Angel* in 1993, "her phenomenal revival in popularity across age groups and lifestyles proves she was no mere shooting star" (Nassour 1993), and she is more popular now around the world than she was even at the peak of her career.

Cline, however, was not alone. Kitty Wells, who became a star a few years before Cline, had hits in the early 1960s, and Brenda Lee, who used Cline's producer Owen Bradley, also played a part in bringing country music to pop audiences. Cline, though, has endured as the symbol of crossover success, partly because of her early, tragic death, which occurred just as she was starting to come into her own, and partly because of her vocal talent. Cline's voice conveyed a knowing sadness in much the same way Billie Holiday infused her own sense of sorrow into her singing. Somehow, though, Cline has transcended her short career and taken on a nearly mythic tragedy, and unfortunate circumstance did not just surround her death. Her life was difficult, and she encountered many challenges when it came to her career, her image, and ownership of her music.

Cline's personality was big and bold: She was outspoken and unafraid to seek success. Yet Cline spent much of the early part of her career fighting against other people's ideas of what she should record and how she should sound. For example, she initially disregarded and did not want to record songs that would make her a big star. Cline was a trailblazer—prior to her breakthrough, women in country music were largely relegated to "window dressing" roles. As described by Dottie West, a contemporary singer and friend of Cline's, "Patsy could be soft and feminine, but she could hold her own against any man. It was common knowledge that you didn't mess with 'the Cline.' If you kicked her, she'd kick right back" (Nassour 1993, xi). In the 1950s and early 1960s, Cline was an anomaly in American culture and especially the music business—strong, sexy, somewhat reckless with her personal life, and fiercely determined to become a famous singer no matter what the cost, personal or professional.

Cline's voice was smooth and full. She was unique because she could embody the song and truly inhabit it. Although she sang many songs that were written by other people, from Hank Williams to Willie Nelson to countless others, those pieces she popularized have become identified with her and not the composer. Cline is known for many songs, most notably her first hit "Walkin' After Midnight" as well as "I Fall to Pieces," "Crazy," and "She's Got You." Most of her albums appeared on the *Billboard* charts posthumously. The first to appear was 1963's *Patsy Cline Showcase*, which hit the seventy-three slot on the Pop Albums chart. *The Patsy Cline Story*, also released in the same

*Patsy didn't let nobody tell her what to do. She done what she felt, and if a man got in her way she let 'em know they couldn't stand there.*
—Loretta Lynn

year, hit seventy-four on the pop chart and nine on the country album chart. After *Patsy Cline's Greatest Hits* peaked at seventeen on the country chart in 1967, time passed before any of her records popped up again. In 1980 *Always* hit twenty-seven on the country chart, *Greatest Hits* went to eight in 1982, and finally *Sweet Dreams* went to six on the country chart in 1985. After that point none of her records reached the top ten on any chart. Due to the nature of the time in which she came to fame and the nature of Nashville, Cline was more known to audiences through her singles than albums. For instance, "Walkin' After Midnight" hit number two on the country singles chart and twelve on the pop singles chart in 1957. Subsequent hits like "A Poor Man's Roses (Or a Rich Man's Gold)," which hit number fourteen on the country chart, and most of her other singles afterward, such as "Crazy," "I Fall to Pieces," "Imagine That," and "She's Got You," all took up significant slots on various charts, such as Adult Contemporary, pop singles, or country singles. The year 1961 was especially remarkable—"I Fall to Pieces" went to number one on the country singles chart, number six on the Adult Contemporary chart, and number twelve on the pop singles chart all in the same year. At the time, it was unusual for an artist to achieve positions on several charts simultaneously.

Cline never received any Grammy Awards or any Country Music Association Awards during her lifetime, but ironically, Loretta Lynn received one for Album of the Year in 1977 with *I Remember Patsy*. Patsy Cline's records have arguably sold more than what the Recording Industry Association of American (RIAA) database suggests because a label must pay to have its sales audited. One source alleges that *Greatest Hits* sold 6 million copies, and another suggests 8 million (Hazen and Freeman 1999, foreword). *The Patsy Cline Collection*, released in October 1991, was on the charts for over eight years. It was certified gold and hailed by many critics for its comprehensiveness; *Heartaches* (1985) was certified gold in 1994; and *Patsy Cline Sings Songs of Love* (1995) was certified gold in 2006. A long-form video, *The Real Patsy Cline*, received platinum certification in 1994. In 1992 Cline received a Grammy Awards Recording Hall of Fame induction for "Crazy," and in 1993 a commemorative stamp was issued. Her accomplishments and her legacy are all the more remarkable considering only three albums of her were released during her lifetime: *Patsy Cline* (August 1957), *Showcase with the Jordanaires* (November 1961), and *Sentimentally Yours* (August 1962).

## EARLY YEARS

*Patsy was born for show business. Her life was singing. When you saw her perform, you knew that nobody else came close. . . . She had a charisma that was equal to Elvis or Johnny Cash.*

—Dottie West

Cline's father, Samuel Lawrence Hensley, met her mother Hilda when he was forty years old and she was thirteen. He was a widower whose first wife, Wynona Jones, had died of pneumonia in 1927 leaving two children, Randolph and Tempie Glenn. Shortly thereafter he and Hilda met at a Sunday school picnic. They married two years later, in 1929. The family moved around when Cline was young. She was born Virginia Patterson Hensley and was referred to as Ginny as a child. She had a younger brother Samuel, who was called John, and a sister Sylvia Mae. When Cline was in the eighth grade, the family finally settled in a modest, working-class neighborhood near Winchester, Virginia. Her parents would often argue because her father would leave for periods of time against her mother's wishes to find work. By some family accounts, her father also had a drinking problem.

Her mother has often been asked about how Cline got involved or interested in country music. "It must have been in her blood. She didn't take after me or her daddy. Patsy's love of music accounted for her drive to become a singer," she said (Nassour 1993, 5). The child actress and singing sensation Shirley Temple was one of Cline's idols growing up, but singing did not immediately enter into the picture. At a very young age Cline asked for dancing lessons, but the family could not afford them. However, to everyone's surprise, she won first place in a dance contest. After her dance success, she started asking to play the piano. Finally, they bought her one when she was seven years old. Her mother says that when she took her daughter for lessons, it quickly became apparent that she could play by ear. The piano teacher told her mother, "She's got a natural gift. You'll be wasting your money. I don't think I could teach her to play" (7).

From that point on Cline was glued to the radio and faithfully listened to the Grand Ole Opry, always telling her mother that she wanted to be a singer like Roy Acuff or Maybelle Carter or anyone else she heard and admired. From a young age, she was driven to be a star. She sang in church choir and even did duets of gospel and religious songs with her mother. Her family, parents, friends, and neighbors kept reminding her how difficult it would be to make it as a country music star, but Cline was undeterred. In fact, it seemed to motivate her even more.

It was sheer determination and fearlessness that drove her into the office of the local radio station, WINC, to see deejay Joltin' Jim McCoy, whose band the Melody Playboys had a live show on Saturday mornings. Cline loved the show, and one morning when she was fourteen she got dressed up, went over to the studio, and asked to see McCoy, unannounced. She boldly told him that she was good enough to be on the radio and asked for a chance to sing without pay. Despite her naiveté—she was green and ungroomed as far as her vocal talent was concerned—he was taken with her gumption and her raw talent, so she became a regular with the group. It also helped that she looked older than she was. Cline was savvy even from a young age and asked for advice from people whenever she encountered a new situation, then took it.

Perhaps on some level Cline knew that she ultimately needed to depend on herself to succeed. Her parents' marriage was starting to fall apart. Her father left the family when she was about fifteen, in 1947. Later, she intimated to others that he "tried something with her one night when he was drunk" (Nassour 1993, 15). His departure put a tremendous financial strain on the family. Her mother, with whom she was extremely close, was a seamstress but did not earn enough to support the family. Cline quit high school as a sophomore to work full-time, first at a poultry factory and then as a waitress at the soda fountain in Gaunt's Drug Store. Her father never lived long enough to hear her sing professionally, although she did see him briefly before he died in December 1956.

Through all this hard work she remained determined and driven to succeed. She sent a letter to the Grand Ole Opry to ask for an audition, and a few weeks later she received a request for a recording and photograph. Through the kindness of people she knew—a local photographer and the owner of a record store—she put together a package and sent it off to the Opry. In the meantime, she sought out Wally Fowler, who ran a program that aired after the Opry on Sunday nights and was known for being a "pioneer of the gospel caravans" (Nassour 1993, 18). Her boldness got her a few minutes with him to audition. Once again, as with her local radio station deejay, Fowler was taken aback by her talent and arranged for an audition with WSM Radio and the Opry officials. While she was in Nashville she met Roy Acuff, and he asked her to sing a song with him on his noontime show. Officials tried to get her to remain in town long enough to sing in front of more people at the organization, but the family had to leave. They traveled in a borrowed car and could not afford to stay over.

Back home Cline kept singing at church socials, carnivals, parties, and anywhere anyone would hire her. Gradually, she gained a name for herself in the region and, by some accounts, a reputation for her "inappropriate" attire and her unladylike mouth: Cline could swear like a sailor, as they say, and then turn on the charm whenever necessary. Some of the men she flirted with started to call her the "honky tonky angel" (Nassour 1993, 27). In 1951, by the time she was nineteen, she was a regular performer with the house band at George and Katherine Frye's Rainbow Inn just outside of Winchester. Shortly thereafter, in 1952, she met a Nashville guitarist named Clarence William Peer who had connections in country music. Peer suggested she change her name to Patsy. He also sacrificed a lot, became enamored of her (despite his own marriage and family), and became her manager. Peer tried hard to get her into Nashville, sending out demo tapes and lobbying on her behalf. Cline, however, did not initially return his affection even though she spent much time with him. Instead, she married Gerald Cline, a man nearly ten years her senior who, according to those close to her, had a womanizing past and nefarious, untrustworthy ways. They met in October 1952 and were married the following March. It seemed as though Cline thought marrying him would help give her some economic stability while she pursued her career, but their marriage was short-lived—Gerald was overprotective and unsupportive. He wanted her at home, not on stage. He also followed Cline and Peer nearly everywhere they went; he suspected their relationship was more than professional, and he was increasingly correct in his suspicions.

Finally, Peer's efforts to assist Cline paid off. Her tapes wound up in the hands of William McCall, president of Four-Star Records. Peer lobbied McCall to sign Patsy Cline and Bill Peer and the Melody Makers. On September 30, 1954, just after she had turned twenty-two, she signed a two-year contract. Cline, overcome with excitement, signed it without reading all the fine print, which turned out to be a costly error. Her royalties were only a little over 2 percent, which after paying for her recordings and the musicians did not amount to much.

Under a deal McCall arranged with A&R rep Paul Cohen at Decca Records, Cline recorded some demos in Nashville. Cohen thought from the start that Cline could have a "pop sound" but still consulted everyone on his roster except her chief rival, Kitty Wells. Finally, they settled on the pop-leaning producer Owen Bradley, and she recorded four songs, including "I Don't Wanna," "I Love You Honey," "I Cried All the Way to the Altar," and "Come On In," the latter of which often became her opening number in live performances. Cohen, however, was unhappy with the results and initially shelved the recording.

During this early phase of her recording career, the sessions involved her singing music that ranged from rockabilly to tearjerker ballads. She had recorded seventeen singles between 1955 and 1960, but "I Love You Honey" and "Come On In" were the only two songs from that Decca Nashville session that turned into singles, though they were released later, in February 1956. The first batch of her singles was released in mid-1955, including "A Church, A Courtroom and then Goodbye" and "Honky Tonk Merry-Go-Round." Both songs ironically mirrored events in her life. She made her Opry debut in June 1955, too, with the former song. Later that year, in the fall, she started appearing on a live entertainment program called *Town and Country Jamboree* based in Washington, DC, as well as making guest appearances on radio shows. Her performances on *Town and Country Jamboree* gave her a slowly growing but devoted regional following. In fall 1955, she told Peer (who had divorced his wife that summer) that she was leaving the band for good, that she needed to focus on *her* career, which meant his tenure as her manager was over, too. Peer was heartbroken. They did not speak for a while but eventually reconciled. By the following year, Cline's marriage was deteriorating and she and Gerald separated.

## CAREER PATH

### Getting the Big Break and Finally Finding Love: 1956–1957

Cline's personal life complicated her professional life and vice versa consistently throughout her career, perhaps due to the fact that her personality was unusually outgoing and uncompromising when compared with other women of her era, and especially compared to Southern women. Her magnanimous personality, love of life, and devotion toward singing often took her to extreme places, extreme people, and extreme situations. But when she met Charlie Dick in April 1956, it sealed the fate of her marriage to Gerald. Cline wrote in letters to a friend that in June 1955 she had left Gerald for six months, although in November they tried to make it work. She writes that some of the problems were that she was his third wife, and he was about ten years her senior and did not want children, although at the time her extra-marital interests certainly complicated the story, too. Perhaps these pieces of information were too thorny and/or embarrassing to admit, which may explain why she did not divulge her relations with Peer to her friend. Dick, though, had a bit of a wild reputation as a ladies' man. He pursued her persistently, and once they started spending time together they were smitten with each other. His brother, Mel recalled that Charlie and Patsy were such a good fit because "they were always on the go and looking for excitement" (Nassour 1993, 84).

She was getting frustrated with her career, though—things were not happening quickly enough. Her contract indebted her to Decca and McCall, but she was not satisfied with what they were doing or what they were *not* doing. She had a recording session in which she did takes on the rockabilly song "Stop, Look and Listen," a weepy ballad called "I've Loved and Lost Again," and two gospel numbers that were not released during her lifetime. Often, she would be so moved by the music and so immersed in the performance that she would end up in tears afterward. But still, she was restless and felt as though something was wrong.

One of the musicians present for that session in April 1956 said that she was upset. Musician Teddy Wilburn recalled her saying "Everybody knows what I should and shouldn't do, but nobody listens to me. It's all in the material and I ain't got no decent material" (Nassour 1993, 84). Still, Decca released the rockabilly song and the weeper on July 8, and she was able to debut the record on a radio program that was part of what the Opry carried on the NBC radio network. That summer, she went to Los Angeles to sing on another program and promote her record. In late fall, after receiving no response from deejays and suffering minimal sales of her albums, she took some initiative and had Charlie drive her to New York to audition for *Arthur Godfrey's Talent Scouts*. She did not receive a slot—someone she thought less talented, George Hamilton IV, did. It enraged her.

When she was in California, she met struggling songwriter Donn Hecht, which changed everything about her career. McCall had Hecht listen to Cline's recordings and complained that she had "bombed" every time he spent money on putting her records out (Nassour 1993, 95) Her contract was about to expire, and McCall was not sure whether or not he should renew her. As crass as it may sound, McCall had spent thousands on her and was not seeing a return on his investment, but he was not quite ready to say goodbye to her. McCall asked for Hecht's opinion, who told him something similar to what Cline had been saying: The material was not right. Hecht told McCall that she was not a country singer, that she should not be singing hillbilly music, but that he should keep her. So McCall asked him to write a song for Cline and make it a hit. Hecht wrote "Walkin' After Midnight." Ironically, when McCall called Cline and played the demo over the phone with a singer, she reportedly hated it and refused to record it. But because she was contractually obligated, she did. They continued to argue during the production process; she said it was a pop song and reiterated that everyone kept pushing her on material that she had no say in and then blamed her when it didn't work out. Cline and Hecht worked out a deal with McCall: If he let her pick the B-side of the record, he would release the songs back to back. If his pick went over well, she had to promise that she would not bother him about material choice again; if both selections were failures, they would part company (Nassour 1993, 98–99).

Before she finished recording though, she had to ask for money. McCall advanced her some cash in exchange for a one-year extension of her contract, which was set to expire in September 1957. Cline was locked in through September 1958. Cline's financial situation only got worse as they recorded a handful of songs in fall 1956 and Christmas approached. Broke again, she called McCall, who advanced her more money and tacked on two more years, moving the contract expiration date to September 1960 (Nassour 1993, 90–100). Cline's career shows us how difficult it was to be a recording artist in an era when sales were measured more in terms of hit singles than in artistic development over the course of several albums and many years. It also shows us how difficult it was to be a female artist who was trying to be true to herself but also become successful.

Finally, Cline broke through. She got her big break when she sang "Walkin' After Midnight" on the *Arthur Godfrey Talent Scouts* program in 1957, which was her national network television debut. Godfrey had seen her appearance on the *Town and Country Jamboree* around the holidays in 1956 and wanted her to appear on his show. She was not excited about performing the song; she may have buried it among roughly thirty other songs until someone in Godfrey's office pulled it out and requested she sing it because of its potential for broad appeal. But she performed her heart out, and the audience responded with thunderous applause that brought her to tears. Godfrey asked her to sing another song, so she got her wish for country material, singing Hank Williams' song "Your Cheatin' Heart" much to the audience's delight.

She was dubbed an overnight sensation, orders poured into the label for her single, and she began to appear on Godfrey's show regularly. "Walkin' After Midnight" was the only certified hit she had of those seventeen singles she recorded between 1955 and 1960. Around this time, when she started to make it and become recognized, she reportedly said, "Damn, it's about time, I've paid my dues" (Nassour 1993, x).

### Riding High On the Charts and Trying to Find Her Way: 1957–1960

The year 1957 was good for her personally, too. In January 1957, soon after she appeared on television, Gerald Cline filed for divorce, which was granted in March. Soon after, Charlie proposed. Cline married Charlie Dick on September 15, 1957, at her mother's home in Winchester. Although they were in love, when they fought they fought hard; he reportedly got violent and would sometimes physically abuse her, so their relationship was far from perfect. In letters to Treva Miller, Cline admitted, "I've never loved a man so much in my life. He is my life, my world, just my everything" (Hazen and Freeman 1999, 163). Within a few months, Cline was pregnant and daughter Julie Dick was born August 25, 1958. Two and a half years later Cline had a son, Randy Dick, on January 22, 1961. Unfortunately, Charlie had a nasty streak, drank a lot, and according to some of Cline's confidants, he sometimes flirted with other women while they were married. Although much of the press and writing about her talked about her bold and occasionally uncouth ways, Cline was also a traditional, warmhearted country girl. She was deeply devoted to her children and Charlie, despite how complicated they made her life and regardless of whatever reservations Charlie may have ultimately had about his wife being on the road so frequently.

Still, though, Cline was not happy with Godfrey's show, because they saw a future for her with pop, blues, and jazz, which she fought against. She wanted to dress in her country-western gear and let loose the occasional yodel. Her stubbornness ultimately got her fired, so she left New York and went back home. There, she begged for her old slot back at *Town and Country Jamboree*, from which she had also been fired when she overslept and failed to show up for a rehearsal. Eventually, she was hired back. She began making personal appearances and singing on variety television programs and in large venues across the country, such as state fairs.

Soon, she began to be seen as a sex symbol and went from traditional country-western attire to clothing her full figure in gold and silver lamé clothing that fit tight around the hips, high heels, and skirts a little bit shorter than what most women wore. "It kind of went with her. It was the full package," said Minnie Pearl of Cline's appeal (Nassour 1993, 125). In April 1957, *TV Guide* wrote a story about her rise, and it seemed that fame, something she sought so desperately, was overwhelming her. "I'm beginning to wonder if I can keep up with all this," she said (*TV Guide* 1957).

*You wouldn't have to tell Patsy anything about this women's lib business. She could've taught them a thing or two.*

—Owen Bradley

In general, though, Cline's career improved once she had a hit, regardless of the arguments and creative differences between her and McCall, Godfrey, or anyone else who had a say in the direction of her career. When "Walkin' After Midnight" was released in February 1957 she had both a pop and country hit on her hands; in just a couple of weeks it sold 200,000 copies (Hazen and Freeman 1999, 146). In all, it spent nineteen consecutive weeks on the *Billboard* country charts and sixteen on the pop chart, outselling the Platters, Bill Haley, and Jerry Lewis.

Writing about the song years later in the *Washington Post*, critic Geoffrey Himes attested to the song's longevity when compared to other songs from 1957 with the words, "[I]t refuses to be pinned down to a particular style; it combines the emotional transparency of country, the robust tonality of Tin Pan Alley pop and a hint of gritty R&B into a sound that was Cline's alone" (November 15, 1991). Himes described Cline's vocal as "strutting" into the song after Don Helms's honky-tonk-sounding steel guitar. "She slides into the flatted blues note, jumps on the syncopated swing accents and promises her departed lover that she won't be sitting at home waiting for him; she'll be out looking for him" (Himes 1991). Owen Bradley must have sensed that the lyrics, too, would ultimately resonate with Cline, as the narrator evokes a person who proactively takes charge of her affairs, personal or otherwise.

Cline also appeared on the Grand Ole Opry again, subsequent to the release of "Walkin'" and once again audiences loved her. After Connie Gay of *Town and Country Jamboree* disparaged her on television, Cline decided not to agree to his terms for a contract to appear on the show; in her letters to Treva Miller, she gave the impression that Gay wanted to pay her less than union scale and that he seemed ungrateful about the fact that her performances raised the show's profile. There was speculation that she would appear on the *Steve Allen, Art Linkletter, Perry Como,* and *Ed Sullivan* shows, but none of those plans came to fruition, which underscores the idea that Cline's career was as much about near-misses as it was about hard work in its small steps toward success. She started recording again in late spring, with about a half dozen songs. Decca also released a follow-up record to "Walkin'" called "Today, Tomorrow and Forever," with "Try Again" on the flip side. She did some touring, sharing the bill with Brenda Lee and Porter Wagoner. The only other song of hers to chart in 1957 after "Walkin'" was "A Poor Man's Roses (Or a Rich Man's Gold)," which reached number fourteen on the country singles chart and was on the flipside to "Walkin' After Midnight." However, in 1957 she received four awards for Most Promising Female Country Artist, from *Cash Box, Billboard, Juke Box,* and *Jamboree* magazines. Critics were taking notice.

Despite how busy she was, Cline's limiting contract with Four-Star influenced what she could record and with whom she could work. She felt as though the contract was keeping her from really seeing the financial fruits of her labor. Cline groused about not having control over her material and her career and claimed McCall was a bastard who was making a lot of money off her. Even though she had a hit, by November of 1957, newly married, she was as broke as ever. After all her expenses were deducted, she received very little from royalties. Her profile continued to rise, but it would be several years before she had another significant hit, crossover or otherwise.

### Sassy and Strong Women of the South: The Dixie Chicks Live Cline's Legacy

Since 1998, the country trio the Dixie Chicks boasted multiplatinum sales and a strong country following, but in March 2003 they gained even more attention when singer Natalie Maines expressed the group's displeasure with the war in Iraq, telling an audience in London that they were ashamed to be from Texas because President Bush was from there, too. Although Maines later apologized, saying she should have criticized the war, many country music stations banned them and accused them of being unpatriotic, perhaps the biggest infraction a country musician can commit.

A publicity campaign was mounted, and the controversy exposed them to a larger audience and illustrated exactly how much of an international crossover pop success the Chicks had become; plus, mainstream audiences had become much more sophisticated about country music, and the band's misgivings about current affairs had become more mainstream. The experience even inspired a documentary called *Shut Up and Sing*. Initially, *Home*'s sales suffered; in the first full week following the flap, sales dropped 43 percent to 72,000 copies, but it stayed the number one country album for the seventeenth week in a row.

Their 2006 follow-up *Taking the Long Way* debuted at number one, sold more than 500,000 copies in its first week, and won four Grammys, including Record and Album of the Year. The album's anthemic winner, "Not Ready to Make Nice," is a pointed jab at their critics. In the chorus, they sing, "I'm not ready to make nice/I'm not ready to back down."

The Chicks share more than just country crossover status with the likes of Patsy Cline and Dolly Parton, exceedingly honest women even when it is unpopular. Cline and Parton were trailblazers, and the Dixie Chicks, as part of that legacy, set new standards for modern, country-based pop music.

The late 1950s can be characterized by country music suffering somewhat in sales and popularity against the rising popularity of rock and roll. Cline continued to work during her pregnancy with her first child, Julie, throughout 1958. She had four recording sessions, which yielded the single "Walkin' Dream," released toward the end of the year with "Stop the World" on the flipside.

The folks at Decca told her it was selling well, but Cline was hoping it would chart well, which it did not. Also, "Let the Teardrops Fall" and "Never No More" came from these recordings, but none of the songs had much impact. She toured a bit and played in Nashville, Minnesota, and even Hawaii and continued to appear on Arthur Godfrey's show and the *Ozark Jubilee*. In a letter to her fans, she said she recorded the song "Just Out of Reach" with the Anita Kerr singers, known for their backup work for Brenda Lee, and entreated her fans to buy her records so she could "put some shoes or boots on this youngin," referring to her unborn child (Hazen and Freeman 1999, 212). In December of that year, Decca released her 1956 recording of the song "Dear God," but it failed to connect with audiences. She described it as her "first real religious record" (Hazen and Freeman 1999, 224). After Julie was born, Cline was prepared to start singing and working again, but the gigs were not coming and the bills were rising.

After Julie's birth, though, Cline's workload didn't increase significantly. In her letters to Miller she described how she was waiting until her contract was set to expire in May 1959—but she was mistaken, as it did not expire until 1960. The time leading up to Julie's birth and shortly thereafter, until the contract expiration, was transitional for Cline. In the early part of 1959, she slowly resumed working and started recording with producer Owen Bradley using stereo technology for the first time. It marked the first time the Jordan-aires started appearing regularly on her songs with backing vocals. Biographer Margaret Jones said that their "low chords and soft spiritual sound counter-pointed Patsy's vocal power and broad range" (1994, 167). When she recorded "Yes I Understand," she used the new technique of overdubbing vocals. That song, along with "Cry Not For Me," was released in February 1959. The work did not result in a big hit, but it was an important step in the formulation of the orchestrated pop sound that would dominate her later hit record-ings. In late summer, the Clines moved to Nashville to be in the heart of the country music scene—a move that seems almost ironic in hindsight—and she sought out a manager in the form of Randy Hughes. Cline wanted to come back into the country music business. In a letter to Miller in January 1959—the last one published—Cline wrote that Bradley wanted to offer her 6 percent on any terms that she wanted, such as the right to choose her material.

### Great Change and Great Success, Followed by Great Tragedy: 1960–1963

Most authors, journalists, and music critics look favorably on Cline as they describe the terms of her arrangement with Four-Star. In its online biography of Cline, *All Music Guide* described her arrangement as one that exploited her talent and limited her to recording songs from only one publishing company. In those days, though, that situation was not unusual. Music publishers owned the artists who signed with them. Once her Four-Star contract was up, she would be able to (and did) select material that was better for her and better for her finances, thanks to the help of Owen Bradley. Cline's return to musical form was serendipitous, because Bradley had been promoted to A&R head at Decca in spring 1958.

During 1959 and 1960, when she was trying to regain her footing after all of these changes—label, managers, childbirth—her pay was low and she traveled long, grueling hours with other Nashville musicians, most of whom were men. She persevered because Hughes kept his word and kept her busy working. Cline also appeared regularly on the *Ozark Jubilee*, which was known as *Jubilee U.S.A.*, from 1959 to September 1960. These times were difficult, as in the earlier years of her career, but complicated in new ways. After the birth of Julie, though, Cline's marriage got rockier, and she suffered from depression. Her weight fluctuated frequently and it was not uncommon for her to go on a crash diet (Jones 1994, 185). It was also not uncommon for her, or other Nashville musicians at this time, to take amphetamines, or speed, to endure the rigors of traveling and performing.

Many of those television-performance agreements allowed her to pick her own material, so despite the fact that the records that Four-Star put out in 1959 did not chart, it is arguable that Cline was choosing the likes of Neal Sedaka, Connie Francis, and country standards such as "Lovesick Blues" because she was open to trying a good song, no matter what the genre. Her final Four-Star session took place in January 1960, and probably as a concession to Cline, Bradley let her do country tunes. She recorded the Tin Pan alley standard that Hank Williams popularized, "Lovesick Blues," along with several other tracks: "How Can I Face Tomorrow?," "Crazy Dreams," and "There He Goes."

In April 1960, when she learned she was pregnant again, Cline was deeply ambivalent about the news, unhappy with her marriage to Charlie (who at this point was having affairs), and worried about the possible negative impressions her pregnancy would have on her career. That summer, however, she signed a three-year contract with a two-year option with Decca; she had developed a sense of trust with Bradley. In November 1960 she recorded "I Fall to Pieces," which was out for at least six months before it reached any significant position on the charts. At first Cline thought the tune, written by Harlan Howard, was damaged goods, or at least bad luck. She also resisted recording the bluesy, sad number because she did not see herself as a balladeer. Many other artists had also refused to sing it, from various popular male singers of the day to Brenda Lee.

Surprisingly, "I Fall to Pieces" was one of the first few country-pop crossovers during this second, newly invigorated stage of her career. Bradley managed a mix of vocal backup that were de rigueur for pop recordings of the time, but lest we forget Cline was a country singer at heart, he allowed a steel guitar to surface, too. There is irony in the way Cline delivered the opening line—she sings "I Fall to Pieces," but she controls those words so carefully that you almost cannot believe her, except for a slight hesitation when she sings the word "fall." The song does not contain much in the way of verses, but each time she repeats the title phrase, it's rendered slightly differently. By the end of the song, the shifts are subtle but significant, and it feels as though she is reconsidering the idea with each rendering.

Cline continued to work with Bradley, who helped create some beautiful orchestral arrangements and enlisted backup vocalists The Jordanaires, who had also lent their signature harmonies to Elvis Presley's early RCA recordings. His influence gave her work a pop sensibility. With Bradley, Cline worked hard to develop a ballad style. It is no accident, then, that her final hits were country music torch songs—deeply emotional, heart-tugging ballads. Because Nashville was rife with excellent musicians who knew each other, Cline had the best of the city's session players at her disposal—Hank Garland on guitar, Floyd Cramer on piano, and Buddy Harmon on drums. Throughout these sessions and despite her success, when Cline was initially presented with tunes such as "I Fall to Pieces," "Crazy," and "Leavin' On Your Mind," she kept insisting they were pop songs. But Bradley kept encouraging her to sing them in her own style. Of course, she did just that. "I Fall to Pieces" was released shortly after the birth of her second child, Allen Randolph, on January 30. After extensive employment of independent promoters, it made a modest appearance on the *Billboard* charts in April, but then reached number one in August on the country chart and slowly climbed up the pop chart to reach number twelve in September. Cline was able to fend off creditors and pay for a car, a refrigerator, and other amenities in cash. With her first royalty check, she bought her mother a new refrigerator and stove; she later bought her a new Cadillac. Cline was so grateful that she bought a small gift for Howard, thanking him for the wonderful song. Cline's hard work, constant promotion, and performances behind the song paid off.

Much about Cline's life has become the stuff of popular music mythology. Sometime after the success of "I Fall to Pieces" she had a hunch that she was going to be involved in a car accident. In April 1961, she drew up a will and left nearly everything to her mother, including the care of her two children. To her husband, she left a few material possessions, including her car, some furniture, a record player and albums, and a television set. Her prediction came true. She was driving with a friend in the rain in Nashville on June 14 and was thrown through the windshield. She needed major reconstructive plastic surgery.

This severe car accident produced a spiritual reawakening in Cline, who believed that she had seen Jesus and that he had told her that it was not her time yet, there was still work for her to do. The accident nearly killed her and left her with visible scars on her head and her face. Friends reported that she seemed less bawdy, more mellow and grateful after the accident. Oddly, the accident brought out the best in her husband Charlie, who tended her at her hospital bedside. Once it was clear that she was on the mend, radio deejays started playing "I Fall to Pieces" more frequently, as a goofy homage. She was flooded with visitors, cards, letters, flowers, and well-wishers. She made an appearance at the Opry in a wheelchair during the week she came home from the hospital in July and returned to the Opry on crutches for her singing debut shortly afterward.

*Patsy Cline's music will live forever because she sang from the heart, she lived the words of her songs.*
—country singer Trisha Yearwood

Part of the Patsy Cline mythology includes the now-legendary stories about the songs she recorded, how they were recorded, and how those songs were chosen. For example, "Crazy," written by Willie Nelson, was recorded in October 1961, not too long after her car accident. One story says that she initially hated the song; other stories say that she loved it instantly. She reportedly spent about four hours in the studio on that song, which was unusual for those days; she could not hit the high notes because of pain in a broken rib. The musicians recorded it, and then a couple of weeks later Cline returned to the studio after resting and did many takes of the song to get it just right. "Crazy" is rather unusual for a country song—it features more than three chords and certainly Bradley's treatment turned it into a swooning, emotionally charged ballad. It has been noted that Bradley's guidance transformed Nelson's song for Cline. Nelson had a difficult time finding the right singer for it; Bradley was charged with making Cline a household word in all demographic markets but especially New York. That song did the trick. When "Crazy" was released on October 16, it went to number two on the Adult Contemporary chart and number nine on the pop singles chart.

Cline's career was at its high in 1961 and 1962 when her recordings of "Crazy" and "She's Got You" became country hits and pop hits. At this point much of her material was provided by the likes of Willie Nelson, Hank Cochran, and Harlan Howard, and she had recorded versions of songs popularized by Frank Sinatra and Gene Autry. She, along with other Nashville and country music notables including Bill Monroe, Minnie Pearl, and Jim Reeves, appeared at Carnegie Hall for the Opry's debut as a benefit concert in November 1961. Although country music at Carnegie Hall was not unprecedented, it was still remarkable. Just in time for her Carnegie Hall appearance, Decca released *Patsy Cline Showcase* on November 27, 1961. Cline was happy with her hits and wanted to keep them coming, for the sake of her children—everything she did was for them. By the end of the year, she was exhausted but had already recorded her next hit, "She's Got You," which was released in January 1962 and hit number fourteen in February.

Cline spent about fourteen months as the main female vocalist for *The Johnny Cash Show*, but she also traveled for shows on the road in the East, Midwest, and Southwest. She also performed at the Hollywood Bowl that year—an accomplishment for a female singer—and had a string of dates in Las Vegas. She was making enough money so that there was some left over to lend to friends such as Loretta Lynn for groceries or rent. (She and Lynn were both somewhat iconoclastic for their time, and they got along well.) Because of

Cline's success, her husband Charlie even quit his print shop job, which irritated her, and she bitingly referred to him as "Mr. Patsy Cline." Around this time, she had an on-again, off-again affair with her manager Hughes, who was extremely good to her and good for her, as well as other flings on the road. Five other country hits were released that year, and Cline was arguably at the height of her career.

After spending all of 1962 touring, she finally bought her dream house. During the summer of 1962, however, she unexpectedly gave friend Dottie West her scrapbooks, telling her that she never thought she'd live to be thirty. She was not quite accurate. She also told June Carter that month that she knew she was going to die soon and gave Carter instructions about what to do with her body and how she wanted her children raised. There are other eerie facts about her death; for instance, "Leavin' On Your Mind," was released in January 1963, making it the last single before her death. Cline was killed in a plane crash on March 5, 1963; Cowboy Copas, Hawkshaw Hawkins, and Randy Hughes were also in the plane. The crash took place somewhere off Highway 70 about three miles west of Camden, Tennessee. The entertainers— all Opry stars—were on their way from Kansas City, where they had performed at a benefit concert, to Nashville.

The last album she recorded, *The Patsy Cline Story*, was released posthumously in June 1963. It is loaded with Bradley's string arrangements and contains pop songs such as "Does Your Heart Beat for Me?" along with a Hensley family favorite, "Bill Bailey." Her version of "Sweet Dreams" was recorded in early February, a month before she died in a plane crash at the age of thirty; the song had already been a hit three times over by other artists.

## MISSION, MOTIVATION, PROCESS

Cline entered the male-dominated world of Nashville and emerged strong, swearing, sassy and seductive. Her friend and fellow country singer Dottie West described the time as challenging for women. "The women singers didn't have the clout or the money-making potential they do today. . . . We were mainly used for window dressing. Patsy broke the boundaries. Her massive appeal proved women, without men by their side, could consistently sell records and draw audiences" (Nassour 1993, Foreword). Although West admitted she could never duplicate Cline's appeal and abilities, she did learn a lot from her. West said that Cline "would tell her 'Find one person to sing to and sing to just that one.' When I got that down, Patsy added, 'Now make each person out there think he or she is that one and cast a spell over them'" (Nassour 1993, Foreword). West's story attests to Cline's native intelligence and ambition but also her generous heart. It also shows Cline understood what the audience wants out of an entertainer.

West described how when Cline would sing, you could sometimes see her cry. She asserted it was sincere; Cline was singing from the heart and was in touch with the emotions that propelled her music. In one particular session, in spring 1956, she recorded the rockabilly song "Stop, Look and Listen," the cry-in-your-beer ballad "I've Loved and Lost Again," and two gospel songs, "He Will Do For You (What He's Done for Me)" and "Dear God." The latter two were not released during her lifetime, but musicians recalled that she was in tears after she performed them. Opry announcer Grant Turner remembered that "she'd do those sacred songs with such feeling, there'd be silence at the end. Patsy's face'd be covered in tears. She was as moved as the audience" (Nassour 1993, 87).

Her performances took a step further in the country music idea of hearing the "teardrop" in the voice. During her career, Cline's chief competitor was arguably Kitty Wells, who recorded "It Wasn't God Who Made Honky Tonky Angels" in 1952 and followed it with other country hits. In 1991, critic Nick Kimberly, writing for London's *The Independent*, examined Cline's voice, saying that her voice was "softer, more sophisticated—more urban" but that the two share this "teardrop," which can take the form of anything as subtle as a break in the voice, a stifle of a sob, or a "willingness to sing a note flat or through clenched teeth" (Kimberly 1991). Although Brenda Lee had more success in the pop market—her records, too, boasted Bradley production— her work was geared toward a younger audience. With the ache in her voice and her romantic material, Cline could not be matched when it came to country listeners, although she ultimately won fans for her pop material, too.

A raw talent who seemed to forge her identity through her own devices, Cline in some ways seems so singular and original it is hard to think that she would mimic someone else. Early advocates talked of her ability to phrase as well as to really belt out a song. Others, such as Jimmy Dean, saw that she was looking to develop her own style, like many singers do, by trying out the sound of others. Dean said, "Patsy sang her butt off. She was a huge fan of Kay Starr's and had a lot of her style" (Nassour 1993, 75).

Cline once told a reporter that she attributed her talent to a childhood illness. When she was thirteen she had rheumatic fever, and she was very ill; her doctor put her in an oxygen tent. "The fever affected my throat and when I recovered I had this booming voice like Kate Smith's" (Jones 1994, 15). Other female singer influences that biographers discuss include Rubye Blevins, a.k.a. Patsy Montana, the yodeling cowgirl; and Helen Morgan, who appeared in the musical *Show Boat*. Cline liked to sing Morgan's songs, according to producer Owen Bradley. Biographer Margaret Jones asserted that "as a child she could safely channel all her emotions into music" (Jones 1994, 15). Singing became a way for her to do just that. Cline was by and large a singer and interpreter. Although she could play piano, she never took a singing lesson and never really learned to read music. When she was in California in 1957, though, she was asked by the owner of a motel in which she was staying to put music to words of a song he had written, called "A Stranger in My Arms." According to the *Winchester Star*, which wrote a story about her in April 1957, she had planned to include it on the album she was scheduled to record in New York. But label and management disagreements kept it and other songs from that session—including one she co-wrote, "Don't Ever Leave Me Again"—from being released until it appeared years after her death on compilations of her work. She is credited under the name Virginia Hensley for the song "Don't Ever Leave Me Again," in 1957, along with Lillian Clarborne and James Crawford. These are the only known releases in which she was a songwriting collaborator. In January 1959, Cline told Miller that she wrote her first song, called "A Sometime Marriage," but it was never recorded (Hazen and Freeman 1999, 256).

During recording sessions, especially in the early days when she was trying to find the best people to manage her and release her music and the most suitable material for her voice, Cline could be difficult to work with. Although Cline was professional, prepared, and usually on time for recording sessions, she had a mind of her own and was never shy about speaking it, especially once she had the audience and record sales to give her some clout and authority. "I soon discovered I had to place myself firmly in control otherwise she would take over," said Bradley of their early recording sessions in the late 1950s (Nassour 1993, 136). Don Helms, a steel guitarist who also worked with Hank Williams, recalled her as being particular; she knew which musicians she wanted. "She had her ideas about tempo and arrangements. . . . Patsy could be stubborn, especially when she saw something a certain way. . . . It might be embarrassing, but she was usually right," said Helms (Nassour 1993, 136).

## LEGACY AND OTHER INTERESTS

The songs that Patsy Cline helped popularize have been recorded by many artists, male and female, from jazz singer Madeleine Peyroux's honky-tonk, sax-driven, loping, take on "Walkin' After Midnight" to a dramatically different version by the Cowboy Junkies on their 1988 album *The Trinity Session* to covers by country singers such as Loretta Lynn, Dwight Yoakam, and even the Oak Ridge Boys. Some artists have gone beyond mere covers of singles. In 1977, Lynn recorded an album called *I Remember Patsy* as a tribute. The Canadian singer k.d. lang recorded *Shadowland* with Owen Bradley in 1988, as a deliberate homage to Cline's early 1960s period. Certainly, the career of jazz-pop surprise sensation Norah Jones, with her multiplatinum album *Come Away With Me* and its subtle, sleepy mix of country, jazz, pop ballads, and blues, would not have been possible without a trailblazer such as Cline, who, despite her early insistence on singing country and not pop, achieved success in the pop world. Cline's voice was simply too big, too smooth, and too indebted to jazz and blues singers to stay in the limited world of country; her voice was bigger in some ways than perhaps she initially realized.

In 1991 the release of her box set, *The Patsy Cline Collection*, gave fans and newcomers alike a comprehensive look at her career. On its release,

Geoffrey Himes wondered in the *Washington Post* why the country music industry had not produced a great singer "with the same full-throated tone, rocking sense of swing and bluesy assertiveness in the 28 years since Cline died" (Himes, November 22, 1991). He then examined current albums from artists such as Reba McEntire, Shelby Lynne, Patty Loveless, Paulette Carlson, Lorrie Morgan, and Karen Tobin, and found traces of Cline's legacy. He has even compared her to Elvis Presley in terms of her "reckless confidence" in her abilities (Himes, November 15, 1991) If country music has not been able to produce someone else like Cline, this inability merely reinforces her singularity and the idea that, despite how classic and timeless her appeal may be, a singer like Cline could only really be formed under extraordinary social circumstances.

> *I got me a hit record and I ain't never made a cent from it.*
> —Cline, about "Walkin' After Midnight"

Judging from the amount of compilations of her material alone—Cline's entire recording history has been mined and much of her sessions, live performances, radio program appearances, and the like have been issued—almost all of the material she recorded has been released posthumously. In fact, after the boxed set was released in 1991, dozens of compilations of her music have been released on various labels.

A group of Cline fans and Winchester residents is dedicated to preserving her childhood home and turning it into a living museum by restoring the house at 608 Kent Street in Winchester, Virginia, to its 1950 status. This nonprofit organization, Celebrating Patsy Cline, held a concert called "Crazy for the Blues" in 2002 sponsored by the Preservation of Historic Winchester, and half of the proceeds went toward purchasing the home. In February 2003 there was a memorial celebration in Camden, Tennessee, and in March of that same year, Jim Stutzman Jr., president of CPC, announced a national campaign for the Patsy Cline Museum project. In September 2003, a tribute CD was released called *Remembering Patsy Cline*, with appearances from the diverse likes of Natalie Cole, Norah Jones, Diana Krall, Michelle Branch, Lee Ann Womack, k.d. lang, Terry Clark, Amy Grant, Patty Griffin, and Martina McBride, among others. At press time, the museum's first phase is planned for an existing building on Loudoun Street in downtown Winchester, in the historic part of the town. It will include artifacts, photo murals, montages, and a chronological exposition of her career and life.

Cline has also been immortalized on the silver screen when Jessica Lange took on the role of Cline and Ed Harris played Charlie Dick in the 1985 film *Sweet Dreams*. Prior to that, she figured prominently in the 1980 film *Coal Miner's Daughter*, which chronicles the life of Loretta Lynn, played by Sissy Spacek. Lynn and Cline, played by Beverly D'Angelo, were close friends. In 2005, a documentary directed by Gregory Hall aired on television called *Patsy Cline: Sweet Dreams Still*, which featured archival footage of performances, photographs, and other memorabilia. Fans who want to pay homage to her life in a more personal way can visit her gravesite in Shenandoah Memorial Park where a bell tower stands in memoriam. Several highways in the Winchester area have been named in her honor.

## SELECTED DISCOGRAPHY

*Patsy Cline*. Decca, 1957
*Showcase with the Jordanaires*. Decca, 1961
*Sentimentally Yours*. Decca, 1962
*The Patsy Cline Story*. Decca, 1963
*Patsy Cline's Greatest Hits*. Decca, 1967
*Patsy Cline Collection*. MCA, 1991
*Patsy Cline Sings Songs of Love*. Universal, 1995
*Walkin' After Midnight: The Original Sessions*. Dualtone, 2003

## FURTHER READING

Beyer, Susan. "Patsy Cline: Through the Years." *Ottawa Citizen* (November 30, 1991).

Celebrating Patsy Cline. Nonprofit organization. Available online at www.patsycline .com.

Hazen, Cindy, and Mike Freeman. *Love Always, Patsy: Patsy Cline's Letters to a Friend*. Berkeley, CA: Berkeley Press, 1999.

Himes, Geoffrey. "How Patsy Cline Put Pieces Together." *Washington Post* (November 15, 1991).

Himes, Geoffrey. "Desperately Seeking Country's New Cline." *Washington Post* (November 22, 1991).

Jones, Margaret. *Patsy: The Life and Time of Patsy Cline*. New York: HarperCollins, 1994.

Kimberly, Nick. "Vocal Heroes: Tears of a Cline." *The Independent*, London (December 16, 1991).

Nassour, Ellis. *Honky Tonk Angel: The Intimate Story of Patsy Cline*. New York: St. Martin's Press, 1993.

*New York Times*. "Grand Ole Opry To Perform Here." (November 8, 1961).

*TV Guide*. "Patsy Cline . . . No Time on Her Hands." Partially reprinted article (April 6, 1957). Available online at www.patsified.com/articles/tvguide5657.htm. Accessed July 2008.

Unterberger, Richie. "Patsy Cline biography." *All Music Guide*. Available online at www.wc05.allmusic.com/cg/amg.dll?p=amg&token=ADFEAEE47817D8 49AA7E20C79A3E52DBB57DF702FE5AFB86112F0456D3B82D4BBD0E4FE0 6BC2AB81B0E577AB7BAFFF26E85B05D2CBE452FBCC0640&sql=11:0vfixqr 5ld6e~T1.

*Winchester Star*. Partially reprinted article (April 1957). Available online at www .patsified.com/articles/wincstar1957.htm.

AP/Wide World Photos

# Ani DiFranco

*I think people who know me*
*perceive me as bit of a pixie.*

## OVERVIEW

Over the course of almost twenty years, the feisty, fiercely independent, and outspoken singer and songwriter Ani DiFranco has remained consistently prolific and is one of the most influential independent singer/songwriters of her generation. In that time period, DiFranco has released an impressive array of material—eighteen studio albums, three EPs, two concert videos, almost a dozen albums in collaboration with other artists, and eight official bootlegs. Known at times during her career more for her independent streak than her music, at least in terms of mainstream press coverage, DiFranco espoused the punk rock do-it-yourself ethos from the beginning. She also founded Righteous Babe Records—located in her hometown of Buffalo, New York—at the age of nineteen so she could release her own work. Throughout her career, DiFranco consistently rejected several overtures and copious sums of money from major labels to release her material.

As her career progressed, DiFranco used the label as a platform not only for her own music but to promote and release the albums of similarly left-of-center folksingers, world music, and spoken-word artists who combine music and poetry in their performance such as Utah Phillips and Sekou Sundiata. Uncompromising—although some critics have called her a control freak—for most of her career she has been the sole producer of her albums, never ceding the reins to another person until Joe Henry produced half of 2005's *Knuckle Down*. However, DiFranco has consistently worked with some of the same engineers and mixers throughout her career. Her intensely personal music, by and large, is situated at the threshold of folk and punk, reflecting a heavy dash of social consciousness with humor and self-righteousness thrown into the mix. In short, politics and art are inseparable for this artist. Her songs tackle issues such as rape, abortion, sexism, and the evils of capitalism, and her voice and her songs are simultaneously compassionate, angry, and empowering, with lyrics that are poetic without resorting to pretense. As one writer for Salon .com put it, "DiFranco's sound could be described as folk you can dance to, or maybe punk for the poetry crowd" (Leibovich 1996).

Few artists have offered the press, fans, and critics such an open roadmap to their personal and emotional lives as has Ani DiFranco, and to the extent that she has made herself open, striving for a connection with fans, she has become a target for criticism and speculation. Such is the risk for being honest, but DiFranco knows no other way. Much of the content of her songs calls to mind the concerns of folk music—she owes much to Woody Guthrie—stream of consciousness lyrics focusing on politics and relationships. Her sound marries her lyrics with a uniquely percussive approach to playing the acoustic guitar that she does with a dexterity that is in a class all its own. An outspoken feminist, her early concert appearances at college campuses across the United States were almost entirely attended by female fans; if there were any men, they were usually the boyfriends of the women in attendance. At her concerts, during the more mellow tunes her fans are so devoted that it is possible to hear the proverbial pin drop. Her career is the definition of grassroots success, touring incessantly, selling her music out of the trunk of her Volkswagen, and finally, when Righteous Babe was founded, releasing albums like clockwork, once every twelve to sixteen months or so. DiFranco proved that she could work as hard as any male performer and be just as successful but on her own terms.

DiFranco's appearance, sporting tattoos and a nose ring, has caused her much attention. Her hair has taken on a variety of hues and lengths, including green, as seen on the cover of *Spin* magazine, as well as dreadlocks and a buzz cut in the early part of her career; all of these choices add to the ambiguity of her appearance and her willful disregard for the conventions of what a successful female musician should look like. For instance, when she appeared on the cover of *Spin* and then *Curve* (February 1995), a lesbian magazine, she gave equal time to each publication. In fact, her appearance on the cover of *Curve* was the first major magazine cover appearance of her career, probably owing to her open bisexuality. Consequently, DiFranco has become an icon for both gay and straight pop culture, each claiming some ownership of her image and success and claiming her as a hero, or heroine.

Although DiFranco is not necessarily known for one particular standout hit, she gained attention vicariously when the singer Alana Davis covered her song "32 Flavors," which with slightly different production than DiFranco's original version became a radio hit in early 1998, peaking at seventeen on *Billboard*'s adult Top 40 chart. DiFranco didn't have a mainstream breakthrough until the 1996 release of *Dilate*—her eighth album. Since that album appearance on the *Billboard* charts, every subsequent album placed somewhere on various *Billboard* charts throughout the late 1990s and early 2000s. Despite her critical acclaim, her legendary devoted fans, and her success as an independent artist, DiFranco's lone Grammy Award is for Best Recording Package for 2003's *Evolve* and not for her music, suggesting that this artist still manages to fly below the radar in the eyes of popular culture. *Educated Guess*, however, received two nominations in 2004, one for Best Contemporary Folk Album and one for Best Recording Package. Her collaboration with folksinger and activist Utah Phillips, *Fellow Workers* (1999), received a Best Contemporary Folk album nomination as well.

Toward the late 1990s, critics started calling her work didactic and over the top, but fans have remained faithful. By the late 1990s, specifically around the release of *Up Up Up Up Up* in 1999, it seemed some critics were growing weary of DiFranco's approach. In 1999, Alisha Davis wrote a review in *Newsweek* that said, "You may tire of her message, but her plaintive voice, and the way she attacks her guitar, stay with you."

DiFranco's fan base is extremely devoted. As honest as she is in her music, her fans have returned that honesty right back to her, which has resulted in an unusually possessive relationship at times whereby her fans projected a sense of who she should be—gay, straight, bisexual—based on their own ideas. DiFranco developed a rabid following early on through gigs at college campuses, folk festivals, and coffeehouses and bars. That grassroots effort enabled her career to grow at a manageable pace and provided her with more feedback and support than she could have imagined. Fans, transformed by her music, consider her an icon, inspiring the name "Ani Lama," a humorous permutation of the Dalai Lama.

## EARLY YEARS

Ani DiFranco grew up in the working-class mill town of Buffalo, New York. Her parents, Elizabeth and Dante DiFranco, have backgrounds that have little to do with music; her mother, who grew up in Montreal, graduated from Massachusetts Institute of Technology with a degree in architecture and was one of very few women in her class. Her father is a research engineer, and he too graduated from MIT. She described her parents as "workaholics" and by way of explaining her breathless recording and touring pace, told *Cincinnati Weekly*, in 2006 "I think I am a workaholic by nature. . . . I learned it early on." But even with all that work, DiFranco described her early childhood as idyllic, saying that her parents were creative and interested in the arts.

Early musical influences include The Beatles, John Lennon especially. DiFranco was exposed to folk music by her parents who created a haven for touring musicians. Unusually, DiFranco says that when she was young, she was not exposed to recorded music—probably because she saw so much live music in her own house. Listening to live music impressed on her the idea that music is a social act and not exclusively a commodity. Her parents did not have a stereo, and she did not buy records until she was in college.

She got her first gig when she was just nine years old—so to speak. Her parents bought her a child's guitar, and at the store she met local musician Michael Meldrum. After they met, he started bringing her up onstage during his gigs and she'd play with him. He helped her land her first gig playing a set of Beatles covers at an area coffeehouse.

For a brief period in her preteen years, DiFranco abandoned music to pursue ballet, but at age fourteen she returned to the guitar and started writing her first songs. During this time, the tenor of her life at home changed, and she has described her home life as "a mess" and "one scary scene after another" until her parents separated when she was eleven. But DiFranco credited her sense of possibility and her independence to her mother, who told her growing up that she could do whatever she wanted. "It's crazy shit to tell a kid, but she was always incredibly supportive, one of those parents that thought whatever I did as fabulous" (Papazian 1996).

As a child, DiFranco was precocious and not fond of rules and restrictions. Because she was so independent she became self-sufficient, which helped her through her parents' separation. Perhaps the independent streak was a defense mechanism. Rules and regulations were difficult for her. She would leave the house in the morning, but even coming home as late as when the street lights came on was stifling to her.

During these formative years, music helped her find herself. She developed her signature percussive acoustic guitar style, enabled by the application of long acrylic press-on nails secured with electrical tape. Meldrum, the thirty-year-old local folksinger and guitarist who became her mentor, was responsible for exposing her to professional musicians. Meldrum also worked as a concert producer, booking acts that were popular in New York City such as Suzanne Vega, Michelle Shocked, and Rod MacDonald.

When DiFranco started writing her own songs, Meldrum was impressed and quickly started planning concerts for her in the Buffalo area. Playing over the din of bar noise, it was hard not to pay attention to her. Using what was at her disposal—the ethos of folk music with the delivery and appearance of punk rock—she created a name for herself. When asked repeatedly by interviewers why she felt the need to play in clubs beginning at such a relatively young age, she told them that she just needed to get away—anywhere out of the house.

By the time she turned fifteen, her parents were divorced. Her mother had moved to Connecticut, and DiFranco chose to stay in Buffalo and live at the homes of various friends. At this point, she had been playing locally at the Essex Street Pub every Saturday night and with the help of Meldrum started getting gigs at other bars and coffeehouses. Many of her friends were older than she was, but their common interest was folk music.

Still, the ad hoc support system could only take her so far; she was destined for bigger things. After DiFranco graduated from Buffalo Academy for Visual and Performing Arts, she attended Buffalo State College and studied painting and art for a year before dropping out. She was ready for her next move. In addition to the immediate lack of opportunities for musicians in Buffalo (and the fact that she had exhausted her gigging options there), DiFranco's sexually frank lyrics and seemingly uncategorizable sexuality made things tricky in a blue-collar, conservative town. "I experience love in a really primal, ungendered way. I've written about it that way, I use both he and she pronouns, I write about people that intrigue and attract me," she told *The Advocate* (Obejas 1997). But that honesty made things difficult and created misperceptions. People called her a man-hater. No matter what DiFranco did in her private life—because it was fodder for so much confessional, brutally honest songwriting—she could not escape inquiries about her sexual preferences. Staying in Buffalo became a no-win situation for her. In 1997, she told *The Advocate*, in response to a direct question, she identified herself as bisexual. She further elaborated and said that she really preferred the word "queer" because it carried a connotation that is more "open-ended. It means, like, the kind of love I experience is not the kind of love that's on TV" (Obejas 1997).

It is worth noting that her appearance during the early years of her career, which included a shaved head and combat boots, was a direct reaction to her experience as a teenager, when she wore her hair long, looked more feminine, and received a lot of attention from men. The impression her feminine appearance gave was not conducive to performance, so she altered her appearance, which in turn helped change the vibe of her concerts. Consequently, in subsequent years after her first few albums, when she felt like wearing a dress onstage young girls in the audience would see her and scream "Sellout!," unable to process the seeming juxtaposition of such uncompromising lyrics and point of view with an article of clothing. But if anyone could make wearing a dress a political statement, DiFranco could.

As a struggling artist, she had considered sending out demos of her material to record labels, but her independent music-promotion philosophy developed over the years as she focused on politics. Part of that development no doubt stemmed from a fortunate introduction to local rock critic Dale Anderson when she was in her late teens. When Anderson, who had been watching DiFranco for years, heard that she was ready to move to New York, he was concerned that someone would take advantage of her talent. He arranged for her to meet with an entertainment lawyer who explained the challenges of a career in the music business—specifically, how contracts worked and how she could potentially lose the rights to her music. There was much to consider, because by the time DiFranco turned nineteen, she had written more than 100 songs of her own.

## CAREER PATH

### A Righteous Babe is Born

Armed with the legal knowledge of potential pitfalls of the music business, DiFranco left Buffalo for New York City. After she moved, she played gigs and worked different part-time jobs. She briefly studied art at the New School for Social Research where her favorite teacher was poet Sekou Sundiata. (She would release one of his albums many years later, on Righteous Babe Records.) She developed an infectious, grassroots musical following, and in response to requests from fans, she started making tapes of her performances. On her own, she recorded a demo and made 500 copies of a self-titled album, *Ani DiFranco*. She emptied her bank account and borrowed from friends to finance the album's production. DiFranco used the studio of friends of hers and worked with Anderson on a demo that she not only could be proud of but also could sell. Righteous Babe was born in 1990. "It was like a joke in the beginning," DiFranco later said, "very theoretical, like, 'I have my own record company,' which means that I just put out a tape independently" (Papazian 1996).

The album has a rough, raw quality to it, with just DiFranco and her guitar, and her voice expresses a range of emotions, depending on the song. She can sing high and sorrowful on ballads but change to a low, angry growl as the song necessitates. The debut featured "Lost Woman Song" about a relationship with an older man that dissolved when she became pregnant and then had an abortion. Dedicated to poet Lucille Clifton, the song is an honest, difficult snapshot of her time in the waiting room and walking through a picket line to get to the clinic. The song exemplifies her ability to show the ways in which the personal is political and the political is personal as it manages to simultaneously discuss abortion rights and a personal loss.

In the early days, word spread through friends and friends of friends, and the folk community and college campuses were first to heartily embrace her. "Whole campfuls of people in Maine had seventeenth generation Ani DiFranco tapes they were playing over and over again," Anderson recalled. "It was not like she was an entertainer. She was a person who changed your life. And people really did feel empowered listening to her music" (Papazian 1996).

Although DiFranco started her own label as a pragmatic move born of necessity, she acknowledged its implications. "I just don't think you can say something meaningful within the corporate music structure. And I know I don't want to be a part of that structure. I don't want to support it, and I want to do everything I can to actively challenge it on a daily basis"(Gillen 1997). Doing things independently, although it required much hard work, was paying off. Fortunately, sales of the first album generated enough money so that she could pay off the recording fees and finance a second release; DiFranco, due to her prolific and independent nature, was able to release six albums in four years, a pace most artists, even those on major labels, cannot and do not match. And when fans would discover her via one album, remarkably, they would then seek out and purchase her entire catalog up to that point.

As early as 1993, DiFranco was getting calls from major label executives, especially Danny Goldberg, then-president of Mercury Records, who was responsible for finding and launching the career of groundbreaking Seattle grunge band Nirvana. Between 1996 and 1997, every major record label approached her with offers but she turned down every single one of them. During these early years, Anderson operated as DiFranco's manager.

By 1994 Anderson had departed, and DiFranco hired Scot Fisher, a lawyer and an old friend who had worked with death row prisoners in Texas, to become president of Righteous Babe. She needed all the help she could get, because she was on the road three-quarters of the year and gaining more attention at each stop; media requests started to flood the office. Before the label got its own designated office space in downtown Buffalo, DiFranco was selling albums via a toll-free number she had established (800/ON-HER-OWN)

*I can't stop. I'll keep making music until someone makes me stop. I love what I do, and if everything else that goes along with making music went away, I'd still be standing onstage in some dive, singing over the chatter.*

*My guitar taught me to sing in textures, from the roundest lingering harmonic to the sharpest snap of a pulled string. Being a percussion instrument as well as a melodic instrument, my guitar also teaches me about the relationship between rhythm and melody.*

and through mail order. Her music was distributed in the early days by one fan phone call at a time or by cassette sales at her shows. Record stores started to become besieged with requests for her records, and retailers would call, asking for a copy, then five, and then ten, and then a catalogue. "It was what you dream of—people wanting to hear the music who kind of forced the stores to carry it, and then the stores saw this was a good business, and so we kept making music and they kept buying it," DiFranco said (Gillen 1997). In the early 1990s, the business was more or less run out of her living room, but within a few years, by the time Fisher was hired and by the time she was fending off phone calls from major labels, she had hired a staff and was selling her own merchandise—T-shirts and posters mostly along with cassettes and CDs—from the downtown Buffalo office.

It is difficult to understate the importance of the story of Righteous Babe, which is integral to the story of her success. In the early to mid-1990s, DiFranco's music was distributed through her own 800 number and through independent distributors such as Goldenrod and Ladyslipper, until their own direct-mail operations became unable to accommodate the rush of expanding interest and orders. In 1995, Righteous Babe made a deal with the larger distributor Koch to increase its connection with retailers.

By 1997, though, three-quarters of a million copies of her nine solo albums had been sold—an impressive feat for essentially a one-woman (and several office people) operation. By 1997, the label beefed up to a full-time staff of twelve people. She kept on the road in support of new releases, clocking nearly 200 shows a year, and was regularly touring with bassist Sara Lee (who had played bass with the B-52s, among others) and drummer Andy Stochansky. Around the office, DiFranco was referred to as simply "the folksinger" or "the little folksinger."

### Finding Her Way: The First Six Albums

One of the benefits of independence as a musician is the freedom to pursue a career in the business on one's own terms yet still be successful. The low-fi nature of some of her early recordings meant that she was not spending a whole lot of money on them—she wanted to just get the music out to her fans. As a result of this utilitarian approach, DiFranco's first few albums are raw and uneven, but her talent is unmistakable. It took recording and touring in support of those first few albums for her career to gain some momentum.

The song "Both Hands," a classic DiFranco examination of a dissolving relation-ship, is one song that especially holds up and bears repeated listening; it has become a concert staple. Perhaps what is most noteworthy about these early albums, when she was playing with minimal accompaniment, is that she often played all of the guitars—electric, acoustic, and bass—with the only musical assistance coming from drummer Andy Stochansky, who started playing on her albums starting with 1993's *Puddle Dive* and ending with 1999's *Up Up Up Up Up Up*. Some early tours only featured her and Stochansky; occasionally, bassist Sara Lee would join them, too.

When listening to her first six albums—*Ani DiFranco, Not So Soft, Imper-fectly, Puddle Dive, Like I Said,* and *Out of Range*—it becomes apparent that DiFranco was trying to find her way both as a songwriter and a producer. It is also clear that she has a keen sense of humor. Always quick with self-deprecation, DiFranco reflected on her studio technique—she was embar-rassed about some of her recordings. On *Imperfectly*, she teased listeners about their inquiries about her sexual preferences with the song "In or Out." The press latched onto her image but the attention, for her, was limiting, because she felt it distracted people from the real content of her material or caused them to take her less seriously.

### Finding Her Voice, Keeping Her Sense of Self While Living in a Fishbowl

*Not a Pretty Girl* signaled the appearance of an album that was as complex and multidimensional as she. It is also the album that was made in response to the sudden forceful media and music business attention that courted her with money and promises. DiFranco's independent mind and assertiveness kept her uninterested.

Concerned with personal strength, the difficulties of human relationships, and ultimately an empowering listen all around, the album is practically com-prised of one small manifesto after another, starting with the jazzy, sassy first track "Worthy," in which DiFranco taunts the listener, "I'm not worthy of you/You're not worthy of me." It is a refrain that could easily be directed at fans who were starting to expect too much from her, or an undeserving ex-lover. In the spoken word "Tiptoe" DiFranco painfully describes the anticipation of an abortion. By mid-album the title track surfaces—it too is another song that lacks a legitimate, tangible chorus—and DiFranco starts off by declaring, "I am not a pretty girl/That is not what I do." In subsequent verses, she tells listeners she is not an angry girl, and calls people out—probably the media—on their own reactions to her music.

Because one assertive song deserves another, DiFranco follows the title track with the fury-filled "The Million You Never Made," a direct assault on the major label executives who pursued her, allegedly for her talent but really for their own monetary gain. DiFranco's voice, suggesting both confidence and an occasional sneer in "Not a Pretty Girl," transforms into a full-fledged, accusatory snarl in "The Million You Never Made." She repeats the last phrase, "I can be the million that you never made," several times, the guitar playing becomes more furious and faster, and the drumming louder and more emphatic. It is probably one of the most concise and eloquent kiss-offs to the commercial music business of its day.

Many of DiFranco's songs follow atypical structure that adheres to her own rules for songwriting. For the most part, the verses are often long, sometimes irregularly so, and the choruses many times do not contain any discernible refrain—often they consist of repeated phrases, such as "la-di-dah-de-hey-yeah" in "Worthy" for example. In "The Million," the song title becomes a battle cry and the closest thing to a traditional chorus, but because she saves it for the end, its meaning makes a forceful impact on the listener. In "32 Flavors," which appears toward the end of *Not a Pretty Girl*, DiFranco asks people to look more closely at her, to realize she is "32 flavors and then some" in the very first verse. The song celebrates one woman's multiple sides, viewpoints, and inconsistencies as an act of resistance against the cookie-cutter, sound bite–driven, one-dimensional image that some of the mainstream press had started to use as her description. It is unfortunate that singer Alana Davis had the hit when she covered this song and not DiFranco herself, because the former's rendering is soft, poppy, and toothless, devoid of the nuances and perspective that can only come from the songwriter herself.

The liner notes for *Not A Pretty Girl*, though, offer listeners some insight into how important her fans had become to her and how important it was, too, for fans to be able to reach her personally. DiFranco thanked them for sending her things such as "letters, albums, CDs, tapes, poems, crayon-scrawled stories . . . escaped journal entries . . . dinner invitations . . . action figures . . . jewelry, T-shirts," among other items, and apologized for being unable to respond to each person individually.

The brutally honest *Dilate* came out in 1996 comprised of eleven songs suggesting the major relationship troubles and psychological repercussions of fame. On the album opener "Untouchable Face," she chronicles a dysfunctional relationship in which her lover has found someone else. The chorus is brash; she spits out "Fuck you/And your untouchable face" and toward the end, her voice turns soft, begging for consideration when she asks, "Who am I? Somebody just tell me that much." The album shows a woman who is not as certain of her place in the world, someone in transition, trying to grapple with her changing world, changing self, and changing relationships. Nearly every song on the album is a sonic gem; for example, the dexterous, fluid guitar playing on "Super-hero," in which she claims her inner strength is gone—"I used to be a superhero/ I would swoop down and save me from myself"—and laments that she is now just like everybody else. Lest anyone peg her as an angry young woman any longer, DiFranco ends the album with hymn-like "Joyful Girl." It is a succinct expression of her inspiration and her worldview, with a clever turn of phrase.

Many of the lyrics and songs were inspired by her relationship with a man whose identity she closely guarded during their early days, the cryptically nicknamed "goat boy" Andrew Gilchrist, who eventually became her husband in 1998. When she started dating him, the queer community was disappointed in her and felt abandoned. Fans would call her a sellout and harass her at her own shows. But when she would talk about loving women in mainstream music magazines, she got a lot of flack for that, too.

The mid- to late 1990s—when DiFranco was experiencing the height of her acclaim, success, and attention—was also a fortuitous time for women in rock music in general. Some might cynically say that "women in rock" simply became a marketable trend. Canadian singer and songwriter Sarah McLachlan formed Lilith Fair, an all-women music festival that toured the United States and Canada during three consecutive summers, from 1997 to 1999. When DiFranco was offered a spot on Lilith Fair, she demurred, saying that her shows were between her and her fans. No doubt that to DiFranco an event such as Lilith Fair, which was rife with marketing, sponsorship, and media buzz, represented the worst part of being a female musician: turning it into a commodity that outweighed any potential warm and fuzzy feelings about a women-centric music business experience. She said, "Lilith Fair is not the festival that I would put together if I were coming up with a chicks-making-noise festival. I think I would have a somewhat more diverse group of woman musicians" (Mervis 1998).

One could question such a move and think it selfish and unsupportive of such a historic event. By early 1998, interviews with DiFranco had already appeared in *Spin, Rolling Stone, Swing,* the *New York Times, CMJ,* and *Ms.* magazine, among others. When *Little Plastic Castle* came out in 1998, the cover art said it all: DiFranco was depicted in a fishbowl in a goofy but pointed image that poked fun at the idea that fame is like living in a fishbowl in which one is subject to endless scrutiny. Overall, the album was more adventurous, and the songs took more sophisticated turns and incorporated new instruments for DiFranco, including a banjo and a horn section, showing a broader musical palette. Other critics said it was her most accessible album, a point that confused her a bit, as though her music up to that point had been abstract or difficult. Additionally, the record marked a turning point in terms of production.

The title track shows one way in which DiFranco finds herself looking at her life from different viewpoints. She tries to take an outside-the-fishbowl perspective and dissects the way she has been portrayed in the media. She considers the way people are quick to judge character such as when "what I happened to be wearing the day someone takes a picture is a statement for all of womankind." In the song, which does not have a necessarily strict verse, DiFranco sardonically describes life in the fishbowl, "the little plastic castle is a surprise every time."

### The Live Vibe: Ani in Concert

From the beginning, DiFranco's live performances have held the key to understanding her appeal. Her stage persona is warm, self-deprecating, and lively.
In the early days, her audience was comprised of young feminists and sensitive
young men. To the uninitiated listener, a live Ani DiFranco album is probably
the next best way (apart from a live concert) to get to know her beyond what
her songs' lyrics. From her goofy, in-between song patter to the response of
the fans, who can go from raucous and supportive one moment to quiet-as-a-
pin-drop the next, DiFranco commands an unusual level of rapt attention—
and respect—from her audience.

Her two live albums, *Living in Clip* and *So Much Shouting, So Much Laughter*, encapsulate her live performances, although the former is more distinctly
organized into a beginning, middle, and end. When *Living in Clip* was released
in 1997 as her first live double album, it received what was the largest rollout
of her albums to date: 80,000 to 100,000 shipped. Many retailers kept tabs
on copies for fans by way of waiting lists in anticipation of selling out. In
addition to giving fans a glimpse of her personality, her live shows (and consequently, the live albums) also highlight her ability to constantly improvise,
change the instrumentation of her songs and her phrasing, and seamlessly
segue from one song into another. In other words, live shows demonstrate her
incredible facility with music, her flexibility of mind, and her restless approach;
she rarely plays the same song the same way twice.

The release of her second live double album, *So Much Shouting, So Much
Laughter*, occurred in 2002. The title was borrowed from her song "Cradle
and All" from *Not a Pretty Girl*. The albums' two dozen tracks are taken
from performances between 2000 and 2002.The album also includes a rendering of "Self Evident," a poem she wrote about being in New York during
the September 11, 2001, attacks and which underwent much revision during
her touring that fall. From 2004 to 2006, DiFranco released a handful of
what she calls "official bootlegs," live albums from individual concerts, from
Boston to Portland to Sacramento to Rome to New York City's esteemed
Carnegie Hall.

### Transitions and Reactions, Political and Personal

After waiting a year and a half for a new release—an eternity for DiFranco
fans—the double-CD *Reveling/Reckoning* arrived in 2001. The album marked
a turning point for DiFranco, she told *Rolling Stone*, because it was the first
time she wrote an album with the idea of her band in mind, and because it
also spans a number of different musical styles, especially jazz, more so than
previous releases. She described the set as two albums but "one story is being
told" (Baltin 2001). *Reveling* is, as its title suggests, slightly more raucous,
with bluesy, funky tunes; *Reckoning* is a more somber, contemplative batch

of songs. DiFranco said she initially conceived of *Reveling* as a dance record. Overall, though, the two records allow her to exhaustively delve into a number of issues with songs ranging from suburban sprawl to personal relationships. In 2001, *Time* magazine remarked on her evolution with this ambitious double-album set, saying that her music displayed a sense of nuance and texture.

In *Evolve*, released March 11, 2003, DiFranco used more jazz-styled arrangements and showed that she was poised to explore a new genre and infuse its language into her own approach. This time around, she used what at that point was her regular band—keyboardist/vocalist Julie Wolf, bassist Jason Mercer, drummer Daren Hahn, a trio of trumpeters (Ravi Best, Shane Endsley, and Todd Horton), and saxophonist Hans Tuber. She says the process of creating the album was largely collaborative. Barry Walters noted that the record also marked an aesthetic journey that perhaps cost her some of her older fans while attracting newer ones who were impressed with her talent. "*Evolve* speaks to both camps with a succinct summation of her experimental side, here focused and more refined" (Walters 2003).

*Educated Guess*, which was released January 2004, contains songs in which she is redefining and reinventing herself yet again. A reaction against extensive touring and being a bandleader, *Educated Guess* is a stripped-down affair with no outside collaboration or interference. DiFranco played all the instruments, sang all the vocal tracks, and recorded and mixed the album by herself in her home studio on an eight-track, reel-to-reel tape recorder. This deliberate move was admittedly a response to the pressure of working with a band and an engineer while touring constantly and keeping up her prolific pace. DiFranco said that it takes "a colossal amount of time and energy to be a bandleader, to be an arranger, to get five people up and at 'em every night" (Orloff 2003). For *Educated Guess* she decided against using a band, and also makes a reference to her husband, whom she divorced in 2003. Yet again, the album chronicled her own journey trying to get back her sense of self and come to terms with solitude, empowerment and independence. *Rolling Stone* online called it "one of her sharpest, most honest works to date" (Orloff 2003).

*Knuckle Down* followed in 2005 with production on half the album from producer and songwriter Joe Henry, who toured with her in 2003. The album bore the emotional residue of the break-up of her marriage and the loss of her father; she deals with the former in the moving album capper "Recoil." Critics hailed the album's lush textures and its sense of focus. Her assessment at the time of *Evolve*'s release about her sound changing was true: The subsequent albums showed a more sophisticated approach to songwriting and more compelling instrumentation that borrowed freely and unapologetically from blues, jazz, and a bit of New Orleans funk. The evolution, so to speak, shows her reinvention of herself and her facility with trying new approaches and mixing in new genres.

*I think political work comes
in all sorts of forms and one
of the least impressive is that
of the politician.*

DiFranco took time off from touring and performing in 2005 to allow the carpal tunnel syndrome in her hands and wrist to heal. She started working on her next album, *Reprieve*, in mid-2005 but had to abandon the process because she was recording at her home in New Orleans when Hurricane Katrina hit in August of that same year. The dozen songs on *Reprieve* were produced by Mike Napolitano, whom DiFranco had started dating. The record, recorded in the midst of the tragedy, reflects a political sensibility as it grapples with displacement, mourning, and frustration. The song "Millennium Theater" ends with DiFranco saying "New Orleans bides her time" but was written before the storm occurred. She expressed her anger to *Rolling Stone* about what happened, saying that Katrina came as a result of "human neglect, racism, incompetence and greed" (Orloff 2006).

## MISSION, MOTIVATION, PROCESS

In her songwriting, DiFranco has often stood up for the underdog, the little guy—or perhaps more appropriately, the girl—who has been underrepresented, repressed, or otherwise silenced. Without a hint of self-consciousness, DiFranco has used her platform as a performer to call to light various issues and causes throughout her career and to champion progressive politics. DiFranco takes a directly activist approach to her own career, so it makes sense that her songwriting would follow suit. It is this approach that has garnered her so many ardent followers, but it is also something that has made her a lighting rod for criticism of being too preachy and heavy-handed. DiFranco does not see her music as issue-oriented at all. Instead, it's pragmatic and automatic; the personal is political.

Before she became a musician full-time, she worked in politically active organizations such as a Central American solidarity movement in New York and the pacifist group War Resisters' League. Once she was able to play music full time, however, it became the channel for her activism.

DiFranco's position gives her a natural and unique platform to help inform and inspire young people and to take part in some old-fashioned, 1960s-style consciousness raising, but she admitted that she feels responsibility not because she is an artist but as a human being. On the song "Face Up and Sing" from *Out of Range*, DiFranco urges her listeners to take responsibility for their lives and to start making noise about the injustice and corruption in their own worlds. DiFranco insists that when she writes songs, she does not start off with an agenda. She has to process what happens to her before she puts words to paper, and then the song appears. Although DiFranco's specific style is unmistakable, her songs reflect universal topics that happen to be personal, through the filter of her experience. The road affords her little privacy or the time needed to undergo the solitary process of writing, so she keeps a journal. When she's home, she can absorb the thoughts that she has jotted down in it and develop songs.

But some pieces, such as "Self Evident," directly respond to events in the world and get a more public process of revision and refinement as she performs them and fans respond to them. DiFranco said that after the terrorist attacks on U.S. soil on September 11, 2001, many people cancelled tours, but she soldiered on and kept performing. "There was a palpable energy everywhere I went, everyone thinking of the same thing, searching for alternative voices beyond the t.v. [sic] propaganda and the deflating messages from the powers that be" (Ehmke 2002). The song first emerged as a poem, delivered onstage with a feeling of urgency, describing that morning. DiFranco said she started reciting the poem before she even finished it, let alone memorized it. "I felt that since this was something we were all working on together as a nation, I could be a little less introverted with my process" (Ehmke 2002). The song was even covered by rapper Chuck D and soon after she heard that version, she tooled with it so that it began to feature a little more instrumentation. Ultimately, she ended up with a pared-down band arrangement. When the instruments kick in, the song morphs into something resembling a rap, as DiFranco sends out a toast to people living in war-torn regions (Afghanistan, Iraq, El Salvador), abortion clinic workers, inmates on death row, and other underrepresented, politically endangered groups.

"Self Evident" is not her only song written in response to politics. "Subdivision," which appeared on 2001's *Reveling/Reckoning*, merges her personal and political concerns via a commentary on America and its aging urban, industrial infrastructures. She sings, "America the beautiful/Is just one big subdivision." However, the song, like most of her best work, is also about something specific; in this case, her hometown of Buffalo. DiFranco fought to save some of the architecture of Buffalo, specifically a Gothic Revival church that was slated for the wrecking ball. She sunk $2.7 million of her own money into renovating the church, which she and Scot Fisher envisioned as a space for the company as well as a concert space and like-minded arts organizations. Hallwalls, an offbeat contemporary arts center, moved into the building in 2006 and Righteous Babe relocated there in early 2007. DiFranco has since renamed the building Babeville.

Indeed, DiFranco does not forget her roots easily; a March 2002 concert in Newport, Rhode Island, raised $20,000, half of which went directly to the Buffalo performing arts school from which she graduated. The rest of the proceeds went to other schools in the district whose arts programs had been scaled back due to budget cuts.

During events at the turn of the century—especially after September 11, 2001, with President George W. Bush in office and the nation at war in Iraq as of March 2003—it was not uncommon to find DiFranco headlining benefit concerts or spearheading new awareness initiatives. In January 2003, she teamed up with Chuck D, Michael Franti and his band Spearhead and many others for Not in Our Name, an antiwar concert in San Francisco. The performers signed a pledge to stand up against injustices committed by the United States government. Another noteworthy effort was the Vote, Dammit! tour in 2004, which visited swing states during early fall 2004 and featured appearances from comics, activists, and satirists; DiFranco also invited the Indigo Girls and Dan Bern to join her, which they all did for specific portions of the tour. Vote, Dammit! was part of her partnership with the Feminist Majority Foundation's "Get Out Her Vote" campaign, designed to spur audience members to register to vote. (As a side note, when she was writing the songs for *Knuckle Down* she was campaigning for presidential candidate Dennis Kucinich and doing the Vote, Dammit! tour and continued to lend her support to his 2008 Democratic nomination bid in fall 2007.)

During eight days in July 2004, DiFranco took a trip to Burma and Thailand with Irish singer/songwriter Damien Rice to visit refugee camps. At that time, more than 1 million Burmese had fled the militaristic regime in Burma. DiFranco visited a camp, met with orphans whose parents were killed by the regime, and held meetings with Burmese activists in the hope that she would raise international awareness about the humanitarian crisis. She was the first American musician to visit the refugee camps and meet with activists there.

Both DiFranco and Rice donated a song to a benefit CD designed to raise awareness of the Burmese capture of 1991 Nobel Peace Prize recipient Aung San Suu Kyi. DiFranco has also appeared with activist Angela Davis and singer MeShell Ndegéocello at a Critical Resistance benefit against prisons protesting the death penalty.

## LEGACY AND OTHER INTERESTS

DiFranco's record label has released several dozen albums in addition to her own by artists Utah Philips, Hamell on Trial, Sekou Sundiata, bassist Sara Lee, Andrew Bird (formerly of Squirrel Nut Zippers), Arto Lindsay, and Toshi Reagan. She also has collaborated with Prince and Maceo Parker on their albums. DiFranco's choice of opening acts during her tours has brought many singer/songwriters to the attention of her fans, which has helped further the careers of some artists on her label such as Sundiata and Phillips. DiFranco also recorded two albums with Phillips, *The Past Didn't Go Anywhere* in 1996 and 1999's *Fellow Workers*. One of those songwriters for the album was the witty, acerbic, Bob Dylan-esque songwriter Dan Bern. When DiFranco was approached by Sony's subsidiary Work to produce Bern's album *Fifty Eggs*, after much wrestling with whether or not she wanted to collude with what some perceive to be the enemy, she gave in to her desire to work with someone whose material she respected.

The company that started out of her living room and the back of her car remains in her hometown of Buffalo, New York. Many journalists have asked her why she decided to base the business where she was born. "It's basically a way of realizing on a personal level that adage to 'think globally, act locally.' . . . I was living in New York City but we didn't think that New York needed another little business; but Buffalo did" (Kidd 2002). DiFranco has done everything on her own terms—for instance, the stipulations she places on Righteous Babe products such as T-shirts. In 1993 she caved in to the demand for T-shirts, realizing it would give her enough financial flow to get some tour help, with the restriction that neither her name nor her image were to appear on her T-shirts. Her first T-shirt featured a poem, instead, and all subsequent T-shirts have also been tastefully designed, many emblazoned with the Righteous Babe logo, a darkened silhouette of a triumphant woman raising her fists in the air. In recent years, DiFranco has relaxed her initial objection and her likeness has appeared on T-shirts.

In a time when recording artists signed with most major label receive between $1 and $2 for every album sold (not including royalties) it is estimated that on average, DiFranco receives about $4 for every record she sells. The model for Righteous Babe is Peter Gabriel's imprint Real World, which famously signed singer Joseph Arthur after Gabriel left him a voice message on his machine. She said: "I know I can trust that label to expose me to some amazing stuff, and I want people to feel that way about Righteous Babe, too" (Gillen 1997). Her savvy and business acumen earned her accolades from *Ms.* magazine, which heralded her as one of "21 Feminists for the 21st Century," and acclaim from *Forbes*, *Financial News Network*, and the *New York Times* as a young entrepreneur. Additionally, her trailblazing has inspired many other female artists to strike out on their own (see sidebar).

Always one to put her money where her mouth is, DiFranco established the Righteous Babe Foundation in 1999 to support a number of issues. The foundation works through the Southern Center for Human Rights in Atlanta to fight against capital punishment, for instance, but also donates to Hurricane Katrina victims and other cultural, grassroots, and political causes and organizations. DiFranco's Foundation also donates to small nonprofit organizations such as Hallwalls, a combination gallery and performance space, and the Squeaky Wheel art center, both in Buffalo.

By 2000, Righteous Babe was employing fifteen people full-time, Scot Fisher continued to run the label as president, and DiFranco continued her aggressive touring pace. By 2003, her songs had appeared in films, on television, and she had produced nineteen albums of her own. The Righteous Babe label, as of fall 2007, has sold 4 million records but, like other small labels, is not immune to the whims of the music business and the effects of rampant free downloading. Renovating the church, for example, shows that Righteous Babe is growing and giving back to its community in a palpable way that preserves and celebrates the arts. The move also suggested that the company's

## Independence Day: Other Female Artists Follow DiFranco

Successfully building a career as an artist through her own independent label, DiFranco's opinion of the corporate music industry has been clear. Founded in 1990, Righteous Babe Records has sold more than 4 million copies of her many albums. Taking the do-it-yourself mantra of punk rock to a new level, DiFranco, whose songs have always been political, turned that perceived obstacle into an advantage. Instead of handing her art over to a mega-conglomerate record company to accumulate a fan base, DiFranco grew a grassroots following through extensive touring and selling albums at shows via her own label, which now represents thirteen other independent musicians.

DiFranco's independent move more than fifteen years ago was prescient. The industry has been through tremendous change and the major label system is threatened by Internet downloading. Not only did she circumvent the system, a move that has been beneficial for her career, but it also opened up other avenues normally blocked by the corporate monoliths, which influenced other artists to follow in her footsteps.

Singer/songwriters Aimee Mann, Jonatha Brooke, and Imogen Heap exemplify this trend. Unhappy with unsuccessful promotion and artistic interference by her record label, Mann founded her own label, SuperEgo Records, in 1999 and her own company, United Musicians, with songwriter husband Michael Penn, now home to several other acts. Although originally signed with Elektra Records, Jonatha Brooke began releasing her albums in the late 1990s through her own label Bad Dog, paving the way for her current independence. And the trend continues. Imogen Heap—a member of short-lived but acclaimed band Frou Frou—released her second solo record, 2005's Grammy-nominated *Speak for Yourself*, through her own Megaphonic Records. The record was critically hailed and showed up on the television show *The O.C.*, undoubtedly thanks to the momentum from Frou Frou's placement on the Grammy-winning soundtrack to the film *Garden State*.

reach—and DiFranco herself—extends far beyond just the music she makes, and combines the personal and the universal in a compelling, socially conscious manner.

## SELECTED DISCOGRAPHY

*Not So Soft*. Righteous Babe, 1991
*Not a Pretty Girl*. Righteous Babe, 1995
*Dilate*. Righteous Babe, 1996
*Living in Clip*. Righteous Babe, 1997

*Reveling/Reckoning*. Righteous Babe, 2001
*Evolve*. Righteous Babe, 2003
*Reprieve*. Righteous Babe, 2006
*Canon*. Righteous Babe, 2007

## FURTHER READING

Baltin, Steve. "DiFranco Revels in Two CDs." *Rolling Stone* online (April 17, 2001). Available online at www.rollingstone.com/artists/anidifranco/articles/story/5931766/difranco_revels_in_two_cds.

Carson, Mina, Tisa Lewis, and Susan M. Shaw. *Girls Rock! Fifty Years of Women Making Music*. Lexington, Kentucky: University Press of Kentucky, 2004.

Carter, Sandy. "An Interview With Ani DiFranco." *Z Magazine* (January 1996). Available online at www.zmag.org/zmag/articles/jan96carter.htm.

Dansby, Andrew. "DiFranco Evolves on New Album." *Rolling Stone* online (January 2, 2003). Available online at www.rollingstone.com/artists/anidifranco/articles/story/5933591/difranco_evolves_on_new_album.

Davis, Alisha. "'You Can't Fence Her In.' Review." *Newsweek* (January 18, 1999).

DiFranco, Ani. "Songwriter Musicmaker Storyteller Freak." *New Internationalist* (August 2003).

Ehmke, Ronald. "Ani DiFranco Talks About the Making of her Album So Much Shouting, So Much Laughter." Ani DiFranco official artist Web site (June 28, 2002). Available online at www.righteousbabe.com/ani/sms_sml/sms_interview.asp

Farley, Christopher John. "Reckonings and Revelations: Ani DiFranco's New CD offers a Little Folk, a Little Funk, A Bit of Jazz, and All-Around Great Songs." *Time* (April 23, 2001).

Gillen, Marilyn. "Righteous Babe an Indie Success Story: Ani DiFranco's Label Rises Up from the Grass Roots." *Billboard* (April 12, 1997).

Hirshey, Gerri. *We Gotta Get Out of This Place: The True, Tough Story of Women in Rock*. New York: Grove Press, 2001.

Keast, James. "Ani DiFranco: the L'il Folksinger that Could." *Exclaim!* (December 2002). Available online at www.exclaim.ca/articles/multiarticlesub.aspx?csid1=43&csid2=9fid1=1340.

Kidd, Rocky. "Anything but the Grrrrl: An Interview with Ani DiFranco, founder of Righteous Babe Records and Folk-Punk Troubador of the Secular Left." *Sojourners* (May/June 2002).

Kuronen, Darcy (curator). "Foreword" by Lenny Kaye, photographs by Carl Tremblay and others. *Dangerous Curves: The Art of the Guitar*. Boston: MFA Publications, 2000.

Leibovich, Lori. "'Ani DiFranco, *Dilate*.' Review." Salon.com (June 3, 1996). Available online at www.salon.com/ent/music/review/1996/06/03/music960603/index.html?source=search&aim=/ent/music/review.

Mervis, Scott. "Ani-Maniacs: Indie 'Folksinger' Has a Special Bond with Her Fans." *Pittsburgh Post-Gazette* (June 26, 1998).

Obejas, Achy. "Both Sides Now." *The Advocate* (December 9, 1997).

Orloff, Brian. "DiFranco Goes Alone on 'Guess.'" *Rolling Stone* online (October 31, 2003). Available online at www.rollingstone.com/artists/anidifranco/articles/story/5935565/difranco_goes_aloen_on_guess.

Orloff, Brian. "Ani DiFranco Salutes New Orleans." *Rolling Stone* online (April 25, 2006). Available online at www.rollingstone.com/artists/anidifranco/articles/story/10114009/ani_difranco_salutes_new_orleans.

Papazian, Ellen. "Woman on the Verge; Ani Difranco." *Ms.* (November/December 1996).

Post, Laura. *Backstage Pass: Interviews with Women in Music.* Chicago, IL: New Victoria Publishers, 1997.

Righteous Babe Records official Web site: www.righteousbabe.com.

Roberts, Michael. "Ani DiFranco, Musician." *Miami New Times* (July 2, 1998).

Rothschild, Matthew. "Ani DiFranco." *The Progressive* (May 2000).

Wethington, Kari. "Ani DiFranco: The Punk-Folk Songwriter Chats with us about the Hurricane, Her New Album, and Choosing a Set List." *Cincinnati Weekly* (June 14, 2006).

Courtesy of Photofest

# Missy Elliott

*Missy is tangible to her audience. It's never been just about her songs. It's always been about being someone her fans could relate to and identify with.*

—Mona Scott, president of Violator Management and Elliott's manager

## OVERVIEW

In the 1990s, Missy "Misdemeanor" Elliott distinguished herself in the world of rap and hip-hop not only because of her gender but because of her nonconformist attitude, her status as a songwriter and performer, and increasingly, as the decade progressed, as a producer. When hip-hop exploded in the 1990s female singers were usually scantily clad background dancers for their male, bling-wearing counterparts or erotically dressed, booty-shaking solo artists. Missy Elliott's creative ascension is refreshing because she refused to cater to racial or gender stereotypes—she wears what she wants and does what she wants, whether that means wearing unconventional outfits in music videos or controlling the course of her career. During her career's early days she wrote songs (and hits), alongside her longtime producer Timbaland, for other artists such as Aaliyah ("One in a Million," "If Your Girl Only Knew") and the lesser-known 702 in 1996. In 1997 her debut, *Supa Dupa Fly*, showed that she herself was a force to be reckoned with as a performer—the record unleashed several hits such as "The Rain." Her debut went to number one on the R&B/Hip-Hop chart and number three on the *Billboard* 200.

Although she had name recognition as a songwriter, which led to her solo debut, Elliott's music and her image were equally remarkable and trend setting (see sidebar). Part of her appeal is attributed to her strong visual sense, which she brings to her music videos, along with her playful, no-holds-barred approach. With her oversize hoop earrings, baseball cap, unapologetic use of make-up, and pristinely clean and unending supply of sneakers, Elliott looks something like a sassy tomboy girl-next-door and performs irreverent and forward-thinking music by throwing together unique samples and sounds. Elliott's lyrics are usually marked by her wicked sense of humor, which is sometimes shown through the use of double entendres but can be more overt, such as a song dedicated to the self-gratification made possible through her "Toyz." In the *New Rolling Stone Album Guide*, a reporter captured her essence by saying that her records have the same kind of formula, of "sexy beats and vocals, Virginia swamp-funk hip-hop production from Timbaland, plenty of filler, a couple of terrible R&B slow jams, and Elliott talking wild shit in between songs" (Sheffield 2004). Equally formed by her Baptist upbringing, hip-hop culture, science fiction, and Japanese anime, Elliott's music is too singular to have been a creation of any kind of record label other than her very own, The Gold Mind, which she has run from day one of her solo career in 1996.

All of her studio albums have at least peaked in a Top 10 chart; each of her first three—*Supa Dupa Fly* (1997), *Da Real World* (1999), *Miss E . . . So Addictive* (2001)—remarkably hit number one on the *Billboard* R&B/

## Hip-Hop Style Keeps Fans Guessing

One look at Missy Elliott's many fashion statements and people knew she was bringing a unique sensibility. Dressed in what appeared to be a blown-up trash bag, Elliott's first and most prominent display occurred in her music video for her debut single, 1997's hit "The Rain." For her 1999 music video "She's a Bitch," she went bald. Instead of dancing around in heels, she is usually wearing sneakers and a tracksuit. From the beginning, Elliott showed that women in hip-hop could be viable creative forces who made their own rules; they didn't have to simply appear in videos wearing next to nothing and sing, or appear as eye candy and fawn over male stars. She prides herself on innovation, so such sartorial gestures are not surprising.

But hip-hop culture knows a thing or two about the power of clothing. Since its inception, hip-hop has consistently and obsessively launched a number of outrageous fashion trends. Videos for Busta Rhymes and OutKast showcase crazy costumes. Bright colors, goofy hats, and fur coats are often seen on the backs of many an emcee. Tracksuits and oversize jeans are also de rigueur, not to mention shoes, mainstreamed by Run-D.M.C.'s trademark Adidas shell-tops immortalized in their video for "Walk this Way" and the eponymous "My Adidas" from 1986's *Raising Hell.* Flavor Flav's big clock necklace has recently re-entered pop culture. And then there's the bling.

Elliott brought back that "old school style" of tracksuits and sneakers propagated in the early 1980s and appropriated it for her own one-of-a-kind creative style: unapologetic and assured. That attitude has garnered a lot of praise from women and men alike and set a new standard.

Hip-Hop chart. The next position for her subsequent record, 2002's *Under Construction*, was nothing to be ashamed of either—it went to number two, and 2004's *This is Not a Test* peaked at number three. Elliott has even made an impact on the Canadian charts, with the success especially of *Miss E . . . So Addictive*, peaking at number eight. As to be expected with such consistently stellar record sales, her albums have launched nearly two dozen *Billboard* singles across a multitude of charts—standard R&B, Top 40, Dance Music, *Billboard* Hot 100, and Hot Rap Tracks. Three songs have hit number one spots on different charts simultaneously. "Work It," however, is her biggest hit to date, topping at number one on the Hot Rap, Rhythmic Top 40, and R&B/Hip-Hop charts and achieving more mainstream chart success, too, by hitting number two on the *Billboard* Hot 100 and number three on the Top 40 Mainstream.

Elliott has received four Grammy Awards. Her 2001 song "Get Ur Freak On" won the Best Rap Solo Performance award; "Scream a.k.a. Itchin'" (2002) and "Work It" (2003) both netted a Best Female Solo Rap Performance award; and "Lose Control" earned her a Best Short Form Music Video Grammy in 2005. All of her albums have at least received gold status, but *Supa Dupa Fly, Da Real World, Miss E . . . So Addictive, Under Construction*, and *This Is Not a Test* have achieved platinum status. Thus far, she has collaborated with, produced tracks for, or otherwise made a guest appearance on a song with artists such as Mariah Carey, Ginuwine, Mya, Pink, Whitney Houston, Justin Timberlake, Janet Jackson, Christina Aguilera, Lil' Kim, Destiny's Child, Monica, and most recently Ciara. Her label launched the career of the platinum-selling artist Tweet in early 2002. She has reportedly refused deals to work with Sean Combs under his auspices with Bad Boy Records, because she would rather chart her own destiny than follow someone else's vision, but most importantly, Elliott admitted that she's too ambitious for such a move.

## EARLY YEARS

Missy Elliott was born in Portsmouth, Virginia, in 1971 as Melissa Arnette Elliott. Her father spent time in the Marines, and her mother Patricia worked as a dispatcher for the local utility company. The family also lived in North Carolina in a mobile home community during her youth. Young Missy spent her afternoons playing outside, singing and performing songs of the Jackson 5 until her mother would call her in for the day. Money was tight growing up: She has told stories about the rats that they would have to keep out of their home. Missy was also the victim of domestic abuse. Her father pulled a gun on her and her mother, and she witnessed her father hitting her mother on more than one occasion as well as being hit once, too. Elliott was afraid to leave the house to visit friends or stay overnight because she wanted to protect her mother. She later reported that she had been sexually abused by a cousin of hers, information that she shared with readers of *Teen People*. Elliott was raised as a Baptist, however, and maintained that her faith has helped through challenging times.

Elliott is exceptionally smart and after an IQ test revealed her high intellect, her school skipped her from second grade to fourth. The change was so difficult socially that her mother requested she move back to second grade, which the school permitted. She has told of her wild imagination as a child, in which she envisioned that Michael and Janet Jackson would find her at school and whisk her away from her difficult home life. When she was fourteen, her mother left her father, and she reports being inspired by her mother's strength.

While in high school, Elliott was a well-adjusted, funny, and creative teenager. She often wrote lyrics, sometimes on her bedroom walls (initially to her mother's dismay). Her songs reflected her life—experiences at school and stories she overheard other people tell. But she was fortunate, because her childhood friend Tim Mosley, who by the time she was in high school was using the name DJ Timmy Tim, became a collaborative partner. He would later record and produce under the name Timbaland. She says that when she met him, he was using a tiny Casio keyboard. The first song they wrote together is called "Wonder Funky Groove," but it was never recorded.

When graduation approached, her mom wanted her to go to college or enter the military, but Elliott had other plans. Along with some friends— LaShawn Shellman, Chonita Coleman, and Radiah Scott—Elliott formed a group called Sista, which performed her songs to Mosley's music. They eventually put together a demo tape with his help. Her career really began in earnest when DeVante Swing, a member and producer of the band Jodeci, heard their music one night when he was in Portsmouth on tour. He took them to New York City and signed Elliott and Sista to his label Swing Mob, an imprint of Elektra Records, and signed Mosley to produce the songs they wrote. The girls worked together for several months and recorded the album *4 All the Sistas*, but the record was shelved for reasons that have never been specified. The group fell apart, but undeterred, Elliott stayed in New York, continued to write songs, and turned to her friend Timbaland. Elliott lived in Brooklyn with R&B singer Faith Evans, who encouraged her to be proud of her songs and to keep writing. Together, Elliott and Timbaland wrote for Jodeci, Raven-Symone, and 702. Elliott quickly became known for her ability to write a song under nearly any circumstance, like clockwork, and for using the odd range of materials on which she would write—a Styrofoam cup, a napkin, whatever she could get. Working with Timbaland was formative; he would construct the rhythm or basic beat sequence—he is known for his pronounced percussive tendencies—and she would write lyrics to fit. She needed to hear the music first. The melody would guide her feelings.

At first her lyrics did not meet with much positive response from the industry, because she was writing about topics that were more "real world" than the love and money themes that were getting radio play. When she tried to change her style and write more about the traditionally commercial themes, she said it was not satisfying. Their next break came when they were asked to write songs for the up-and-coming R&B singer Aaliyah on her 1996 album *One in a Million*. Elliott's work on this record was crucial, because it became a tremendous seller (it went double platinum) and spawned several hits, including "If Your Girl Only Knew," which was an R&B smash. She was also contributing songs to Mariah Carey and Brandy's career.

Elliott also worked as a guest vocalist for Gina Thompson's song "The Things That You Do" in 1996 along with MC Lyte's "Cold Rock a Party," which showed her potential as both a lyricist and a singer. Both successful songs were produced by Sean Combs and gave her even further exposure. In fact, he had hoped to sign her to his own Bad Boy record label. A veritable bidding war ensued among labels that wanted to sign her. Elektra Records' Sylvia Rhone, chairman and CEO, took notice of this prodigiously talented and productive woman and offered Elliott both a recording contract plus the ability to run her own label. She seized the deal, knowing that it was of the

*I find it a blessing that my name is everywhere.*

utmost importance for her to be able to control her own destiny. In the world of hip-hop, it was heretofore unprecedented for a woman to be taken seriously as a creative and commercial force, and Elliott's deal literally opened the doors for many other female artists and groups to walk through. At this period in the industry, women were perceived almost exclusively as props—provocative eye candy in music videos and awards shows or backup singers at best.

Elliott's imprint, called The Gold Mind, Inc., not only releases her records but has expanded to promote other artists, too, including the 2002 debut of Tweet. The label brought her to the attention of Mona Scott of Violator Management, who became Elliott's manager. Initially, Scott said Elliott did not want to be a performer, and described her as being painfully shy when they first met. By the end of the 1990s, Elliott was earning up to six figures for her songs. It was a shock for her; she never anticipated that she could earn that kind of a living, and she felt blessed.

When asked later about her unorthodox career path and the fact that she worked behind the scenes before she emerged on her own, she told *Rolling Stone* that it actually helped her. Elliott said that most people wanted to see a light-skinned, long-haired woman with a "Janet Jackson six pack" (Eliscu 2003). By the time people heard her on other people's work, looks did not matter as much.


## CAREER PATH

Critics speculated that despite the fact that Elliott was successful writing songs with other people singing them, the industry was not ready for a performer who was more on the plus side in terms of physique. Elliott's talent quickly disproved that notion. She did not initially jump into the process of working on an album of her own material; her first months on the job with Gold Mind involved signing other acts, such as Nicole Ray. She vacillated. She told a reporter in 1997 that the past rejection of Sista stung. Ultimately, she decided to record and once she did, the album came together in one remarkable week in a small studio in Virginia Beach. She and Timbaland kept a pace of finalizing one song in less than an hour. Before the record's release, she was hopeful about its potential to break new ground.

Released in 1997, *Supa Dupa Fly* was a super-duper success. Though "The Rain" hit the charts and helped propel the album to top spots, the variety of material on the album and Elliott's own versatility—she could sing, rap, and write music—ensured it was a critical success. Steve Huey, in *All Music Guide*, held back nothing when he declared it "a boundary-shattering postmodern masterpiece. It had tremendous impact on hip-hop and an even bigger one on R&B, as its futuristic, nearly experimental style became the de facto sound of urban radio at the end of the millennium." The record earned her accolades from mainstream music magazines as well as rap and hip-hop publications such as *The Source* and *Rap Pages*. Matt Diehl of *Entertainment Weekly* proclaimed her "a wickedly innovative singer-rapper who favors expansive song structures and trip-hoppy textures." *Rolling Stone* was equally generous in its assessment, noting in particular her personality, saying she was sexy and that Timbaland's production "marries hip-hop beats and succulent R&B with a cool, uncluttered glaze that flatters the rhythms instead of flattening them" (*Rolling Stone* 1997). Elliott believes she and Timbaland as a team created a fresh, innovative approach that brought a new sound to radio. Both retail and radio liked it. The record was a number one hit on the Top R&B/Hip-Hop Albums chart and a number three debut on the *Billboard* 200. It spawned two hit singles, with "The Rain (Supa Dupa Fly)" peaking at number eighteen on the Rhythmic Top 40 and "Sock it 2 Me," appearing on four separate charts, peaking at number twelve on the *Billboard* Hot 100 and reaching its highest spot on the Hot Dance Music chart at number three.

Her songs, with Timbaland's production, are often characterized by their itinerant stopping and starting, with arrangements that are at times unusual. In "The Rain (Supa Dupa Fly)" for example, there are layers of sounds that work together carefully to create a mesmerizing rhythm not unlike a slow, steady rain: a sample of Teena Marie, the sound of thunder, pizzicato strings, a bass line that sounds similar to a video game, all interrupted periodically by Elliott's curiously phrased rapping. Her music videos, too, offered her singular visual style; in the video for the song "The Rain (Supa Dupa Fly)," she appeared in what looked like an inflatable space suit that seemed to be made of plastic garbage bags, alternating with other futuristic outfits and sparkling, oversized sunglasses. Elliott is not an artist who is afraid of looking silly. Instead, this video and the many others that came after it showcase her creativity and her fun-loving personality, which resulted in three nominations for MTV music video awards.

Shockingly, the album entered the *Billboard* charts at number three, which made it one of the highest-ranking debuts of a female hip-hop artist at the time. The record also showed that Elliott, in between celebratory raps and references to herself and/or Timbaland, could actually sing and that she was not afraid of explicit lyrics, suggestive sighs and moans, and wicked double entendres. In the song "Don't Be Commin' (In My Face)" she recalls her own experience, tells a lover to get lost and that it's too late, she urges in the third verse that "all my bitches who sat home crying" disappointed by their lovers to "shake 'em off like Jell-O." Later in "I'm Talkin'," she reflects on her process, while multi-tracking vocals feature her singing in the chorus, "My style's the bomb diggy" as the same medium-tempo rhythm repeats. Overall, *Supa Dupa Fly* is a slow and heavy mesmerizing affair, with smart lyrics and observations that illustrate her uncompromising and steely persona.

Instead of touring in support of the record, Elliott got back to work. A shy person by nature, she was not interested in or comfortable with the idea of performing in front of large crowds. Luckily, her record sales did not need any additional boost nor did she need much in the way of industry validation to confirm that her first foray was an unqualified success. More to the point, she was in charge, and so she could decide whether or not she wanted to tour. In the meantime, though, Elliott did perform a little bit; she became the first hip-hop artist to appear on the Lilith Fair tour in 1998.

For Elliott, there was no perceivable sophomore slump. Her 1999 follow-up *Da Real World* spawned a few hit songs, namely "She's a Bitch" and "Hot Boyz." Unafraid to take on her own peers in her songwriting, she points out the limitations of hip-hop culture's clichés in "She's a Bitch." In the song, Elliott takes an insulting term that's commonly used in hip-hop and redefines it for women who are strong and know what they want. Elliott talked about her subversive approach, saying, "I became a bitch in power because when I walked in, I asked for what I wanted. And at the end of the day, if this is the way I want it, this is the way I'm going to have it. I wanna be like a female Quincy Jones" (Good 2001, 151). Using it as a term of empowerment was a striking move for a female artist in a male-dominated field. She called attention to the double standards for women who are clear about what they want but who are often maligned for the unwavering strength and clarity of their purpose. Consider "She's a Bitch" as a sonic, ironic funky representation of just that.

By this point, her work with Timbaland was so influential, they were hyper-attuned to the fact that other people were copying their approach. She addresses that in "Beat Biters," saying that others were "stealin' our beats like you're the one who made 'em/Timbaland's the teacher and I'm the one who grades 'em."

Elliott's persona continued to evolve with this album, and offered some contradictions for her listeners. Eminem, a white hip-hop artist whose lyrics can be interpreted as misogynistic, makes a surprising appearance on the song "Busa Rhyme." Elliott pokes fun at hip-hop conventions even as she establishes new ones for women hip-hop moguls. In "Hot Boyz," she narrates in first person as though she were a gold-digging woman looking for her next male victim. Elsewhere, the record features other players and rappers, including Redman and OutKast's Big Boi, along with Aaliyah and Da Brat, who appeared on her debut. Timbaland is at the helm again, ensuring the same futuristic sound and breakbeats and adding unusual creative touches, such as incorporating a "Speak and Spell" toy to electronically spell out her name on the song "Mr. DJ."

Again, she earned her accolades, with *Entertainment Weekly* giving the album an A– and *Rolling Stone* writer Touré applauding it, saying that "it all comes off like a soundtrack for a dark future where humanoids escape the pressures of intergalactic war by unwinding to hip-hop funk." His one reservation, however, was that alongside other MCs with serious rhyming skills, Elliott paled in comparison; her lyrics were sometimes just too simple. "It's only her rare sense of rhythm, timbre and delivery that make a silk purse out of the sow's ear that are her words. How strange to find an artist so innovative musically, so lucid rhythmically and so unfocused lyrically" (Touré 1999). Ultimately, he suggested—as have other critics since then—that perhaps Elliott was more interesting and important as a producer and businesswoman than as a performer of her own music. Regardless, the album was a number one hit on the Top R&B/Hip-Hop Albums chart, a number ten hit on the *Billboard* 200, and it generated three singles in "All N My Grill" (with a top slot of number twenty-nine on Rhythmic Top 40), "She's a Bitch" (top spot of nineteen on Hot Rap Single), and "Hot Boyz," an even bigger hit. That song went to number one on Hot Rap Singles, Hot R&B/Hip-Hop Singles, and number five on the *Billboard* Hot 100.

> *If ecstasy is the hottest drug, then consider me your pusher.*

After the release of *Da Real World*, Elliott lost thirty pounds and stopped smoking marijuana to keep herself healthy and in good shape for touring and recording. Her new slimmed-down image raised some eyebrows among fans and critics who wondered if she were feeling the need to pander to popular culture by intentionally sexing-up her image. She discussed the issue with the press and acknowledged that her mother, with whom she is extremely close, would be surprised by the fact that she was smoking pot at all. During this time, she was building a new home for her mother in Virginia, and they were living together in Elliott's New Jersey home. She was not shy about sharing her thoughts about her faith in God, continuously thanking him every day for blessing her.

By the time *Miss E . . . So Addictive* was ready to be released in May 2001, Elliott was looking forward to doing some touring and performing in support of her record. She also decided to do more to promote the record herself by appearing on radio and at retail outlets and generally making herself more available in the months leading up to her release. The move was smart, because it put her in close contact with her fans, and they appreciated the gesture; it also jolted her fans and created a buzz months before its release. Additionally, her previous records had sold a little more than a million copies, and Elektra thought her third could hit the 3 million mark. Still working with Timbaland, even though he had branched out and worked with some other artists in the interim, the record was another platinum-selling success with several remarkable singles. The record featured guest MCs and other singers and rappers ranging from Method Man, Ludacris, Ginuiwine, and Busta Rhymes to Nelly Furtado and Jay-Z as part of her indefatigable mix over sixteen tracks.

The biggest hit on the record is the song "Get Ur Freak On," striking in its energetic rhythm, Far East melody line, and jungle beats. A dance remix of the song featured vocals from the pop singer Nelly Furtado. "People are going to bug out when they hear it. Nelly's hot on the pop side, but R&B people are going to respect her when they hear this," Elliott said (Collins 2007, 64). In a

2001 *Rolling Stone* review, writer Rob Sheffield called the album's single "Get Ur Freak On" "the weirdest, loudest, funkiest and just plain best single of the summer so far, a sonic orgasmatron of Indian tablas and Dirty South future-shock funk." The album is noteworthy because Elliott showed that she could burn up the dance charts, too, with hot club tracks such as "Scream a.k.a. Itchin'" and "4 My People." Two other songs, "Dog in Heat," and "One Minute Man," full of sexual lyrics, no doubt contributed to the album's warning label of explicit content—a designation that was not alien to her. However, *Miss E* is a typical balancing act, with a ballad, "Take Away," thrown in for good measure. Some thought it was her best effort yet, and *Spin* magazine rated the record an eight out of ten. "Get Ur Freak On" won her a Grammy Award for Best Rap Solo Performance, and "Scream a.k.a. Itchin'" nabbed her a Best Female Rap Solo Performance Grammy. The record was a number one hit on the R&B album chart, made number two in the *Billboard* 200, and even entered the Canadian *Billboard* album chart with a top eight position. Four singles made it onto *Billboard*'s various charts, including "Lick Shots," "One Minute Man," and "Take Away." But "Get Ur Freak On" cemented Elliott's status as a genuine genre buster, popping up on Canadian, R&B, dance, Latin, *Billboard* Hot 100, Top 40, and rap charts and earning a number three position on two of them.

The video for "Get Ur Freak On," earned a nomination for Best Female Video at the MTV Video Music Awards in 2001. It showed that Elliott was still committed to pushing boundaries and exploiting her active imagination. Part ode to Michael Jackson's groundbreaking video "Thriller" and part science fiction nightmare, the video finds Elliott in a hollowed-out, cobweb filled underground universe with hip-hop fly girls and boys dressed in quasi-military gear, dragging their bodies around with zombie-like dance moves. Additionally, the video shows her sense of humor with its self-conscious use of animation in a few places.

Just one year later, in 2002, Elliott released her fourth record, *Under Construction*. For this record, she and Timbaland decided to pay homage to the early days of hip-hop. Beyoncé Knowles of the all-female R&B trio Destiny's Child made an appearance, along with Jay-Z, TLC, and Timbaland himself. It yielded two more smash hits, "Work It" and "Gossip Folks." In "Work It" she adopts the posture of sexual predator, thus stretching the boundaries of what is normally a male role in hip-hop music, and sings onomatopaeia-inspired lyrics to simulate physical sounds. In "Gossip Folks," she takes a shot at those who have been gossiping about her weight loss, saying "Girl I heard she eats one cracker a day." Ludacris takes a section of the song and raps about his life and his career; Elliott gives him, through this appearance, an opportunity to clear up rumors and gossip that surround him, too. On "Nothing Out There For Me," the song is set up like a telephone call between two girlfriends, with Elliott trying to get Knowles to come out of the house, away from a man she fears is controlling her friend, and hit the clubs. Elliott takes the part of a cautious friend, but Knowles asserts that there's "nothing out there for me."

*Under Construction* elevated her profile yet again, the way that only a double-platinum album can. It sold 4 million copies worldwide and exposed her to an even wider audience. *Rolling Stone* writer Gavin Edwards called it "uninhibited and unpredictable" and "her best yet." The record netted her a BET Award in 2003, along with two Lady of Soul Awards, including one for Song of the Year for "Work It," whose video won an MTV Video Music Award. Elliott also won Artist of the Year at the Radio Music Awards, along with two other nominations for American Music Awards.

Some of her most strident messages come through on this record, namely that she wants rappers to stop killing each other and MCs to dance like they did in the older days of hip-hop. Elliott also asserts that women have a right to be as aggressive and raunchy as men by asking for what they want from their partners and getting satisfaction on all counts. She humorously references a certain part of male anatomy by sampling an elephant roar. But Elliott is not afraid to also be a bit sentimental on *Under Construction*, although the move is jarring in an album full of heat. In "Can You Hear Me" she collaborates with TLC to honor its member Lisa "Left-Eye" Lopez and also pay tribute to Aaliyah, both of whom had recently passed away. In *Rolling Stone*, Edwards said that the "the track sounds like high-fructose corn syrup" whereas the rest of the album "sounds like habañero peppers, cinnamon and sweat."

While she was readying her next album Elliott sang as a guest on Gwen Stefani's work, "Cop that Sh#!" In summer 2003, Elliott also started appearing in a national television and print advertising campaign alongside Madonna for the clothing retailer The Gap. People liked the ads, which exposed her to an even wider audience. In November 2003 *This is Not a Test* appeared. Although the album's material is still progressive and interesting, there are no real showstoppers as on previous releases. Again, Timbaland produced, and the songs have embellished beats that are achieved by the incorporation of unlikely sources—echo chambers, ring modulators, torpedo tubes, and rusty pipes. The most arresting tracks are "I'm Really Hot," which was a radio hit, and her duet with Nelly, "Pump it Up." "Pass the Dutch" is a hot, throbbing dance track. The record continues the preoccupation with early 1980s hip-hop that permeated *Under Construction* and boasts a bevy of guest stars like Jay-Z, R.Kelly, Beenie M, and Mary J. Blige, but once again, Timbaland and Elliott's presence permeate the disc. Elliott is still self-effacing and honest, with an homage to everything from her vibrator ("Toyz") to full-figured women (the bonus track "Pump it Up") to Big Daddy Kane and Fred "Rerun" Berry. And once again, Elliott's record is full of shout-outs and thank yous that provide useful insight into who and what informs and participates in her creative process.

Elliott stayed busy and expanded her interests beyond the studio by launching her own line of clothing with Adidas in 2004 called Respect M.E.—the first such venture with a musician since the rap group Run-D.M.C. endorsed

its famed sneakers. In early 2004, Warner Music Group restructured and consolidated Elektra and Atlantic Records Groups, causing Sylvia Rhone to leave
her post as chairman/CEO of Elektra. Elliott initially thought she would leave
the label if Rhone was not there, but she changed her mind, citing the success
of the label's handling of many other artists. Around the release of her 2005
record *The Cookbook* she told *Billboard*, "I don't feel like I'm walking into a
bad situation. They're willing to allow me to do whatever, because they respect
what I've done. This is my last album [for WMG]" (Hay 2005).

*The Cookbook* debuted in the number two position, giving it a superstar
status. The record featured another smorgasbord of guests like Ciara, Slick
Rick, and Mary J. Blige, along with television show *American Idol*'s winner
Fantasia. This time, though, Elliott herself produced the extremely successful
and relentlessly fast-paced "Lose Control." Like the rest of her best singles,
she earned attention for the video and was nominated for six MTV Video
Music Awards. She won two for best dance video and best hip-hop video. The
video also helped her nab a Grammy for Best Short Form Video and the song
earned her four Grammy nominations. The video itself is a striking collection
of alternating images of people dancing in different situations, whether it's in
the middle of the desert or lined up in matching warm-up gear dancing
together in a way that calls to mind a chain gang.

On *The Cookbook*, Elliott seems at ease and the material shines through
even though there is a change in her usual recipe because of the production,
backing, rapping, sampling, and contributions from many new people. She
did not completely abandon her partner Timbaland, but she consciously
mixed it up to bring in other sounds and vibes. She did not neglect Timbaland
though, saying that she checked in with him for feedback and asked him to be
directly involved with "Joy" and "Partytime."

Yet again, Elliott seemed unable to contain herself and cooked up sixteen
tracks for her fans. Jackie McCarthy in *Billboard* said that *The Cookbook*
suffered from a lack of economy, "serving up all you can eat when one full
plate would suffice." Some critics believed it was her least unified album yet,
confused by efforts from new producers such as the Neptunes on the futuristic-
sounding "On and On" and others that at times yielded uneven results. Still,
it's hard to deny her sheer energy; the album bursts out of the gates with "We
Run This," which playfully incorporates a sample from an early 1980s Sugar
Hill Gang song "Apache." Elliott stakes her self-deprecating claim on her
artistic turf at the song's onset, saying "My style can't be duplicated or recycled/
This chick is a sick individual."

In 2006, she released a collection of her greatest hits called *Respect M.E.*
The past few years have found Elliott expanding her horizons even further
than her clothing line. She scored some music for the Disney children's film
called *Stick It* about gymnastics. In 2007, she also produced a few songs for
Whitney Houston's yet-to-be released comeback album. Fans who were nervous
that Timbaland and Elliott would not work together on her next record
launched a page on the social networking Web site MySpace called "Reunite

Missy and Timbaland." The fans were responding to a reported statement from Timbaland that her sixth album was too "over the top," and they worried that her next release, slated for early 2008, would not include him. But Elliott laughed and told *Rolling Stone* he was "saying that in a good way. Like, I'm so far left, people might not be ready for me. . . . I never want to give them another 'Get Ur Freak On' or another 'Work It.' We're trying different stuff, just going in blind and hoping that people will be with it" (*Rolling Stone* 2007).

## MISSION, MOTIVATION, PROCESS

Much of Elliott's career has been defined by her collaboration, perhaps even more so than the average singer or songwriter of her generation because hip-hop encourages ceaseless permutations of singing, guest rap spots, guest producing, and other involvements. The community is tight but competitive, and her relationship with Timbaland has been a boon to her career from the start. Still, when asked about whether working with women is more difficult than working with men and if women are more competitive, Elliott takes a pragmatic approach and speaks fondly of working with the artist Eve. "We need more women like her. It makes sense that if you're hot and I'm hot we should make a record together. Because then we'll both be hot and we'll both have a lot of money" (Eliscu 2003).

It is remarkable that Elliott received her own imprint under Elektra before she even proved to the label that she was a bankable artist in her own right: She was signed based on the commercial strength of her collaborations with other bankable artists. Elliott's sense of possibility is what helps her become a visionary artist. Although other artists may be able to sing beautifully or rap with a remarkable dexterity, Elliott excels with the rhythm that she gives listeners and the wordplay that she engages in. Her keen sense of rhythm has enabled her music to successfully permeate the charts of rap, hip-hop, and dance music. Additionally, Elliott has become known for writing songs quickly and with relative ease. Her prolific nature has aided her career and will undoubtedly help secure her longevity as an artist.

After the platinum success of *Under Construction*, journalists frequently lauded her work ethic, which directly propels her consistent success. She appeared on the MTV Video Music Awards with Christina Aguilera, Madonna, and Britney Spears for its star-studded opening performance, won two awards, and was in the midst of finishing up her fifth album in just six years. She told *Rolling Stone*, "Not to say that I'm the hardest-working female out there, but I do work very, very hard, and I don't even feel like I do anything else but be in the studio. I have not had a vacation since I've been an artist. I always gotta be doing something or I would just get bored" (Eliscu 2003). Some might perceive her as overextended or overexposed at times, but Elliott's pace is a direct result of equal parts ambition, creativity, and talent; sitting still represents complacency and lack of progress.

*I do think I get more females asking for songs, because they can pretty much relate to the issues. They feel it's their testimony . . .*

With her sixth release, *The Cookbook*, Elliott offered listeners a batch of songs that are far-reaching. On her official Web site, she said it is a challenge and described it as "finding that in-between space"—not so far out there that people cannot relate to it but not so safe that it's not interesting or a rehash of material she's already created. The first track on the album starts with a blast of horns and ends with a full-fledged marching band sound, with a complete horn section. On "Irresistible Delicious," she conjures the rapper Slick Rick but with her own twist. Elliott self-produced the song "Lose Control," a party song if ever there was one. But the album is not just a creative pastiche of the now-and-then of hip-hop; it's noteworthy, too, because it contains one of her most personal contributions to date. "My Struggles" is a reflection on her trials growing up with an abusive father. Elliott wrote that the song is "close to me. . . . I'm talking about what my home was like with my father being abusive to my mother. I wasn't born into being a superstar. I went through a lot" (Missy Elliott official Web site). She added that it reminded her of Grand Puba and Mary J. Blige on Blige's similarly confessional "What's the 411?," and it is no surprise. *The Cookbook* has the same sprawling, freewheeling, celebratory feel as Blige's album *What's the 411?*, along with its honest autobiographical moments. And so Elliott collaborates with those two artists to tell her story of survival and her own hard-won fame. Looking back, though, that sense of gratitude and of paying tribute has always been present in her records. On "Missy's Finale," which ends her first album, she sings about her faith in God and thanks him for "staying with me through my ups and downs and through my whole period of doing this album."

The story of Missy Elliott, however, is a story of a work in progress. Elliott keeps people guessing because she is so forward-thinking and sets high creative standards for herself. She considers herself a young artist with much still ahead of her, despite her extremely productive ten years recording. And as much as Elliott is clearly her own woman, she admires the career path of her friend Queen Latifah, a singer and actress who has worked in television and film and recorded albums with music that ranges from hip-hop to jazz standards. In 2003 she told *Newsweek*, "I love the way she planned out her whole career. She was an artist, then a management company, then a sitcom and movie star. She was nominated for Oscars! Ten years ago I'm quite sure she never imagined she would have lasted this long" (Ali and Ordonez 2003).

## LEGACY AND OTHER INTERESTS

As a female artist who maker her own rules about beauty, sexuality, and femaleness, Elliott is a new icon. She has told journalists that women continuously thank her and tell her that they're tired of seeing excessively thin women in television. Around 1999 to 2000, Elliott actually lost some weight, and some thought perhaps it was an attempt to appear more attractive, a notion she disputes. She lost the weight for health reasons. Additionally, she told reporters she did not diet—she upped the ante on exercise. Her healthy attitude about her body image is inspiring and refreshing, but in the past few years, she has looked increasingly glamorous and buff in her music videos, so that an ardent fan or even just a skeptical observer cannot help but wonder if there is more of a makeover going on behind the scenes than Elliott is admitting to.

Elliott continues to bequeath her legacy as an innovator by mentoring other artists through their work, whether it's younger stars who emerged after she did, such as Ciara, Fantasia, Raven-Symone, Keyshia Cole, and Destiny's Child, or the likes of Janet Jackson, an artist who has struggled to regain the traction her career once had in the 1980s and early 1990s. Elliott believes, though, that this work with other artists, specifically through the auspices of her Gold Mind, informs her own songwriting process.

During the course of her career, Elliott has balanced her attention between charitable and commercial interests. Elliott has worked as spokeswoman for the organization Break the Cycle, whose mission is to enable young people to stop domestic abuse. After her first few albums were released and the industry felt the impact of her strong image, she did not shy away from expanding her image and branding it in more public ways. To that end, she has appeared in campaigns for Adidas, The Gap, Virgin Mobile, Vanilla Coke, and MAC Cosmetics. These activities elevate her profile and position her as part of mainstream American culture. Elliott even has her own shade of lipstick, appropriately called Misdemeanor, with Iman Cosmetics and donates part of the proceeds to help battered teens. Additionally, she has taken on small roles in films such as *Pootie Tang* and *Honey*. In 2004, she started Respect M.E., a line of clothing with Adidas, a portion of whose sales are donated toward Break the Cycle. One year later, she launched a reality program on UPN called *The Road to Stardom with Missy Elliott*, a musical talent competition of which she is a judge and a co-executive producer. In response to concerns that she was becoming overexposed, Elliott seemed unconcerned; she was committed to staying true to herself. With an eye toward ensuring that her image is well-represented on celluloid, Elliott is slated to appear in a film about her life, set to be produced by Robert DeNiro's company Tribeca Films.

## SELECTED DISCOGRAPHY

*Supa Dupa Fly*. Elektra, 1997
*Da Real World*. Elektra, 1999
*Miss E . . . So Addictive*. Elektra, 2001
*Under Construction*. Elektra, 2002
*This is Not a Test!* Elektra, 2004

## FURTHER READING

Ali, Lorraine, and Jennifer Ordonez. "The Marketing of Missy: The Electrifying Ms. Elliott Gets Commodified." *Newsweek* (December 8, 2003).

Collins, Tracy Brown. *Hip-Hop Stars: Missy Elliott*. New York: Chelsea House Publishing, 2007.

Diehl, Matt. "Missy Elliott. Supa Dupa Fly. Review." *Entertainment Weekly* (August 8, 1997). Available online at www.ew.com/ew/article/0,,288987,00.html.

Edwards, Gavin. "Under Construction. Review." *Rolling Stone* 911 (December 12, 2002). Available online at www.rollingstone.com/artists/missyelliott/albums/album/88784/review/6067498/under_construction.

Elliott, Missy. Official artist Web site. www.missy-elliott.com.

Good, Karen Renee. "Feeling Bitchy: Missy Elliott." *Hip Hop Divas*. New York: Vibe Books/Three Rivers Press, 2001.

Hay, Carla. "The Last Word: A Q&A with Missy Elliott." *Billboard* (February 26, 2005).

Huey, Steve. "Supa Dupa Fly. Review." *All Music Guide*. Available online at wc10 .allmusic.com/cg/amg.dll?p=amg&token=ADFEAEE47817D849AA7E20 C79A3 E52DBB57DF702FE5AFB86112F0456D3B82D4BBD0E4FE06BC2AB8 1B0FA6AB57FB0FD2EA45D43D2CAE456FBD667382DFC93&sql=10:hbfexqu hldke.

Jones, Steve. "Elliott Takes Off with 'Supa Dupa Fly.'" *USA Today* (September, 1997).

McCarthy, Jackie. "Missy Elliott: The Cookbook. Review." *Billboard* (July 16, 2005).

Paoletta, Michael. "Elliott: Running at Full Throttle. Review." *Billboard* (December 13, 2003).

*Rolling Stone*. "Missy Elliott. Supa Dupa Fly. Review."(December 17, 1997). Available online at www.rollingstone.com/artists/missyelliott/albums/album/118971/review/6067401/supa_dupa_fly.

*Rolling Stone*. "Fall Music Preview 2007: Bruce Springsteen, James Blunt, Alicia Keys and More." (September 7, 2007). Available online at www.rollingstone.com/photos/gallery/16296997/fall_music_preview_2007_bruce_spr/photo/27/large.

Schnuer, Jenna. "Mona Scot, Missy Elliott: Once 'Painfully Shy' Performer Steps Out Front With Adidas and Gap Deals and Adoring Audience." *Advertising Age* (March 1, 2004).

Sheffield, Rob. "Miss E . . . So Addictive. Review." *Rolling Stone* 871 (May 29, 2001). Available online at www.rollingstone.com/artists/missyelliott/albums/album/202317/review/6067560/miss_eso_addictive.

Sheffield, Rob. *The New Rolling Stone Album Guide* (2004). Available online at www.rollingstone.com/artists/missyelliott/biography.

Sheffield, Rob. "This is Not a Test. Review." Rolling Stone (December 25, 2003). Available online at www.rollingstone.com/reviews/album/296896/review/6067976/thisisnotatest.

Touré. "The Real World. Review." *Rolling Stone* (July 9, 1999). Available online at www.rollingstone.com/artists/missyelliott/albums/album/280440/review/6067699/da_real_world.

Frank Driggs Collection/Getty Images

# Aretha Franklin

## OVERVIEW

Aretha Franklin, perhaps more than any other singer of her genre and generation, managed to blend blues, soul, gospel, rhythm and blues, and other roots music into her own heady style, garnering herself the nickname "Queen of Soul."

She is what is commonly referred to as a living legend. Franklin's career is a testimony to her diverse musical interests and her singular vocal talent, both formed by an early life spent singing gospel music in church and listening to her charismatic father preach. Although Franklin started off her recording career with Columbia Records when she was just a teenager, her career really saw its peak in the late 1960s through the early 1970s when she was releasing records with Atlantic, with hits such as "Respect," "I Never Loved a Man," "Baby I Love You," "Chain of Fools," "(You Make Me Feel Like) A Natural Woman," "I Say a Little Prayer," "Think," and "The House that Jack Built." This remains her most productive, commercially viable, and critically acclaimed recording period. As the 1970s wore on, her albums became more mature and more thought out, yet she went through a lull toward the end of the decade. Franklin capped off the decade by falling somewhat of a victim to current musical trends by recording a disco album in 1979 called *La Diva*, seemingly predicting or cementing her transition from queen of soul to full-fledged diva. In the 1980s, she changed labels again, moving to Arista, and as the decade progressed she experienced another burst of commercial success with *Jump to It* and more significantly *Who's Zoomin' Who?* The 1980s saw three Top 10 hits, including "Freeway of Love," "Who's Zoomin' Who?," and the duet with George Michael "I Knew You Were Waiting (for Me)."

During the 1960s and into the 1970s, Franklin became an important symbol of the powerful African American female, a woman whose performance persona exuded confidence during the decade of civil rights, the Black Panthers, women's liberation, and other humanitarian movements. She and her family, because of her father's minister-celebrity status, were close with many important cultural figures of the day, including Martin Luther King Jr. Anthems such as "Respect," despite what some may say, are not strictly feminist—it is impossible to separate the sentiments from equal rights and black pride. Even the course of Franklin's career can reflect the changing times, as seen through the various chart names that *Billboard* used from the early 1960s through 2000s: her earliest hits landed on "black singles" lists that were later labeled rhythm and blues. With idols such as Sam Cooke, Clara Ward, Mahalia Jackson, and Dinah Washington, Franklin saw evidence before her of musical excellence and of artists who were able to achieve success in multiple genres. The crossover success of gospel singer Sam Cooke was especially important to her career.

In 2003, *Billboard* published an article chronicling her achievements and concluded that Franklin has the most Top 10 and number-one rated R&B

albums of any solo artist and the most charting R&B albums and Top 40 R&B albums of any solo female artist, with seventeen Top 10 hits, twenty-two Top 40 *Billboard* 200 albums, twenty number one R&B/Hip-Hop singles and tracks, and ten number one R&B/Hip-Hop albums. These numbers put her in a league of her own (*Billboard* 2003). Franklin has won seventeen Grammy Awards, starting in 1967 for the song "Respect," which garnered her Best Female R&B Vocal Performance and Best R&B Recording/Best R&B Performance. Eight more Grammy Awards would follow in the ensuing six years: She netted her first Grammy for the 1972 album *Amazing Grace*, which got Best Soul Gospel Performance, and in 1972 she also earned a Best Female R&B Performance Grammy for *Young Gifted and Black*, which took its title from a Nina Simone song. The mid-1980s were also good to her; "Freeway of Love" in 1985 nabbed her Best Female R&B Vocal Performance (she has won this Grammy eleven times) and 1987's "I Knew You Were Waiting (For Me)," a duet with British soul-pop singer George Michael got them both a Best R&B Performance by a Duo or Group with Vocal. Her return to gospel with *One Lord, One Faith, One Baptism* in 1988 earned her Best Soul Gospel Performance-Female for the album. Her most recent Grammy, for Best Traditional R&B Vocal Performance, was awarded in 2005 for the song "A House is Not A Home."

Franklin, twice divorced, still lives in suburban Detroit and may derive some comfort from the area as a safe haven in the midst of her fame and accomplishments, disappointments and heartbreaks. In her own autobiography, she alludes to her Cancer moon as part of why she enjoys domesticity and cooking. Her children are grown and many of them are talented musicians. Franklin, however, bristles at the notion that she is "hiding" in Detroit or even that she is more confident there, but the truth is that she has slowed down considerably in the past ten years and has reduced her touring and recording.

## EARLY YEARS

Although she was born in Memphis, the family did not stay there long; they moved to Buffalo and then Detroit, on the north end, and then to the west side.

Franklin's musical roots are firmly planted in the world of gospel. From a young age, Franklin was exposed to music, religion, and ideas of equality. Franklin grew up with two sisters, Carolyn and Erma, both of whom had recording careers, and she is the fourth of five children. Her brother Cecil has worked as her manager. As children, the three sisters would sing in the Detroit church of her Baptist minister father, Reverend C.L. Franklin. Her mother, Barbara Siggers, was a well-known gospel singer and worked as a nurse's aid. Her parents separated when Franklin was just six years old, and her mother moved to Buffalo without the children, who would often visit her in the summertime.

Her parents decided her father should be charged with raising and providing for them; his salary afforded that. When Franklin was ten years old, her mother died of a heart attack, which shocked and saddened young Aretha.

Music, however, specifically the gospel music of the church, was a tremendous comfort. Her father, who was by most accounts charismatic and charming, was a prominent advocate for civil rights and a well-compensated speaker with a propensity toward Cadillacs and alligator shoes. Franklin said he often was referred to as the "black prince" because he was so sharply dressed (Franklin and Ritz 1999, 13). He was often called away from the family for speaking engagements at other churches, and during those times, the children were often looked after by family friends such as gospel vocalists Frances Steadman, Marion Williams, or Mahalia Jackson, who became an inspiration to Franklin. Her father was responsible for bringing Martin Luther King Jr. to Detroit for an event that many consider the template for the famous march on Washington, DC, later in the decade. Her father has had perhaps the most singular influence on her life, and she continued to seek his guidance throughout difficult times. His skills as a minister—which in some regard is a performance—also came in handy when the young Franklin was nervous or insecure.

Living in Detroit in the 1950s meant fertile ground for singers and performers. When Franklin was about eight or nine years old, she started messing around with the piano while listening to Eddie Heywood on the record player. Encouraged by her interest in music, her father gave her piano lessons, but Franklin hated it, saying that it felt too much like school. Eventually, she taught herself how to play and learned, too, that she could sing. Jackson's presence in her life often meant visits from famous artists such as Dinah Washington, Art Tatum, Sam Cooke, James Cleveland, and Clara Ward. Cleveland became one of her earliest mentors. He taught her how to reach notes that previously were out of her range. Clara Ward's performance at the funeral of one of Franklin's aunts had an impact on her too; after being wowed by Ward's performance, Franklin knew she wanted to sing. Growing up, watching Sam Cooke's career take off, Franklin saw that a career shift from gospel to soul music was possible. Franklin had her first solo in church at age nine or ten. Around this time, she was modeling herself after Ward, who also sang and played the piano in church; Ward was also a close friend of her father. During the time she sang as a soloist in church, she was paid $15 a week. Other childhood passions included roller skating and boxing—she would watch boxing matches on television with her father.

As a young teenager, from about the age of thirteen to sixteen, Franklin spent time as part of a traveling gospel road show with her father and her siblings, which was a result of his growing celebrity. As his celebrity status as a preacher increased, he recorded sermons on Chess Records and appeared on radio programs around the country. The experience of being on the road gave her early insight into discrimination, the rigors of touring, and a dose of responsibility, all of which would come in handy later as her own career started to take off. But Franklin's childhood was not necessarily easy, even if she had found her muse early. She became pregnant and had a baby at the age of fourteen; Franklin has remained silent on the identity of the father. Likewise, the family has refused to discuss why Franklin's mother left. Her teenage pregnancy experience was unfortunately somewhat of a foreshadowing of the thorny nature of Franklin's relationships with men; for example, the details of her second divorce have barely been discussed publicly. Franklin has been shy her entire life; some have mistaken it for arrogance. But the death of her mother, according to some family friends, accounts for the change in her previously outgoing personality to being wary, shy, and introverted.

Franklin made her very first recording at age fourteen as a gospel singer, which took place at a church in Oakland, California, as part of a service her father at which her father was appearing. In 1956, Chess Records released a compilation of her gospel performances from the New Bethel Baptist Church at home in Detroit under the title *Songs of Faith*. She sang several standard tunes, but reinterpreted them with the accompaniment of the church choir swelling behind her and even at the age of fourteen showed she was capable of making them her own. Reportedly, Motown Records wanted Franklin to sign with them in its early days; Billy "Tyran Carlo" Davis and Berry Gordy Jr., the latter of whom went on to found Motown, were two young songwriters who regularly came to hear Franklin sing at church. Prior to founding Motown, the pair wanted her to sign a production deal with Chess Records and sing their songs, fresh off their success with Jackie Wilson. Her father vetoed the idea, saying she was too young. Instead, they prepared her older sister, Erma, for a session, with Aretha on piano. Motown, too, reportedly had expressed an interest, but Franklin said that she and her father had their sights set on bigger things, which is rumored to have angered some members of the African American community in Detroit (Jackson 2005, 166).

When Franklin had a child at age fourteen, she dropped out of high school. In her autobiography, she alludes to the father as a neighborhood boy she was in love with but gives him an alias and has never identified him (Franklin and Ritz 1999, 58). Franklin named her son after her father, Clarence Franklin. She also had another child, Edward, a couple of years later.

During the time when she was home with her new baby, in the late 1950s, Franklin decided she wanted to model her career after Dinah Washington's, whose move from blues to jazz made her a spectacular success thanks in part to the help of Clyde Otis from Mercury Records. Ted White, who would later become Franklin's first husband, visited the Franklin house with Washington. Franklin was taken with Washington and decided that it was time to pursue her own career. Her father was initially reluctant for her to leave Detroit for New York City, because she left the baby behind in the care of her father's mother and also left behind gospel music for secular. Once in New York, bass player Major "Mule" Holly produced a demo of her singing a blues tune.

Franklin auditioned for Jo King, who became her manager, and Holly got the demo into the hands of John Hammond at Columbia Records, who had a strong track record among jazz artists. After hearing her, he wrote in his memoir that he thought her voice was the best he'd heard in quite a while. Franklin was just eighteen years old. To say that his approval was fortuitous would be an understatement: Hammond discovered Billie Holiday, was responsible for some of Bessie Smith's final recordings, and signed big band leader Count Basie, all prior to meeting Franklin.

## CAREER PATH

### *The Columbia Years*

Franklin signed with Columbia, thanks to John Hammond, for a six-year contract that resulted in a prolific output: ten albums and two "greatest hits" collections. Her contractual arrangement was unprecedented and provided her with a "substantial royalty rate" according to Buzzy Jackson (Jackson 2005, 166). Her first Columbia record, *Aretha*, came out in 1961 and featured her take on a smattering of styles—pop, jazz, blues, and show tunes—recorded with the Ray Bryant jazz group. Hammond wanted to develop a following among jazz audiences but still retain the gospel quality of her voice. The first four tracks, "Over the Rainbow," "Today I Sing the Blues," "Right Now," and "Love is the Only Thing," were live takes in the studio, meant to feel spontaneous and intimate. In October 1960, "Today I Sing the Blues" was the first song released before the album, and it found an audience with R&B fans and became her first Top 10 single. "Won't Be Long" was released in February 1961, and went to number seven on the R&B chart, crossing briefly over to the pop chart to hit number seventy-six.

When her debut album was released in March 1961 it garnered favorable reviews. *Billboard* remarked, "[S]he brings a true and strong gospel accent into a fine full-blown blues" (Bego 2001, 47). Franklin started taking piano, voice, and dance lessons, as well as other classes, under the guidance of Jo King. She spent a good portion of 1961 touring to promote her album, playing mostly in dark, smoky rooms along the jazz circuit of the United States. *Down Beat* magazine pronounced her "New Star Female Vocalist" in 1961. Franklin never saw herself as strictly a jazz singer; her sights were set higher and across genres. Although much of her Columbia material is jazz-based, she also covered more blues-based material, such as Dinah Washington's "Soulville." Critics noticed how natural such music seemed to come to her and, although they were quick to assign her fluidity with the blues to real life experience, it is just as likely that Franklin's performances during these early years were equally influenced by her father's impassioned sermons and by growing up in a veritable incubator of musical creativity and expression—the church.

On visits back home to Detroit to visit family, Franklin became reacquainted with family friend Ted White. Things between them progressed so quickly that she was married in 1961 at the age of nineteen. She was captivated by his sophistication—he was a Detroit-based music promoter. Shortly after their marriage and through the mid-1960s, he became Franklin's manager and would bring in new musicians to back her. He also became the father to her third child.

For her second album with Columbia, *The Electrifying Aretha Franklin*, Hammond changed his approach, surrounding her with a big band, complete with horns and strings. Released in 1962, it produced three hit singles. Franklin is confident on "You Made Me Love You" and noteworthy on "I Told You So," and the record also contains some blues-oriented tunes such as "Blue Holiday" and "Just For You." The album produced her lone Top 40 pop single during the Columbia years, "Rock-a-bye Your Baby with a Dixie Melody." During the summer of that year, she appeared at the Newport Jazz Festival along with Carmen McRae, Duke Ellington, Clara Ward Gospel Singers, and the Thelonius Monk quartet, among other musical luminaries.

Some critics contend that during her Columbia years, Franklin wanted to continue with gospel material but that the label was pushing her toward pop-oriented material and production values. Hammond, however, was clear from the beginning about his intentions of producing Franklin as a jazz singer with gospel roots. As Franklin's career progressed, Hammond became less involved. Executives thought he was too out of touch with the youth and not able to create a huge hit for her, but Hammond said that Columbia wanted to turn her into a pop star, a move he disagreed with. Hammond contended that he always knew she had potential to be a real musical powerhouse, with the ability to write, arrange, and sing.

Once Hammond was out of the picture, Robert Mersey worked on her next three albums, including the August 1962 release *The Tender, the Moving, the Swinging Aretha Franklin*, which features a take on "Try a Little Tenderness," and the Billie Holiday standard "God Bless the Child." Another track, "Don't Cry Baby," spent a week on the pop chart at number 92, and "Try a Little Tenderness" hit number 100. Things continued in a generally tender musical direction with *Laughing on the Outside*, an album of all ballads, including Johnny Mercer and Hoagy Carmichael's classic "Skylark," for example, and a song she and White wrote together, "I Wonder (Where You Are Tonight)." Her final album for Columbia, *Unforgettable*, released in March 1964, was a tribute to Dinah Washington who died unexpectedly in December 1963. It has been referred to as her most inspired and serious project for Columbia. After Mersey, she was turned over to producer Clyde Otis, whom Columbia thought would bring Franklin to a wider audience via pop and R&B material. Their first album together, *Runnin' Out of Fools*, released in late 1964, hit eighty-four and became her second-highest charting album at the time. Columbia hoped that those who were buying Dionne Warwick albums would start buying Franklin ones, too, but it didn't happen. Most of the later releases for Columbia were the result of the label scrambling to cash in on whatever material they had from previous recording sessions, and they are, according to critics, for the most part artistically unremarkable.

The Columbia years can best be characterized by a continual experiment with jazz, big band, show tunes, and blues material. These years do illustrate her versatility but do not yet show her strengths at the piano or her potential as a creative collaborator. Additionally, Franklin was frustrated by the label's erratic marketing strategy, which seemed to change with each new release. About these years, Franklin said in her autobiography, "I've never been easy to categorize, nor do I like being categorized, but I suppose you could say my early style was a combination of blues, gospel-based jazz, and rhythm and blues" (Franklin and Ritz 1999, 86). Despite these issues, Franklin's career was gaining her attention, and by most accounts, she seemed patient and confident of her eventual success.

Her career thus far showed how many men were involved in deciding her fate, and the degree to which they helped or hurt her could be debated. For example, White, her husband-manager, admitted he had a hand in getting Hammond out of the picture (Bego 2001, 54). By the end of the decade, her relationship with White became especially contentious. As her manager, he made money from her career and often fought with her father (who opposed their union to begin with) and with Columbia (which often considered White a hindrance and did not like his headstrong ways). Franklin found herself frequently in the middle, but when she contested White's authority, he often became abusive. Franklin's career was at an early crossroads; her marriage would come to one later in the decade.

### The Atlantic Years

By the time her contract with Columbia was up, Franklin had garnered a fair amount of attention and praise, but she had not seen a fair amount of money, partially because of White and partially because of erratic sales and marketing. Those years were not nearly as successful as her time with Atlantic would be. Franklin seemed ready for a change. About this juncture, she has said, "It's the rough side of the mountain that's easiest to climb. The smooth side doesn't have anything for you to hang on to" (Jackson 2005, 169). Producer Jerry Wexler at Atlantic Records pursued her and offered her a significant $30,000 signing bonus. Franklin had an interest in the label, which was home to Ray Charles, Ruth Brown, Isaac Hayes, Otis Redding, and Wilson Pickett.

Wexler quickly went to work and connected her with a small recording studio, Fame Studio in Muscle Shoals, Alabama, with arranger Arif Mardin and engineer Tom Dowd. He went back to basics, with the strategy of putting Aretha back on the piano and letting her "wail." Additionally, Wexler had Franklin choose or write all the material for the album—something that had not happened on her Columbia albums, even though she did have approval over the material selected for her. She worked harmonies out with her sisters, Erma and Carolyn, on her Fender Rhodes keyboard at home. Her first single was "I Never Loved a Man (The Way I Love You)," whose success became the stuff of legend. Reportedly, Franklin came in, knew what she wanted to do, and arranged, performed, and recorded the song in two hours. Wexler pressed a handful of copies and distributed it to some deejays, who started playing the song before the rest of the album was even finished. Much of Franklin's work during the latter part of the 1960s was with the Muscle Shoals Rhythm Session. Richie Unterberger of *All Music Guide* summed up the sessions thusly: "The combination was one of those magic instances of musical alchemy in pop: the backup musicians provided a much grittier, soulful and R&B-based accompaniment for Aretha's voice, which soared with a passion and intensity suggesting a spirit that had been allowed to fly loose for the first time" (Unterberger).

Franklin's career really took off with Atlantic records. She had ten Top 10 hits in about an eighteen-month time period, starting in early 1967. She also had a fairly consistent production of other respectable hits over the course of the next five years. Her years with Atlantic, characterized by the helpful hands of Wexler, Mardin, and Dowd, were exceptionally productive. Her choice of material helped keep her career artistically interesting and creatively stimulating, as she went from originals, gospel, and blues to pop and to rock covers, encompassing such diverse artists as Sam Cooke and the Drifters to The Beatles and Simon & Garfunkel. It seemed that Wexler "got" her and was able to work with her talent, finding homes for her songs.

Franklin's image has very much been shaped by the messages contained in her hits. "Respect," for example, can be read as an anthem—she certainly sees it that way—a declaration of black pride, feminist strength, or at the very least, personal dignity in the face of an unjust relationship characterized by a power imbalance. Franklin conveys a no-nonsense, smart, strong persona, one who refuses to be a victim. Throughout the legendary song, Franklin asserts that she has the upper hand, singing in the first verse "All I'm askin'/Is for a little respect." Flipping the gender perspective—the song was written and recorded by Otis Redding in 1965—added a whole new meaning. Her sisters are credited with adding the refrain "sock it to me," further personalizing what has become perhaps her most well-known song. Franklin was riding high— "Respect" hit number one on both the Pop and Black singles charts, and the record it appeared on, *I Never Loved a Man (The Way I Love You)*, peaked at number one on the Black Albums chart and number two on the Pop Albums chart. Such success was no small feat for a debut on a new label, but no doubt it also substantiated not only the groundwork laid by her Columbia years but also her own hard work and that of the studio gurus who let Aretha be Aretha.

Less than six months after *I Never*, Atlantic released *Aretha Arrives* in August with eleven new songs. Again, Franklin's sisters Carolyn and Erma

*That little girl done took my song away.*

—Otis Redding, upon hearing Franklin's version of "Respect."

sang backup on some selections. One of the singles, "Baby I Love You," written by Ronnie Shannon, became another million-seller like "Respect." Franklin was finally becoming a huge star, but she was focused on her music and bored by its business aspects. She was a tremendous success, toured heavily in North and South America, and finally got to play the Apollo Theater. The city of Detroit designated February 18, 1968, Aretha Franklin Day, and Dr. King, for whom she had sung at rallies in the past, came to pay her a surprise visit, solidifying her importance as an African American icon.

Her next record, *Lady Soul*, was released in January 1968 and was chockablock with hits, too, from the funky love-obsession theme of "Chain of Fools," written by Don Covay, to the Carole King and Gerry Goffin composition "(You Make Me Feel Like A) Natural Woman," another song with which she is strongly identified. Mark Dobkin called the album "a perfect expression of her musical personality" (Dobkin 2004, 233). "Chain of Fools" went to number one on the *Billboard* black singles chart and number two on pop singles and "Natural Woman" hit number two on *Billboard*'s black singles and eight on pop singles. Franklin's sister Carolyn wrote "Ain't No Way" for the album and Franklin wrote "Since You've Been Gone (Sweet Sweet Baby)." She also sang the Ray Charles tune "Come Back Baby" and Curtis Mayfield's "People Get Ready." *Lady Soul* proved Franklin was indeed the Queen of Soul, peaking at number one, two, and three on the black, pop, and jazz charts, respectively. Franklin was on a roll—*Aretha Now* followed, her fourth record in two years with Atlantic, and it, too, was a number one record on the black album charts. *Aretha Now* included a stellar cover of Dionne Warwick's "I Say a Little Prayer," which hit number three on the black singles chart. The continued success enabled her to tour Europe; *Aretha in Paris* came out in 1968 too.

During these years, however, Franklin was having a difficult time in her personal life. *Time* magazine put her on the cover in June 1968 and printed what Franklin termed erroneous information about her mother abandoning the family, which she said Cissy Houston (who was singing backup frequently during these years for Franklin with the Sweet Inspirations) and Gladys Knight fabricated. The *Time* article also contended that White had been violent with her. He even went so far as to sue the magazine. Franklin also said *Time* posited the idea that she sang particular songs because of her experience, another idea she disputed, saying, "I am Aretha, upbeat, straight-ahead, and not to be worn out by men and left singing the blues" (Franklin and Ritz 1999, 123). Many critics, however, agree that it is easy to imagine she was singing the blues because she was living them and that her family was concerned about her during this time. Around the time of the article, Franklin was twenty-six years old and had achieved remarkable success. But she had dealt with the tragic deaths of two of her idols, Dinah Washington and Sam Cooke, who

was shot by a motel owner in what can be best clas-
sified as a misunderstanding. She also had had her
third child, Teddy, but because of her career's
demands left childrearing duties largely to her father
and grandmother "Big Mama."

> *Inside every woman, there's an Aretha Franklin screaming to come out.*
>
> —Lena Horne

Her relationship with White was failing and to cope
she was chain-smoking, overeating, and having trou-
ble with drinking (Bego 2001, 114). The stress played a contributing role in
the cancellation of tour dates. To add to her stress, while she was going through
her divorce in 1969, her father was fighting tax evasion charges and was
arrested for possession of marijuana. Producer John Hammond once reportedly said that Franklin had "terrible luck" with men; somehow, they all made
her suffer. Wexler said that Franklin's personal life is so sad that he called her
"the mysterious lady of sorrow" (Bego 2001, 8).

Things were rough for Franklin, except for her career. *Soul 69,* released in
1969, earned some accolades, even if, despite the misnomer of the title, it was
a deeper deviation into what Stanley Booth, writing in *Rolling Stone,* called
"jazz-blues." Booth wrote that "Aretha is more exciting and more believable
than any other lady now singing" and commended Arif Mardin for "beautiful" arrangements. He also acknowledged Wexler for gathering members of
the Miles Davis Quintet, the Count Basie Orchestra, and some of the usual
players from her Memphis group, on a re-recording of a song she recorded for
Columbia, "Today I Sing the Blues," and the Smokey Robinson tune "Tracks
of My Tears" (Booth 1969). A greatest hits package, *Aretha's Gold,* came out
in 1969 while she took some time off before working on *This Girl's In Love
With You,* which was released in 1970. The album had some heartbreaking
material, including her own composition, the ballad "Call Me," which she
wrote after watching two lovers depart, and a cover of the Beatles song "Elea-
nor Rigby," a rumination on loneliness that must have felt appropriate for her
and which hit number seventeen.

If *This Girl* was her catharsis, *Spirit in the Dark,* which also was released in
1970, could be considered her rebirth. Franklin took on B.B. King's "The
Thrill is Gone" and the strong and sassy "Why I Sing the Blues." *Spirit in the
Dark* boasts a record five songs written by her, including the title track. The
abundance of horns shows a decidedly funkier vibe. "You and Me" became a
number five *Billboard* R&B hit and peaked at thirty-seven on the pop charts,
and her B.B. King cover nabbed her a number three R&B hit. Indeed, the
record fared better on the R&B chart, peaking at number two, whereas it
stopped at twenty-five on the pop album chart.

Indeed, it seemed with White's controlling methods out of the picture,
Franklin was better off. In 1970 she had her fourth son, Kecalf, out of wed-
lock; the father was Ken Cunningham, an entrepreneur who served as her
road manager in the late 1960s and who she nicknamed "Wolf." She credits
Wolf and his strong black pride for her return to a more natural look; she lost

*I never left church. And never will. Church is as much a part of me as the air I breathe.*

weight, stopped shaving her eyebrows, and wore her hair in an Afro. The pair stayed together for about six years. Franklin spent much of the 1970s embracing diversity, with turns singing pop-oriented material, gospel, funk, and soul. In the early 1970s, she started to expand more into pop material: Some of her most notable hits include "Spanish Harlem," which hit number two on the pop chart and number one on the R&B chart, and a cover of the Simon & Garfunkel song "Bridge Over Troubled Water," which was a tremendous success when she sang it at the Grammy Awards telecast in 1971. At this time she also produced two well-regarded albums, *Live at Filmore West*, and the 1972 double gospel album *Amazing Grace*, recorded with James Cleveland and the Southern California Community Choir. It proved that Franklin was indeed still in touch with her gospel roots since the album hit the Top 10 and is regarded as one of the most successful gospel-pop crossover releases ever recorded.

She had a few more hits after the success of 1972's releases, including "Angel" from *Hey Now Hey* (1973) and the Stevie Wonder song "Until You Come Back to Me" from *Let Me In Your Life* (1974), which hit number one on the Black Singles chart and three on the pop charts in 1974. Franklin produced the album with Mardin and Wexler, but the inconsistent *Hey Now Hey*, in which Franklin herself shared production credits with Quincy Jones, was her first Atlantic album not to make the top twenty-five. Her historic and productive span with Wexler came to an end, and her career entered something of a lull; their final two projects are *With Everything I Feel In Me* (1974) and *You* (1975). There were conversations about having her sing disco, but the energy did not seem right. Franklin lamented that many of the traditional R&B artists had trouble in the days of disco.

Ahmet Ertegun of Atlantic Records presented Franklin with producer options for her next album, and she chose Curtis Mayfield, who produced 1976's *Sparkle* and 1978's *Almighty Fire*, with 1977's *Sweet Passion*, an album of show tunes, standards, and ballads, thrown in between. Franklin reflected on her choice as a good one, saying that *Sparkle*, for example, "proved the permanent power of rootsy rhythm and blues" (Franklin and Ritz 1999, 161). Around this time, Franklin and Wolf moved from their swanky apartment in New York City to Los Angeles in the hopes that a change of scenery would help matters, but they would soon go their separate ways.

The next ten years were difficult. Franklin and Wolf parted, and in 1978, after dating for a year and a half, she married actor Glynn Turman. Her father officiated at the ceremony. They did not have children together, and the marriage did not last long. In 1982 they separated, and in 1984 the marriage was officially dissolved. Her brother Cecil had become her manager, and sometimes his decisions were contested by Wolf, creating tension. Franklin sang at the funerals of both Clara Ward and Mahalia Jackson, and while performing in Las Vegas in June 1979 learned that her father had been shot in a botched burglary in his Detroit home. Her father slipped into a coma and stayed in it for five years.

### Zoomin' into the 1980s with Pop Music, Securing Her Diva Status

Much of the discussion of Franklin's success seems to have been centered around the talented men, such as John Hammond and Jerry Wexler, she encountered who could make great things possible in her career. At the end of the 1970s when her contract with Atlantic was about to expire, she signed with Clive Davis's new label, Arista, with the approval of her brother. Franklin said she needed money to take care of her father and wanted the personal involvement and expertise of Davis. (Her twelve years at Atlantic had been tremendously good to her; she earned more gold records and Grammy Awards than any other female African American performer at the time.) But toward the end of her stint with Atlantic, she expressed some frustration that her songs weren't hitting, and she felt that her later releases were not adequately promoted. It was time for a change. We can add Clive Davis, president of Arista Records, to the list of men in high places who gave Franklin's career a boost but this time in the pop milieu. Franklin yet again proved in the 1980s that she could transcend the standard she had established for herself, probably because that standard was based on diversity to begin with.

As if to send a message that she was seeking even wider audiences for her work, Franklin started off the decade by appearing alongside other great artists such as John Lee Hooker in the blues comedy film *The Blues Brothers*. In this cult hit starring Dan Akroyd and John Belushi, Franklin performed another one of her blockbusters, "Think," and her appearance in the film was well-regarded.

Her first release for Arista, 1980's self-titled *Aretha*, was filled with samples from the pop music canon, including mediocre covers of the Doobie Brothers "What a Fool Believes" and a disco take on Otis Redding's classic "I Can't Turn You Loose," which garnered her a Grammy nomination. During its most promising moments, though, Franklin's preeminence as a singer is reestablished, especially on "United Together" and "Come to Me." Produced by Chuck Jackson, the record also features a number of songs she wrote or co-wrote. It went to number six on the black albums chart and forty-seven on the pop albums chart. *Love All the Hurt Away* followed in 1981, with more covers such as "It's My Turn," the Rolling Stones' "You Can't Always Get What You Want," and the title track, a duet with George Benson. Some critics thought these records were unimaginative and disappointing, but they show a woman in transition and trying things out with a new label. Still, she was charting, as the album hit number four on the black albums chart and thirty-six on the pop charts. The pop-chart position could not have been what Arista wanted from a superstar such as Franklin, but they had to be pleased when "Hold On! I'm Comin'" gave her a Grammy Award for Best Female R&B Vocal Performance in 1981.

After the relatively tepid label debut Franklin requested songwriter and producer Luther Vandross, who had worked with Diana Ross and Dionne Warwick, to produce 1982's *Jump to It*. The title track on *Jump To It* gave the forty-four-year-old Franklin her first number one hit in the 1980s (on the R&B singles chart; it hit twenty-four on pop singles and four on the club play singles). It also featured two compositions by Vandross: "Love Me Right," which barely missed the Top 20 R&B Singles chart at number twenty-two and "This is for Real." Writing in *Rolling Stone*, Vince Aletti said that "Vandross recaptured the spirit of Aretha's early work—its vibrancy, assurance and emotional impact—by keeping things simple (but quite sophisticated) and finding a common ground of instinct and inspiration" (Aletti 1985). The record peaked at number one on the R&B chart and twenty-three on the pop chart, which was a definite improvement.

Franklin remained productive, following *Jump to It* with 1983's *Get It Right*, which critics contend did not work overall, despite Vandross's involvement and its consistently high production values. Its top spot on the *Billboard* 200 was 126, even though it had peaked at number 4 on the black albums chart and 21 on the Top R&B/Hip-Hop Albums chart. Three singles, though, made the Top 10. Franklin and Vandross parted ways, and it wasn't until 1985's *Who's Zoomin' Who?*, produced by Narada Michael Walden, that once again Franklin was catapulted to superstar status. It features the rock-meets-soul duet "Sisters Are Doin' It For Themselves," with Annie Lennox, and "Freeway of Love," a lighthearted, upbeat soul-based pop song that hit number three on the pop chart. For fans and critics who knew her music for two decades, "Freeway of Love" felt somewhat hollow. Aletti wrote that it felt like "an overcalculated pop song that tries very hard for funky abandon and ends up with a lot more flash than feeling," but remarked that Franklin seemed to enjoy the ride, punching up the song's innuendoes (Aletti 1985). The song also earned her a Grammy Award for Best Female R&B Vocal Performance. *Who's Zoomin' Who?* offers some unexpected choices, with standouts including "Sweet Bitter Love," a twenty-year-old song she recorded first for Columbia that she produced for this version, and "Integrity," which revisits the themes of her chestnut "Respect." Even the title track plays on the ideas of fidelity and trust, with Franklin wisely coming out on top, entreating her love, with a dose of sass, to "take another look and tell me boy/Who's zoomin' who?" The song peaked at number two, and the track "Another Night" slipped into the Top 10 at number nine, which helped expose Franklin to a new generation of fans and signaled a comeback of sorts (see sidebar).

Franklin also had a large hit with the duet "I Knew You Were Waiting For Me," recorded with George Michael, which appeared on the 1986 *Aretha*—the second time she named an album after herself. The pairing was a good combination, as Michael started as one half of the soul-pop British group Wham! and eventually embarked on a very successful solo career. Keith Richards produced her other hit from this record, "Jumpin' Jack Flash," which

## The Comeback Artist

When Aretha Franklin switched labels from Atlantic to Arista in 1980, it marked the beginning of one of the most successful phases of her career. Franklin's reemergence signaled a comeback and suggested that female artists could find a new audience and remain culturally relevant later in their career.

Others have pulled off similar coups, such as Kylie Minogue. The Australian dance/pop singer had languished in relative obscurity with U.S. audiences, although she had been a star in Europe and Australia when her cover of "The Loco-Motion" became a hit in 1987. A number of subsequent albums struggled to connect as well, and she signed with Parlophone, which released the enormously successful single "Can't Get You Out of My Head" in 2001. Minogue won a Grammy in 2004 for Best Dance Recording for *Body Language* at the age of thirty-six.

Mariah Carey's five-octave voice earned her millions of record sales through the 1990s, leading to an $80 million contract with Virgin Records in 2001. But the decade was unkind to her, marked by dismal sales, public episodes of psychological instability, and a poorly received film appearance, *Glitter*. The album soundtrack, her first for Virgin, sold only 2 million copies worldwide compared to the 20 million worldwide of 1993's *Music Box*. Carey established her own imprint, MonarC Music, at Island/DefJam, which released her disappointing 2002 *Charmbracelet*. After a three-year hiatus, 2005's *The Emancipation of Mimi* hit the charts and sold 6 million; Carey was thirty-five.

Janet Jackson struggles to achieve a true comeback after scoring multiplatinum albums starting from 1984's *Control* through an alleged wardrobe malfunction at the 2004 Super Bowl halftime performance that inadvertently exposed her breast to millions of television viewers. *Damita Jo* was released two months later and only sold 2 million copies worldwide.

appeared in the Whoopi Goldberg film of the same name. The album won her a 1987 Grammy for Best Female R&B Vocal Performance, as well as another for Best R&B Performance by a Duo or Group with Vocal for her song with Michael. Her other noteworthy release in the 1980s was her return to gospel with 1987's *One Lord, One Faith, One Baptism*. The record featured appearances by Reverend Jesse Jackson; her brother, Reverend C.L. Franklin; Mavis Staples; and sisters Carolyn and Erma. *One Lord* became a number one–selling gospel album and even appeared on the R&B album chart at twenty-five.

The decade, though, like the ones before it, was not easy for her on a personal level. She and Glynn Turman eventually divorced, and her father finally passed away that year. Shortly before her father's death, she had a negative experience in a small plane that contributed to a fear of flying. In later years,

*She's the voice of old America. Aretha is the blues, is gospel, is down-home, is fried chicken, is chitlins. Aretha is, put your feet up under the table. Aretha is, don't worry about it baby, it'll be alright.*
—poet Nikki Giovanni

fear forced her later to limit touring (she went by bus) and record in Detroit. Her sister Carolyn and brother Cecil also passed away from long bouts with breast cancer and lung cancer, respectively, within eight months of each other in 1988.

## MISSION, MOTIVATION, PROCESS

Critics have had somewhat of a difficult time accurately describing Franklin's talent as a singer. It is almost cliché to say she is passionate and pours her soul into her performances but harder still to pinpoint what about it makes the talent uniquely hers. Additionally, it is inaccurate to simply consider any of the powerful lyrics to songs she made famous without discussing the inflection and strength her voice brings to them. Jerry Wexler had some insight about what makes a great singer; "There are three qualities that make a great singer—head, heart and throat. The head is the intelligence, the phrasing. The heart is the emotionality that feeds the flames. The throat is the chops, the voice. Ray Charles certainly has the first two. Aretha, though, like Sam Cooke, has all three qualities" (Dobkin 2004, 2). Franklin views her singing, regardless of whether she's just come off a performance that was lackluster or whether she has given it her all, as a personal offering. British journalist David Nathan, who has written extensively about Franklin, remarked, "Aretha's phrasing was unlike anyone else's; she fused the emotion of the church with a touch of jazz and added a heavy dose of the blues. The result made her a lasting original" (Nathan 1999, 71).

Franklin's recording career and performing career work hand-in-hand in terms of their inconsistencies. Sometimes Franklin could be spot-on and right in the moment; other times, her performances in concerts seemed disinterested and distracted. But after years of singing mostly jazz for Columbia, *I Never Loved a Man the Way I Love You* represented a pivotal point in Franklin's career. Even though the title track itself took off before the rest of the album was even recorded, that record also included such would-be classics as "Soul Serenade," "Dr. Feelgood," "Do Right Woman—Do Right Man," and the song that worldwide is synonymous with her name almost more than any other, "Respect." The record worked, too, because she does what she does best—sing unrestrained and play the piano. She was closely involved in the recording process, and she had finally found in the Fame Studio band a group of musicians with whom she could really gel. It is a sad irony that the title song tells the story of a woman who is in love with a dishonest, emotionally destructive man; several people have theorized that the song is about her relationship with White, even though Ronnie Shannon (one of White's clients) wrote it, not Franklin.

Additionally, the record is noteworthy because it is the mark of a woman who, not even thirty, had given birth to two children and was in the midst of a difficult marriage. Franklin sings with experience and maturity. It is primarily an album about female sexual desire, something that was previously just the territory of blues artists such as Bessie Smith and Billie Holiday. Franklin took the yearning of gospel, married it to the emotional impetus behind blues, and turned it into genre of her own. Comparing her to other artists, including Diana Ross, Franklin distinguishes herself. "[N]o female singer had yet emerged as a bona fide recording artist, directing the action in the studio, producing cohesive, album-length works, until Aretha Franklin showed the world that forty-one minutes (eleven tracks) of church-influenced soul music could be considered a thematically consistent and lasting work of passion and craftsmanship" (Dobkin 2004, 13–14). Wexler described her during the recording process as searching for herself and thus recording songs that reflected her life, because she kept a hand in selecting them or writing them herself. She had a sense of what she wanted to accomplish, particularly with her version of "Respect," which Wexler said she worked out at home, before coming into the studio. He also attested to how easy it was to work with her in the studio. "With Aretha it always went like cream. If I had something to say that she didn't agree with, we worked it out. There was never an impasse or any ridicule or abrasiveness. She had superb musicality, this gift—so unsophisticated, like a natural child, a natural woman" (Bego 2001, 91).

> *She has her own harmonic concept, where she can go from blues to gospel. She has a very interesting way of melding, mixing up blues chords and gospel chords, which throws the musicians off, until they get to learn the progression. It's almost like Billie Holiday or Frank Sinatra—you can't keep their time.*
>
> —Jerry Wexler

Wexler's guiding hand and musical acumen cannot to be underestimated. In a retrospective article in *Rolling Stone*, he wrote about his strong belief in letting a singer play his or her instrument of choice, even if their skills are not superlative, because it is about "bringing another element to the recording that is uniquely themselves. In Aretha's case, there was no compromise in quality" (Wexler 2004). Franklin asserted in her autobiography, "Look over the selections . . . and you see that soul was the key. There was no compromising, no deliberate decision to go pop. As it turned out, these records crossed over and sold on the charts. But we weren't trying to manipulate or execute any marketing plan. We were simply trying to compose real music from my heart" (Franklin and Ritz 1999, 111). Luckily, the public was receptive to her singular stew of gospel, jazz, blues, and soul. *Rolling Stone* magazine called *I Never Loved a Man the Way I Love You* one of the forty essential albums of 1967. The song of the same title is remarkable because it represents what Franklin is so good at—it is direct and personal but at the same time, the "you" in question is somewhat ambiguous. Is the "you" another man? Is it God? Is it her father? The question is never answered, but the song is alternately propelled and then grounded by the Wurlitzer piano and Franklin's voice.

Franklin, though, is a skilled songwriter, a fact that has been often overlooked because she is such a strong interpretive singer. In her autobiography she remembered the genesis of two songs in particular, "Call Me" and "Day

Dreaming." Franklin was honest, albeit cryptic at times, about her temptations and liaisons with other men, often using pseudonyms such as Mr. Mystique. The ballad "Call Me" came after witnessing a poignant encounter between a man and a woman who were obviously in love. They had to part and told each other "I love you," but their gaze lingered. Franklin said, "Finally, the woman says, 'Call me, call me the moment you get there . . . the hour . . . the minute . . . the second. . . . Call me baby.' It was the story of me and Wolf" (Franklin and Ritz 1999, 133). The song, though, made for an emotionally draining recording session. Musician Jimmy Johnson said she was crying in the studio while recording the vocal. "The tears were splashing onto the music stand" (Dobkin 2004, 234).

It was not the first time Franklin wrote from the heart about romantic experiences. During her time with White she was entangled off and on with Dennis Edwards of the Temptations, but Wolf was secure enough to let her make her own decisions and sort out her feelings. After spending the evening with Edwards riding around in a limousine, Franklin was inspired to write "Day Dreaming," whose lyrics recall "Day dreaming and I'm thinking of you" and the emotionally treacherous declaration "I want to be what he wants when he wants it and whenever he needs it." Looking back on it in her autobiography, Franklin talks about how the lyrics reflect her naïveté. Nevertheless, the anecdotes she shares about her songwriting process do show that Franklin was writing from life experience.

## LEGACY AND OTHER INTERESTS

The music she has created in the 1990s and through the 2000s is best characterized as spotty and inconsistent, with a seven year-gap in between 1991's *What You See is What You Sweat* and her subsequent studio release *A Rose is Still A Rose* in 1998. It is fair to say that nothing can compare to the output of her creative zenith in the late 1960s and through the early to mid-1970s—even her successful work with Arista in the early to mid-1980s pales against the complexity, nuance, and range of those Atlantic years. Nevertheless, Franklin has had some hits lately. In 1998, singer Lauryn Hill, formerly of the hip-hop group the Fugees, wrote and produced the funky, contemporary-sounding title track to Franklin's album *A Rose is Still a Rose*. Franklin reflected on it, saying that it "speaks to women, stressing that self-esteem is not depending on anything else but you and service to others" and understanding that "the deepest validation comes from God" (Franklin and Ritz 1999, 246). The song became a number one dance hit, went to number five on the R&B chart and twenty-six on the *Billboard* Hot 100. Sean "Puffy" Combs, along with Narada Michael Walden and Jermaine Dupri, lent his hand at producing. The record topped out at number seven on the *Billboard* Top R&B/Hip-Hop Albums and hit thirty on the *Billboard* 200—no small feat for a woman in her late fifties.

Also in 1998, Franklin sang the Puccini aria "Nessun Dorma" as Luciano Pavarotti's replacement at the Grammy Awards, a performance that surprised crowds. She discussed a cookbook she has planned, *Switching in the Kitchen with Ree*, and her own production company under Crown Productions and World Class Records, which at one point had planned to make a film about the Reverend Jesse Jackson and a documentary about her father.

In early 2001, Franklin was feted by VH-1 in a live performance show called *Divas*. Younger artists such as Mary J. Blige and Jill Scott paid tribute to the Queen of Soul along with other diva-like singers such as Shania Twain, Celine Dion, and Mariah Carey. In September 2003 she released *So Damn Happy*, which found her pairing up with Blige for a couple of songs, with esteemed producer and songwriter Burt Bacharach. Additionally, the album featured "Everybody's Somebody's Fool," a contribution from Jimmy Jam and Terry Lewis, whose work in the 1980s with Janet Jackson made her a star. In an interview with the *New York Times*, Franklin was enthusiastic about the record, her first in five years, saying "some of it is hip-hop, some of it is traditional. It just works" (Weinraub 2003). Franklin even embarked on a limited tour in support of the album's release. In spring 2007, Franklin oversaw auditions for the musical based on her life, *Aretha: From these Roots*, expected to open in Detroit.

Franklin became an icon of African American success and female empowerment, partially due to the message of her music, her father's job, and her relatively middle-class upbringing, despite her teen pregnancies and deceased mother. The early 1960s were also a time of increasing politicization in American culture. Because her father was friends with Martin Luther King Jr. and Adam Clayton Powell, Franklin sang at fundraisers in support of the burgeoning civil rights movement. Like many artists, Franklin parlays her beliefs into causes that help others. Franklin has donated to many charities, including Jesse Jackson's Operation Breadbasket, the NAACP, Operation PUSH, UNICEF, and Easter Seals. She established the Aretha Franklin Scholarship Foundation, which awards scholarships to minority students in the Detroit area to help pay for college tuition.

Because she grew up knowing from an early age that she was talented, Franklin felt it was just a matter of time before she became a big star—it was not a question of "if," it was a question of "when." That ambition truly sets her apart. In the later part of her career she has been honored repeatedly; her historic penchant for performing in ornate evening gowns, along with her legendary status, has earned her the title of "diva," a moniker she happily embraces. Indeed, Franklin is a living legend whose work continues to inspire artists and find younger audiences. Without Aretha, the careers of scores of other female soul singers simply would not be possible—chronicling her legacy would inadvertently require a mentioning of every female artist from Tina Turner and Diana Ross to Jennifer Lopez to Beyoncé Knowles to Mariah Carey and Alicia Keys, Missy Elliott, and Mary J. Blige.

## SELECTED DISCOGRAPHY

*Aretha.* Columbia, 1961
*I Never Loved a Man The Way I Love You.* Atlantic, 1967
*Aretha Arrives.* Atlantic, 1967
*Lady Soul.* Atlantic, 1968
*Aretha Now.* Atlantic, 1968
*Soul '69.* Atlantic, 1969
*Aretha Franklin at the Filmore West.* Atlantic, 1971
*Aretha's Greatest Hits.* Atlantic, 1971
*Young, Gifted and Black.* Atlantic, 1972
*Amazing Grace.* Atlantic, 1972
*Jump to It.* Arista, 1982
*Who's Zoomin' Who?* Arista, 1985
*One Lord, One Faith, One Baptism.* Arista, 1987
*Queen of Soul: The Atlantic Recordings.* Rhino, 1992
*A Rose is Still a Rose.* Arista, 1998

## FURTHER READING

Aletti, Vince. "Who's Zoomin Who? Review." *Rolling Stone* 455 (August 29, 1985). Available online at www.rollingstone.com/artists/arethafranklin/albums/album/206141/review/5944690/whos_zoomin_who.
Bego, Mark. *The Queen of Soul: Aretha Franklin.* New York: DaCapo Press, 2001.
Booth, Stanley. "Soul 69. Review." *Rolling Stone* 28 (March 1, 1969).
Caulfield, Keith. "Aretha Franklin Has Most Top 10, No. 1, R&B Albums." *Billboard* (October 4, 2003).
Dobkin, Mark. *I Never Loved a Man the Way I Love You.* New York: St. Martin's Press, 2004.
Franklin, Aretha, and David Ritz. *Aretha Franklin: From These Roots.* New York: Villard, 1999.
Jackson, Buzzy. *A Bad Woman Feeling Good: Blues and the Women Who Sing Them.* New York: W.W. Norton, 2005.
Nathan, David. *The Soulful Divas: Personal Portraits of Over a Dozen Divine Divas, from Nina Simone, Aretha Franklin and Diana Ross to Patti LaBelle, Whitney Houston and Janet Jackson.* New York: Billboard Books, 1999.
Unterberger, Richie. "Aretha Franklin biography." *All Music Guide.* Available online at wm04.allmusic.com/cg/amg.dll?p=amg&token=ADFEAEE47817D849AA7E-20C79A3E52DBB57DF702FE5AFB86112F0456D3B82D4BBD0E4FE06BC2AB81B0E57CAB7BAFFF26E85B0FD9CAE75CFDDA764C40&sql=11:jifpxqe5ldke~T1.
Wexler, Jerry. "Aretha Franklin." *Rolling Stone* online (April 15, 2004). Available online at www.rollingstone.com/news/story/5940015/9_aretha_franklin.

Courtesy of Photofest

# Emmylou Harris

## OVERVIEW

Although she came into the music business in the late 1960s, roughly around the same time as many other female singers and songwriters who went on to sell more records and earn a higher level of international acclaim than she (most notably her friend Linda Ronstadt), few artists have made the kind of impact on country and roots music as Emmylou Harris. Throughout her career, Harris has been known as a seeker of songs, for her gift for phrasing, and her beautiful, crystalline voice. Perhaps because her work on the whole is subtle and smart, larger commercial success has eluded her. Despite the fact that these attributes have not made her a household word, Harris's accomplishments and her approach have influenced scores of other artists, earning her a coveted spot as a favorite artist among fellow musicians and songwriters, as well as music critics. Many other songwriters and singers revere her voice; most notably, she has been a collaborator with Gram Parsons and Neil Young. She started as a folk singer, but her country-rock work with Parsons sparked her curiosity, and her voice was noticed by Linda Ronstadt, who was instrumental in bringing Harris to the attention of the larger music community.

From album to album, sometimes released against the current of popular music's trends, Harris has followed the music that has interested her and, as the mark of a true artist, is not strictly guided or overwhelmingly concerned about album sales or whether a particular sound fit a particular genre; her integrity guided her, along with her terrific instincts. Harris is a trailblazer, and by the time her 2007 comprehensive retrospective album *Songbird: Rare Tracks and Forgotten Gems* was released, Harris became a genre unto herself, in a niche that she worked hard to carve out for herself, quietly and without excessive fanfare, over thirty years. Her approach to country music allowed many people to see beyond the stereotypes of the form, thus showing how inviting its history and its wealth of material could be to other artists who would then, in the 1990s, mine it for inspiration, stylistic cues, and songs to cover during live shows, as a signifier of their roots-music credibility.

Harris benefited early on by working in the early 1970s with her mentor, the pioneer of "cosmic American music" Gram Parsons. He opened her eyes to the possibilities of country and rock and inspired her own exploration of the hybrid genre through a series of excellent, critically acclaimed, and commercially successful albums, starting with 1975's *Pieces of the Sky* through the next decade. Her work as part of Trio with Ronstadt and Dolly Parton resulted in two albums and showed her gift for collaboration and harmony. She also has collaborated with numerous other artists from diverse genres of music, most recently a 2006 release with Mark Knopfler of Dire Straits, *All the Roadrunning*, which ended up on many critics' best-of lists.

Among critics and journalists, the word "crystalline" consistently surfaces as a description of her voice. In fact, Harris is continually sought out to sing backing vocals or duets on dozens of recordings with artists such as

Willie Nelson, Roy Orbison, Bonnie Raitt, Bob Dylan, David Bromberg, Guy Clark, Neil Young, Elvis Costello, Rodney Crowell, Trisha Yearwood, Patty Griffin, Roseanne Cash, Lyle Lovett, Bonnie Raitt, Garth Brooks, Vince Gill, and many others. Her trailblazing ways have helped the careers of Lucinda Williams, Gillian Welch, Alison Krauss, Neko Case, and other female artists who incorporate varying degrees of country, rock, folk, and bluegrass in their music, tinged with a sense of loss, melancholy, self-reflection—and varying degrees of Southern gothic—in their lyrics. Harris has lent her voice to backing vocals on albums by the now-defunct, all-female indie hip-hop band Luscious Jackson, as well as on *City Beach*, the solo album of one of the band's songwriters, Jill Cunniff. She has also co-written several songs with Cunniff, who appears as a guest performer on Harris's album *Red Dirt Girl*.

> *It's always great to get together with women, too; when you spend most of your life on a tour bus with men, it's really nice to have some girl talk and girl time.*
> —on the side benefits of working with Parton and Ronstadt

Whereas Harris has been a reliable and valued collaborator for many artists—her voice instantly lends an element of beauty and grace to a song—her own body of work also has been critically hailed; she seems incapable of releasing a bad album. Harris has earned twelve Grammy Awards and record sales of more than 15 million albums worldwide. She has been nominated for twenty-four Country Music Awards and won three. Harris's career had a serious jolt as a result of appearing on the soundtrack to the quirky 2000 Joel and Ethan Coen film *O Brother, Where Art Thou?* (see sidebar). Records that she released subsequent to appearing on the monstrously successful, award-winning soundtrack also saw a significant rise in sales, especially the earthy but lush *Red Dirt Girl*, which was released just a few months before the film, and 2003's *Stumble Into Grace*. Harris's longevity as a woman whose music transcends genres seems assured. Her tone has been described as immaculate, her phrasing gentle in *The New Rolling Stone Album Guide*, which may not sit well with purists of rock or country.

## EARLY YEARS

Harris was born the second of two children to a military family stationed in Birmingham, Alabama. Her father, Walter "Bucky" Rutland Harris was a Marine Corps pilot and her mother, Eugenia Murchison Harris, came from a family of farmers in Alabama. She spent much of her childhood moving around until the family moved to Woodbridge, Virginia, while she was a teenager. But when she was about ten years old, her father was fighting in the Korean War and was taken as a prisoner. After being held for over a year, her father returned, but the experience left a lasting impression on her. He was honored by the Marines for his efforts and passed away in 1993.

Harris learned the piano as a child and played saxophone in the high school marching band. Before she discovered folk music, she felt a kinship with Edith Piaf and Billie Holiday's work. She was attracted not only to their voices but also the drama and tragedy associated with their personal lives. As a teenager, she started to learn guitar after a cousin received one for Christmas in the early 1960s. Inspired by the work of Bob Dylan, Joan Baez, Judy Collins, and Pete Seeger, Harris asked for one too, and her grandfather gave her a Kay guitar, which she has kept. She also listened to country music, albeit some-what unintentionally—her older brother was a fan of it, and it was always on the radio. Because of her brother she heard Buck Owens, Kitty Wells, and bluegrass. She also credits artists like Hank Williams and the work of Ian and Sylvia as part of her influences.

In high school, she was a cheerleader and won beauty contests. She gradu-ated from high school as valedictorian. A serious student, Harris admitted that she did not really go out on dates in high school and eventually parted ways with her cheerleading set of friends. Harris yearned for something more bohemian or left-of-center. "You were either a homecoming queen or a real weirdo. I was a 16-year-old WASP wanting to quit school and become Woody Guthrie" (Brown 2004, 17). Harris won a theater/drama scholarship to the University of North Carolina at Greensboro as a result of winning the Miss Woodbridge beauty pageant in her hometown. There, she began to study music seriously, learning the songs of Bob Dylan and Joan Baez. She acquired a Gibson J-50 that was easier to play than her Kay. Her first paid performance took place in summer 1965 at a roots festival in Steele, Alabama. She was paid not in cash but with a platter full of ripe fruit. In college, she started lis-tening to Tom Rush, Robert Johnson, Son House, and other acoustic blues artists. She frequented a place called the Red Door, which featured live music. There, she met student Mike Williams with whom she formed a duo, but eventually they parted ways. Harris was feeling out of sorts and restless, and she was tired of doing the right thing and being good. With no interest in the social scene of partying and drinking and with a waning interest in the pos-sibilities of a drama career, Harris turned her attention to music.

Eventually, after a few semesters Harris quit school and decided to pursue music full time. She moved to New York to join its folk music scene, which was waning and changing to a psychedelic, more rock-oriented music. She stayed in New York and worked in the clubs in Greenwich Village, where she became a regular at Gerde's Folk City. Some of her similarly thoughtful folk musicians and songwriters from this period include Tom Slocum, David Brom-berg, Paul Siebel, and Jerry Jeff Walker. Harris was invited to perform a few songs for A&M Records, the label of the Flying Burrito Brothers, in 1968, but they didn't sign her.

In 1969 she married songwriter Tom Slocum, and by the next year released her debut LP called *Gliding Bird*—an apt description of her soaring, beautiful voice. It was described as a folk record, but one that bore the influence of Joni Mitchell. Harris wrote a few of the songs but also covered Bob Dylan's "I'll Be Your Baby Tonight," and, at the urging of her producer Ray Ellis, the Hal David/Burt Bacharach tune "I'll Never Fall in Love Again." Selecting a Hank Williams song and a Dylan tune showed that her instincts for material were good. Harris was admittedly green and has said she did not have a direction and did not receive sufficient guidance from her label; the album was recorded in a mere three days.

Her life, however, and her career quickly became more complicated. Jubilee Records, the label that released her album, went out of business not too long after its release, and Harris became pregnant with a daughter. During her pregnancy, her marriage began failing. After moving to Nashville, the pair divorced after about two years of marriage. Struggling to make ends meet while being a single mom, Harris worked in Nashville waiting tables and singing occasionally, but ultimately moved back to live with her parents, who had a farm near Washington, DC. Fewer than 2000 copies of the record were reportedly sold at the time, and until its reissue in 1980, it was extremely difficult to acquire. Harris has, for the most part, disowned it as part of her collection and has been disinclined to discuss it; she is equally taciturn when it comes to questions about her love life and her marriages, of which there have been three.

She worked during the day and at night, gradually, she started to perform again, finding a vibrant musical community, especially bluegrass, in the DC area. Her first foray was as part of a trio with guitarist Gerry Mule and bassist Tom Guidera. During one of their gigs at a club called Clyde's, some of the members of the country-rock group the Flying Burrito Brothers were in the audience. Parsons, who was the band's founder, had recently left the group, but Chris Hillman, its current leader and a former member of the Byrds, was taken with Harris's voice. She was singing "It Wasn't God Who Made Honky Tonk Angels." Reportedly, he considered asking her to join the Burrito Brothers but instead, he quit the group and joined Stephen Stills's group Manassas. In the meantime, he suggested to Parsons that he meet with Harris; he had been looking for a female singer for his solo work. They had trouble figuring out how to find Harris, but thanks to her babysitter, who was at a Flying Burrito Brothers concert and had given Parsons Harris's phone number, a connection was made. Parsons and Harris met—he and his wife came up to see her and her trio play, and they instantly hit it off. He joined her in the second set of material. He was especially taken with her ability to articulate the nuances of country singing, even though she had much to learn yet. Harris said on her official Web site that she has no idea what would have happened if Parsons hadn't come into her life. He introduced her to country music in a new way. She said she got into it "more by osmosis—I didn't really feel it in my heart. I didn't really understand it until I worked with Gram" (Skanse 1998).

## CAREER PATH

Her career started to take off once she started working with Parsons, who was starting at the time to really bring together country music. She sang harmony on his debut solo record *G.P.*, released in 1972. She then toured with his backup group, the Fallen Angels. In 1973, she worked with him on his stellar album *Grievous Angel*. Unfortunately, though, Parsons passed away a few weeks after the recording sessions for the album were complete. He died on September 19 of a drug- and alcohol-related overdose in a hotel room outside the Joshua Tree National Monument in California. Harris was bereft; at the time of his death, she had left California and gone back to DC, with the intention of moving to California with her daughter Hallie. Instead, Harris stayed in DC and regrouped with Tom Guidera to form the Angel Band. Don Schmitzerle, who worked at Warner Brothers, heard Harris on a Parsons record and sent an A&R rep, Mary Martin, to investigate. She called Brian Ahern, who had recently worked with Anne Murray and had helped her hit the pop charts. He met with Harris in Maryland where he recorded four sets of her and her band at the Red Fox Inn with a portable device. It was enough to pique his interest in producing her record; in fact, Ahern worked with her on her next ten records and soon after the release of *Pieces of the Sky* became her second husband.

Signed by Warner Brothers to the Reprise label, the band moved to Los Angeles to work on her major label debut, *Pieces of the Sky*, released in February 1975. The album's material comes from an array of covers from artists such as The Beatles and Merle Haggard. There was no great groundswell of response to the album's first single, the waltzy, weepy ballad "Too Far Gone," so Warner Brothers brought in promotional folks from the pop side of the label and an independent promoter, Wade Pepper, who had worked wonders with Anne Murray's "Snowbird." Consequently, in 1975, the album's second single "If I Could Only Win Your Love," a cover of a Louvin Brothers song, became her first top five hit. Nearly four years later, Warner Brothers re-released "Too Far Gone," which that time peaked at number thirteen on the country charts. *Pieces of the Sky* contained only one Harris composition, an ode to "fallen angel" Gram Parsons called "Boulder to Birmingham." Harris's version of the Beatles tune "For No One," was reimagined with a slower, more ponderous pacing; it feels more contemplative than the original. Harris showed a sign of whimsy, too: She sang "Queen of the Silver Dollar," a song by children's author and songwriter Shel Silverstein.

In the early part of Harris's career, she could not escape being mentioned by critics in nearly the same breath as Linda Ronstadt. Her *Pieces of the Sky* was compared to Linda Ronstadt's record *Heart Like a Wheel*, which also dabbled in country sounds. But more than Ronstadt's record, Harris's album looks back at country's "old warhorses," as they were called, and their voices are different. Harris's voice, although feminine like Ronstadt's, sounds more fragile; at times her reedy soprano sounds like glass that is about to break. Critics thought the more challenging the material became, the more moving Harris's performance became. Through the years, her voice would gradually morph into something richer, and occasionally rougher, but it would always possess that pure, unfettered quality.

> *If you live by the charts, you die by the charts.*

*Pieces of the Sky* marked Harris's first in a long line of either gold or platinum releases that would ensue through the rest of the 1970s. *Elite Hotel*, *Luxury Liner*, and *Quarter Moon in a Ten Cent Town* continued to showcase her talent and helped develop her reputation as a country-rock pioneer. Harris's second album, *Elite Hotel*, was released in 1976 and used the Hot Band as her backup group. The Hot Band boasted some musicians who had worked with Elvis Presley—James Burton and Glen D. Hardin—along with a songwriter, little known at the time, named Rodney Crowell, who also played rhythm guitar. *Elite Hotel* featured smart covers of Patsy Cline's "Sweet Dreams" and Buck Owens's "Together Again," both of which became number one country hits in the first year of the record's release. Here, too, Harris takes on Flying Burrito Brothers with "Sin City" and "Wheels" but Stephen Holden of *Rolling Stone* said, with a tone of disappointment, that she brought a "honeyed sadness" to those tunes, whereas the originals suggested "an ongoing personal battle with the cosmos" (Holden 1976). But such differences in interpretation inform the motivation of an interpretive singer—she leaves her own indelible emotional blueprint on the song. Overall, it is a consistently engaging album, with smart use of a backing band and smart material, including another Beatles cover, "Here, There and Everywhere."

In a review of *Elite Hotel*, Holden wrote that "Harris sings like a more ethereal and fragile Linda Ronstadt, her voice perpetually on the edge of tears" (Holden 1976). Although the comparison to Ronstadt is apt—the singers are friends and tread in similar circles and style—Harris's voice, while sweet like Ronstadt's, is slightly more reserved than the rich fullness of Ronstadt's. The difference between the two singers is more like comparing a weathered, aged whiskey to a full-bodied, rich, and deep red wine. Soon after, Harris released the Christmas song "Light of the Stable," which had vocals from Neil Young, Dolly Parton, and Linda Ronstadt. Harris sang on Young's and Ronstadt's albums frequently, songs such as "Star of Bethlehem" and "The Sweetest Gift," respectively.

She also sang on Dylan's album *Desire* and appeared in Martin Scorcese's documentary film of the Hot Band's final performance. In 1977, Harris released her third album, *Luxury Liner*, which became yet another number one country album and went to twenty-one on the pop album charts. Critically, it was well-regarded. *Rolling Stone* reviewer Peter Herbst said that *Luxury Liner* was her "apex; superbly chosen songs, hot picking, and a definitive representation of her plangent, romantic sensibility" (Herbst 1977). On the album she visits more material from the Louvin Brothers with a song called

"When I Stop Dreaming" and also has a selection from the Carter Family. Her interpretations of Townes Van Zandt's "Pancho and Lefty," about a pair of grifters, and Chuck Berry's "(You Can Never Tell) C'est La Vie," which was a number six country hit, continue to show a musicologist's gifted approach to unearthing smart material. The Parsons-penned title track, for example, was relatively unknown, appearing on an album by one of his early bands. Her backup band for *Luxury Liner* consists of Crowell, Ricky Skaggs, and Albert Lee. The album cover, too, is striking. It is a close-up of Harris, with the light hitting the side of her face and her long, dark hair framing her face beautifully.

Harris's fourth record, *Quarter Moon in a Ten Cent Town*, came out in 1978 and produced her third number one single, the spunky country barroom declaration, written by Delbert McClinton, "Two More Bottles of Wine." The album marks the first time she does not cover Parsons material and the first time she does not include any pop music covers, rendered country style. Instead, Harris returns to Parton's oeuvre with "To Daddy," which nabbed her a number three spot on the country charts, and takes on a couple of Crowell songs and two by Jesse Winchester, including "Defying Gravity" and "My Songbird." Greil Marcus, a rock critic with very particular taste and one who seems to sense the subtleties of an artist such as Harris, dismissed her singing as too tentative and unoriginal, and *Quarter Moon* as "a make-out album for the sensitive" (Marcus 1978). Regardless of Marcus's opinions, the record was a number three country hit and a number twenty-nine pop album hit, even though it did not yield any significant charting singles. After this record, Crowell left the group, and Ricky Skaggs stepped in to become his replacement as her singing partner. For Harris the addition of Skaggs just meant there were more possible influences to investigate and more possible directions to take her career. In a way, *Quarter Moon* can be interpreted as an album that shows the inklings of the more traditional material she would focus on in the near future.

Harris's 1979 album *Blue Kentucky Girl* shows a movement toward bluegrass and more traditional, unfettered country music, which reinforced the idea that at her heart she was defining herself as a country artist. "I'm considered a pop artist, but I don't really get played on pop stations. I've never had any pop hit singles. I consider myself a country artist, but country artists consider me pop," Harris said at the time (Brown 2004, 125). Harris took on Willie Nelson and the classic "Save the Last Dance for Me," as well as "Even Cowgirls Get the Blues," for which she received harmony assistance from Dolly Parton and Linda Ronstadt. *Rolling Stone* reviewed the album, which seemed to echo some of the sentiments Marcus expressed about her previous release, claiming that her approach was too measured; she was singing the songs, but somehow remained removed from their emotional content. Nevertheless, *Blue Kentucky Girl* nabbed another number one single for "Beneath Still Waters," a Grammy for Best Female Country Vocal Performance, and hit number three on the country chart and forty-three on the pop album chart. The Grammy Award actually helped propel the album sales, which had initially lagged for several months.

The next year's work, the 1980 album *Roses in the Snow*, continued to delve further into traditional music and was best described as an acoustic bluegrass album. Working with the multitalented Ricky Skaggs again, the record came together easily. Harris said that her label intimated that the record would seal the end of her career, so risky was the material. In 1980, she recorded a duet with Roy Orbison, "That Lovin' You Feelin' Again," which became a Top 10 hit, and one that sounds more like a soft-rock hit than a rootsy country tune. Nevertheless, the pair won a Grammy for Best Country Vocal Performance, Duo or Group. The record hit number two on the country charts and twenty-six on the pop album charts. She released *Light of the Stable* at the end of the year, which is a holiday collection. On the heels of that release, Harris stopped touring to raise her second daughter, Meghann. To hold over fans, the records *Cimarron* and *Evangeline* were released in 1981 and comprise mostly previously unreleased songs, duets, and outtakes from the Trio sessions with Dolly Parton and Linda Ronstadt. *Cimarron* became a number six *Billboard* country album and yielded two country singles, "If I Needed You" and "Born to Run"; *Evangeline* hit number five on the country album charts and twenty-two on the pop album charts.

*Look what she's accomplished: She freed country music from stereotypes and showed rockers that country music was okay.*

—Country Music Hall of Fame and Museum director Kyle Young

### The 1980s: Years of Transition

In the early 1980s, punk and new wave started to chip away at the music-buying audience, and country music was starting to develop a more slick, unabashedly pop-crossover sound, with Dolly Parton leading the way. After *Evangeline*'s release in 1981 Harris lost Skaggs to his solo career. He was replaced by Barry Tashian, who had been the front man for the rock band the Remains, popular in the 1960s. In 1982 drummer John Ware left the group. She and The Hot Band released a live album *Last Date*, named as an homage for its successful single "(Lost His Love) On Our Last Date," which set lyrics to Floyd Cramer's instrumental song. Harris's marriage to Ahern was starting to dissolve. Her final release with Ahern as producer was the 1983 release *White Shoes*. It was a surprising mix of material, even for the eclectic Harris, with covers of Donna Summer's disco hit "On the Radio" and Sandy Denny's "Old-Fashioned Waltz." The album peaked at twenty-two on the country charts and produced three separate charting country singles in "Drivin' Wheel," "In My Dreams," and "Pledging My Love." The latter two were number nine hits, and "In My Dreams" earned Harris a Grammy Award for Best Female Country Vocal Performance.

Harris moved to Nashville with her daughters and met up with Paul Kennerley, a singer/songwriter on whose album *The Legend of Jesse James* she had sung backup. The two worked together on her 1985 album, which was a commercial failure but of autobiographical importance. Called *The Ballad of Sally Rose*—Harris's alias/pseudonym—the concept album was inspired by Bruce Springsteen's *Nebraska*; other critics noted that it seemed to emulate the Willie Nelson album *The Red Headed Stranger*. Each song tells the story of a character, or persona, and each persona has characteristics that can be read as an embodiment of Harris herself: a young girl from a small town with expectations of a better life joins a band and falls in love with another musician who is ultimately killed. The series of songs are not strictly autobiographical but rather a fictionalization of some of her experiences. Dolly Parton and Linda Ronstadt make appearances. *The Ballad of Sally Rose* is useful when looking at her whole repertoire because it marks a strong songwriting effort even though it was not financially successful.

Despite the difficulty, the album did yield some happiness for her personal life, albeit inadvertently. As with her previous collaboration with Ahern, her work with Kennerley led to marriage—the pair wed shortly after they toured in support of *The Ballad of Sally Rose*. He suggested her next album put her voice as the centerpiece, and the album *Angel Band* was a quiet, introspective collection of country music gospel-spirituals, issued in 1987, which peaked at twenty-three on the country charts. *Angel Band* featured Carl Jackson, Vince Gill, and Emory Gordy and came on the heels of 1986's *Thirteen*, which fared even better on those charts, hitting number nine but staying off the radar of most pop audiences at 157 on the *Billboard* 200.

In 1987, the most eagerly anticipated project from Harris finally came to fruition: *Trio*, the collaboration among Harris, Linda Ronstadt, and Dolly Parton. Harris arguably had the lowest profile of the three in the eyes of the average record buyer, who would know Parton from country music and film and Ronstadt from her seeming unending appetite for good songs. But for these three gilded-voiced females, the project earned them all a certain cachet and plenty of critical accolades. Harris and Ronstadt, friends since the early 1970s, both loved the work of Parton and describe the first time the three sang together as "magical." The trio approach worked so well because they share a love of that mountain music sound. The record earned all three women a Grammy for Best Country Performance by Duo or Group with Vocal. Before the end of the decade, she released 1989's *Bluebird*, which is a somewhat uneven collection.

### Reaching a New Generation, Reinventing Herself Again

In 1990, Harris released *Brand New Dance*, which more than anything else shows her as an artist in transition; the material was good but not outstanding. Harris had left much of her previous sound behind, but she had not yet met with the artists and producers who would invigorate her career and give her new directions. With the group the Nash Ramblers, an acoustic bluegrass group, Harris released a live album in 1992 called *At the Ryman*, named for one of country music's well-known concert halls at the Grand Ole Opry. The album was recorded there and a television special aired that contained footage from performances and recording sessions. The record earned her a Grammy. After that release, she switched to Elektra Records. Her first release with them was called *Cowgirl's Prayer*, which *Rolling Stone* said "goes to the heart of her talents as an interpretive singer," showcasing covers of Leonard Cohen and Lucinda Williams (Coleman and Kemp 2004). In 1994, Warner Brothers released *Songs of the West*, a related collection of previously released work that is tied to ideas of the West—mythological, musical, or otherwise.

In the mid-1990s, rock musicians with progressive, prolific tendencies such as Old 97s, Wilco, Ryan Adams, and others were putting out records that bore country influences, and the mish-mash of folk, rock, and country came to be known as alt-country or Americana. Emmylou Harris's career received another jolt when she turned in another artistically intriguing direction with the release of her 1995 album *Wrecking Ball*. The moody, atmospheric sound can be attributed to production from Daniel Lanois, known for his work with U2 and Peter Gabriel. Her choice was important for a number of reasons. Harris admitted she was looking for a change in her musical direction and knew of Lanois's work with Bob Dylan. Of the process of working with Lanois, she said, "It was rejuvenating on a lot of different levels: he introduced me to more turbulent rhythms, yet in songs I was still very comfortable with. As a singer, it was very stimulating emotionally." *Wrecking Ball* was not likely to gain her continued airplay on country radio. Harris was not concerned. "[M]y attitude by then was: 'You think you're breaking up with me, but actually I'm breaking up with you'" (*Sunday Herald* 2006).

And what a smooth break-up *Wrecking Ball* became. Harris was at the point in her career where many other artists are content to survive on greatest hits releases and other less rigorous or creatively engaging work. Instead of resting on her laurels and forging a career as a guest vocalist for perpetuity, in *Wrecking Ball* she presented an adventurous work that embraced world rhythms and acoustic instruments. It also felt more singularly grounded in a folk/roots feel that softly pushed the boundaries of country music and rock music. The hand of Lanois can be felt in the prominent role of percussion, something that is emphasized especially in his work with U2, whose drummer, Larry Mullen Jr., plays on the album. The title track, penned by Neil Young, features his backing vocals. The combination of their voices, along with the lyrics in the chorus, is haunting: A request to meet at the wrecking ball is followed by "I'll wear something pretty and white/And we'll go dancing tonight." The song evokes the sense that the narrator is willingly walking into a difficult emotional situation—the idea of a wrecking ball is a powerful, pervasive metaphor for the album, which came on the heels of her split from Kennerley. Other standout covers on the record include a take on Jimi Hendrix's "May This

Be Love" and her takes on songs by Steve Earle ("Goodbye") and Bob Dylan ("Every Grain of Sand"). She also makes Lucinda Williams's "Sweet Old World" even more of a heartbreaker. In Harris's hands these works are re-envisioned, reworked, and turned into singular and haunting songs; the melodies remain intact, uncluttered for the most part, with a subtle, spellbinding effect.

The songs on *Wrecking Ball* are spare, raw portraits that are unflinching in their honesty, a balance of the earthy and the spiritual. *Wrecking Ball* could be the album Harris had been trying to make her entire recording career. It was a risky piece of work. Such compliments are not uncommon—many critics are given to superlatives when it comes to Harris's voice. Although *Wrecking Ball* was not a tremendous seller for Asylum, the label that released it—the album peaked at number ninety-four on the *Billboard* 200—she received a Grammy for Best Contemporary Folk Album. *Wrecking Ball* is important, also, because it marks the beginning of a territory Harris would begin to chart for the next ten years on her own solo works, many of which are marked by similarly haunting, atmospheric production coupled with her own equally haunting, piercing voice, palpable especially on 1999's *Red Dirt Girl* and 2003's *Stumble Into Grace*.

After *Wrecking Ball*, which also caught the attention of a new, younger generation of listeners, Harris participated in several collaborative works before releasing her next solo studio album. A reprise of her work with Parton and Ronstadt took place for *Trio II* in 1998, along with collaboration with Ronstadt on *Western Wall: The Tucson Sessions*, released in 1999. Both were received relatively well by critics and fared well on the country charts, hitting number six, and Internet charts, hitting number seven; it peaked at seventy-three on the *Billboard* 200. Warner Brothers released a three-disc retrospective compendium called *Portraits* in 1996, and two years later she worked on a record with Willie Nelson called *Teatro*. Additionally, a live album called *Spyboy* was released. The title refers to her band's name, but it directly references the jester who's charged with running ahead of the Mardi Gras parade. The rhythm section of her band on *Spyboy* comes from New Orleans, and *All Music Guide* described the project as awe-inspiring for its range of material and the live renderings, especially her takes on the Parsons track "Wheels," and the Parsons-inspired "Boulder to Birmingham."

After 1998's *Spyboy*, Harris took some time off to write the material for her next solo record and left her management and her label. *Red Dirt Girl*, released in fall 2000 on Nonesuch, is the first record to feature songs written almost entirely by Harris herself, although *The Ballad of Sally Rose* featured a majority of her own work. But *Red Dirt Girl*'s beauty and depth signaled yet another facet of her talent had been uncovered. After working for decades alongside skilled songwriters, it seemed like a natural progression to delve more deeply into songwriting herself. For an artist who took about two decades to put together an album of work that she herself had written, she certainly made a formidable impression, leaving many critics to wonder why she had waited so long to make such a compelling artistic statement. Her attempts were validated by both the music-buying public and the larger music business, for the record received a Grammy for Best Contemporary Folk Album, peaked at number five on the country album chart, three on Top Internet Albums, and fifty-four on the *Billboard* 200.

*Red Dirt Girl* featured some appearances from Guy Clark, Buddy and Julie Miller, Bruce Springsteen, Patty Scialfa, and Jill Cunniff in various forms—either as co-writers, backing musicians, backing vocalists, or some combination thereof. One of its few covers is her tense, understated take on Patty Griffin's "One Big Love." Harris charts diverse emotional territory, from sadness and melancholy on "Bang the Drum Slowly," an elegy for her father; the smart, resistant, "I Don't Wanna Talk About It Now"; or the autobiographical and reflective title track.

*Rolling Stone* described Harris on *Red Dirt Girl*: "Her ethereal voice, with its silken core and ragged edges, is the perfect delivery system for the tastefully chosen songs she has purveyed for three decades" and called the album "stiflingly exquisite" (Berger 2000). Each song is a set piece and tells its own story. After *Red Dirt Girl*, Harris seemed dedicated to following her songwriting muse, and took part in the Grammy-winning soundtrack to the film *O Brother Where Art Thou* (see sidebar), which also spawned a tour called Down From the Mountain; she also appears in the documentary film about the concert.

Lanois's protégé and producer Malcom Burn, who helped mix and who played several instruments on *Wrecking Ball*, takes pains to preserve the same kind of spacious, spare sonic territory developed on that record with her 2003 album *Stumble Into Grace*. The material here is beautifully treated; mature, wise, and insightful, it features a number of outstanding contributions from like-minded artists such as Gillian Welch, Jane Siberry, and Linda Ronstadt. The lilting and sweet "Little Bird" is the result of collaboration with Canadian folksingers Kate and Anna McGarrigle. Harris co-wrote, along with Jill Cunniff of Luscious Jackson, the song "Time in Babylon," whose rhythms and lyrics snake their way into your head and make you think. The song is a poetic indictment of consumerist, apathetic American life, likening it to Babylon, but ultimately, the narrator seeks redemption. Finally, thanks to an intact thirty-year friendship, Harris pairs up again with Ronstadt on an ode to one of country music's female icons, June Carter Cash, on "Strong Hand (Just One Miracle)." Harris pays tribute to her marriage to Johnny Cash, marveling, "And it's a miracle/How one soul finds another." Harris wrote or co-wrote all but one of the album's eleven tracks. The record is another strong effort from Harris in this vein. "I'm a little surprised I've been able to do two albums that way. I'm a card-carrying interpreter. It gives me a great deal of satisfaction, and I hope I'll be able to live in both worlds" (Devenish 2006). Throughout, the material and even the title, *Stumble Into Grace*, reflect an artist who is starting to really master her craft as a songwriter and one who is trying to get through her life, acknowledging its foibles, flaws, and missteps,

### *O Brother,* It's Bluegrass: A Soundtrack Spawns Record Sales

Throughout her career, Emmylou Harris has been sought out for her cool, steely voice by other musicians, often for collaborations across genres. However, bluegrass and roots music in general received a tremendous boost after the release of the film *O Brother, Where Art Thou?* in 2000, directed by Joel and Ethan Coen, and its subsequent soundtrack. The film is an interpretation of Homer's *Odyssey* set in Depression-era Mississippi. Put together by respected producer and musician T Bone Burnett, the music exposed country, bluegrass, gospel, folk, and blues to a whole new generation of listeners and had a ripple effect on the record sales of those artists involved. The film featured many bluegrass legends such as Ralph Stanley, Fairfield Four, and the Whites, and younger artists such as Gillian Welch and Alison Krauss, who along with Emmylou Harris sang a chilling a capella "Didn't Need Nobody But the Baby."

In addition to the Grammy Awards the *O Brother* soundtrack garnered, including the coveted Album of the Year, it boosted the career profile of Alison Krauss and Union Station, whose aptly titled 2001 release *New Favorite* was not only a critic's darling but a number one bluegrass album and number three country record and earned three Grammy Awards.

Harris's fall 2000 release *Red Dirt Girl* marked a significant upturn for her, earning a Grammy for Best Contemporary Folk Album, and it became her first record in the Top 10 since 1986's *Thirteen*. The positive acclaim helped pave the way for the 2003 *Stumble Into Grace*, which received accolades from the critics and peaked at number six on the country chart and a respectable fifty-eight on both the *Billboard* 200 and Top Internet Albums chart.

but still seeking peace and deeper meaning. Many critics could not help but remark on her vibrato; Farber said it had never sounded quite as regal. The title, too, is a bit ironic, considering how poised, groomed, and positively radiant the silver-haired Harris looks on the cover. The album reached number six on the country chart and peaked at fifty-eight on both the *Billboard* 200 and Top Internet Albums, an accomplishment for a record that is tough to classify and that comes from a woman who was approaching sixty. She received a Grammy nomination for Best Contemporary Folk Album.

Proving again her ability to choose (and be sought out by) compelling collaborators, and also to enrich many songs by adding her silken voice, the 2006 album with Mark Knopfler, *All the Roadrunning*, was an intriguing pairing. With his subdued, understated raspy drawl and her light but rich voice, the rootsy songs, mostly ballads and mid-tempo tunes that chronicle love and loss, suggest a lifetime of history, especially the touching, tense "This is Us." Over the course of several years, the songs were slowly put together—most of them duets and most of them written by Knopfler—with a richness and natural intimacy that prompted Farber to declare that their work together called to mind the duets between Johnny Cash and June Carter Cash or Tammy Wynette and George Jones. Arguably, Knopfler, who had been the lead singer and guitarist for the band Dire Straits in the 1980s and released a few solo albums, benefited from working with Harris. Farber wrote that Knopfler needed something to "liven up his increasingly drowsy guitar playing and somnambulant singing" (Farber 2006). Critics were somewhat surprised by the collaboration, but as Harris told it, when she and Knopfler sat down and started to get to know one another, they shared a folk background that was "very song-oriented. We like a lot of the same artists, we were both fans of each other, and our voices blended together very easily from the beginning" (*Sunday Herald* 2006).

In fall 2007, Rhino Records released an extremely comprehensive, seventy-eight-track four-CD package, and one DVD called *Songbird: Rare Tracks and Forgotten Gems*, which is a collection of rare tracks, previously unreleased songs, and noteworthy collaborations. The albums work in chronological order, offering selections from over the years on the first two discs. It shows off unissued outtakes such as "Softly and Tenderly" from the Trio II sessions; the song "In the Garden," which was recorded for the film *All the Pretty Horses* (it didn't make the cut); and three songs from the Gram Parsons tribute album she produced, *Return of the Grievous Angel*. Appearing for the first time is her favorite song of Parsons, "Angels Rejoiced." (Her last conversation with him was about that song.) Duets with Patty Griffin, Mark Knopfler, George Jones, and other artists are also included. The accompanying DVD includes nine videos and a duet of "Love Hurts" with yet another vocally unlikely collaborator, Elvis Costello. The song was recorded at the Grand Ole Opry in 2006.

## MISSION, MOTIVATION, PROCESS

Much of Harris's process, like that of any musician, comes from what she learns from others and what she allows herself to be open to discover. Much has been made, for example, of the influence of Gram Parsons on the direction of the early part of her career and of the collaborative nature of her work in general. But the work with Parsons was different from later work; it was the beginning of her career, and there was much to learn. "In singing with him I felt that he really honed my voice and my style, which until that point had basically consisted of me trying to copy Joan Baez and Judy Collins." She says that she learned a country style of "restrained approach and very, very delicate phrasing, which really does enable you to bring a lot of emotion to a song, without actually emoting as such," she said (*Sunday Herald* 2006).

When she was putting together her breakthrough album *Pieces of the Sky*, Parsons had passed away unexpectedly. But Harris continued her educational process, listening to Merle Haggard, George Jones, and Tammy Wynette. She would jot down ideas and songs and lyrics in her notebook. As *Pieces of the Sky* producer, Ahern appreciated Harris's depth and that she was "more interested in important compositions." That led him to the material of songwriter Rodney Crowell, whose song "Bluebird Wine" leads off the album. Her voice startles for its clarity and its upper-register fluidity; in contrast to her later years, Harris's voice is almost girlish on this album, resembling Dolly Parton's. In fact, Harris even covers Parton's signature autobiographical tune "Coat of Many Colors."

While assembling the musicians, they chose many who were not country musicians per se but excellent players nonetheless; some had even worked with Parsons. Harris and Ahern stressed to them that they were looking to do something innovative, so the musicians should not worry about what category the songs would ultimately fit into. "We were trying to reinvent the music we loved, because what's the point of doing something exactly the way it was done earlier? If you are a song interpreter, you must come up with something different" (Clark 1975). And that is exactly what they did. They rented a large house in Beverly Hills, and Ahern transported his mobile studio from Toronto on a flatbed tractor trailer. Once they got started, it was Ahern's mission to record more than was essential for one album, so that there would be no pressure to include subpar material and also plenty to choose from for future projects. Harris's contributions were rich and seemingly unending. That curiosity is a testament to her continued success and why many artists continually cite her integrity.

One of the album's standout tracks happens to be one that Harris wrote with some assistance from Bill Danoff. "Boulder to Birmingham" was inspired by the notorious Topanga Canyon fires that were raging at the time, consuming the landscape and offering their own palette of color and smoke, but also by the death of Parsons. "When you are very raw and in the throes of deep grief, there's an unreality of being in the world when someone that used to be with you is suddenly no longer there. I think the combination of those things is what got the song started," Harris said (Clark 1975). Some of the lyrics relate that landscape, and other parts talk about what the narrator would do "[i]f I thought I could see/I could see your face." Another verse is chilling and seems directed to Parsons's death. Harris sings, "Well you really got me this time/And the hardest part is knowing I'll survive."

Harris continued to write songs as she got older, and her work in the past ten years consists more of her own material than covers of other artists. For most of her adult life she has worked as a musician, other than short stints waiting tables in the early days. Life certainly informs her songwriting. In 2006, she told a writer for the *Daily Post*, a Liverpool, U.K., publication, "Everything that happens to you affects you in some way, it's there in the memory and becomes part of everything. But I don't really write songs about characters, although I suppose there was Lillian [from her song "Red Dirt

Girl"], but that was a composite of people I knew. For the most part, I usually just write about myself" (Key 2006). As for her guitar chops, Harris claimed in this same interview that she only knows four or five chords, but the veracity of this statement feels suspect, especially considering how quickly other musicians attest to her unsung skills on the guitar.

*I look at my voice and my abilities as a gift. I don't feel that I can even take any credit for it, but it's such a huge presence in my life.*

In the studio, Harris is content to let the experts do the producing and mixing, but she is more inclined to keep things organic. "I do prefer to record live with everyone in the room, but it's often nice to just put something down with a beat box or bass or something" (Key 2006). Throughout the process, though, she remains an unparalleled collaborator, suggesting perhaps that something has guided her and protected her. "I do believe like souls attract like souls. I was fortunate in that I had this creative safety net, people who trusted my instincts and supported me," Harris said, looking back on her career (Gleason 2007). She feels similarly about the instant kinship she must feel with a song before she will sing it. "I think they find you, somehow. It's been a very serendipitous thing. . . . I don't waste my time with songs that don't absolutely floor me. . . . I think you have to create a magnetic field, in a sense, that draws the songs that shimmer for you. But I'm always looking" (Brown 2004, 11).

## LEGACY AND OTHER INTERESTS

One of the causes that Harris has championed through her career deals with Vietnam veterans' affairs. In 1997, Harris visited Cambodia and Vietnam with Bobby Muller, the president of the Vietnam Veterans of America Foundation; he is also the cofounder of the International Campaign to Ban Landmines. The visit inspired her to do something to affect change, and she has fought for landmine eradication. Along with like-minded artists such as Steve Earle, John Prine, and Nanci Griffith, Harris participated in a benefit album called *Concerts for a Landmine Free World*, which was released in spring 2001. The album comprises live performances from these artists and others, including Kris Kristofferson and Mary Chapin Carpenter. The concerts took place in December 1999 and were initiated by Harris, who contributes the album's first track, "The Pearl." Her work was nationally recognized by the Vietnam Veterans of America Foundation when, on behalf of the organization, Senator Patrick J. Leahy presented Harris with a humanitarian award named after him on behalf of landmine victims. At the ceremony, Harris was honored by her artist friends, many of whom had appeared at these benefit concerts, and she performed as well. Harris expressed her gratitude for a career that enabled her to illuminate causes and issues that concern her. "I'm so, so grateful for the opportunity to be able to do that. Because that's the

*As both a truly venturesome, genre-transcending visionary and a provocative guardian of country music's living heritage, Emmylou Harris has uncompromisingly advanced the cause of roots music in our nation and its artistic and cultural resonance around the world.*

—Timothy White, editor of *Billboard* magazine

only way I know to be really thankful for my blessings" (Margolis 2002). In 2004, she served as the narrator for a U.S. Department of State–supported documentary calling attention to the issue called *First Steps: The International Response to the Global Landmine Crisis,* which was aired on PBS.

An animal lover who owns numerous cats and dogs, Harris is also an advocate for animal rescue efforts and fundraising, including support for PETA programs. Since 2002, Harris has run a dog rescue and adoption organization called Bonaparte's Retreat, which is based in her home community of Nashville, where she has lived for more than twenty years. She started the shelter in her backyard in memory of her own poodle-mix dog, who spent much time with her touring on the road and lived to the age of fifteen. After Hurricane Katrina hit New Orleans in fall 2005, many animals, too, were displaced. Harris made a donation to and worked with the Humane Society of the United States for relief efforts in that area, which helped about 10,000 animals. Harris adopted a Katrina dog, Keeta, who travels with her. "Animals can teach us how to be better human beings. They certainly taught me that" (Humane Society of the United States official Web site). Harris organized a benefit concert for the Nashville Humane Association, which was held in the city's Ryman Auditorium and has performed at other events for Tony La Russa's Animal Rescue Foundation.

Harris gives to her community in other ways as well. In 2002, she organized a benefit concert to help with repairs of Holy Trinity Episcopal Church, a Gothic revival structure in Nashville that also happens to be the church her mother attends. She has also donated time and energy to Nashville's Second Harvest Food Bank. Since 2002, budding guitarists who idolize Harris have been able to purchase a Gibson that the company named in her honor. The L-200 Emmylou Harris Model is styled after the SJ-200 she had been playing for most of her career and is a smaller instrument that travels easily.

Her impact on other female artists is seemingly infinite. Harris, in short, is a genre unto herself, and her ability to seamlessly blend and embody many genres in one career and one voice is a model for other artists who have been inspired by her. Artists from Sheryl Crow to Lucinda Williams borrow her twang, her sorrow, and her ability to fuse country and rock. Bluegrass purists with beautiful voices such as Gillian Welch and Alison Krauss benefit from Harris's trailblazing ways, too. And younger, independent-minded artists with country twang but more rock/pop-oriented tendencies such as Garrison Starr, Kasey Chambers, Alison Moorer, Neko Case, and Jolie Holland owe much to her style, too. She is credited, alongside artists such as Steve Earle and Lucinda Williams, as embodying a genre loosely called Americana, whose lineage can be traced back to Johnny Cash, a legendary talent who combined elements of rock, folk, and country, and even to Parsons himself, who called his sound "cosmic American music." Rodney Crowell is absolute in his declaration of her influence, saying that "every woman artist now in this business has in some way been influenced by Emmylou and her dignity of spirit" (Brown 2004, 10).

## SELECTED DISCOGRAPHY

*Pieces of the Sky*. Reprise, 1975
*Elite Hotel*. Reprise, 1976
*Luxury Liner*. Reprise, 1977
*Quarter Moon in a Ten Cent Town*. Reprise, 1978
*Blue Kentucky Girl*. Reprise, 1979
*Roses in the Snow*. Reprise, 1980
*The Ballad of Sally Rose*. Reprise, 1985
*At the Ryman*. Reprise, 1992
*Wrecking Ball*. Elektra, 1995
*Spyboy*. Eminent, 1998
*Red Dirt Girl*. Elektra, 2000
*Stumble Into Grace*. Nonesuch, 2003.
*The Very Best of Emmylou Harris: Heartaches and Highways*. Rhino, 2005
*Songbird: Rare Tracks and Forgotten Gems*. Rhino, 2007

## FURTHER READING

Ankeny, Jason. "Review of Gliding Bird." *All Music Guide*. Available online at www
    .allmusic.com/cg/amg.dll?p=amg&sql=10:kjfrxqq5ldae.
Berger, Arion. "Review of Red Dirt Girl." *Rolling Stone* 850 (September 28, 2000).
    www.rollingstone.com/artists/emmylouharris/albums/album/119307/review/
    5947007/red_dirt_girl.
Brown, Jim. *Emmylou Harris: Angel in Disguise*. Kingston, Ontario: Fox Music
    Books, 2004.
Clark, Rick. *Pieces of the Sky* liner notes. Nashville: Warner Brothers, 1975.
Coleman, Mark, and Mark Kemp. *The New Rolling Stone Album Guide*. New York:
    Simon & Schuster, 2004. Available online at www.rollingstone.com/artists/
    emmylouharris/biography.
Devenish, Colin. "Emmylou Finds 'Grace': New Album Honors Carter, Cash, Features
    Old Friends." *Rolling Stone* online (September 16, 2003). Available at www
    .rollingstone.com/artists/emmylouharris/articles/story5935869/emmylou_finds_
    grace.
Farber, Jim. "It's a Three-For-All! It's a Key Day for Record Releases." *New York
    Daily News* (April 25, 2006).
Flippo, Chet. "Emmylou Harris is Century Honoree: Country Artist to Receive Bill-
    board's Highest Honor." *Billboard* (May 8, 1999).

Gibson Guitars official Web site. "Gibson, Emmylou Harris Introduce L-200 Travel/ Performance Guitar." Available online at www.gibson.com/whatsnew/pressrelease/ 2002/jan8a.html.

Gleason, Holly. "A Soulful Survivor Takes Stock: Emmylou Harris Begins a Year's Hiatus as She Reflects on the People and Places that were Part and Parcel of her New Multidisc Retrospective." *Los Angeles Times* (September 16, 2007).

Harris, Emmylou. Official artist Web site. See www.emmylouharris.com.

Herbst, Peter. "Luxury Liner review." *Rolling Stone* 235 (March 24, 1977). Available online at www.rollingstone.com/artists/emmylouharris/albums/album/223808/ review/6067959/luxury_liner

Holden, Stephen. "Elite Hotel review." *Rolling Stone* 207 (February 26, 1976). Available online at www.rollingstone.com/artists/emmylouharris/albums//album/5165089/ review/6210136/elite_hotel.

Humane Society of the United States. "Emmylou Harris: A Beautiful Voice for Change." 2006. Available online at www.hsus.org/humane_living/memorial_and_ planned_gifts/hsus-special-friends/emmylou_harris_her_lifes.html.

Key, Philip. "Country Living: Emmylou Harris Talks to Philip Key about 35 Years in Music." *Liverpool Daily Post* (June 2, 2006).

Marcus, Greil. "Quarter Moon in a Ten Cent Town. Review." *Rolling Stone* 260 (March 9, 1978). Available online at www.rollingstone.com/artists/emmylouharris/ albums/album/114489/review/6212668/quarter_moon_in_a_ten_cent_town.

Margolis, Lynne. "Emmylou Honored in D.C." *Rolling Stone* online (November 13, 2002). Available at www.rollingstone.com/artists/emmylouharris/articles/story/ 5935661/emmylou_honored_in_dc.

Pendragon, Jana. "Spyboy Review." *All Music Guide*. Available online at wc06.allmusic .com/cg/amg.dll?p=amg&sql=10:hvfexqujldae.

Scoppa, Bud. "Pieces of the Sky. Review." *Rolling Stone* 184 (April 10, 1975).

Skanse, Richard. "Restless Angel: It's Taken A Year for Emmylou Harris to Catch Up to Her Vacation." *Rolling Stone* online (December 10, 1998). Available online at www.rollingstone.com/artists/emmylouharris/articles/story/5922324/restless_ angel.

*The Sunday Herald*. "It Takes Two, Baby: A Skilled Solo Artist, Emmylou Harris Has Also Thrived When Working With Others." Glasgow, Scotland (July 30, 2006).

Courtesy of Photofest

# Debbie Harry

*I was hugely influenced by
Debbie Harry when I started
out as a singer and songwriter.
I thought she was the coolest
chick in the universe.*

—Madonna

## OVERVIEW

As the lead singer of the post-punk band Blondie, Debbie Harry brought a trendsetting fashion sense and an energized yet cool, almost reserved, vocal approach to the group. Blondie was the most commercially viable band of the punk/new wave era that started during the late 1970s and into the early 1980s. The band articulated a smart and witty attitude with its lyrics, and its music was unafraid to dip into other styles and moods—rap, reggae, rock, and disco, to name a few. Despite its influential New York City punk pedigree, the group had an incredibly melodic sound that avoided pretense yet did not pander to the Top 40 sensibility of the day. Instead, Blondie did its own thing, and the band, along with Harry herself, became extraordinarily popular in the United States and the United Kingdom. As part of Blondie, Harry helped make the sound of punk palatable to the masses. Thirty years later, many songs such as "Rapture" and "The Tide Is High," often show up on television and film and receive mash-up treatment with other artists and remix treatment by deejays and producers.

Through her years with Blondie—a name that refers self-consciously to a persona Harry created and to her hair color as well—she and the band experienced an ebb and flow relationship with success. She and band mate/boyfriend Chris Stein wrote most of the material together, which became increasingly eclectic. At the height of the band's popularity, she released a solo album. Then, Stein became struck with a rare illness that threatened his life, and musical endeavors went on hiatus for a few years in the early 1980s. Harry began acting in films and releasing more albums on her own, to varying levels of critical and commercial acclaim. When Stein regained his strength later in the decade, the band reunited. The resulting tour and album were both tremendously successful and are a testament to the band's longevity, influence, and iconic status, in no small part due to Harry's personality and image as a steely, sexy blonde. Despite the fact that Harry appeared to be "pop's ultimate blow-up doll, she sniggered underneath, fooling middle America, nay the world, into thinking she was the fantasy, a shiny, modern Marilyn Monroe. Blondie, it seemed, were [sic] the ultimate Warholian mix of art and commerce" (O'Brien 2002, 139).

Deborah Harry became an icon in no small part because she purposefully played with the expectations and bleached-blonde images of Hollywood—her natural hair color is brown—by invoking the glamour and then taking control of it in a self-directed form of empowerment that suggests that she would readily objectify herself before she would allow others to do it to her. She intentionally courted attention, but on her own terms; Stein would send risqué pictures of Harry to magazines. As rock critic Evelyn McDonnell said, there are two ways of looking at her: "Deborah Harry brought a pin-up, starlet sensibility to rock and roll, or Deborah Harry brought a punk sensibility to the pin-up/starlet. Or both" (Che 2005, xv). But Harry has never simply reduced herself to a vapid object of desire; she represents a smart and sexy female star who is aware of herself. She plays with the expectations of her audience but also shows her audience that she too is a work in progress, the subject of her own creation. It is a posture that is not without irony, but she also shows audiences she can have a lot of fun, too.

*It's great to be back in the hot seat. It keeps your ass warm.*

Given Blondie's tremendous success as a group, it was inevitable that when Harry transitioned into a solo career and the band went on hiatus in 1982 she encountered tough criticism. Speaking strictly in terms of commercial sales, Harry was most successful with Blondie; most of her solo releases were not tremendous sellers, but *KooKoo* did hit gold status. *Rolling Stone*'s biography of her, written by Arion Berger, even went so far as to say that her "fake-tough-girl act on her solo records proves that Deborah Harry needs her ex-Blondie songwriting partner, Chris Stein, like a fish needs gills" (Berger 2004). When the band reunited for two albums and a tour in the late 1990s, the records sold well and the tour sold out. The group's successful reunion, too, proved that their music was still vital, even if the sound and the musical landscape had altered—their reconnection and its attendant album and touring helped expose them to a new generation of fans. Harry brought to Blondie's reunion another dimension to the band and her role in it.

To some extent, Harry's image overshadowed her own talent and the talent of her bandmates, and that stress took its toll. Years later, when the group reunited, she told rock critic Ann Powers, "What keeps me happy now is focusing on the music. I lost that focus at some point or another; all the attention pushed me away from it"(Powers 1999).

## EARLY YEARS

Harry was born in Miami in 1945 and was adopted and raised by Richard and Catherine Harry in the suburbs near Paterson, New Jersey. When she was an adult, she tried to find out some information about her biological parents, but her father had passed away and her mother did not want to speak with her. Much about her childhood is unknown, but biographer Cathay Che explains that for the most part it was happy. Harry had a sister named Martha, enjoyed singing, and seemed well adjusted, albeit somewhat shy and a bit introspective. In other words there was little about her upbringing that would foreshadow the kind of noncomformist streak that would later develop once she started taking music seriously. She and her mother did disagree about Harry's fashion sense; she wanted to put her sneakers on backwards and wear things that were more outrageous than the preppy look her mother envisioned for her. Although Harry hated going to school and did not like the pressure to perform, she was always curious and interested in her work.

Her relationship with music started with the radio, which she listened to all the time. She also sang in the church choir but did not have any vocal training while growing up. Harry was influenced by the diversity of music on the radio more than specific records or artists, as she never had much money to buy albums. That love of radio and the impact it made no doubt must have influenced the way the band created its own music; Harry never lost sense of what made a great song.

In 1965, Harry moved to New York City as soon as she graduated from college with the aspiration to become a painter. Her first foray into music in the late 1960s came as the singer with Wind in the Willows, a folk-based rock group formed in 1966 by former civil rights activist Paul Klein. Writer Robert Christgau, then working at *The Village Voice*, chronicled the story of the band, which helped catch the attention of manager Peter Leeds. The group recorded one self-titled album. Released by Capitol in 1968, it did not have much of an impact on listeners so a second one was never released. The group broke up in 1969, but the band's tongue-in-cheek, somewhat campy sensibility later surfaced in her work despite the lack of commercial or critical traction.

After the Willows broke up, Harry went through a rough period. Within about a year, she moved out of New York City, first to upstate New York, and then back to her parents' house in New Jersey where she kicked a drug habit she had developed. Harry worked a number of jobs while she explored her options. She also entered beauty school—a move that made sense in light of the evolution of her image once she started experimenting in rock bands. During her transitional years, before Blondie was formed, Harry worked as a Playboy bunny briefly at the Playboy Club, and worked as a waitress at the New York restaurant Max's Kansas City. That job put her in a prime spot—the punk rock scene of the 1970s.

During the early 1970s glam-punk was emerging as something of a backlash to the hippie folk music sensibility that had started to dominate the 1960s. Harry became part of a downtown New York City scene that played at the legendary punk rock club CBGB's, now closed, and included artists such as Patti Smith (who was working hard to create an image of poetic androgyny), Lou Reed, David Byrne, along with groups such as the Ramones and Television. Harry had incredible, crippling stage fright, but she eventually moved past it when Blondie was in its formative stages of performing at CBGB. She forced herself to confront it with the logic that you don't know whether or not you can do something unless you try. In 1973, she was playing in an all-female rock group called the Stilletos when she met Chris Stein, an artist who had graduated from the School of Visual Arts and whose connection to her soon became both artistic and romantic. She left the Stilettos and formed Angel and the Snake with Stein. By 1974 they had changed the group's name to Blondie and added Clem Burke on drums, Gary Valentine on bass, and Jimmy Destri on keyboards. The band's name did not stem from Harry's hair color per se, but rather from the term "Blondie" used by lascivious catcalling truck drivers who called out to her on the street.

Stein had the smart idea to photograph Harry for the underground magazine *Punk*, which was featuring the likes of Johnny Rotten, Patti Smith, and other punk artists who vied for its attention. In a centerfold, she appeared naked with a guitar and was referred to as "punkmate" of the month. The photograph was both cheeky and insider-ish—a self-conscious allusion to Harry's previous short stint as a Playboy bunny. Her appearances in the magazine caught the attention of people before the group had taken off; in fact, the photographs may have helped Blondie nab a recording contract. The group was getting other press in the New York scene, which also helped, even though many other emerging bands discounted them because the band's sound, enthusiasm, and lack of chops, seemed to relegate them to the pop category rather than any kind of artful participant in the punk scene. In the world of punk rock, ambition and enthusiasm were not revered attributes.

The group's first single, "X Offender," was produced independently by Richard Gottehrer and Marty Thau. Gottehrer was known for his work on a CBGB compilation and more significantly with the 1960s group the Crystals on their song "My Boyfriend's Back," and Thau had worked with the Ramones. Gottehrer and Thau sold Blondie's single to the label Private Stock. The song's topic was risqué—a sex offender—but the sound was enticing and melodic, complete with female backup vocals reminiscent of the 1960s. Despite the fact that the single didn't really connect with audiences even though it got radio airtime, Gottehrer persuaded the label to release the group's self-titled debut, *Blondie*, in December 1976. After cementing a cult following in New York, Blondie played in Los Angeles to sell-out crowds. There was not much of a scene in LA but the radio station KROQ had started to create a slow buzz about the group by playing its single. The group played a week with the Ramones and opened for Iggy Pop on his national tour in winter 1977, followed by their own United Kingdom concert debut.

The group had signed on with Private Stock without the benefit of a manager or legal representation. Private Stock told Blondie that the deal was decent and that they should simply sign the contract. Because they couldn't afford a lawyer or manager, they did. Luckily, that situation changed in 1977 when Peter Leeds signed on. He worked with the group for two years and wrested control of the band's deal with Private Stock from the company. In October 1977, Chrysalis Records bought out the group's contract and re-released their debut. By this point the band was in the hole at least a half a million dollars for production costs and tour expenses typically associated with such an arrangement and faced hard work and extensive touring to pay off the debt. Leeds was motivated to take the band to the next level of success and viewed Harry as the key to their image.

> *I made my own image, then I was trapped in it.*
> —in 1993, about "Blondie"

Writing in *Rolling Stone*, critic Ken Tucker described the debut album as "a playful exploration of Sixties pop interlarded with trendy nihilism. Everything is sung by Deborah Harry, a possessor of a bombshell zombie's voice that can sound dreamily seductive and woodenly Masonite within the same song" (Tucker 1977). Tucker's description captured Harry's appeal: Some of the album's content suggests a sci-fi or tabloidesque unbelievability, such as "Kung Fu Girls," "The Attack of the Giant Ants," and "Rip Her to Shreds," all of which are rendered in an oddly playful and energetic manner. Overall, the songs are irreverent and sexy, a balance of aggression and retreat, teasing and truth-telling. Unsurprisingly, such a left-of-center, unorthodox approach—a punk-leaning rock band with a sense of humor and a sense of darkness—did not nab them much airplay. Their aggressive pop, driven by an equally aggressive female singer, was unusual and new. Consequently, Blondie was subjected to an unofficial radio boycott.

Harry's intentional move to take control over image creation rather than leave it to her label, a man in power, or the media had its costs. Some listeners were confused and thought Harry's name was Blondie. Some missed the irony altogether. One promotional poster for the song "Rip Her to Shreds" played off the playful-yet-aggressive sex kitten image that Harry had cultured for herself, asking "Wouldn't You Like To Rip Her To Shreds?" Such reductive behavior in the marketplace took the attention away from the music and placed it strictly on superficial appearance. Still, Harry was purposeful. "I wanted to inject film-star glamour. And I didn't want to be portrayed as a victim" (O'Brien 2002, 141).

Before the release of the second album, Gary Valentine left the band. Chrysalis released *Blondie*'s follow-up, *Plastic Letters*, in early 1978, which was also produced by Richard Gottehrer. It, too, contained a number of songs whose titles suggested supermarket tabloid headlines, such as "Youth Nabbed as Sniper," "Bermuda Triangle Blues," and others. A review in *Rolling Stone* faulted the release by saying its trashiness was "too studied" and its mania "too high-pitched." Some music critics point to the album as a typical sophomore slump with uneven material, yet the release yielded the group's first charting hits. Their initial success came in the United Kingdom with the upbeat "Denis," a remake of Randy and the Rainbows 1963 hit "Denise." Blondie changed the gender, and Harry sings a verse in French. The song broke through on the UK chart, hitting number two in early 1978. It hit the Top 10 and propelled the album to the same spot. "Denis" was followed by "(I'm Always Touched By Your) Presence, Dear," which went into the Top 10 in the United Kingdom. Stateside, the record entered the *Billboard* 100, topping out at seventy-two on the pop albums chart.

## CAREER PATH

It was *Parallel Lines*, the group's third album released in September 1978, that exposed their music to a much larger audience and, most importantly, in their home country. Producer/songwriter Mike Chapman took the helm, and the band emerged less as a raw variation on punk and new wave than as a bona fide pop band. For instance, "Picture This," written by Stein, Harry, and Destri, hit the Top 40 and "Hanging on the Telephone" hit the Top 10—both on the UK charts. In the United States, "Hanging on the Telephone" was closer to straightforward smart pop than the usual snarky punk/new wave hybrid that attracted only the most underground of music listeners. Like the best of Blondie's hits on the album, it was a terse blast of well-produced pop music confection, clocking in around three minutes. Listeners could see past the ironic, sometimes silly B-movie imagery of its first couple of releases and embrace the band for its melodic pop music.

The record's success is most attributed to the smash "Heart of Glass," written by Harry and Stein, which became easily one of the band's most recognizable songs. With a subtle but unmistakable disco beat, the song is infectious, memorable, and danceable—qualities that helped it be the first Blondie song to make the number one slot in the United Kingdom and the United States. "Heart of Glass" was a respectable dance hit, and "Sunday Girl" hit number one in the United Kingdom. "One Way or Another," in which Harry adopts the persona of a snarling, sneaky stalker, determined to nab a love interest, starts off with the statement that the singer is going to find the listener and then "getcha getcha getcha getcha." "One Way or Another," with its signature guitar lick, was a Top 40 hit, going to the twenty-four spot. Harry wrote the song with bassist Nigel Harrison and released it as a single on the heels of "Heart of Glass." The record ultimately sold 20 million copies worldwide and peaked on the pop albums chart at number six. Even though the singles were blockbuster hits, the other, lesser-played tracks were equally strong, from the slightly dreamy "Fade Away and Radiate," to "Sunday Girl," an up-tempo love song with handclaps, to the imploring "Will Anything Happen?" The latter is narrated from the perspective of a backstage groupie, starstruck and hoping to get lucky. The song's questions "Will anything happen? Will I see you again?" evade easy answers: Is she talking about the rock star's impending fame or her smoldering passion for him? "Hanging on the Telephone" and "Will Anything Happen?" are noteworthy, too, because they were written by Jack Lee, who was not a member of the band.

The band's platinum-selling fourth album *Eat to the Beat* followed in 1979 and was also produced by Mike Chapman. The album is unapologetically pop driven, but remains engaging because of the band's adept musicianship and Harry's strong vocalization. She distinguishes herself among other female rock vocalists of the time because she actually sings rather than emote any tough but hurting, bluesy female personas that were popular then. "Dreaming," "Union City Blue," and "Atomic" were all sizable hits in the United States and the United Kingdom, and "Atomic," which manages to meld disco beats and surf rock riffs, hit number one in England. "Dreaming" especially uses electronic overdubbing and multitracking, which creates an echoing wash of

Harry's voice in pleasant conjunction with Clem Burke's fast-paced drumming that rises and breaks, almost like waves, as the simple guitar riff of the song's main melody floats above it.

Even though *Eat to the Beat* peaked at seventeen on the pop albums chart, William Ruhlmann of *All Music Guide* called it a "secondhand version of their breakthrough third album." Even if some critics thought the album was half-successful creatively speaking—Ruhlmann even went so far as to call it "corporate rock without the tangy flavor that had made *Parallel Lines* such ear candy"—*Eat to the Beat* was still a huge commercial success and feels more muscular, layered, and polished. The song "Victor," for example, predates the kind of dark sonic noise of Frank Black and the Pixies' underground, abstract punk-rock songs that would earn headlines in the late 1980s. But themes of Blondie's earlier records are also present in *Eat to the Beat*, though they take on different meanings in light of the group's fame. The cheeky "Die Young Stay Pretty" with its electronic-reggae lilt foreshadows a later hit ("The Tide is High"). It can be read as an indictment of the culture that ultimately enabled the group's fame and as a tongue-in-cheek comment on the way in which Harry willfully put herself up for scrutiny, albeit on her own terms.

The year 1979 was also significant because Leeds departed as the group's manager. In the Harry and Stein biography *Making Tracks: The Rise of Blondie*, they assert that Leeds often did not consult them before making decisions. For his part, Leeds does not dispute that but contends that he wanted something more for them than just playing at CBGB's and other small dives in New York (Che 2005, 46). Indisputable, however, is the fact that the group rose to stardom while he was their manager.

In the meantime, Harry collaborated with European disco producer Giorgio Moroder on the song that became one of the group's enormous hits, "Call Me," which was the theme to the coming-of-age 1980 film *American Gigolo*. The song, released in February of that same year, became the group's second U.S. chart hit and another number one pop smash. Later in the year, Blondie released *Autoamerican*. From the very first track, "Europa," it is clear that Blondie was looking for a different musical direction. It's a sonic experiment that starts off with film-score-worthy orchestration and gradually adds a moody guitar before devolving into a mess of distortion, electronic bleeps, and Harry performing some spoken-word piece about the ways in which the automobile has negatively impacted contemporary life. From that first track, which borders on artful noise, Blondie moves into the disco-pop of "Live It Up" and the loose cabaret throwback "Here's Looking at You." All this self-consciousness and willful genre-hopping would almost be too much to bear, until we get to "The Tide is High," followed by "Angels on the Balcony," and realize that the Blondie we know is alive and well.

*Autoamerican*'s sales were boosted not only by the group's strong fan base but also by the fact that Blondie kept a steady recording pace by releasing five albums in as many years. Its two gigantic hits—a sunny cover of the reggae tune "The Tide is High," which went to number one in the United Kingdom and the United States, and "Rapture" helped the album go platinum. "Rapture," a slinky tune with a cool, bass-heavy groove, marked another innovation when Harry experimented vocally, employing a technique that is a cross between spoken word and rap. This song marks an early pop embrace of rap, the burgeoning New York musical style. However, the record overall shows experiments in form, sound, and style that are not always consistent. By this point, many fans had declared that the group sold out, but the point is that Blondie had started off by consciously playing on preexisting genres and ideas. Somehow, the band lives comfortably in the contradictions that its fame and high profile have presented: Blondie is a band with its roots in an avant garde scene in New York that writes commercially palatable and memorable pop songs. *Autoamerican* peaked at number seven on the pop albums chart.

However, change was afoot, and fans and critics knew it, though details of Harry's first solo album were closely guarded before its debut. *KooKoo* was released in 1981 while Blondie was still technically together even though some of its members already were engaged in other musical endeavors. Harry told the *New York Times* that she and Stein, still her boyfriend and songwriting partner, wanted to "wait and see what everybody falls into," before releasing the album and admitted her interest in Broadway and film (Palmer 1981). Production help came from R&B gurus Nile Rodgers and Bernard Edwards, who had worked with Diana Ross and Chic. Some critics thought that because of the high caliber of players, the record's offerings should have been much better than they were, but other critics saw that Harry was trying to synthesize the styles Blondie had been playing with on its previous release. Some critics thought *KooKoo* was a successful exercise; the long-time connection between Harry and Stein is heard throughout.

The funky "Backfired" is reminiscent of "Rapture," with its dominant bass and horn section and speak-sing vocals. As the album's single, it surfaced on the dance, R&B, and pop charts, faring best on club play. Harry had a part in writing four of the album's eleven songs, "Jump Jump," "Inner City Spillover," "Chrome," and "Military Rap." Regardless of any perceived critical shortcomings or songwriting failures, the record hit number twenty-five on the pop albums chart and ultimately went gold.

In fall 1981, the group released *The Best of Blondie*, which was another success, achieving the number thirty spot on the pop albums chart. In spring 1982, the group released *The Hunter*, which was created to satisfy its contract with Chrysalis. The album was a flop in comparison to the band's earlier work. "Island of Lost Souls," something of a rehash of "The Tide is High," peaked at thirty-seven, barely making it into the *Billboard* pop singles chart, and was the only single from the album in the United States. Some critics believed the material was inferior and that the lyrics were disjointed and difficult to understand. With *The Hunter*, it seemed as though the band was running out of ideas. Even the arena tour it launched that summer was a disappointment: the

*New York Times* urged the group to basically regroup. The record went to thirty-three on the pop albums chart. Interpersonally, Blondie was suffering, too. Prior to the release of *The Hunter*, Infante sued the group, whom he felt was trying to purposely cut him out by excluding him from rehearsals, meetings, and recording sessions. The suit was settled out of court, and Infante remained in the group.

### Solo Work, Acting, and Other Endeavors

Blondie got some time off, but not necessarily for artistic reasons. Stein was suffering from the rare genetic disease called pemphigus, and Harry took time off to take care of him. His illness, from which he ultimately recovered, changed their lives, however. Harry would not release another solo record for nearly five years. They were both exhausted by the illness, and their romance did not make it. "I didn't know who I was anymore. I was really lost and very, very depressed. Chris was trying to recover, and I was trying to recover. There just wasn't room for two recoveries," Harry told *People* magazine (Helligar 1999). Periodically she appeared on record and in films, but many things happened in the landscape of pop music in the interim that also affected her solo career.

Wisely, even before Blondie officially went on hiatus, Harry started to turn toward other endeavors, a move that in hindsight looks as though she were laying the groundwork for other career possibilities. For the next ten years or so, her career took shape in the form of solo albums, acting stints, and even a foray with a jazz group. In 1980 she starred in a small role in the independent, pseudo–film noir *Union City*, reminiscent of the 1944 genre standard-bearer *Double Indemnity*. Chris Stein contributed music and Harry starred as Lillian, the wife of a man who is headed for a breakdown. She garnered favorable reviews for her performance, which enabled her to take the time to choose among acting offers. She started using her full name, Deborah Harry, rather than her nickname Debbie, for her acting work. Harry had auditioned for a part that actress Cathy Moriarty ultimately got in the Martin Scorcese film *Raging Bull*. In 1982, she appeared in a starring role as a radio talk show host in a film by David Cronenberg called *Videodrome*, followed by a role in the off-Broadway play *Teaneck Tanzi: The Venus Flytrap* in 1983. She took a memorable role as Velma Von Tussle in John Waters's campy 1988 film *Hairspray* and a bit part in the 1989 series of short films *New York Stories*, directed by Francis Ford Coppola, Woody Allen, and Martin Scorcese. She also appeared in three episodes of the crime drama show *Wiseguy* in 1989 as a struggling singer in New Jersey and on Showtime's *Body Bags* in 1993.

Harry's next solo release was *Rockbird*, in 1986, which was not a critical success in spite of her famous interpretive abilities on songs. As her first output since Stein regained his health, Harry co-wrote all but one of the songs. The catchy song "French Kissin'" was a mild hit on the radio, but the record barely made an impact, hitting ninety-seven at its peak on the *Billboard* 200. Like much of Blondie's music, Harry's song fared better in the United Kingdom, peaking at number eight. The arrival of Madonna on the pop music scene a couple of years earlier, who arguably took some fashion cues from Harry but shaped her music in a much more dance-oriented direction, diverted attention away from Harry. Harry felt that her label saw them as competition and perhaps did not know how to really distinguish them sufficiently enough to promote them distinctly. Ironically, Madonna's blonde bombshell image was made more palatable for intense commercial success by the experimentation Harry herself did in the early years of Blondie.

After her departure from Chrysalis, the label released *Once More Into the Bleach*, a collection of remixes of her own hits and Blondie classics. Her official third album, *Def, Dumb & Blonde*, came out in 1989 on Sire—fifteen innocuous, fun-loving tracks of Euro-styled dance music produced with Mike Chapman. The record only hit 123 on the *Billboard* 200. One notable track is the synthesizer-guitar rock of "I Want That Man," during which Harry proclaims "I wanna be the queen of the U.S.A. . . . What I really want I just can't buy." Again, the British were kind to her, and the song went to number thirteen on the UK charts. Harry snarls with sass and catcalls on "Bike Boy" and shout-raps in the guitar-heavy "Get Your Way." In both songs she is so convincing and true to her roots that it is easy to forget that she was forty-three.

In the 1990s, Harry appeared in the film *Heavy* (1995) and *Six Ways to Sunday* (1999). In the midst of all of this varied activity, she managed to release another album, *Debravation*, in 1993. The album contains a collection of eclectic songs that were written in conjunction with Chris Stein, such as "Stability," "Mood Ring," "Dancing Down the Moon," and "The Fugitive." On "Stability," Harry is still cool and wry; it is one of the album's few standout tracks. She collaborated with R.E.M. on "Tear Drops" and "My Last Date (With You)," and novelist William Gibson wrote lyrics for the industrial-sounding experimental song "Dog Star Girl." The record did not fare well and is thought to suffer from too many guest producers and contributors. Harry let her hair go back to her natural brown color and, at the age of forty-seven, was not as thin or glamorous as perhaps her fans were accustomed to. Still, her voice retains its signature nuances, even if on this album her interpretations suffer, and her charisma is still evident.

*Debravation* would be Harry's last solo record for fourteen years, but her music career took another intriguing turn in the mid-1990s, when she connected with the New York–based group the Jazz Passengers, a quasi–avant garde group that takes a postmodern look at jazz, standards, and original songs. Over the course of several years, she has sung on a few tracks of the group's records, including "Dog in Sand" on its 1994 release *In Love* and on *Individually Twisted* in 1997, which was billed as "The Jazz Passengers Featuring Deborah Harry." The album includes a reworked version of "The Tide is High" and Elvis Costello and Harry duet on "Doncha Go Way Mad."

*The comfort level with Blondie is great, but in most cases, the audience wants to hear the old music from us, rather than the future, and that is death for an artist. You have to keep moving forward.*
—on release of her 2007 album

## The Return and the "Curse" of an Aging Blondie

During their years apart, band members had taken part in other musical endeavors ranging from playing in other bands to producing. Although 40 million records had sold worldwide by the early 1980s, many of their profits were tangled up in legal tussles and tax problems, so perhaps a reunion was inevitable. In 1998, Blondie reunited and in 1999 released its first album in seventeen years, *No Exit*. The single "Maria" reached fourteen on the adult Top 40 chart, and appeared on the dance music chart at the top slot of number three. The single "No Exit," which features rapper Coolio, went to eighteen on the *Billboard* 200. Although the sales pale in comparison to the group's heyday, the release helped create a new generation of Blondie fans. The supporting tour was so successful, it inspired a live record, *Live in New York*, which was also released in 1999.

The title of 2004's *The Curse of Blondie* serves as a tongue-in-cheek reference to its own difficult history. The tour that was launched was a success, although the record barely slipped into the *Billboard* 200, never faring better than the 160 position. Some critics called it the first strong effort from the group since *Autoamerican*. The sharp, sexy "Good Boys," got great airplay on the Dance Music/Club Play chart (peaking at number seven), and disco guru Giorgio Moroder took a turn at mixing the single version. The fourteen tracks, produced by Steve Thompson, manage to sound both modern and classic Blondie. The band toured through 2003 and 2004, returning to the United Kingdom as well in 2005 for the fourth time in four years.

Harry continued to maintain her edgy downtown cachet. In 2000 she was cast in a New York premiere of *Cast*, a dark work by English playwright Sarah Kane, which featured the use of four voices as chamber pieces. Reviews pronounced Harry as well-suited to her part, by her ability to reveal a tension between depth and surface in her character. Several years later, along with other artists who emerged from the CBGB scene in the late 1970s, Harry appeared and performed at a few concerts and rallies designed to raise money and save the club from closing; owner Hilly Kristal had been involved in rent disputes. Despite the momentum and awareness that developed and the protests, the club's lease was not renewed by the Bowery Residents' Committee, and Kristal was forced to shutter it.

After a long recording absence Harry released *Necessary Evil* in 2007. In an interview on television with CNN, Harry said self-effacingly, "I really felt like I had to be creative, and get out of that lovely comfortable rut that I was in" (CNN, Showbiz Today 2007). Harry worked with New York producers Super Buddha and also with Stein as a collaborator even though their romance had long ago fizzled out. Harry also collaborated with Roy Nathanson, a musician she worked with in the Jazz Passengers, on "Dirty and Deep." The straightforward, fast-paced rock tune "Two Times Blue" peaked at number thirteen on the Hot Dance Music/Club Play and was her first chart hit in nearly fifteen years, since 1993's number two dance hit "I Can See Clearly." Harry's acting career continued to keep pace in 2007, with a role in the thriller *Anamorph* and a small role in the drama *Elegy* starring Penelope Cruz and Ben Kingsley based on Philip Roth's novel of the same name.

## MISSION, MOTIVATION, PROCESS

Harry and Stein have been songwriting partners since the formative stages of Blondie: She primarily contributes lyrics and he contributes the melody and music. "The method of writing a hit song is to f---ing die and then come alive again," Harry said in the beginning of *Making Tracks*, which she wrote with Chris Stein and photographer Victor Bockris—the latter of whom was the subject of the Blondie song "Victor" (Harry, Stein, and Bockris, Prologue, 1998) Although she was being a bit flip, the sentiment makes sense: It is important to experience as much as possible in life, and then turn it into something new and worth remembering in musical form.

Harry's purposeful exploitation of the Blondie image may have gotten more attention than her singing. Even though one aspect of Harry-as-Blondie was indeed image-driven, the music had to work for the group to have left such an impact on listeners. In 1999, reflecting on how she cobbled together her sound, Harry said that when she was in her early twenties, it was difficult to sing because she was "all bottled up." To combat that, she listened to all types of singers, but it was her work with the same group of people—the band—that helped her develop her style.

Part of the tension in the early days of Blondie came from manager Peter Leeds's belief that the band was nothing without Harry; he reportedly would threaten to replace many of the male players if they complained about the way things were being handled. But the group worked well together, and it was especially insulting to Stein and Harry, who, along with Burke and Infante, really formed the backbone of the band. The group worked best when it worked together, and to his credit, Leeds connected Blondie with producer Mike Chapman, who was responsible for the sound of its breakthrough record *Parallel Lines*. Harry admits that Chapman challenged the band and demanded a level of professionalism and rigor that was new for them in the studio. Under his tutelage, their arrangements became tighter, making them more commercially viable. At this point in the band's career, there were hits in the United Kingdom and Australia, and they had toured all over the world, but American radio hits eluded them. The charismatic Mike Chapman changed that with his skillful development of *Parallel Lines*.

When it came time for recording "Heart of Glass," they spent over three hours just getting the bass drum right. Putting together "Heart of Glass" was especially difficult, because although Harry and Stein had written it together in 1975, it was decidedly uncool at the time among their musical crowd to write a disco-funk song. Ironically, it was the album's U.S. third single—a move that seemed desperate after releasing two songs that charted better in the United Kingdom—but it wound up being a big hit.

When the record was released, it was imperative that the album sell well. The band was often kept in the dark or otherwise deceived, and this time they were told that they needed to break through in the United States to make any money on the album. Because Leeds handled every aspect of their business, they had no way to determine if he was manipulating them or not. Leeds's mishandling of the album's cover image was the final straw. He had wanted all of the men in the band to smile and for Harry to frown, an idea the band was not too keen on. He also wanted to photograph them in such a way that it looked as though they were fading in and out of these "parallel lines," a concept the group liked. It was decided that everyone would pick out the image he or she wanted, and the cover art would be spliced together accordingly. However, Leeds disregarded the selections of the group members and did what he initially wanted. Harry looks stern and the male group members are mostly smiling. The band was furious.

Throughout her career as a lyricist and singer, Blondie has put together some reportedly semi-autobiographical songs—"English Boys" and "War Child" from *The Hunter*, for example—and Harry admitted that "Sunday Girl" was written by Stein when she was out on the road meeting radio deejays before the release of *Parallel Lines* trying to promote the band. When it came time for her first solo album in over a decade, *Necessary Evil*, Harry found herself synthesizing her many years of experience as a band member and solo artist, characterized by dabbling with various musical genres. Harry was involved in nearly every aspect of the production, producing her own video for the album, choosing musicians and collaborators, and selecting the company to master the material. At age sixty-two, she's more than earned the right to take the reins. The record's material ranges from neo-noir torch material to pop-rock to 1960s girl group sounds to danceable beats and showcases her many talents and interests. She admits that she is not sure if compiling her various personas was a conscious choice. Like many songwriters, much of life and events around her are absorbed and influence her work. Overheard conversations, personal experience, items in the news all get turned into a new narrative, with a fresh approach and sound.

She was vocal about two songs in particular on *Necessary Evil*, "Love with a Vengeance" and "What is Love," as keys to understanding what the record is about. On her Web site, she explained that since the 1960s, we have lost the ability "to look at life with love." She hoped that bringing the concept of love into the conversation that her songs create would help people look at each other and the world with kindness.

In an interview near the release of *Necessary Evil*, Harry discussed her past with Blondie and how many artists half her age consider her an inspiration, from her trashcan punk rock fashion aesthetic to her good looks and her ironic cool stance. Harry demurred, though. "It's hard for me to think that Blondie was so completely original. I don't really think that I'm an icon. I think an icon is a statue, something that's frozen, you know. I don't feel like that" (Ryzik 2007).

## LEGACY AND OTHER INTERESTS

Harry was one of the first artists in the music industry to become involved in fundraising concerts for AIDS awareness and research. In 1987, billed as Tiger Bomb, she and Stein appeared alongside artists such as Phillip Glass, Laurie Anderson, and poet William S. Burroughs at a concert for the AIDS Treatment Project. Harry sang a duet with Iggy Pop on the *Red Hot + Blue: A Tribute to Cole Porter* album (1991), which benefited AIDS research. She with her cool voice and he with his gravely growl turned in a particularly campy but enjoyable rendition of "Well Did You Evah," which is one of the record's highlights. In 2006, the designer Marc Jacobs created a series of T-shirts to honor Blondie's induction into the Rock and Roll Hall of Fame. The T-shirts featured a silk-screened, Warhol-like image of Harry available in ten colors. Proceeds were donated to her charity of choice—Riverkeeper, an environmental organization whose mission is to protect the Hudson River and New York City watersheds. A wildly popular design, Marc Jacobs reprised the shirt in 2007, with proceeds donated to the Provincetown Art Association and Museum. Her image is currently used in a campaign by the cosmetics company MAC Viva Glam VI, which donates sales of the Viva Glam lipsticks to the MAC AIDS Fund, a worldwide resource for people living with HIV/AIDS. Harry also lends her support campaigning for gay rights and human rights, appearing alongside Cyndi Lauper in the True Colors Tour for the Human Rights Campaign in 2007.

The legacy of Blondie shows up in curious places, including the 2007 opening of the Rapture Café in downtown New York, named for the band's hit. Overall, its impact on the New York downtown music scene cannot be understated. The prologue to *Deborah Harry: Platinum Blonde* by biographer Cathay Che begins with the scene of an all-female rock tribute band performing Blondie covers in an anonymous New York basement club to a very engaged, enthusiastic crowd. Harry and Stein stand in the back of the room, curious. The musicians onstage include women from various rock, indie, punk, and other bands, all influenced by the assertive, strong presence of Debbie Harry herself. Kate Schellenbach, drummer for the influential but short-lived all-female band Luscious Jackson, which was popular in the 1990s, said that Blondie inspired her to frequent the seminal club CBGB as a teenager. There, she met her future bandmates, which changed her life. Schellenbach even played at a show in New York with Blondie in the late 1990s when regular drummer Clem Burke could not make it. Harry returned the favor and appeared on the band's album *Electric Honey*.

Many other artists have tackled Blondie's best hits. But perhaps the most unusual interpretation of "Heart of Glass," other than the one by Chet Atkins, comes from the postmodern jazz-rock trio The Bad Plus, whose thoughtful deconstruction of the song swings, slides, and pauses where the original consistently propels and pulsates. The trio resists the urge to indulge the song's signature melody line until nearly the very end, when drummer David King throws the song full-steam into the signature rhythm, crashing cymbals and all. It's a playful, intuitive, and surprising interpretation of a classic pop song.

From tribute bands to inspired covers to her influence on fashion (see sidebar), Debbie Harry's legacy proves that Blondie is more than just a band

### Punk Rock Fashion Icon

With an uncanny ability to turn unlikely items such as trashcan liners and zebra-print pillowcases into fashion statements, Deborah Harry established her status as an icon for the punk/new wave set during the 1980s. Her sense of style, culled from Europe, New York, and punk rock's do-it-yourself ethos certainly helped, along with her facility in taking charge of her image, a skill she honed while in beauty school.

During Blondie's heyday in the late 1970s and early 1980s she often donned miniskirts, jumpsuits, and work by international designers such as Kansai Yamamoto, Thierry Mugler, and Claude Montana. Harry epitomized a certain kind of downtown chic, making creative use of clothing and embracing young designers, most notably the work of American Stephen Sprouse in the late 1970s, whose initial designs incorporated elements of 1960s attire with day-glo colors and an urban touch, such as graffiti-inspired prints. With angular bangs, a choppy haircut, black leather, and makeup that favored kohl-rimmed eyes and bright and/or glittery eye shadow, Harry's overall look was entirely New Wave. The nascent form of music videos became yet another venue to hone her image. In the "Hangin' on the Telephone" video she appears in a stylish black sheath dress. She dances around in the video for "Heart of Glass" looking glamorous, twirling a diaphanous sheet of material to the disco beat.

Harry's approach to image-making was complex and well considered; she could seamlessly transition from underground fashion renegade to old-fashioned movie star glamour, especially with her blonde hair as an accessory. Her ability to incorporate seemingly disparate design elements or trends has most noticeably impacted other blonde bombshells, whether it's the leather, short skirts, and appropriation of underwear as outerwear of Madonna, or punked-up plaid and bare midriffs by Gwen Stefani, who has her own fashion line, L.A.M.B. Both Madonna and Stefani acknowledge Harry as an influence. All three women take pieces of various cultures and movements and transform them into something unique, often with a heavy, ironic wink toward Marilyn Monroe.

that married garage rock and girl group sensibilities. Its balance of art and commerce proves that one need not sacrifice the former to achieve the latter. Vocally, Harry's versatility was a manifestation of a desire to self-consciously toy with conventional ideas of female singers: kitten, vamp, tigress, and everything in between. Many female singers who grew up revering new wave, punk, outspoken females or some combination thereof owe some debt to Harry, especially the spate of 1990s indie rock bands with prominent females such as Belly, the Breeders (themselves an offshoot of the Pixies), Hole, and L7. Notably, Harry's influence touches both independent and commercial music, from the punk-pop (and risqué fashion antics) of Karen O of the arty and aggressive New York band Yeah Yeah Yeahs to the extraordinarily successful image-renovator Madonna. Additionally, Harry's longtime friendship and collaboration with Stein, spanning thirty years, is an indication of her artistic merit, and her bravery in releasing a pop album at the age of sixty-two testifies to her interest in creating smartly crafted pop music.

## SELECTED DISCOGRAPHY

### Blondie

*Plastic Letters*. Chrysalis, 1977
*Parallel Lines*. Chrysalis, 1978
*Eat to the Beat*. Chrysalis, 1979
*Autoamerican*. Chrysalis, 1980
*No Exit*. Beyond, 1999
*The Curse of Blondie*. Sanctuary, 2003

### Solo

*KooKoo*. Chrysalis, 1981
*Rockbird*. Geffen, 1986
*Def, Dumb & Blondie*. Sire, 1989
*Debravation*. Sire/Reprise, 1993
*Necessary Evil*. Eleven Seven Music/ADA, 2007

## FURTHER READING

Bayley, Roberta. *Blondie Unseen: 1976–1980*. London: Plexus Publishing, 2007.
Berger, Arion. "Debbie Harry biography." *The New Rolling Stone Album Guide*. New York: Simon and Schuster, 2004. Available online at www.rollingstone.com/artists/deborahharry/biography.
Brantley, Ben. "A Playwright Foretelling her Doom." *New York Times* (November 11, 2000).

Che, Cathay. *Deborah Harry: Platinum Blonde, A Biography*. London: Carlton Publishing/Andre Deutsch, 2005.

Christgau, Robert. "Necessary Evil. Review." *Rolling Stone* online (October 18, 2007). Available at www.rollingstone.com/artists/deborahharry/albums/album/184464/review/5943316/debravation.

CNN. October 21, 2007. "Deborah Harry's Necessary Evil: Blondie Frontwoman Releases Her First Solo Album in 14 Years." Available online at www.cnn.com/video/#/video/showbiz/2007/10/21/quan.soundcheck.deborah.harry.cnn.

Cohen, Debra Rae. "Eat to the Beat. Review." *Rolling Stone* 305 (November 29, 1979). Available online at www.rollingstone.com/artists/blondie/albums/album/210132/review/6067915/eat_to_the_beat.

DeCurtis, Anthony. "Rockbird. Review." *Rolling Stone* 492 (January 29, 1987). Available online at www.rollingstone.com/artists/deborahharry/albums/album/124056/review/5940805/rockbird.

George-Warren, Holly, Patricia Romanowski, and Jon Pareles. "Blondie Biography." *The Rolling Stone Encyclopedia of Rock & Roll*. New York: Simon and Schuster, 2001. Available online at www.rollingstone.com/artists/blondie/biography.

Harry, Debbie, Chris Stein, and Victor Bockris. *Making Tracks: The Rise of Blondie*. New York: Da Capo Press, 1998.

Harry, Deborah. Official artist Web site. See www.deborahharry.com.

Helligar, Jeremy, and Helene Stapinski. "Bleach Blond: After 16 Years Apart, Blondie Takes To the Comeback Trail With a New Album and a U.S. Tour." *People* (January 11, 1999).

McDonnell, Evelyn. "Debravation. Review." *Rolling Stone* 667 (October 14, 1993). Available online at www.rollingstone.com/artists/deborahharry/albums/album/184464/review/5943316/debravation.

O'Brien, Lucy. *She Bop II: The Definitive History of Women in Rock, Pop and Soul*. London: Continuum Press, 2002.

Palmer, Robert. "The Pop Life." *New York Times* (November 28, 1980).

Palmer, Robert. "The Pop Life." *New York Times* (July 15, 1981).

Powers, Ann. "Blondie Proves (Again) It's a Group, Not a Girl." *New York Times* (February 21, 1999).

Rachlis, Kit. "Plastic Letters. Review." *Rolling Stone* 262 (April 6, 1978). Available online at www.rollingstone.com/artists/blondie/albums/album/178492/review/5946643/plastic_letters.

Rockwell, John. "The Pop Life." *New York Times* (October 12, 1979).

Ruhlmann, William. "Eat to the Beat. Review." *All Music Guide* online. Available online at www.allmusic.com/cg/amg.dll?p=amg&token=ADFEAEE47817D849AA7E2 0C79A3E52DBB57DF702FE5AFB86112F0456D3B82D4BBD0E4FE06BC2AB 81B0FA6AB571B0FD2EA45D43D0C0EA53F6D8642D5DF0&sql=10:0ifuxqq 5ld6e.

Shepherd, Richard. "Spoofing Mysteries." *New York Times* (September 26, 1980).

Tucker, Ken. "Blondie. Review." *Rolling Stone* 236 (April 7, 1977). Available online at www.rollingstone.com/artists/blondie/albums/album/248822/review/5941424/blondie.

Courtesy of Sire/Photofest

# Chrissie Hynde

*It's not that I wanted to go to bed with the Beatles or the Rolling Stones, it's that I wanted to be like them. They were wild and free, with this sense of adventure—everything you want when you're young.*

## OVERVIEW

As lead singer for the rock group the Pretenders, Chrissie Hynde occupies a unique spot as an icon—she is the female focal—and vocal—point for an otherwise all-male group. Although she came of age in the post-punk late 1970s she also grew up listening to British Invasion bands such as The Beatles, the Rolling Stones, The Who, David Bowie, and the Kinks. Hynde took in all of those influences and filtered them into her own particular worldview, musically and lyrically. Indeed, Hynde also distinguishes herself because most of her influences—explicit and implicit—have historically been male. Because of her group's strong UK leanings and success abroad coupled with the fact that Hynde was the only American in the band in its first incarnation, many Americans have mistaken the group for an entirely British rock outfit. As a vocalist, she brings a cool, knowing female perspective to the music and as a musician, she offers guitar skills generally regarded as among the best in the business, regardless of gender. With her ragged, long bangs; kohl-rimmed eyes and evasive way with eye contact; and simple but effective clothing such as jeans, black T-shirts, leather (which at times was controversial, given her animal rights record), and boots, Hynde made herself over in a slightly androgynous version of a male rock star.

The genesis of the band's name reveals a sense of play, of aspiration, and of humor, too. Hynde told *Billboard* in 1995 that she was in a room with a biker at a motorcycle club who played a song for her behind locked doors, because he didn't want his friends to hear how important it was to him. That song was the Sam Cooke version of "The Great Pretender." The moment was so moving that it inspired her band's name.

The band itself reached nearly immediate commercial success with its first record. Its 1980 debut, *Pretenders*, landed on *Rolling Stone* magazine's Top 500 Albums of All Time list at number 155. Sustaining that level was not easy as childrearing, band member deaths, and personnel changes forced Hynde to take time off, reconsider, and bring in new ideas. But for the better part of thirty years, the group released records that have done well critically and commercially and performed live shows that were a particularly important component to understanding its energy and ambitions. The Pretenders as a group cannot boast a prolific output, but, rare among many musicians, it can boast respect and admiration of its peers, and it can boast a fairly consistent commercial and critical acclaim for the mere eight studio albums released in nearly thirty years together, several of which went platinum.

All of the Pretenders albums have appeared on some *Billboard* chart, but arguably the group's most successful records, commercially speaking, came in the early 1980s and early 1990s. However, a new chart, Top Independent

Albums, rated 2002's *Loose Screw* as number eight, proving that the Pretenders could not only retain an audience but also find a new one in the changing landscape of the major label system. Their songs "Brass in Pocket," "Don't Get Me Wrong," and "Night in My Veins" all deal with love, sex, desire, passion, ambition, and all the blurry lines in between in an intelligent, wry manner, with unflinching honesty. Articulating lyrics in "Brass in Pocket" such as "I'm special . . . So special/I'm gonna have some of your attention, give it to me" in your first Top 20 hit certainly helps set your agenda and establish a direct sense of purpose. Still, surprisingly, the Pretenders have not been recognized with a Grammy Award.

And then there's the simple matter of Hynde's iconic status. Some critics contend that through the years, the Pretenders music has become less edgy and hard—calling it softer and more pop-oriented—but the songwriting and Hynde herself never let things devolve into mediocrity. Although Hynde was not the first female to front an all-male rock band, her tough-but-cool demeanor has influenced a number of other bands with a similar male-female ratio or mix and a similar aesthetic on both sides of the Atlantic, whether it is Garbage, Elastica, or Sonic Youth. Solo artists such as Courtney Love, the singer and widow of Kurt Cobain from Nirvana, and younger stars such as Avril Lavigne bear some of Hynde's influence, too. Famously, Hynde once made a how-to list of ten things budding female rock stars should do, a ten commandments of sorts. One of them decreed: "Don't think that sticking your boobs out and trying to look f---able will help. Remember you're in a rock and roll band. It's not 'f--- me,' it's 'f--- you!' " (Johnson 2003). Decrees like that have secured her an unassailable reputation in rock and roll history as tough, smart, and uncompromising.

The group's lineup has changed considerably over the years, but Hynde herself has kept the band together. Thus it is synonymous with her name and her image more than any other member. A reluctant icon, Hynde insisted that the idea of a band is about what can be created as a group, not as an individual. She has also spoken in ways that somewhat deny her gender. When asked by Holly George-Warren in *Rolling Stone* if there are double standards for men and women in rock and roll, Hynde said no, but her remark was starkly idealistic. "That's the beauty of rock. It's what Charles Mingus described as 'the colorless island that musicians live on' that goes beyond these distinctions and discriminations" (George-Warren 1997).

## EARLY YEARS

Hynde grew up as the second child in a working-class family in Akron, Ohio. She has an older brother named Terry. Her father, Melville "Bud" Hynde, worked at the telephone company and her mother, Dolores, worked part time as a secretary and also owned a hair salon. Her father's father worked for a rubber company and her mother's father was a cop. Growing up as a child of the 1960s she admired The Beatles and the Rolling Stones, the Kinks, Jimi Hendrix, Bob Dylan, and Iggy Pop of the Stooges. She read a guitar book that taught her chords, and she said she never played along with records. Early experiences had an unusually strong impact on her. Being exposed to live music at the age of fourteen changed her irrevocably. She went to see Mitch Ryder and the Detroit Wheels at an outdoor venue near her hometown in northeastern Ohio. At the end of the afternoon set, a fight broke out onstage, and, entranced, she stayed for the evening show. Still, even though she was captivated by the dramatic antics, she did not necessarily idolize those who were on stage; instead, she wanted to be them. As Scott Cohen described her in *Spin* magazine in 1986, Hynde cannot imagine herself as anything or anyone else, nor does she seem comfortable with her own stardom, success, or fame, illustrating the sometimes uneasy relationship between one's image and ambition. However, he wrote, "there isn't anyone she would want to be, not even for a moment, but there are people she wouldn't mind smelling for a moment, or being near, or touching . . . "(Cohen 1986). Ambivalence would become something her music would explore.

Other early experiences had a formative impact on the sort of adult female rocker she would become. Getting her period at age thirteen enraged Hynde, who thought it would not happen to her, which suggests an uneasiness about femininity. An assignment she completed in class at age twelve—she was asked to think of a word and then write a poem about the word—prompted a contemplation on England, where she eventually would move and live for most of her life. Its rural landscape, she would reflect later, resembled the hills of Ohio of her youth.

When it came time for college, Hynde initially wanted to be a painter and was accepted at Ontario College of Art in Toronto. However, she didn't enroll, because she couldn't afford to do so. Instead, she chose Kent State University in Ohio and happened to be a witness to the tragic killings in 1970. While she was at Kent State, she formed her first official band, and some of its members went on to form the group Devo. She waitressed at a diner when she was in college and listened to a lot of Velvet Underground, the Stooges, and similar bands. For her twenty-first birthday her parents wanted to give her a watch, but she asked for a Melody Maker guitar. It was the beginning of a lifelong obsession with guitars.

She didn't last long in college, and seeking inspiration elsewhere, Hynde went to London in 1973. She left with a copy of *New Music Express* that contained an article about Iggy Pop, three records—*Raw Power, Fun House,* and *White Light, White Heat*—and about $500. She lent the records to someone and never saw them again, and while she was lamenting this at a party where she knew no one, someone chimed in and said he knew Iggy Pop. That someone was *NME* journalist Nick Kent, who took a liking to Hynde. Kent helped her get a start in London, and for a period of time, Hynde became a rock critic. She found herself in the middle of the United Kingdom's punk rock explosion and even worked for a time at Malcolm McLaren's SEX boutique. While abroad, she befriended the members of what would become the Sex Pistols (notoriously influential despite the fact that they only released one album) and the Clash, but she was not able to put together her own group. She moved back to Cleveland around 1975 and waitressed for a while, but she had trouble being polite, she had trouble serving people meat, and she had trouble remembering to get people their checks on time.

Hynde formed a group called Jack Rabbit, which did not last long, and then moved to Tucson, which also did not last long. However, while in Tucson she received a phone call from someone in Paris whom she'd met who asked her to sing in a band he was putting together. She went to Paris and joined the Frenchies and stayed there for a bit in 1976 but then wound up back in London, acting on a hunch that it was where she was supposed to be. Malcolm McLaren hired her as guitarist in the band Masters of the Backside, but she was dismissed after a few months of rehearsals. She kept working by singing backup and/or playing guitar with a number of artists, many of them members of either the Heartbreakers or the New York Dolls, and Nick Lowe. Hynde remained committed to music and eventually gathered enough material for a demo tape of original work.

It is impossible to talk about Hynde's career without talking about the Pretenders, but before she found the members, she met manager Tony Secunda. She played him the chords for what turned into "The Phone Call," and he decided to champion her cause and try to get her a record deal. Hynde needed a band and she needed money, so he helped pay her rent. After a time, however, they had a falling out, and she was back on her own. Hynde contacted Greg Shaw, someone she hung out with during those years, and he put her in touch with Dave Hill, who was a manager and also the founder of Real Records. He became her manager and fronted her the money to audition members and put together a band.

Hynde formed the group in 1978 after writing songs with Mick Jones but some of that material ended up on the first record by his own band, the Clash. Initially, she envisioned the band as more like a motorcycle club than a band. The original incarnation of the Pretenders included bassist Pete Farndon, guitarist James Honeyman-Scott, and drummer Martin Chambers. Farndon had spent time playing in a band in Australia before he returned to England. She liked Farndon because he didn't play bass with a pick; meeting him led her to Honeyman-Scott, whom Farndon knew. They hired drummer Gerry Mackleduff as a session musician and recorded two of her songs, "Precious" and "The Wait," along with a Ray Davies song, "Stop Your Sobbing." Farndon and Honeyman-Scott knew drummer Martin Chambers from their shared hometown, Hereford. Hynde managed to persuade Nick Lowe to produce a single of "Stop Your Sobbing" in fall 1978, with a B-side called "The Wait," based on the demo version she sent to him. The Pretenders then went to Paris for its weeklong performance debut.

## CAREER PATH

*I don't think we'll ever be mainstream. And I'm very grateful for that.*

In January 1979, "Stop Your Sobbing" was released in the United Kingdom and became the band's earliest exposure to radio audiences. The single is a mostly faithful take on the Kinks's 1964 song, but this time, it's drenched in a fair dose of reverb and jangly guitars. Hynde suffuses the track with subtle shifts in her mostly no-nonsense efficiency, and by the song's end, she admonishes her overly effusive lover with cries of "Stop! Stop! Stop!" Her personality was established to listeners early on through this song, suggesting that one would be wise to do as Hynde says. The song hit the British Top 40 first, but did not make much of an impact in the United States. The follow-up song, "Kid," which Hynde wrote and Chris Thomas produced, did well in the United Kingdom too, and another song, "Brass in Pocket," which Hynde wrote with Honeyman-Scott, was a U.K. chart topper. By the spring, the band was playing to sell-out crowds throughout the United Kingdom.

The momentum grew, and finally, in May, they started to work on their debut in earnest. Hynde wrote nearly all of the album's dozen tracks, except for the Davies cover and three that she co-wrote. *Pretenders* was released in January 1980 and became an instant classic, showing the group's full, deep range of influences. The album showcases how the Pretenders took the hard, rough edges of punk and finessed them into an accessible, melodic version of rock. The album's true gem, however, and breakthrough hit in the United States was the song "Brass in Pocket," which featured a cheeky narrator with her sights set high for herself and her love life. The well-known lyrics Hynde sings have her declaring "I'm gonna use my arms/Gonna use my legs . . . gonna use my imagination." The video helped cement Hynde's image as she appears as a reluctant but seductive waitress at a diner, intermittently waiting on members of the band. You get the feeling she'll bring your meal when she's good and ready to do so, and you'd be wise not to ask for it twice.

One of the strengths of the Pretenders songs, on display throughout the debut, is that the music itself so clearly and immediately correlates with the complex emotional terrain Hynde's voice and the lyrics set forth. Hynde's voice takes command, but the group itself is more than up to the task of playing with her authoritative, assertive styling. Songs often employ just a few chords or ideas, but the group takes the songs to new and innovative places.

Other standout tracks on the album include the first track, "Precious," a word that is used in a mostly sarcastic fashion. In the simple, rough, fast-paced song Hynde says in the first line, "I like the way you cross the street 'cause you're precious," but she lets the title word slither out in a way that suggests she means otherwise. Ultimately, though, she rejects the object of her affection, declaring that she's "too precious/F*** off!" In "Mystery Achievement" we get some small clue about the band's name. The "mystery achievement" could easily be interpreted as a lover, or even her career. In the last line of the song, Hynde says "but you know me/I love pretending." The song "Private Life," employs a reggae-like guitar riff that sounds like it was pulled from a B-side of a record by the Police, one of the group's contemporaries. Overall, the record's twelve tracks represent a reasonable template for the emotional and sonic terrain the Pretenders would traverse over the course of the next twenty or so years.

*She's a tough broad, the ultimate role model.*
—feminist scholar
Camille Paglia

In the United States, "Private Life" was a Top 20 hit, going to number fourteen on the pop singles chart; in the United Kingdom, where they had more name recognition, it went to number one; it also hit number one in Australia. Its success, though, was not so easy for Hynde to endure; she was embarrassed by it. *Pretenders* fared extremely well for a debut—its best position was number nine on the pop albums chart and it sold a million copies. The group was distinguished by its 1960s-style pop sound, which was a perfect foil to Hynde's sassy lyrics and erotic delivery.

After a year and a half, the second album, *Pretenders II*, was released in August 1981. With some mixed reviews from critics, it nevertheless fared well commercially and peaked at number ten on the pop albums chart. Critics thought that their sophomore attempt lacked the edginess and sexual aggressiveness of the debut but that in some ways, *Pretenders II* was even more daring. The Pretenders's strength is not from stellar musicianship or innovation but rather from Hynde and her ability to play a character—to pretend, shall we say.

The record has some great songs, ones that mostly show a logical progression from the debut. "Message of Love" is punctuated by jagged guitar riffs that remind one of the Clash. The song went to number five on the mainstream rock charts. In *Pretenders II* Hynde and the band are charting slightly more moody and unpredictable waters, navigating fame, isolation, love, and sex. In the midtempo "Talk of the Town," Hynde exhibits some existential angst, saying "you've changed your place in this world" and "it's hard to live by the rules/I never could and still never do." Elsewhere, another Ray Davies song made it onto the record, "I Go to Sleep," which was not much of a surprise; Hynde had been dating her idol Ray Davies and appearing on the road with the Kinks.

When Chambers injured his hand in October 1981, the Pretenders had to postpone a tour. Sadly, *Pretenders II* would be the last record to feature the original incarnation of the group's lineup. In June 1982, Farndon was kicked out of the group because his drug habit was interfering with the band's commitments, and two days later, James Honeyman-Scott died in his sleep after a cocaine overdose. Ten months after that, Farndon met his fate and died of a drug overdose too. It was a time of tremendous change—Hynde was pregnant by Ray Davies and in 1983 gave birth to a daughter, Natalie. Hynde and Davies never married.

Chambers and Hynde were deeply affected by their bandmates' deaths. When pressed for comment, Hynde only told the Associated Press she was "shocked." She and Chambers reassembled the Pretenders with bass player Malcolm Foster and guitarist Robbie McIntosh, whom Scott had recruited earlier when the band had considered adding another guitarist.

They worked together on a song in time for Christmas, "2000 Miles," and put together a successful third release, *Learning to Crawl* produced by Chris Thomas, in 1984. With a polished sound throughout, the record's material eulogizes the deaths of the two members and also finds Hynde angry about the rampant development of her Ohio hometown, thus infusing the material with a sense of righteousness. "Middle of the Road" leads off the album and finds Hynde as feisty as ever. Audiences liked it too, and it garnered a fair amount of radio play to reach number nineteen on the *Billboard* Hot 100. In "My City Was Gone," about her hometown, she laments the loss of the downtown, the train station, and her favorite places, "reduced to parking spaces." The song hit number eleven. Hynde was never one to resort to simple sentimentality, and instead, in a song like "Middle of the Road," she just plainly tells us that she's "standing in the middle of life/with my past behind me." The directness of such a lyric is disarming and deeply affecting.

The album's second track, "Back on the Chain Gang," was a tremendous hit. Hynde had started the song years before and revisited it as a eulogy to Honeyman-Scott. The bittersweet, instantly catchy song starts off with the lyrical reminiscence, "I found a picture of you/Oh oh oh oh" and laments the loss of a loved one. Hynde likens the return to making music and reforming the band to a chain gang, but it's an affectionate moniker; she talks about "a circumstance beyond our control" and "the wretched life of a lonely heart." The song appeared in the mainstream rock and pop singles charts, topping out at number four and number five respectively. It has become one of their most beloved hits. The song was quickly recorded after Honeyman-Scott's death with guitarist Billy Bremner (formerly of Rockpile) and bassist Tony Butler (Big Country) and was a hit before the record was even released.

*Rolling Stone* dedicated lengthy space to its review of *Learning to Crawl*, praising it as a triumph in light of the band's tragic losses and lauding Hynde for her ability to be intimate in a real rock and roll context. But those intimate lyrics also covered topics that few other artists, male or female, were chronicling with such unflinching honesty and nuance—specifically, motherhood and domesticity. These topics receive her wry insights as she unflinchingly looks at them in songs such as "Watching the Clothes" and "Thumbelina" and the heartrending "Show Me." Fans and music lovers responded kindly, as the record was a tremendous success. *Learning to Crawl* achieved platinum status within three months of its release, and reached number five on the *Billboard* 200.

In 1986, instead of hiring full-time band members, Hynde assembled another incarnation of the Pretenders that included McIntosh and session musicians for *Get Close*, the record that they released the following year. Hynde claimed she did not set out to write a whole bunch of songs about the moon—half the songs on *Get Close* contain some element of lunar imagery—but she had lived through a lot of trauma in the previous five years—death, births, a relationship break-up, and then marriage to the singer Jim Kerr of the British group Simple Minds.

The album's song "Don't Get Me Wrong," another knowing pop song about love, went into the Top 10 in 1986. Some critics dismissed it as a trifle and also remarked that *Get Close* sounded nothing like the band, probably because it had seen such an extreme change in personnel. Hynde had gone with a different producer, Bob Clearmountain, known for his extensive work with smart pop bands (including Simple Minds), and the difference in production is pronounced. But Hynde's lyrics are less acerbic than she is known for. Lyrics such as "I'm a peasant/Dressed as a princess," make us wonder, when Hynde has ever really been concerned about looking pretty? Some of the songs here show a fondness for soul and dance music, which can somewhat be attributed to the addition of funk keyboardist Bernie Worrell to the record. Regardless of such complaints, the album achieved gold status, peaked at number twenty-five on the *Billboard* 200, and launched a handful of songs onto the radio—the aforementioned "Don't Get Me Wrong;" "My Baby," which went to number one on the mainstream rock tracks chart and, a year later, number sixty-four on the *Billboard* Hot 100; and "Where Has Everybody Gone?," which landed at twenty-six on the Mainstream Rock Tracks chart. Even Hynde's take on the Jimi Hendrix song "Room Full of Mirrors" hit the charts.

Hynde recorded the Sonny and Cher hit "I Got You Babe" in 1985 with UB40 and in 1988 recorded her second duet with them, "Breakfast In Bed." An ad hoc kind of greatest hits collection, *The Pretenders: The Singles* came out in 1987 and fared reasonably well, hitting sixty-nine on the *Billboard* 200. The late 1980s were turbulent, though. The Pretenders launched a tour of the United States in 1987 and had trouble maintaining a steady line-up; musicians were fired and replaced. Even McIntosh was gone by the end; former Smiths guitarist Johnny Marr was hired to replace him. Hynde was the only original member left.

### The 1990s to Current Day: New Decade, New Transitions

When she started gathering material for 1990's album *Packed!*, Hynde was essentially the only Pretender left, and the record did not seem to some reviewers to be as strong an effort as previous ones. It barely made it into the Top 50, peaking at forty-eight on the *Billboard* 200, but one of its songs, "Never Do That," fared well on the modern rock chart. Some of the songs deal with unrequited love, which is a departure from the usual perspective of Hynde's lyrics. *Packed!* isn't full of just love songs; the lilting ballad "Criminal," for instance, was written when she was visiting Akron and reflects a sense of Hynde's hometown, as does the rocking, complex homage "Downtown (Akron)." The conclusions about the album's material, though, are not altogether unfounded; her marriage to Kerr dissolved that same year, 1990. (The pair have a daughter together, Yasmin, who was born in 1985.) The record did not even chart well in the United Kingdom, which had previously been a receptive market for the band's music.

In 1993, the *Best of the Pretenders* sold well, which was a strong indicator of the group's longevity. However, some members of the press saw the group's next album, *Last of the Independents*, as a comeback of sorts. In 1994, the group reformed after a period of losing key players and seeking replacements, including guitarist Adam Seymour and bassist Andy Hobson. *Last of the Independents* was released in May with original drummer Martin Chambers back in the line-up; many fans and critics had speculated that she had fired him around the time of *Get Close*, which would help explain his absence. The Pretenders sounded like a band again for the first time in a decade. Of the process of regrouping, Hynde joked with *Billboard*, saying that "some women need a man—I need a band!" (Bessman 1994).

*Last of the Independents* reinvigorated the Pretenders. The song "I'll Stand By You," a torchy ballad that's sentimental by Pretenders standards, turned up on a number of different *Billboard* charts (Adult Contemporary, Modern Rock), but reaching number eleven on the Top 40 chart. Other standout tracks include the sexy "Night in My Veins," which was a number two modern rock hit. The success of these two songs helped the album land at number forty-one on the *Billboard* 200—an admirable accomplishment for a group that had not released a studio album in four years.

In 1995, the same lineup of the Pretenders released an acoustic record, *Isle of View*, which was a result of two evenings' worth of live recordings with the Duke String Quartet. For the casual fan, this album probably escapes notice— *Isle of View* went to 100 on *Billboard* 200—but for fans who are interested in spare versions of some of the band's hits, it is a worthwhile investment.

Twenty years into the band's career, the Pretenders appeared at Lilith Fair and proved, with kudos from other performers, that the group was still influential and fresh. Songs from *Viva El Amor!*, released in June 1999, were performed during Lilith Fair and played with a strange mix of laid-back energy. For many of the women on the tour circuit with Lilith Fair the Pretenders's participation gave them the opportunity to play alongside one of their idols.

*Viva El Amor!*'s arresting cover art, in black and red and white, was styled after a propaganda poster, with Hynde raising her fist in the air. The photograph was taken by the late Linda McCartney. The album fared respectably on the charts and was reviewed well. Hynde's sexy but angry voice and phrasing once again are balanced by the band's tight backing, which complements her lyrics in unexpected ways. The result is clean, tough, and compelling. For example, the song "Human" is a matter-of-fact, upbeat contemplation of one's foibles and strengths without sounding simple. Radio liked it so much that it peaked at number thirty on the Adult Top 40. Elsewhere, "Popstar" is snarky and sinewy, and the lyrics indict those who are aspiring for fame. One of her favorite guitarists, Jeff Beck, makes an appearance on the full-throttle "Legalise Me." Throughout the record's dozen tracks, Hynde does not indulge in sentimentality, and the record retains a fairly consistent feel even if there are no monstrous pop hits that demand attention or, for that matter, bring the record to anything better than a 158 position on the *Billboard* 200.

> *I've adapted along the way, but philosophically, I'm the same vegetarian hippie musician I was when I left home for London with everything I owned in one suitcase . . . except now I'm more comfortable with everything.*

In 2002, the laid-back, reggae-influenced *Loose Screw* was released on Artemis Records. The content shows maturity—at fifty-one, with two grown daughters (ages eighteen and twenty at the album's release), Hynde has learned a few things, yet her voice sounds as young and timeless as ever, and Hynde is just as fiery. Much of the content remains somewhat consistent—love, sex, death, infidelity, alienation—which is rendered with her own archness fused with defiance and fury, especially on the sharp riffs of "Lie to Me." With a chorus that repeats the threat "if you lie to me again" several times, it's a more grown-up version of "Stop Your Sobbing." Still, an aging rocker cannot escape contemplating how time changes things and how one becomes wiser, and those elements are especially evident on "Fools Must Die" and "The Losing," both of which deal with mortality. The single "Complex Person" comments on guns, construction workers, and feminism with ease. And in the bass-heavy reverb in "I Should Of," she wishes for the benefit of hindsight when looking back on the failures of a dissolved relationship. Hynde pulls no punches; she is firmly secure in her persona. Hynde even covers a Latin song, "Walk Like a Panther." Many of the tunes were written in the wake of the break-up of her second marriage to Colombian sculptor Lucho Brieva.

The band toured in early 2003 in support of *Loose Screw*, since through its history, touring has proven to be a crucial component of its success. In a time when music videos are increasingly rare and television seems to cater to younger artists or the older, multimillion-selling artists for appearances, a group like the Pretenders must sustain itself in new ways. The challenge in the music business still remains for artists who are older and who came of age when radio play made a difference and people more regularly bought albums based on that exposure. The model is breaking down somewhat, thanks to the advent of the Internet, but commercial radio does not quite know what to do with the Pretenders other than to lump the band into "classic rock," which it is not. With the rise of Internet downloading and label consolidation, legacy artists such as the Pretenders do not often receive much airplay and are often not the priority of labels seeking to turn a maximum profit with minimal effort. When *Loose Screw* was released, the record business was a much leaner

*Rock 'n' roll gives us the sense of community we lack, but the commercial importance we sometimes place on it shows how vapid people have become spiritually.*

and more fiscally conservative enterprise, generally speaking, than when the Pretenders released its debut. Hynde made a small number of television appearances to promote the band, but her frustration was evident.

The Pretenders were inducted into the Rock and Roll Hall of Fame in 2005. The honor was especially poignant considering the museum's location in Cleveland in Hynde's home state, but also because of the affirmation of the longevity of their career. Drummer Chambers accepted the induction in honor of the original band members Farndon and Honeyman-Scott. In 2006, the Pretenders's first ever box set was released, called *Pirate Radio*, boasting four discs and more than five hours of music along with a DVD of rare performance footage. The group had never completely stopped touring, but a comment Hynde made in 2006 was taken out of context; some fans thought she said she was going to retire after she said at an Atlantic City, New Jersey, concert that it was the last show—she meant it was the last show of the tour. Rest assured, Hynde and the Pretenders still have music to make. The band is slated to release a new record sometime in 2008.

## MISSION, MOTIVATION, PROCESS

As much as Hynde is a front woman, she is, more importantly, a band member and functions best as part of a tight, musically in-sync unit, no matter how singular her image may be. The model of the Pretenders even paved the way for other similar, female-fronted bands (see sidebar). To some extent, the difficulty of keeping a band together over the course of many years can be attributed to the periods of time during which the group did not record or when records that did not fare well. After the deaths of two key members, it quickly became apparent that if the Pretenders were to keep making music, Hynde would need to take an active role in ensuring its longevity, and her steely determination has enabled that to happen. David Wild of *Rolling Stone* once asked her if she ever thought of becoming a solo artist, and she demurred, saying that despite the struggle over the years maintaining a good lineup, "I've never had any interest in Chrissie Hynde, and I wouldn't go see her. I like bands" (Wild 1994).

Yet as much as Hynde might be perceived as a solo artist with a band, she truly thrives on the dynamic among the band members. For the first time in nearly a decade, after the success of several Pretenders records, band tragedy, and personnel changes, Hynde reunited with drummer Martin Chambers for the group's album *Last of the Independents*. Adam Seymour was added on guitar. The collaboration of Chambers and Hynde had a substantial impact

## Behind Every Woman Stands a Group of Men

Although the personnel has changed considerably through the band's twenty years together, Chrissie Hynde is singlehandedly recognized as the Pretenders. With her tough but sexy persona as the lead singer of an all-male band, Hynde paved the way for many other front women to follow in her path. Whether it is Justine Frischmann of the U.K. rock band Elastica, Gwen Stefani of No Doubt (who has since launched a highly successful solo career), or the Deal sisters in the punk-infused band the Pixies, most of whose members are male, Hynde became a model for how other women could navigate the sometimes murky and sexually charged waters of fronting a band—or playing a significant and visible role at the very least—comprised of men.

The rock band Garbage, fronted by Scot Shirley Manson, hit it big with its 1995 debut self-titled album, abetted by the hit "Stupid Girl." Like the Pretenders, the three other members of the band are men, and Garbage became known for its grungy pop-rock sprinkled with samples and loops, delivered with Manson's sultry voice and angry lyrics. Nominated for seven Grammys, Garbage is frequently referenced by critics as a band that bears the influence of the Pretenders. In fact, Shirley Manson even wrote a song called "Special," which cribbed a line from the group's "Talk of the Town," and Garbage's lawyers urged them to remove it. But they sought and received permission from Hynde herself. Manson, along with seminal punk artist Iggy Pop, also paid tribute to the group at a 2006 *VH-1 Decades Rock Live* television special and appeared with her idol to share the stage during the Pretenders song "Talk of the Town" and the Garbage song "I'm Only Happy When it Rains."

on the album, particularly via "Money Talk," "All My Dreams," "977," and "Love Colours."

Hynde seems to downplay the role of bandleader at times and also downplay her own ability as a rhythm guitarist with a career-long preference toward Fender Telecasters. She said she had trouble playing along with records, and because she couldn't, it inadvertently jump-started her songwriting career. She does not use a tape recorder and does not save anything on a laptop computer. Her process is to strum some chords till she either finds the right inspiration for the song in mind or until she gets stuck. Sometimes, she'll pass the work-in-progress off to a guitar player who will take it in another direction and breathe life into it. Such trust in collaboration is in keeping with her band mentality. Plus, when it comes to the qualities of what makes a good song, she believes what matters is not money, technology, or knowledge of chords or how to do it at all. Hynde emphasized the importance of how the song feels, and noted that if it sounds too clean or polished, the song sometimes loses a sense of truthfulness.

Hynde has been honest about some autobiographical elements that have filtered into her songwriting. One of the Pretenders's biggest early hits, "Back on the Chain Gang," opens with the lyric and recurring statement "I found a picture of you." The song morphed from two places; first from a photo of ex-relationship Ray Davies and then from the death of Honeyman-Scott. Although she put together the material for *Loose Screw* in the wake of the break-up of her second marriage to Brieva, Hynde disagreed with some writers and interviewers who suggested it was a break-up album. "The Losing," for example, stems from a friend who bets on horses.

Like many artists, Hynde has been influenced by her upbringing and her environment and has discussed the connection she still feels to her industrial hometown, Akron, Ohio. She says the smell of burning rubber from a nearby Goodyear plant and the aroma of oatmeal from the nearby Quaker Oats are burned into her memory. In 1995, after living in England for most of her adult life, she told *Billboard* about how she returns to Akron regularly with her children to visit family. The title of the acoustic versions of Pretenders hit singles and rarities, *Isle of View*, comes from her perspective on an island, living in England. It also, she said, sounds like "I love you" when spoken.

## LEGACY AND OTHER INTERESTS

In 1988, Hynde became a founding member of a group called the Ark Trust, an environmental/animal rights group that is now part of the Humane Society of the United States. Hynde, as one of its founders, became embroiled in a public controversy when she jokingly suggested in 1989 that its members should firebomb McDonald's; she had spoken out previously against the fast food chain. Hynde, with her laid-back approach to singing and playing, is nonetheless a staunch advocate for animal rights and Greenpeace. Most notably, she has lent her support to PETA and does not eat meat.

Her efforts have frequently garnered her headlines as well as legal trouble. In 2000, she and other members of PETA were accused of creating about $1000 worth of damage to a New York Gap clothing store and charged with criminal mischief and disorderly conduct, destroying leather and suede goods. In 2003, she was briefly detained, along with other protesters, after partaking in an animal rights demonstration outside a KFC restaurant in Paris. That same year, she was part of a Greenpeace-led lobby of Spanish authorities regarding the impounding of a Greenpeace ship from the port of Valencia. Activists had chained themselves to the ship to protest and to block the import of timber from Cameroon's rainforests.

Hynde no longer lists her idols but rather admits to admiring certain musicians such as Neil Young and Bob Dylan. She started off idolizing the male rock stars of her youth but only insofar as she could learn from them. Female performers held less inspiration for her. Nevertheless, Hynde's career has come full circle; it's not likely that female singers who front all-male bands can truthfully say they were not influenced by females, because Hynde made that path seem not only possible but attractive, too.

## SELECTED DISCOGRAPHY

*Pretenders*. Sire, 1980
*Pretenders II*. Sire, 1981
*Learning to Crawl*. Sire, 1984
*Last of the Independents*. Sire, 1994
*The Isle of View (Live)*. Warner Bros., 1995
*Viva El Amor!* Warner Bros., 1999
*Loose Screw*. Artemis, 2002

## FURTHER READING

Associated Press. "British Rock Star Dies." (June 17, 1982).

*BBC News*. "Hynde Defiant After Court Let-Off." (May 24, 2000). Available online at news.bbc.co.uk/2/hi/entertainment/761995.stm.

*BBC News*. "Hynde Asks Spain to Free Ship." (July 2, 2003). Available online at news.bbc.co.uk/2/hi/entertainment/3039178.stm.

*BBC News*. "Police Break-up Hynde KFC Demo." (July 16, 2003). Available online at news.bbc.co.uk/2/hi/entertainment/3072265.stm.

Berger, Arion. "Viva el Amor! Review." *Rolling Stone* 816–817 (July 8, 1999). Available online at www.rollingstone.com/artists/pretenders2/albums/album/212250/review/5940684/viva_el_amor.

Bessman, Jim. "Pretenders Return with Album, Tour; Hynde Recruits New Band for Sire Set." *Billboard* (April 2, 1994).

Carson, Tom. "Pretenders II." *Rolling Stone* 353 (October 1, 1981).

Cohen, Scott. "Hynde Sight." *Spin Magazine* (December 1986).

Erlewine, Stephen Thomas. "Pretenders Biography." *All Music Guide*. Available online at wm06.allmusic.com/cg/amg.dll?p=amg&token=ADFEAEE47817D849AA7E20 C79A3E52DBB57DF702FE5AFB86112F0456D3B82D4BBD0E4FE06BC2AB8 1B0FA6AB779B0FD2EA45D43D6C0EC5EF6DE612D5DF0&sql=11:0ifuxqr5ldhe.

Erlewine, Stephen Thomas. "Viva el Amor! Review." *All Music Guide*. Available online at wm10.allmusic.com/cg/amg.dll?p=amg&token=ADFEAEE47817D849AA7E 20C79A3E52DBB57DF702FE5AFB86112F0456D3B82D4BBD0E4FE06BC2A B81B0FB6ABC66ADFF2EA3160ED9C9EB5CFDDE765D40&sql=10:hpfrxqq kld6e.

Gabarini, Vic. "Get Close. Record Reviews." *Playboy* (February 1987).

George-Warren, Holly. *The Rolling Stone Encyclopedia of Rock & Roll*. New York: Simon and Schuster, 2001. Available online at www.rollingstone.com/artists/pretenders2/biography.

George-Warren, Holly. "Chrissie Hynde." *Rolling Stone* 773 (November 13, 1997).

Graustark, Barbara. "A Pop-porri of Recordings: Pretenders." *Newsweek* (June 9, 1980).

Holden, Stephen. "The Pop Life: Pretenders and Rock's Direction." *New York Times* (November 19, 1986).

Hynde, Chrissie. "Rolling Stone. Top 500 Albums: Pretenders." *Rolling Stone* online (November 1, 2003). Available online at www.rollingstone.com/news/story/6599010/155_pretenders.

Hynde, Chrissie. "Rolling Stone. Behind the Lines. 'I Found a Picture of You.'" *Rolling Stone* online (November 14, 2005). Available online at www.rollingstone.com/artists/pretenders2/articles/story/8798823/chrissie_hynde_on_back_on_the_chain_gang,

Johnson, Brian. "The Great Pretender." *Maclean's* (February 24, 2003).

Loder, Kurt. "Learning to Crawl. Review." *Rolling Stone* 415 (February 16, 1984).

Miller, Jim. "Straight From the Heart." *Newsweek* (April 2, 1984).

O'Brien, Lucy. *She Bop II: The Definitive History of Women in Rock, Pop and Soul.* New York: Continuum, 2002.

*Playboy.* "An Enduring Band: The Pretenders." *Playboy* 30 (June 1983).

Pretenders Archives. Fan-run Web site. See www.pretendersarchives.com/news/News.html.

Swenson, Kyle. "The Pretenders Uninhibited Approach to Pop." *Guitar Player* 33(10) (October 1999).

Tannenbaum, Rob. "The Pretenders. Get Close. Review." *Rolling Stone* 491 (January 15, 1987). Available online at www.rollingstone.com/artists/pretenders2/albums/album/88687/review/5941428/get_close.

Thigpen, David E. "Real Thing." *Time* (June 27, 1994).

Tucker, Ken. "The Pretenders. Review." *Rolling Stone* 315 (April 17, 1980).

White, Timothy. "Pretenders' Hynde Appreciates The 'View.'" *Billboard* (October 14, 1995).

Wild, David. "Chrissie Hynde." *Rolling Stone* 698 (December 29, 1994).

Young, Charles M. "Packed! Record Review." *Playboy* 37 (October 1990).

Courtesy of Photofest

# Indigo Girls

*The Georgia duo the Indigo Girls has given hope to all would-be poets whose careers peaked with the high-school literary magazine.*

—writer Mark Jenkins

## OVERVIEW

As the most prominent female duo in folk-rock music to emerge in the latter third of the twentieth century, the Indigo Girls began their career in Georgia in the 1980s and rose to success with their breakthrough self-titled album in 1988. Their brand of acoustic guitar–based melodic music that has its roots in folk, blues, bluegrass, and rock and roll found them fans around the world. Although in hindsight the idea of two women with guitars harmonizing may not seem so revolutionary, at the time there were few if any prominent female singer/songwriter acts of any merit. What distinguished them was their duality and Emily Saliers's approach, which aligned her with more traditionally introspective songwriters such as Joni Mitchell. In the early years, it was easy to distinguish a track penned by Saliers—her voice is higher and thinner, and her songs are usually more somber with abstract, spiritual, or religious undertones. As a counterpoint, Amy Ray takes her inspiration from rock and roll more than folk music, from such masculine acts as The Jam, the Pretenders, and Husker Du and songwriters such as Elton John and Neil Young. Her voice is lower, raspier, and her songs often feel more urgent, angry, or otherwise faster-paced than those that Saliers writes. In many ways, they are yin and yang, earth and sky, with Saliers's soprano and ethereal, wispy vocals and Ray's earthy alto working in complement.

Although Saliers admits that Bob Dylan and Joni Mitchell are two of her main songwriting influences, the Indigo Girls draw their influence most closely from 1960s- and 1970s-style folk duos and most consistently earn comparisons to Peter, Paul and Mary, The Kingston Trio, and Simon & Garfunkel. Both women have very different performance and writing styles: Ray's more rock approach is balanced by Saliers's sweetness. Regardless of their differences, all of their songs tell poignant stories. More than anything, there exists the possibility of renewal and redemption, personal change, and survival in the music of the Indigo Girls.

Over the course of their twenty-year career, the duo has released eleven studio albums, several live albums, EPs, and other releases. Seven of their releases have achieved at least gold sales status; their most significant release, *Indigo Girls*, is multiplatinum two times over. Worldwide, the band has sold 12 million copies. They have been nominated for seven Grammy Awards, but surprisingly have only received one thus far, for Best Contemporary Folk Album for *Strange Fire* in 1989. It was a promising achievement in the early part of the group's career. The song "Closer to Fine" from *Indigo Girls* is arguably the band's most influential song and is easily identifiable as their own. It found a home on college radio fairly quickly and subsequently inspired legions of young girls to learn how to play the guitar. Despite the fact that their *Billboard* singles charted most consistently from 1989 through 1997, from "Closer to Fine" to "Shame on You," then seemingly fell off the radar of the *Billboard* singles charts, their albums have continued to place on the *Billboard* 200, and the Top Internet Albums. Their 2006 release, *Despite Our Differences*, peaked at forty-four on both the Top Internet Albums and the *Billboard* 200 charts. And despite the lack of strong presence on the singles charts and the fact that their last album to achieve any certification was the 1995 *1200 Curfews*, which achieved platinum status in August 2001, the Indigo Girls have consistently sold out their concerts, maintained their fan base, and continued to sell millions of records. Their songs, quite simply, are infectious, full of energy, and make you want to sing along.

At the time that they hit the music scene, there were only a small number of female artists or female-fronted bands that attempted to discuss political, social, and spiritual issues in their music. Although social commentary is nearly omnipresent in all of their songs, the Indigo Girls avoid coming across as preachy. Their message is often characterized by a sense of poetry, a love of word play (the pair are known for being fans of the *New York Times* Sunday crossword), and at times, a sense of humor. Throughout their consistently appealing output, the Girls have not become too pretentious, although some critics, looking to find fault, have accused them of just that. It is, however, hard to be considered truly pretentious if you are an artist who in the early days of your career becomes identifiable for wearing laid-back clothing such as flannel shirts and denim.

The Indigo Girls are also noteworthy for being some of the first openly gay musicians in the 1980s. The fact that they were out, proud, and progressive helped pave the way for many other female artists who were also lesbians (see sidebar) or attracted a lesbian audience, such as k.d. lang, Michele Shocked, Ferron, Phranc, and even the Swedish band K's Choice.

As two women working together, the Indigo Girls have had a tremendous impact on the music business and established their place in history as a poetic folk-rock act with a social conscience and a love of intricate melodies. Working as a duo has permitted them to explore the duality of the subject matter they write about; their voices often echo, repeat, and work as call-and-response throughout their songwriting, which creates a deeper and broader emotional range.

## EARLY YEARS

As a child growing up in New Haven, Connecticut, Saliers was surrounded by music; it was a constant presence in the family. Father Don and mother Jane led songs during family trips in the car, and Emily's upbringing—she is one of four girls—was marked by singing around the piano and in the church choir. One of Emily's earliest songs was written around the age of ten as a protest about pollution.

Although the Indigo Girls did not start working together until 1983 in Athens, Georgia, as students at Emory University, their friendship started

### Leading by Progressive Example

As one of the most prominent lesbian rock groups, the Indigo Girls have achieved universal acclaim, but their sexuality was rarely an obstacle for their fans. Early on, they were more likely to be pigeonholed as "chick music." They received significant recognition for their first hit "Closer to Fine" and were welcomed enthusiastically by the lesbian community, even though their lyrics never explicitly outed them. Instead, their lyrics concentrate on a variety of political and social messages and usually hint at the redeeming power of love and friendship. The novelty of a female guitar-based, folk-rock duo concerned with progressive issues did not seem like an immediate guarantee of multiplatinum record sales. Yet, they have scored a number of radio hits including 1992's "Galileo" and 1994's "Least Complicated," and they performed all three years of Lilith Fair (1997 to 1999). The duo paved the way for lesbian rockers like Melissa Etheridge and Canadian pair Tegan and Sara.

Nearly twenty years after their first hit single, the Girls are still sticking to the courage of their convictions. On her 2006 album *I'm Not Dead* pop artist Pink collaborated with the Indigo Girls on the political song addressed to President George Bush titled "Dear Mr. President." The song includes the ironic lyric "What kind of father might hate his own daughter if she were gay?" Vice President Dick Cheney's daughter is proudly out, but he has had a complicated public relationship with the issue. The Girls are reaching a younger generation who might not be familiar with them.

But it's the universal themes in their songs that have kept them popular. Their melodic, thoughtful music is essentially hopeful and earnest, even when it is politically charged or socially observant. They must be doing something right: they've sold more than 12 million records.

much earlier, when Ray was ten (and in the fifth grade) and Saliers eleven (in the sixth grade) at Laurel Ridge Elementary School, in Decatur, Georgia, where Emily's family had just moved. However, it was not until high school that they discovered that they liked to play music together, when they took their acoustic guitars to play at a PTA meeting. There, they discovered their gift for harmonization and the chemistry they created singing together. By 1981, they had released a tape, literally recorded in Amy's basement, that consisted mostly of cover songs along with two originals, released under the name of Saliers and Ray called *Tuesday's Children*. In the following year, Ray created a cassette of her own music called *Color Me Grey*. After graduation from high school, Saliers became an English major at Tulane University, and the next year, Ray went to study the same subject at Vanderbilt. However, neither of them enjoyed being so far away from home, and by 1984 they had both transferred to Emory University in Georgia.

While in college at Emory, they performed together as either Saliers and Ray or B-Band and first took the name Indigo Girls in 1985. The name holds no real meaning: Amy chose the word "indigo" from the dictionary because she liked the sound of it.

> *It's like singing with your sister.*
>
> —Emily Saliers, on singing with Amy Ray

Although they had played together off and on for years, it was not always immediately apparent that they ought to do so for a living. In the early days, they begged club owners to let them play and gradually made a name for themselves in the bars around Atlanta, which was a supportive place for musicians. The Indigo Girls gained national attention around the same time and scene from which other bands from Georgia, such as R.E.M., the B-52's, Let's Active, and Drivin' N' Cryin', were also emerging. For the Indigo Girls, their early success can be attributed to years of hard work and a little bit of luck, not because of any established underground rock scene. They played between other musicians' sets and worked hard to develop their sound.

Their very first official release as the Indigo Girls came in the form of a seven-inch single called "Crazy Game," which was followed in 1986 by a six-track EP engineered by a local singer/songwriter named Kristen Hall. The EP was followed by *Strange Fire* in 1987, which had only a 7000-copy print run but which did have the good fortune of arriving around the time that the careers of Suzanne Vega and Tracy Chapman were burgeoning. The arrival of these two artists, with their issue-oriented material and consciousness-raising lyrics, would ultimately make it much easier for an openly gay female duo slinging two acoustic guitars to gain some attention from the mainstream.

As an album, *Strange Fire* is raw and inchoate, lacking the cohesion between the duo that characterizes their later releases. But this imbalance makes sense because they were just starting out as a legitimate musical act. It is easy to distinguish who writes what song, not only because their voices are so different but because of the content of their respective songs. For example, Saliers's contributions are usually marked by slower, more introspective and poetic lyrics, such as the jazzy, whistle-tinged "Crazy Game" and the post-breakup tearjerker "Left Me a Fool." Ray contributes the more fiery, passionate numbers such as the album's opener, which also is the title track, propelled by chiming, heavily strummed acoustic guitars and the lyric "I come to you with strange fire/I bring an offering of love." Additionally, the pair offered a faithful cover of the Youngblood's "Get Together." The album spawned one of their crowd and fan favorites, "Land of Canaan," in which they assert in the chorus, "I'm not your Land of Canaan, sweetheart/Waiting for you under the sun." It's a smart, sassy, up-tempo declaration of standing your own ground and championing your self-worth in the face of a relationship whose prognosis seems less than positive and healthy.

Overall, though, as an early artifact of their career, *Strange Fire* shows an intense, unwavering preoccupation with religious motifs, spirituality, and

> *In a lot of ways we're different. We've got like a yin and yang thing going on.*
>
> —Emily Saliers

poetic explorations of one's own emotional and psychological experiences. The Indigo Girls, in many ways, are not for the faint of heart. Additionally, when one listens to *Strange Fire*, it is hard to resist the temptation to read into their lyrics and wonder if the relationships they are writing about are their own—have they really bared it all for their fans? Although they started off their career with many first-person narratives in their songs, those narratives slowly have become sharper, more personal, and clear.

## CAREER PATH

The Indigo Girls's music caught the attention of producer Scott Litt, who had worked with R.E.M., a band whose popularity was starting to grow with the release of its 1988 album *Green*. The Indigo Girls's tape of material landed on the desk of CBS executive Roger Klein, where it remained unplayed. However, when he was in Atlanta he decided to check out their live show. He came back the next night for more. Within a month, the Indigo Girls were signed to CBS's Epic Records in Atlanta's Buckhead Diner late one evening after a gig in 1988.

The 1989 self-titled *Indigo Girls* earned a Grammy for Best Folk Recording that year, broke into the *Billboard* Top 30, and the song itself gained airplay on college stations. Within six months, the album achieved gold status, and within two years, by the end of 1991, *Indigo Girls* had hit platinum sales. Shortly thereafter, Epic released *Strange Fire* to a wider audience. The album wasn't as well received by critics but was embraced by Indigo Girls fans and did gain the larger audience that Epic had aimed for.

The song "Closer to Fine" was the first track on the album and the one that really broke them through to a wider audience, helping to fuel sales of their records and ticket sales at concerts. The song received heavy airplay on the radio on both mainstream and college stations, as well as on MTV. In many ways, it epitomizes their sound: two acoustic guitars chiming and chasing each other, two voices communicating like a call and response, and an earnest, entreating first line. The song itself tells of a spiritual quest. The climax of the song is positively ecstatic, its traditional formula of verse-chorus-verse-chorus-bridge-chorus unremarkable, but the content and sheer earnestness of their beliefs is irresistible, even years later.

The rest of the album is equally compelling. After the rousing start of "Closer to Fine," the song "Secure Yourself" continues the journey, directing the listener "Secure yourself to heaven, hold on tight the night has come/ Fasten up your earthly burdens, you have just begun." Somehow, though, despite the overly spiritual—call it Christian, biblical, or just plain religious—bent to their songwriting, the Indigo Girls never come across on their debut as preachy. There is an underlying eternal optimism in their music, even as they are writing about the "Prince of Darkness," another stellar cut that explores personal demons, or about the recollection of a childhood's difficult scars in "Kid Fears," which features haunting backing vocals by Michael Stipe of R.E.M. "Kid Fears" actually gained them early college radio play before "Closer to Fine" broke through. Although they were practically neighbors for several years, it took a while for the Indigo Girls and R.E.M. to meet. Once they made friends with Stipe, Saliers and Ray asked the rest of the band to work with them as they were preparing their debut.

In a further endorsement, the Indigo Girls spent three and a half weeks as an opening act for R.E.M. in early 1989, just prior to their major label release. Despite the fact that the two women played acoustic guitars and in the early days spent time fretting about whether to play "too many ballads" when they opened up for hard rock bands, they followed their hearts and were ultimately met with success from fans and critics alike. Audiences were intrigued by the combination, if not immediately besotted, during their early tours with R.E.M.

Of course, once the album came out, critics began to swoon over the duo, praising the unified power their voices create. They were impressed, too, with the "all-stars" who assisted them on their major label debut, including the aforementioned Michael Stipe and members of the Irish band Hothouse Flowers. Additionally, most of the band R.E.M. plays on the jangling song "Tried to Be True," which is the closest thing to roots rock on the album other than perhaps the rousing "Land of Canaan." The album's production is incredibly sharp, compact, and well polished with all margins of error smoothed over even if the lyrics are sometimes are too earnest. The piano-driven ballad "Love's Recovery," for instance, features artfully obtuse lyrics that are puzzling but somehow manage to not distract the listener too much.

Regardless, the album is the stuff of dreams for most artists who make their debut, and Saliers and Ray were greeted by both critical and commercial success. They were surprised by it and had no expectations that it would go gold. The album even earned them a Grammy for Best Contemporary Folk Group, much to their surprise.

### Nomads and Beyond: Sophomore Slump?

The years following the release of *Indigo Girls* were marked by lots of touring, which helped expand the fan base, and much artistic activity. They did several headlining tours, served as the opening act for Neil Young, and played with Joan Baez at summer 1990's esteemed Newport Folk Festival. On the touring circuit in support of their release *Nomads Indians Saints*, they held fans spellbound. Their performance inspired descriptions invoking religious or spiritual fervor because of the emotional connection Saliers and Ray made through their soaring voices. The overall critical assessment of *Nomads* was mixed, however. Some reviewers were generous, but others were unsparing in their criticism of the tightly packed, sometimes awkward lyrics. Other critics thought the material was not as strong overall as on their previous release. An astute reader would observe that attempts to describe the music of the Indigo Girls could often inspire similarly circular, nonsensical proclamations. Regardless of the critics' objections, the album contains one memorable melody after another. For instance, the leadoff song, "Hammer and a Nail," which frames life on earth through the metaphor of manual labor and entreats the listener to take care of one's local and global environment, starts off the album with an inspiring approach and features the admirable feat of Ray singing the harmony below the melody.

Ray's voice has been described as rough compared to Saliers, and although it does have this quality, it is more useful to recognize how she uses her voice to impart a particular emotional experience for the listener. For example, in the urgent waltz "Pushing the Needle Too Far," the raspy vocals impart a sense of desperation along with intricate finger picking on the lead guitar. Saliers joins in for harmony and for call-and-response later in the song. Additionally, the song's strong location toward the end of the album sends a message to listeners about loss of self, losing one's way and, in one anecdote, losing one's mind in the face of life's demands.

The album is loaded with powerful metaphors, chiming acoustic guitars, and thoughtful, introspective lyrics. The production focuses on the voices and guitars; other instrumentation is minimal, deemphasized, and unobtrusive. Still, the yearning and sense of music as an exercise in the spiritual journey comes through loud and clear. The title *Nomads Indians Saints* takes its inspiration from the Ray-written song "World Falls," in which she declares "I wish I was a nomad, An Indian or a saint/Give me walking shoes, feathered arms and a key to heaven's gate." And these themes come through, in "Hand Me Downs," in which Ray declares that "everything I truly love/Comes from somewhere high above." Still, *Nomads* is all about the search. "Watershed" provides another metaphor for life's trials and for reevaulating one's life. In short, it's uplifting, with Ray and Saliers trading off lines one by one in verses that can be summarized by the statement that life is what you make it and that much of our experience is determined by how we respond to what life hands us. The chorus affirms this. Throughout the album, the Indigo Girls demonstrate that despite any criticism about precocious poetics, they do have a talent for clarity and wordplay.

*Nomads*, like its predecessor *Indigo Girls*, got some big league help. Musicians such as Peter Holsapple, John Cougar Mellencamp's drummer Kenny Aronoff, seasoned bassist Sara Lee, singer/songwriter Mary Chapin Carpenter, and R.E.M. guitarist Peter Buck all lent their talents. The immediate success of *Indigo Girls* was a hard act to follow but when *Nomads Indians Saints* (1990) was released, it was nominated for a Grammy, and it eventually reached gold status.

During this time, the Indigo Girls were extremely prolific, releasing three records in as many years. Their EP *Back on the Bus Y'all* was released in 1991 with live versions of what were starting to become some fan favorites, including "Tried to Be True," "Prince of Darkness," and "Kid Fears," along with a live version of "All Along the Watchtower" by Bob Dylan. It, too, became a certified gold record and nominated for a Grammy. The Indigo Girls seemed to be on quite a prolific tear, but releasing the live EP bought them some time to work on the next release.

In spring 1992, *Rites of Passage* emerged and peaked at number twenty-one on the *Billboard* 200 chart, achieving platinum sales by the year's end. Many critics contend that some of their strongest songs and most diverse sounds appear on this album, such as the single "Galileo," which ponders reincarnation and misplaced karma and entreats the listener to "call on the resting soul of Galileo/King of night vision, king of insight" in the quest for enlightenment. Although it is subtle, the song shows a degree of wry humor in the lyric "look what I had to overcome from my last life/I think I'll write a book." The song is noteworthy for a few reasons: It starts off with steel drum, moves to syncopated verses, and is anchored by the swell of violins. It also peaked at number ten on the *Billboard* Modern Rock Tracks and number eighty-nine on the *Billboard* Hot 100. Throughout the rest of *Rites*, as usual the more direct and fiery tracks are penned by Ray and include "Jonas and Ezekial," "Chickenman," and the upbeat "Joking," whose furiously paced mandolin and lighthearted lyrics suggest that perhaps they were able to successfully infuse their songwriting with some humor. The Indigo Girls also contribute a version of the Dire Straits song "Romeo and Juliet," which gains a new dimension as a duet sung by two women: The Indigo Girls infuse it with passion. Additionally, there is the romantic Saliers tune, "Love Will Come To You," that is a hopeful ode to a friend suffering through a broken heart, and also contemplative ballads such as "Virginia Woolf" and the appropriately haunting, strings-tinged "Ghost."

On *Rites of Passage*, the band adds to its list of impressive contributors and guest artists, with bassist Edgar Meyers, Jackson Browne, and fiddler and singer Lisa Germano. Celtic instruments such as bodhrán, uiliean pipes, and bouzouki make an appearance, adding a traditional element to their songwriting.

After recording and touring at a breakneck pace, the Indigo Girls slowed down and took two years before the release of *Swamp Ophelia* in April 1994. The album continued to expand their fan base and debuted at number nine on the *Billboard* 200 chart, their best debut to date. By the end of the year, it went gold. Ironically, Ray and Saliers were interviewed by *Billboard* prior to the release of *Swamp Ophelia*, and expressed doubt about the album's potential for singles or chart positions but did have hope for play on college radio stations. Many critics felt that *Swamp Ophelia* marked a turning point for the band; the eleven songs embody the passion and directness of *Indigo Girls* but stretch the content beyond the usual territory of tearjerker ballads, rambunctious anthems, and the tendency to meander into somewhat didactic territory of *Nomads*. The album was produced by Peter Collins at Nashville's Woodland Sound Studios. Indeed, although the title suggests a sticky, maudlin morass by simultaneously referencing the intractable earth and the tragic Shakespearean figure of Ophelia, who drowned herself, the album itself exhibits more organic sounding instruments with a tone that is not exclusively depressing. Musically, *Swamp Ophelia* continues the vaguely Celtic and intriguing instrumentation that began with *Rites* by adding pennywhistle, cello, trumpet, flugelhorn, and accordion adding to the mix—even experimenting with string sections and electric guitar.

The album's single was the incessantly catchy Saliers tune "Least Complicated," which can be read as a reminiscence of one's sexual awakening, the moment when she realized as a child that she did not fit in with the rest of the kids on the playground. Lyrics evoke a sense of trying to understand oneself when life and school teach you one thing and your personal experience teaches you another. The song is propelled by her powers of narrative and observation, bongos, other percussion, accordion, and other instruments that expand the texture of their music even further than their previous release. The song peaked at twenty-eight on the *Billboard* Modern Rock Tracks chart. Other standout songs include the dark, six-minute "Touch Me Fall" by Ray, with a muscular electric guitar presence that rivals anything that male-dominated Seattle grunge bands were producing at the time. Another noteworthy track includes the ode to partnership, "Power of Two." In fact, in his round-up of top albums of 1994, *Atlanta Journal-Constitution* writer Steve Dollar singles out the Saliers song "Power of Two" as a standout track.

Following the release of the stellar *Swamp Ophelia* and the double live album *1200 Curfews* in 1995, the latter of which features covers of Bob Dylan, Joni Mitchell, and Neil Young songs, the Indigo Girls slowed their work pace a bit. Perhaps, after nearly ten years of writing, touring, and recording and releasing a half dozen albums, they were getting tired.

Some critics and fans started to feel as though their material was getting a bit stale. Looking at the larger context of the times, however, perhaps the Indigo Girls began to seem less novel, less original, because of the mid- to late 1990s influx of and tremendous success with what became a formula of girl-with-a-guitar. Perhaps, too, the tremendous success of Sarah McLachlan's women-only touring extravaganza known as Lilith Fair made the playing field more heavily populated with female artists. The festival drastically improved the musical landscape for female artists, but its pervasiveness must have lessened the impact the Indigo Girls, even as participants in Lilith, could have on new fans and its ability to retain their older ones.

It makes some sense, then, that three years passed between 1994's *Swamp Ophelia* and a new studio album release in the form of 1997's *Shaming of the Sun*. The album wasn't as well received by critics as previous efforts because of a slight formulaic feel to the material. Noteworthy songs include the leadoff

"Shame on You," which packs in references to religion, immigration, and white middle-class ignorance and guilt. But even here the religious metaphors become diluted. In the first verse, Ray sings, "Let's go down to the riverside and take off our shoes and wash these sins away." In the chorus, which quickly follows, the river becomes personified and says to those who enter: "Shame on you." With banjo and electric guitar, it shows their interest in layering rock and folk instruments— a pleasant move—but like many of the album's other

> *In a busy, active, alienating era, it's a very personal alternative. . . . You don't need to plug it in. You can just play it anywhere.*
> —Emily Saliers,
> on using an acoustic guitar

songs, does not do too much to expand the Indigo Girls' oeuvre. Despite the critical disappointment, the album itself went to number seven on the *Billboard* 200 and was certified gold by August 1997. "Shame on You" peaked at number fifteen on the *Billboard* Adult Top 40 and number six on the Top 40 Adult Recurrents; it was the only song to appear on the *Billboard* charts.

*Come On Now Social* was released in 1999, with the appearance of a heavy-hitting and eclectic batch of musicians such as Sheryl Crow, Joan Osbourne, MeShell Ndegéocello, and Natacha Atlas. The album's sound palette is varied, starting with the rocker song "Go" to open up the experience and then hitting on country, old-style folk, and pop along the way and releasing the pleasant folk-pop single tinged with horns called "Peace Tonight." Although in *All Music Guide* Stephen Thomas Erlewine goes so far as to call the album a "fully realized comeback" and it peaked at number twelve on the Top Internet Albums and number thirty-four on the *Billboard* 200, *Come On Now Social* has not achieved even gold status.

### New Label and New Beginning for the New Millennium

The songs on 2002's *Become You*, their ninth album, are stripped down and closer to their roots than some of their earlier efforts and are a testament to the maturity and comfort of their years working together. Their intention was to pare down their arrangements to create a solid acoustic album, and they succeeded. The songs feel effortless; their production and instrumentation come across as natural and unforced. The album brings us the personal "She's Saving Me," written about the death of Saliers's sister Carrie at the age of twenty-nine from pneumonia; "Hope Alone"; the Ray-penned "Yield"; and the thickly layered vocals of the bluesy "Bitter Root." "You've Got to Show" is a sultry, intimate tune underscored by the warm vibrations of a Fender Rhodes piano and a saxophone solo, with the lyric "There are a thousand things about me I want only you to know/But I can't go there, you've got to show." In some ways, at least according to Ray, the album benefited from some of the time she spent working on her own solo album *Stag*, which was released in 2001. *Become You* is also noteworthy because it represents the first time Ray and Saliers actually worked together on songs at Tree Sound

*I keep hearing from reporters that women performers are hot items on the music scene at present but we certainly didn't feel that people were out clamoring for us to sign a recording contract.*

—Amy Ray

Studio in Georgia, thus breaking their historic pattern of writing songs separately and collaborating later. In 2004 they released *All That We Let In*, which was regarded by critics and fans as one of their best efforts in years and a continuation of the fine return to form of their earlier records. It peaked at thirty-five on the *Billboard* 200 and sixty-six on the *Billboard* Top Internet Albums, and although "Perfect World," the quintessential Indigo Girls single—catchy, thoughtful, intriguing use of organic instruments—did not receive high placement on the *Billboard* charts, it, along with other strong songs such as "Fill it Up Again," did signal that the Indigo Girls had not run out of ideas yet. A sonic experiment, the Ray-written "Heartache for Everyone" even dips into ska beats.

After many years with Epic Records, the Indigo Girls signed a five-album deal with Hollywood Records. *Despite Our Differences*, released in September 2006, was produced by Mitchell Froom, who has worked with Suzanne Vega, Elvis Costello, and Paul McCartney, among other prominent artists. The group even invited two artists whose sound diverges significantly from their own—outrageous, outspoken pop star Pink and pop songstress Brandi Carlisle—to contribute backing vocals on a few tracks. (The Indigo Girls returned the favor and appeared on Pink's track "Dear Mr. President" on her album *I'm Not Dead*.) On the whole, the pair took some musical risks for this album that paid off. As a debut on a new label, too, it only makes sense to try something new, to break away somewhat from previous methods, approaches, and sounds. Regardless of the collaborative involvement of so many accomplished musicians, *Despite Our Differences* is very much an Indigo Girls record. After nearly twenty years together, the Indigo Girls have become icons of folk rock with a social and spiritual consciousness.

## MISSION, MOTIVATION, PROCESS

The Indigo Girls' inspirations and backgrounds, musically speaking, are somewhat divergent, although early in their collaboration they bonded over a love of 1960s soul music, Buffalo Springfield records, and Joni Mitchell. Together, though, their songs can be characterized as first-person narratives often with a confessional bent. Superficially speaking, they do not seem to be the most obvious pairing of talent but what began as two young girls who liked to sing together has become a formidable creative duo.

In retrospect, the spiritual and literary qualities of their songwriting seem preordained. Emily Saliers's father taught in the school of theology at Emory University, and Amy Ray majored in religion. Saliers was going to be an English teacher before Ray persuaded her to play music together.

Together, they count William Faulkner, Flannery O'Connor, Herman Melville, and Toni Morrison as favorite writers. Though their music is not religious, per se—they are less concerned with fear, fire, and brimstone than with redemption, higher powers, and the greater meaning of life—it is hard to deny its influence and the multitude of universal images and themes it affords their songwriting.

Although they perform and record as a duo, Saliers and Ray usually work separately on music. Indeed, they are well known for going their separate ways as soon as the touring or recording processes are over, returning to their individual homes. When it's time to work on music, they compose independently and come together to collaborate on harmonies, instrumentation, and guitar parts. A careful reader of the Indigo Girls liner notes reveals that the composer nearly always takes the lead vocal on her own songs. Their writing and singing styles are appreciatively different. Ray is more outgoing, Saliers is more introspective, and it works because they willingly merge their differences into their songs. Saliers told *Guitar Player* magazine in September 1994 that she works out material on her Martin guitar but needs a "quiet space" to get started. "I start collecting these feelings and reaction and responses, and I tuck them away—I don't really write them down"(Mettler 1994). Saliers said the best time for her is either late morning or early afternoon, by herself, with a cup of coffee. She described the process as mostly spontaneous and does not overanalyze the muse. "Obviously, if I start playing something fast on the guitar, I'm not going to write that sensitive love song that I've been holding inside" (Mettler 1994). She also acknowledged that she is inspired often by new things she encounters—people, places, and things. In the *Guitar Player* interview, she reflected on some of the songs that went into *Swamp Ophelia* and said that she was jogging in Germany and thought about its place in history and how in the not too distant past, nearby countries and cities were enemies, "and people we thought we hated were being killed, but now we're all very friendly. There just seems to be no absolute truth about conflict." The cycle of history and the repetition of human actions through time, she said, is "very inspiring" (Mettler 1994).

Ray, on the other hand, writes whenever she is moved. "I don't have much discipline. And I don't know why I write, either. I go by stream-of-consciousness, so whatever pops out is what's most important to me," (Mettler 1994) she says, sometimes using an acoustic Martin guitar and other times her Fender electric guitar. She lets her approach to instrumentation and arrangement be somewhat dictated by the song's feel and message. For instance, when writing "Touch Me Fall," a six-minute progressive-leaning song, Ray started playing acoustically but then turned to her Fender Stratocaster. "I wanted a gutsy sound. The challenge was to give a tangible feel to my abstract thought ['Everything is beautiful'] as well as that feeling's flipside: decomposition," she explained (Mettler 1994).

Although their styles differ, the themes that interest Ray and Saliers unite them, serving as a common starting ground for putting their individual perspectives together. Religion and spiritual matters are a constant thread through their music, but the word "religion" is not necessarily synonymous with Christianity, although images of Christianity do often pervade their songwriting. Ray is more oriented in a view of nature than structured Christianity, and Saliers recognizes the merits of various faiths in her worldview. Arguably, it took the Indigo Girls a few albums to develop skills of irony and humor in their process, but those elements do surface every once in a while. Throughout their time together, too, they have become more confident songwriters, which Ray said has resulted in a more assertive style. As artists, through working together they have developed a fluency with each other and an unwavering sense of purpose. The work they did for some side projects, for example, marked the first time they wrote a song together. For instance, they wrote "Blood Quantum," for the Honor the Earth benefit CD together.

Following up such a stellar major label debut could not have been terribly easy for the Indigo Girls. The content on *Nomads Indians Saints* took the pair a step further in the quest for spiritual enlightenment and redemption that threads through the debut. Their ability to connect meaningfully to their listeners gives them the opportunity to address the delicate issues of life. Ray's message in one of her standout compositions, "Pushing the Needle Too Far," is one of caution that entreats the listener to resist giving in to drugs, suicide, and despair. Such an aggressive address to the listener is a product of their cleaner, more focused writing. Over the years, their efforts directly outside the day-to-day dealings of music—their causes—have helped sharpen and shape their perspective and make them better songwriters.

## LEGACY AND OTHER INTERESTS

Part of what has made the Indigo Girls so successful is their ability to take time off, do other projects, and pursue other interests individually, and then regroup. Amy Ray started her own label, called Daemon Records, based in Decatur, Georgia, in 1990 as a way to contribute to the region and assist the careers of its emerging musicians. It releases records by artists in the Athens and Atlanta scenes. The label's first release came from a band called The Ellen James Society, named after the feminist character in John Irving's novel *The World According to Garp*. In the meantime, the label put out albums from Rose Polenzani and Kristen Hall. About a decade passed, however, before Ray released her own album *Stag* in 2001, a melodic batch of rock-based tunes that allowed her to explore her inner tendencies to write harder-driving songs laced with smart lyrics and strong attitude. The album includes guest appearances by Joan Jett and Kate Schellenbach (drummer for the then-popular, all-female band Luscious Jackson). In 2005, Ray released a second solo album *Prom*, whose cover—you guessed it—features a young girl dressed in a billowy prom dress. Then, in fall 2006, Ray released another solo album called *Live From Knoxville*. While Ray owns a label, Saliers, who enjoys cooking a great deal, owns a restaurant in Decatur called Watershed, which serves seasonal, Southern-inspired food. Its cuisine has received culinary awards and acclaim on both local and national levels since 2000.

Over the course of their career together, the Indigo Girls have donated their time, energy, and music to a number of causes, especially those close to their own interests. Starting in the beginning of their career, the pair made their political and humanitarian interests clear and was identified most closely with Greenpeace. However it would take several years before some of these concerns would begin to pervade the usually personal approach of their songs. On *Indigo Girls*, the liner notes list organizations such as Amnesty International, Greenpeace, and the Coalition for the Homeless as efforts they support. And as early as 1990, a year after the release of their debut, they started supporting these causes with more than just mentions on paper. Their music appeared on an album called *Tame Yourself* in honor of the tenth anniversary of PETA (People for the Ethical Treatment of Animals), along with Chrissie Hynde, Howard Jones, and the B-52s. They've appeared in countless concerts for causes and folk festivals, from Newport Folk Festival to more unusual events such as "A Gathering of Tribes," which took place in San Francisco in fall 1990 and featured musicians from all levels of fame.

> *We don't say to people that they necessarily have a responsibility to be political. . . . Music is such a good way to resist. It keeps you strong. It has dignity.*
> —Amy Ray

The process of raising awareness about local issues on national levels is not easy, they acknowledge. Throughout their career, they have used their position to call attention to issues that have been important, including making a recording called *Jesus Christ Superstar: A Resurrection*, whereby the Indigo Girls reinterpret the songs from the rock opera. The album's proceeds benefited three gun control education groups, including Sarah Brady's Center to Prevent Handgun Violence. The Indigo Girls released *Resurrection* on Ray's label, Daemon Records, and let the charity be chosen by the album's producer Michael Lorant, who had been the victim of a mugging and shooting. In 1995 they spent time on the "Honor the Earth" tour, which raised about $250,000 and generated correspondence to public officials for the grassroots efforts of Native Americans. Concurrent to that, a benefit CD was released called *Honor*, with tracks from not only the Indigo Girls but Bonnie Raitt, Bruce Cockburn, and more. By 1996, their interests ranged from women's issues and the environment to the rights of oppressed, disenfranchised groups such as Native Americans. These progressive issues began to make a more regular appearance in their work, prompting the Indigo Girls to describe their music as "acoustic folk rock with angst" (Perkinson 1996).

Throughout their career, they have also lent their support to the gay community, marching in gay rights rallies and parades. They have never apologized for being out musicians and have also resisted being pigeonholed or stereotyped, too. In 2000, Ray and Saliers participated in Honor the Earth Tour again, which supports the political advocacy for native people who are supporting and protecting the earth. In fall 2006, their music was featured on a benefit album *Safe Haven for the Sexual Minority Youth Resource Center*, an organization in Oregon that benefits, educates, and caters to lesbian, gay, bisexual, transgendered, queer, and questioning (LGBTQQ) youth. In fall 2006, in support of *Despite Our Differences*, the Girls played sets at shows in their home state that benefited a musician's medical expenses and the Georgia Network to End Sexual Assault.

On the lighter side of things, the Indigo Girls have also performed onboard cruises organized by Olivia, a travel organization geared toward lesbians.

## SELECTED DISCOGRAPHY

*Indigo Girls*. Epic, 1988
*Nomads Indians Saints*. Epic, 1990
*Rites of Passage*. Epic, 1992
*1200 Curfews*. Epic, 1995
*Become You*. Epic, 2002
*Despite Our Differences*. Hollywood, 2006

## FURTHER READING

*Advertiser, The*. "At Last, the Girls Get a Chance." (August 24, 1989).

Blake, John. "Sharing Musical DNA, Indigo Girl Emily Saliers and Her Father Tell What's the Same About their Different Styles in Book." *Atlanta Journal-Constitution* (December 4, 2004).

Christie, Brian. "Indigo Girls Perform Live, Discuss Their Career." *CNN News* (April 29, 1994).

Dafoe, Chris. "Inside the Sleeve: Indigo Girls *Indigo Girls*." *Globe and Mail*, Toronto, Canada. (August 17, 1989).

Devenish, Colin. "Indigo Girls Get Back to Basics: Ray and Saliers True to Acoustic Roots on 'Become You.'" *Rolling Stone* online (January 16, 2002). Available online at www.rollingstone.com/news/story/5919110/indigo_girls_get_back_to_basics.

Dollar, Steve. "The Year's Best Music Rock Albums." *Atlanta Journal-Constitution* (December 25, 1994).

Erlewine, Stephen Thomas. "Come on Now Social. Review." *All Music Guide*. Available online at www.allmusic.com/cg/amg.dll?p=amg&sql=10:azfyxqlkldke.

Flick, Larry. "Indigo Girls Ponder Popularity; Epic Readies Push for 'Swamp Ophelia.'" *Billboard* (March 12, 1994).

Foyston, John. "Indigo Girls Serve Up Evening of Intelligent, Provocative Music." *The Oregonian* (October 29, 1990).

Givens, Ron. "The New Kids on the Block: Indigo Girls and Syd Straw Dispense Folk Wisdom." *Newsweek* (August 21, 1989).

Guterman, Jimmy. "Review of *Indigo Girls*." *Rolling Stone* 551 (May 5, 1989). Available online at www.rollingstone.com/artists/indigogirls/albums/album/92738/review/6068072/indigo_girls.

Harrington, Richard. "A Tribute to PETA's Pals." *Washington Post* (November 12, 1990).

Haymes, Greg. "Duo Dynamics: Complementary Styles Help Indigo Girls Keep Music Fresh." *The Times Union*, Albany, NY (March 4, 2004).

Holden, Stephen. "Indigo Girls' Sensibilities." *New York Times* (December 10, 1990).

Hull, Anne V. "Closer to Fame: Indigo Girls' Obscure Days are Over." *St. Petersburg Times* (September 19, 1989).

Indigo Girls official Web site. See www.indigogirls.com.

Jenkins, Mark. "Indigo Girls Dye Everything Poetry." *Washington Post* (November 23, 1990).

Mettler, Mike. "Indigo Girls: The Power of Two." *Guitar Player* (September 1994).

Morse, Steve. "Music: Acoustic Claims a Piece of the Rock." *Boston Globe* (June 4, 1989).

Morse, Steve. "Indigo Girls: Strange Fire, Record Review." *Boston Globe* (December 7, 1989).

Morse, Steve. "Indigo Girls A Team Despite Differences." *Boston Globe* (April 26, 1990).

Morse, Steve. "The Nonmaterial Indigo Girls: Their Folk-Rock Takes You on a Spiritual Journey." *Boston Globe* (December 7, 1990).

Morse, Steve. "The Red-Hot Indigo Girls. Music Review." *Boston Globe* (December 12, 1990).

Morse, Steve. "The Indigo Girls: Taking Stock at 30." *Boston Globe* (May 1, 1994).

Neufield, Matt. "Indigo Girls are the Real Thing." *Washington Times* (November 22, 1990).

Niester, Alan. "Pop Reviews: Protest Recalled with Indigo Girls' Aggressive Folk." *Globe and Mail*, Toronto, Canada. (May 5, 1990).

Owens, Thom. "Shaming of the Sun. Review." *All Music Guide*. Available online at www.allmusic.com/cg/amg.dll?p=amg&token=&sql=10:2ht67ub080jg.

Perkinson, Robert. "The Indigo Girls." *The Progressive* (December 1996).

Popkin, Helen A.S. "Out of the Blue." *St. Petersburg Times* (October 5, 1990).

Sacks & Co. "The Indigo Girls' New Album *Despite Our Differences* Out Now on Hollywood Records." Press release. (January 11, 2007).

Selvin, Joel. "Something Else." *San Francisco Chronicle* (September 8, 1990).

Selvin, Joel. "Folk-Singing Duo Scores Direct Hit at Berkeley Complex, Lyrics Set to Hard-Driving Guitar." *San Francisco Chronicle* (November 2, 1990).

Staggs, Jeffrey. "Indigo Girls' MTV Blues." *Washington Times* (June 24, 1994).

Sullivan, Jim. "'60s Folk Meets '90s Folk in Newport." *Boston Globe* (August 13, 1990).

Tomlinson, Stuart. "Indigo Girls On the Go Rocker, Balladeer Bask In Success of First Album." *The Oregonian* (December 1, 1989).

Tomlinson, Stuart. "It's Like Singing With Your Sister." *The Oregonian* (October 26, 1990).

Courtesy of Photofest

# Janis Joplin

*. . . If Joni Mitchell gave me the idea that a woman could write about her life in a public forum, Janis gave me the idea that a woman could live a wild life and put that out there in a public forum, too.*

—Rosanne Cash

## OVERVIEW

Perhaps more than any other female musician, Janis Joplin's life and career embody the cliché expression "sex, drugs, and rock and roll," albeit in a tragic way. Joplin emerged from the blues musical tradition with a style that shows an influence of the singer Bessie Smith. However, Joplin came of age during the late 1960s, so the influence took on new life when it merged with women's burgeoning sexual freedoms of the decade. Janis Joplin became a voice of a generation, but unlike Joan Baez, another artist and singer closely associated with California's music scene in the 1960s, Joplin was a more emotionally explosive singer and performer. Where Baez was plaintive with her political entreaties through beautiful songs, Joplin infused her singing with a sense of urgency, desperation, pain, and passion that seemed borne out of her need to break out of the good-girl expectations surrounding her upbringing and her community. She rose to stardom as the lead singer for the San Francisco group Big Brother and the Holding Company, but she left this psychedelic rock band in the late 1960s for an influential solo career that was cut short by years of drug and alcohol abuse that ultimately ended her life.

Janis Joplin did much to change the definition and expand the possibilities of women in rock in the 1960s (see sidebar). She was strong, assertive, honest, and at times sexually frank—she was prone to the kind of indiscreet talk that men are more commonly associated with. Her voice and style bore the influence of Aretha Franklin, Bessie Smith, Big Mama Thornton, Otis Redding, and Odetta. Although Joplin died young and her personal life was marked by difficult relationships, her career left an incredible impact on the rest of the music business, on artists who discovered her work posthumously, and on popular culture in general. Joplin's achievements helped make possible the careers of Bonnie Raitt, Sheryl Crow, Joan Osborne, Melissa Etheridge, and Joss Stone—female songwriters and singers who all to some degree fuse blues and rock. Rosanne Cash reflected on Joplin's influence saying that without Joplin, there would be no Melissa Etheridge, there would be no Chrissie Hynde, no Gwen Stefani, that there would be no one.

Her first album, *I Got Dem Ol' Kozmic Blues Again Mama!*, reached number twenty-three on the *Billboard* black albums chart and number four on the *Billboard* pop albums chart. Its follow-up, *Pearl*, reached number thirteen in 1971 on the black album chart and number one on the pop albums chart. The posthumous success continued, with *Joplin in Concert* hitting number four on the pop albums chart in 1972, *Janis Joplin's Greatest Hits* hitting thirty-seven on the same chart in 1973, *Janis* hitting fifty-four in 1975, and finally *Farewell Song* peaking at 104 on the pop albums chart in 1982. She is most identified with the song "Me and Bobby McGee," which was written by Kris Kristofferson

**Days of Psychedelia, Days of Folk Music: Three Joplin Contemporaries**

The late 1960s and early 1970s were an extraordinarily productive time for West Coast–based singers and songwriters, many of whose careers were bolstered by the Monterey Pop Festival, psychedelic drugs, and exploring the boundaries of folk music. The era launched not only Joan Baez and Janis Joplin, but Cass Elliot (Mama Cass), Cher, and Stevie Nicks.

Cass started in a folk trio called the Big Three, with Tim Rose and James Hendricks, and after a few underappreciated records, it morphed into the Mugwumps, which included Denny Doherty. He and Elliot would make music history when they joined John and Michelle Phillips in The Mamas and The Papas in 1965. Many critics attribute the group's success with songs such as "Monday Monday" and "California Dreamin'" to Cass's warm voice and charismatic personality. In fact, her home in California was reputedly a revolving, welcoming door; people came and went at all hours of the day and night.

Before she became known as a pop music diva, Cher's roots were in folk music with her husband Sonny Bono. The pair recorded several albums together as Sonny and Cher, most notably the 1965 anthem "I Got You Babe." Her solo career now spans several decades and includes successful turns in films, especially *Moonstruck*. Stevie Nicks and Lindsey Buckingham toured as the band Fritz and opened up for Janis Joplin, Jimi Hendrix, and others between 1968 and 1971 before joining Fleetwood Mac in 1974. As a singer in Fleetwood Mac with on-again, off-again boyfriend Buckingham, Nicks's flowing, mystical attire and husky voice made her a symbol of sexy 1970s singers, one whose name was frequently mentioned alongside Linda Ronstadt and Emmylou Harris.

and went to number one on the pop singles chart in 1971; the song "Mercedes-Benz," which in the 1990s was used in a car advertisement on television; and "Get It While You Can," which hit number seventy-eight in 1971 on the pop singles chart. "Kozmic Blues" hit forty-one on the pop singles charts in 1969, "Cry Baby" reached forty-two in 1971, "Down On Me" hit number ninety-one in 1972, and "One Night Stand," ten years later, reached thirty-five on the *Billboard* Mainstream Rock chart. Although *Cheap Thrills*, released by Columbia, was certified gold in October 1968, and her debut was certified gold in December 1969, nearly all of her gold, platinum, and multiplatinum certifications took place after her death. *Pearl* was certified gold in February 1971 and multiplatinum (times three) by 1986. Her next album to achieve gold after *Pearl* was *Joplin in Concert* in 1972, and *Janis Joplin's Greatest Hits* in 1975. By 2000, *Pearl* would be platinum four times over, and the aforementioned *Greatest Hits*, seven times platinum by 1999. Joplin never saw much of this success in her lifetime: The bulk of her accolades, album sales, and critical and commercial appreciation came after her death. She did not receive any Grammy Awards. One can only speculate about the shape her career might have taken had she not passed away at such a young age.

In addition to the legacy she left with her own musical style, Joplin unintentionally became a new type of role model for women in the late 1960s—one who was real, flawed, but nonetheless attractive. Joplin literally did not feel comfortable in her own skin—she often felt that her excess weight, her wavy, thick hair, and her troublesome skin were liabilities in an era of thin, straight, long-haired women. Additionally, her own contemporaries, from Grace Slick, the singer for Jefferson Airplane who was a former model, to the tiny and angelic Joan Baez, were traditionally more feminine than Joplin. But she formed her own style by wearing long flowing shirts and somewhat flamboyant beaded tops and boots. Once she started to perform, though, she infused her performance with a raw eroticism that created an unorthodox stage presence for a woman in the mid- to late 1960s. Joplin challenged boundaries, including sexuality; she was open about relationships she had with men and women, including a long-term, off-and-on relation with a woman named Peggy Caserta. In addition to winning fans and gaining attention, especially in the early days with Big Brother, Joplin's ferocious, passionate persona onstage caught the attention of Jim Morrison, Joe McDonald, Kris Kristofferson, Jimi Hendrix, and oddly, Joe Namath, who were all men she is rumored to have slept with.

## EARLY YEARS

Joplin grew up in the small conservative oil refinery town of Port Arthur, Texas, situated in the southeastern corner of the state. At the time that she was growing up, it was a pleasant place to raise a child, and the community was a mix of Mexicans, African Americans, and Cajuns from Louisiana. Her father, Seth, was educated at Texas A&M and moved from Amarillo to Port Arthur to work for Texaco as an engineer. Joplin referred to her father as a "secret intellectual." Her mother, Dorothy, originally came from Nebraska and was the daughter of a cattle rancher turned farmer turned salesman. Joplin's mother was described as industrious and disciplined—a woman with an aggressive temperament and an unwavering decisiveness along with her very shrewd intelligence. As a young child, her parents said that she did not necessarily behave in a way that suggested she craved the spotlight. She sang in choir and glee club but she was not really aware of any musical talent. In fact, Joplin was mostly interested in art, and as soon as she could hold a pencil she started drawing. Her parents arranged for art lessons by the time she was in third or fourth grade. She also enjoyed reading, and her mother said she was a storyteller. When she was six, her mother gave birth to Laura, her younger sister, and to brother Michael when Janis was ten. Although she loved her siblings, her mother said that Janis seemed to need more attention than they did, and if she did not receive it, she grew unhappy. She also pushed herself to be a high achiever. Overall, she was well-liked by her community; she seemed like a bright, well-adjusted, helpful child.

When she got to high school, Joplin started to form her own opinions, including her proclamation in ninth grade that she approved of integration—a bold statement unheard of in that part of the world. It was the beginning of her departure from the innocent, demure, and shy girl of the South and her transformation into a strong-willed, independent young woman. Through most of high school Joplin's grades were high, and she was smart, imaginative, and at times challenging. Her mother wanted her to conform and wished for social approval for her daughter. Her friend Karleen Bennett recalls an incident in which Joplin painted a nude silhouette on her closet door, and her mother forced her to cover up the image. Her teenage years got even more difficult as high school progressed, as her adolescent chubbiness gave way to weight gain, and her skin became plagued with acne. She became extremely self-conscious, and her talent and intelligence did not make up for those perceived shortcomings in the conservative small town of Port Arthur. She became friendly with a handful of boys who were starting to rebel against the strictures of the small town by drinking, rabble rousing, and partaking in general juvenile delinquency—nothing terribly harmful or illegal. Her new male friends applauded her for her ability to blend in as "one of the guys" and engage in loud, crude talk as they were wont to do.

By the time she was a senior in high school, even with the boys as a buffer, she was mocked and made fun of. Her unconventional style of dress raised eyebrows. Her friend Karleen said Joplin often acted as though she did not care what people thought of her, but deep down she just wanted to be accepted and really did want the approval. At the suggestion of her mother, Joplin took a drafting class, thinking it would help her with her painting skills, but she was the only girl in the class. People assumed her affiliation was sexual and began saying that she was chasing the boys. But her difficulty with her parents and her friends really crystallized after she defied her parents and went to New Orleans one evening—she told her parents she was at Karleen's—with a bunch of friends. They hung out at jazz joints and on the way home got into an accident.

Joplin's hometown consisted mostly of Baptists and Catholics with strong ideas about how teenagers ought to behave. Joplin needed attention, and even negative attention was acceptable. Because she hung out with mostly boys and not girls, she started to develop a negative reputation in her conservative town. Her outlandish behavior and her inflated and mostly false claims of sexual exploits gave people the idea that she was loose or wild, but Joplin was actually a smart, creative teenager who felt trapped, which led to restlessness.

Somehow, though, she found refuge in music. Despite her intelligence, she stopped going to school periodically because socially it was so unpleasant. She spent time at the local coffee shop, Pasea's, where she displayed and sold some of her paintings. But during this time, too, she had been listening to jazz; Joplin was influenced by the beat generation and jazz, despite the fact that she was a teenager growing up in the age of The Beatles and Beach Boys. Joplin started singing along with her records around her sophomore year in high school. Musically speaking, as a teenager she sang with folk rock groups, playing sometimes with future Jefferson Airplane guitarist Jorma Kaukonen. Early videos of her performances show that she had started to develop her own style even before she became a part of Big Brother and the Holding Company. At home Joplin would listen to records by Odetta, Bessie Smith, and Willie Mae Thornton and imitate what she heard—her ability to do so was uncanny. Slowly, though, she started to develop her own phrasing, her own inflections.

After graduating from high school, her parents were grateful that she agreed to enroll at nearby Lamar State College of Technology in Beaumont, but it didn't have a much better or more open atmosphere than her high school. She studied for about a year, but during that time, there was an incident in which she ran off to Houston, became extremely intoxicated, and wound up in the hospital with a kidney infection. Psychiatric and psychological counseling also resulted from the event. According to biographer Myra Friedman's account, it seems as though her parents really were not sure what to do about her, or for her, or with her. For a brief period, her mother sent her to live with her sister in Los Angeles. Joplin got a job and moved out to her own place in Venice, where the beatniks were. The experience changed her; she returned to Texas shortly thereafter and tried to convert the middle-class suburban friends she made into hippies too. It helped provide her with an identity. During that year, she had started to sing, beginning with a performance at a Beaumont Club. Initially, she was not met with much of a response, positive or negative, but it did not stop her. Joplin started to sing at the Half-Way House in Beaumont and the Purple Onion in Houston—the same place where she'd lost control of herself. That summer, too, she sang for a bank commercial, set to the tune of Woody Guthrie's "This Land is Your Land," swapping out the word "land" for "bank." It was the first recording she made.

Joplin returned to Lamar in spring of that year and performed well. She lost weight, started wearing make-up, and worked as a waitress. If she wasn't working, she was out with her friend Jack Smith at the beach or dancing. Things were normal and placid for a while, but gradually beer turned to bourbon, and the swimming and lounging at night on the beach turned to driving the car into the water. Finally, she and Jack started going back to Louisiana for the bars, and her personality swung back out of control. She and a handful of her friends somehow ended up in Austin by the summer of 1962, specifically to the University of Texas-Austin. A group of tenement houses called "the ghetto" quickly became her home; it was the center of the Beat scene, too. The music scene of the Beats in Austin revolved around country and blues; the main-stream people on campus were listening to folk music. Joplin started singing around campus with friends Powell St. John and Lanny Wigins, and they called themselves the Waller Creek Boys.

Austin was more important to her career than her life as a student, because she met Kenneth Threadgill, country music singer and proprietor of a place called Threadgill's, a hangout and music spot converted from a gas station. He encouraged her efforts and became her friend. The trio performed there and on campus regularly and she enrolled at University of Texas-Austin as an art student. She was still a wild child, still saying outlandish provocative things to get attention, and still starting trouble. Mostly, she drank a lot, but she did not take psychedelic drugs at this time nor did she smoke pot—her friends recalled her taking Seconal and said she would "run crazy. She'd walk the streets at night and try to get run over and run into buildings with her head" (Friedman 1973, 41). Despite the fact that she had a close group of friends and was starting to perform, the community at large in Austin, on campus and off, did not approve of her. Finally, she reached a turning point when she was rated "Ugliest Man on Campus." She left campus one night in January after performing at Threadgill's. Her parents tried to find her, but it was too late. She had already taken off for San Francisco.

## CAREER PATH

Still entranced with beatnik and then hippie subculture, Joplin was destined for San Francisco. After hitchhiking from Texas to California she arrived with her friend Chet Helms, filthy and broke. Undaunted, the first night Joplin performed at Coffee and Confusion in the North Beach area, which was home to City Lights Bookshop and other beatnik haunts. The small crowd assembled there loved her and she went home with $14. She worked odd jobs and lived on the dole, her parents and friends said, and sang. San Francisco was undergoing a transition between the end of the beat era and the beginning of the hippie era. Regardless, she was at home; in San Francisco, no one thought her grubby attire, loud demeanor, or free, live-and-let-live attitude was un-usual. She started smoking dope, which she'd previously eschewed in Austin, and doing speed. Some other friends contend in the early days of her life in San Francisco she was also doing heroin.

Joplin spent 1963 to 1965 in the San Francisco area and developed a strong, devoted following. But she continued to be misunderstood and receive abuse from other people; one evening, she had a violent run-in with a rough crowd in a back alley; another night, she got into a motorcycle accident. Her rela-tions with men were similarly difficult. She moved to New York and stayed on

*She had a large ego to gratify. She certainly sought and needed other people's acceptance, but she was very definitely an independent person. There was nobody else controlling her destiny, that's for sure.*

—Jim Langdon

the Lower East Side, playing at a place called Slug's. Somehow, her parents became convinced that her career was starting to take shape, but Joplin didn't stay there long and was back in San Francisco by fall 1964. When she returned, she started dealing drugs, mainly speed, which, in addition to her performances on stage, was yet another path to social acceptance.

Unfortunately, the loose, laid back culture of 1960s San Francisco appealed to her too, as she had easy access to drugs and alcohol. By the middle of 1965 she tried to have herself committed to the San Francisco General Hospital. It did not work. She was dating a man whose drug habits were not too dissimilar from her own, although he was in much better physical shape than she was. Eventually, though, the hedonistic lifestyle took its toll on her. Wasted to eighty-eight pounds, Joplin was sent home to her parents by her concerned friends and her boyfriend at the time, himself a speed user. She also went home because she was supposed to be getting married to her boyfriend. Joplin returned to school, wore practical clothing that covered up the track marks on her arms, and attained some level of conformity and stability for about ten months. She wanted to stay off drugs and did not like the edginess and anxiety that it brought her; she talked often of doing "the right thing." Unfortunately, her boyfriend deserted her, so there was no marriage. While she was living in Texas during this time, Joplin kept singing, making trips to Austin to appear at a club called the Eleventh. By 1966, she was able to identify becoming a singer as her chief aspiration but was afraid that the choice would also mean a return to her previously unstable lifestyle.

As she was planning to move to Austin, her friend Chet Helms, who was still in San Francisco, contacted her through a mutual friend and expressed that they wanted her to audition for a band called Big Brother and the Holding Company, whom he was managing. She was only twenty-three years old; it was May 1966. At the time, Joplin kept telling reporters she joined the band not because she was ambitious about her singing career but because of sex. To some extent, that line was a cover—it was hard for her to admit to her ambitions.

Joplin moved back to California and joined the group. In general, she was met with surprise from her audience—surprise that a white woman could sing the blues like she did. When she first arrived, band members were expecting someone more glamorous, rather than the overweight girl with bad skin and rough, mannish clothing. Early rehearsals with Big Brother before performances indicated to her that she needed to sing loud in front of a rock band. There is inherent irony, though, because she was not even initially brought on to be the band's lead singer, but her larger-than-life personality soon demonstrated that she should serve as nothing but just that. Big Brother and the Holding Company tended to play sloppily, and although that style had its appeal critics noticed that Joplin elevated the music to another level. This progression wasn't always recognized, however, because members of the band sometimes remarked that they received complaints about how "terrible" she was—her Texas country rock was a bit at odds with the band's idea of a rock sound. Nevertheless, somehow the band could not help but be transformed by her presence, and Joplin had discovered a joyous, bluesy band to help her find her voice.

Ultimately, despite the fact that Joplin had been clean for about a year, San Francisco's culture started to affect her again, along with the crowd she was hanging out with. Soon, drinking at pool halls with the Grateful Dead turned into doing speed again and then acid with Big Brother, although reports seem to suggest she was not aware it was acid at the time and that overall she stayed away from that drug. Around this time, San Francisco's young population was shifting from beatniks, who wanted to create an alternative to mainstream American culture, toward hippies, whose primary concern was reactive: dropping out of and escaping from mainstream culture. The growing tension between the two was something Joplin experienced; no doubt the hippies' preferences toward LSD, heroin, and marijuana were all around her. Indeed, even the band's name reflected the transition from beatniks to hippies: The "big brother" part was a cynical beatnik reference to George Orwell's classic novel *1984* but the latter half referred to the slang expression "are you holding" as in "are you carrying marijuana?" Joplin lived with the band in a house north of San Francisco, down the street from the Grateful Dead, in which she found a community that was deeply interested in expanding its mind through music, drugs, and intellectual dialogue.

### From Big Brother to Solo Career

The band had a self-titled debut on the Mainstream Label, which came out in 1967. Joplin only appeared on a few tracks singing lead; in others, she is relegated to the background. Her standout tracks include "Bye, Bye Baby" and "Down on Me."

To say that Joplin's addition to Big Brother was an asset is an understatement; many critics agree she was the most engaging part of it. When the band played at the 1967 Monterey Pop Festival she sang the Big Mama Thornton song "Ball and Chain" and captivated the audience. Cass Elliot of The Mamas and The Papas recalled watching Joplin's performance, stunned (Jackson 2005, 219). Joplin's signature whisper-to-a-howling-scream of a vocal approach surprised many. Her body shook, quivered, her hair swung around; Joplin looked as though she were possessed by some force greater than herself. The performance, though, was no act; she was quick to say that singing was liberating for her. Because of her confident onstage persona, reporters were often caught off guard by her offstage demeanor, when her insecurities

*If you can get them once, man . . . I think you sort of switch on their brain. . . . Whooooooo! It's life. That's what rock 'n' roll is for.*

revealed themselves. Some felt protective, but others were alarmed by how needy she could be. The misery and power she portrayed on stage dissolved between performances but her genius was still evident. Joplin herself acknowledged that it was her vulnerability that allowed her to connect with audiences. Her performances were cathartic, startling, and provided a strong, immediate bond for fans who were attracted to her self-destructiveness. But her onstage personality also diverted much of the attention away from the rest of the band members, who were all male and who did not enjoy their newfound invisibility. After Monterey, interviewers all wanted to talk to Joplin, who was none too happy to comply with their requests, albeit with a manipulative twist that showed she wanted to retain the upper hand in her image creation. Joplin perceived it as an opportunity to concoct shocking sound bites and racy details about her life. Regardless of the veracity of her stories, Joplin had the press wrapped around her finger; she made for good copy.

The success of their live performance and the presence of Joplin in the band helped the band sign a deal with Albert Grossman to manage them in early 1968. He set them up with gigs up and down the East Coast. Big Brother made its stunning, successful New York debut in February 1968. B.B. King opened for them as his first performance for a white audience in downtown Manhattan.

The acid rock, *Cheap Thrills*, came out in 1968 and topped the charts, which helped elevate Joplin to star status. *Cheap Thrills* was the band's first album for Columbia Records and was the official commercial breakthrough for the band. The recording process was fraught with difficulty because at its heart Big Brother was a gritty, sloppy garage band. Joplin suggested they record it live, since their live energy was compelling. The idea didn't work—the tapes were a disaster, the audience unresponsive—so they went back to recording in the studio. There, Joplin poured her passion into the sessions and sang her heart out, but the band members remained cool and unflappable. They were in one place, which was laid back and usually out of tune, and she was in another, taking the process much more seriously. Eventually, the studio was turned into a makeshift live environment, so the band could play its parts together at the same time, which was more successful. The band wanted to create a record that made people dance, but Joplin, caught between the band's idea and producer John Simon's desires to put together something in tune and in time, was frustrated. Joplin did her best to rise above the noise, most notably on "Piece of My Heart," but also as part of a simmering exercise in restraint, a cover of the classic George and Ira Gershwin song "Summertime." Unsurprisingly, both tracks were singles for the album.

The success came despite the fact that the band was paired with an unlikely producer, John Simon, a man with exacting musical standards and a background in jazz. *Rolling Stone* expressed disappointment at the inherent sloppiness of the band even under the guidance of one of the best producers in the business. Other critics were much more generous in their assessment by acknowledging that the band's energy made up for the lack of musicianship. Regardless of what the critics thought and whatever perceived missteps were taken in the record's production, *Cheap Thrills* quickly shot up to the number one slot and went gold within just a couple of months of its release. "Piece of My Heart" became a Top 40 hit. At this point, the band was billed as "Janis Joplin with Big Brother and the Holding Company."

Shortly after the album's release, Grossman, who was managing Peter, Paul and Mary and Bob Dylan at the time, encouraged Joplin's solo career and suggested she leave the band. At this point, Joplin was unhappy—the tension in the band was high, and the press had disparaged Big Brother while reserving most of its praise for her. She was ambitious, but her bandmates were overcome with inertia. The decision tormented her, but once she reached it, she actively courted success. There were other elements, though—specifically the collective toll that drugs took on the band members. As Joplin's sister Laura explained, with their newfound income from music, drug use went up and relationships and performances suffered. During Christmas 1968, Janis Joplin and Big Brother played its last gig as a group. So Joplin looked for a better, blues-oriented backup band, one with a seasoned horn section like those who backed Aretha Franklin or Otis Redding. By this stage in her career, Joplin had the undivided attention of the media, which had latched onto her every word and lauded the power with which she claimed the rough side of rock and roll for herself. The only women prior to Joplin who had sung in this way were African American.

Although pursuing life as a solo artist meant losing the support of her surrogate family in San Francisco, Joplin forged ahead. In hindsight it seems a foregone conclusion that she would leave the band, but she faced some challenges and some backlash from fans—hippies thought she was selling out, and Joplin herself was finding it difficult to be a woman out on her own, even in the late 1960s. She continued to give the public the persona that made her famous and continued to hide her native intelligence. Her paranoia about her image and her looks continued unabated as did her use of alcohol. By summer 1968, six months before she left the band, she started using heroin more regularly. Life on the road was taking its toll, but there was a certain self-destructive romance to heroin, because artists such as Billie Holiday had used the drug. There was a belief that it was a path to musical greatness.

Joplin, though, was excited by the prospect of working on her own. Getting musicians together and convincing them to stay with her during the touring and recording process was tricky once again; visions and ideas clashed between Joplin and producer Gabriel Mekler, who had previously worked with Steppenwolf but not any soul bands. Drug use was commonplace among Joplin and some of her band members and was enough to be disruptive to the recording and touring processes. Her first album, *I Got Dem Ol' Kozmic Blues Again Mama!*, featured some of the musicians from Big Brother, including guitarist Sam Andrew, but the group heavily featured horns, too. It was released in September 1969 with only eight tracks; she did a take on the Rodgers and Hart song "Little Girl Blue," wrote the song "One Good Man," and co-wrote "Kozmic Blues" with organist-producer Mekler. The title of the album refers to what she felt was the universality of the blues—Joplin did not feel it was a race-specific state of mind. Although she was brought up white and middle-class and the blues was acknowledged as the music for those dealing with hard times, Joplin distinguished her brand of blues as something more existential that is felt in the gut.

The overall sound of the band was a bit more accomplished and put-together than the shambolic jam rock of Big Brother, but the music itself, a soulful rock, was a new embellishment for her singing. The group played together for months before the album was released—Grossman advised her to not waste any time after her departure. The album was not the biggest success but it did contain her most well-known songs, a take on the Jerry Ragovoy's "Try (Just a Little Bit Harder)" and a cover of the Bee Gees' "To Love Someone." At the time of its release, though, *Kozmic Blues* was not critically hailed, rather it was considered a letdown because it was rough around the edges and showed growing pains because of Joplin's shift in style to a more soulful rock. The band overshadows Joplin's voice in many cases but does so without making up for it with any inspired playing. However, it is more than worth wading through the murky playing because of Joplin's voice. The album received mixed reviews in the United States but better press in Europe; British audiences liked her, and troops stationed in Germany could not wait for her to come and perform for them. Still, in retrospect it is really surprising that a woman who had received so much in the way of accolades had such a tricky time getting decent, consistent producers and competent, smart musicians to back her. It is almost as if on *Kozmic Blues*, her band is simply not worthy of her, continuing a trend from her Big Brother days, but it is more likely that timing and her insecurity regarding her own musical talent hindered her—it was not easy for her to be around more competent musicians. And her voice proved difficult to match to any particular genre.

If one can remove her debut from that immediate historical context and think of the album as the beginning of the career of a woman who was experimenting with her voice and doing something that was relatively new for the time, one is better able to appreciate its accomplishments and its flaws. For example, the record is heavy on horn arrangements, and although Joplin's voice may become too harsh at times, many critics believe that on this album she has achieved a stylistic balance between pure blues and soul. Part of the issue, it seems, is that it is hard to capture her essence in the studio. Consequently, her live performances—even those recorded—are significantly better. It is worth watching the *Woodstock: 3 Days of Peace & Music* documentary directed by Michael Wadleigh just for Joplin's performance of the traditional gospel song "Work Me Lord." Joplin is positively electric. In fact, the strength of her live performance sums up the whole genesis and, some might argue, the point of her career itself, because Joplin had a parasitic relationship to her audience. Then again, the point of much of the music produced in San Francisco in the late 1960s, whether it was Big Brother, the Grateful Dead, or Country Joe and the Fish, was just to play it for other people to enjoy. Spontaneity and experience were more important than studied attention to music theory and the mantra of practice-makes-perfect. Many of the recordings from these bands around the time suffer from such inconsistencies. Nevertheless, the album went gold, but it fell short of generating any Top 10 singles.

There is a sense that she hoped fame would bring her some inner peace. Unfortunately, the path to fame was littered with Southern Comfort, heroin, bisexual experimentation (mostly with longtime companion Peggy Caserta), constant work, and the need to regularly work her audiences into a near-riot stage. By spring 1969—well before her debut record released—Joplin was obviously on her way to self destruction. She had a serious overdose in March 1969, but luckily her friends revived her. In early 1970, she took Dolophine to try to kick her habit and was under the care of a physician. She went to Brazil for five weeks and declared that she was clean, but when she returned, she quickly started up again. The cycle continued, on and off, for months.

By 1970, Joplin had three albums behind her, stellar performances at the watershed festivals at Monterey and Woodstock, an appearance on the cover of *Newsweek* magazine, and countless newspaper and magazine articles devoted to her. Joplin even turned up as a guest on the *Dick Cavett Show* just before her ten-year high school reunion. All of this public acceptance should have made her appearance at the reunion go smoothly—she even brought some of her San Francisco contingent along to help deflect any potential trouble. Her younger sister Laura was there, and Joplin hoped her presence was supportive, but Laura told the press that her parents had lost two of Joplin's records and had not replaced them. Joplin held a pre-reunion press conference, during which she came close to crying several times. Dressed in many layers of colorful clothing and oversized glasses, she looked like a California freak to her conservative hometown. Her entourage behaved badly, and her parents felt embarrassed; Joplin and her mother came to blows and there are uncorroborated reports that her mother suggested that she wished Janis had never been born. Joplin was crushed. But even after this experience, she changed her will so that half of her estate went to her parents and a quarter each to her brother Michael and sister Laura.

There is some evidence that by spring 1970 she was trying to take more responsibility for her career and had cut back on drinking. When she returned from her reunion, she started to work on the next album, which was recorded with a collection of musicians, some with whom she had worked previously, who took on the name the Full Tilt Boogie Band. Finally, Joplin had a band that was not only versatile but that existed to serve her vision. Joplin was excited, looking forward to making more money, taking control of her career, maybe even having a baby with boyfriend-turned-fiancé Seth Morgan. But as time passed he seemed less interested in her and more interested in her money.

The album was titled *Pearl*—the nickname her friends in San Francisco used for her so they would not have to call her Janis Joplin, her public, famous name. Produced by Paul Rothchild, known for his expert work with the Doors, *Pearl* was released in early 1971, four months after her death. He was the first producer to be able to really work with Joplin. She died only three weeks after Jimi Hendrix, who had choked to death after taking an overdose of sleeping pills. Joplin died in a Los Angeles motel on October 5, 1970, of an overdose of heroin and alcohol. Some, such as her sister, have insisted that her death was accidental, that Joplin had taken a very pure dose.

Although Joplin was sometimes criticized for screaming and screeching and neglecting subtlety, it was not in her nature to be demure or quiet. *Pearl*, though, showed that she could ably and equally handle rock, blues, and soul music. It wound up becoming her signature record and a tragic promise of what she could have achieved had she lived. The album gave listeners the classic Joplin songs such as the goofy, tongue-in-cheek ode to consumption "Mercedes Benz," a take on Howard Tate's soul ballad "Get it While You Can," and her own attention-grabbing composition "Move Over" as the opening track. Most notably, though, *Pearl* included the Kris Kristofferson–penned "Me and Bobby McGee," for which she perhaps is most known and which became a number one single in 1971. She covered it in a live performance, just accompanying herself on acoustic guitar, while touring before the album was released. Sadly, it was the beginning and end of her foray into her country roots. Although the song had been recorded by Roger Miller, most music did not cross over at the time into other audiences, so when she sang it, to her audience the song was a new sound. One of the more poignant moments of the album, though, is "Buried Alive in the Blues," an apt metaphor for her relationship to her career, perhaps. There were no vocals for the track, so the instrumental, absent her signature voice, feels like a tribute or an oddly rousing elegy.

### Fame After Death

After Joplin died, her music helped keep her name alive and gain her new fans. To date, *Pearl* has gone platinum four times and *Cheap Thrills* triple platinum, but Janis Joplin's *Greatest Hits* beats them all, coming in at seven times platinum. The album *Joplin in Concert*, in addition to recording her live performances, warts and all, also makes plain the fact that Joplin was starting to fall apart. It includes a number of memorable performances, including "Piece of My Heart" and "Kozmic Blues," going back to some of her work with Big

Brother and ending just a couple of months before her death, especially in her take of "Ball and Chain." The album is difficult to listen to in places when, for instance, Joplin rambles about how things have started to fall apart and the cruelty of life. Even though the audience cheers, the pain and despair in her voice is gut-wrenching. Listening to it now, with the knowledge of her life's tragic end, gives one the chills. Much of her music, in hindsight, becomes an unsettling portent.

Among the other posthumous releases is *Janis Joplin's Greatest Hits* (1973), a spare collection of twelve tracks including a couple of tunes she sang with Big Brother and the Holding Company. It gives listeners a fairly thorough representation of Joplin's art as well as a sense of her finest moments. *Essential Janis Joplin*, has a bigger gamut of material, with eighteen tracks, but does not contain, for example, the original recording of "Me and Bobby McGee." The longer *18 Essential Songs* was released in 1995. But fans who seek a comprehensive catalog of Joplin's work should look into the three-CD boxed set *Janis*, released in 1993, which contains songs with and without Big Brother, including early material such as "What Good Can Drinkin' Do" along with an acoustic demo of "Me and Bobby McGee" and an eight-minute version of "Ball and Chain" from Big Brother's first set at Monterey Pop Festival. This boxed set provides listeners with a comprehensive overview of her career and a healthy dose of extras and rarities.

Subsequent to Joplin's death, her work developed a cult following among those who emerged from the scene and women and men who felt underrepresented among her generation. Fans reacted strongly to her loss because they felt that she was just like them; the outcast who never went to the prom in high school or was asked to participate in anything. She became a warning, though, to those who grew up in the so-called Age of Aquarius who, like her, partied and lived hard. It is poignant that none of them seemed surprised by her death. Critics, however, mourned in their obituaries for Joplin about the needless loss caused by abuse of chemicals by the disenfranchised whose pain was ignored by society.

## MISSION, MOTIVATION, PROCESS

Joplin was not a participant in the acts of racial hatred that many of her peers in Port Arthur perpetuated; instead, she believed in racial equality. When she was in high school, her friends were mostly male who introduced her to blues and jazz, which was risqué and looked down on in her small town because it was practiced by and listened to mostly by African American people. Her musical preferences fed her already growing discontent with her small town— Joplin had already gotten in trouble in school, for example, for speaking up in class in favor of integration. The experience helped her form a sense of her own intelligence and exposed her to music that spoke to her. Her younger sister, Laura Joplin, described Janis's experience with her friends: "They took music very seriously . . . they would have a party and would lie down on the floor with their eyes shut, then someone would put on a cut and they would try to identify it" (Jackson 2005, 206). These friends exposed her to a form of music more expressive than the sterile 1960s pop that permeated the "cheerleader culture" of her hometown. Part of that music was Huddie "Leadbelly" Ledbetter and Bessie Smith, who Joplin considered honest artists and who she preferred to whatever she heard on the radio. Additionally, in the early days, Joplin mimicked Bessie Smith and sang a lot of her songs, but not simply as an exercise in blind adulation. For Joplin, it meant that she was consciously turning her choirgirl soprano into a much more throaty, dusky wail of a voice. Joplin learned from Smith that you could sing not only with some kind of proficiency but that you could sing from the heart as well. Joplin wanted to be tough, but in truth, she was hurting, so the tough-but-tender persona of the blues suited her. For most of her career, she operated with this approach; at first she was self-conscious and answered a lot of questions about it, but as her career started to develop momentum, in particular in her days with Big Brother, she began to internalize the process of mimicking and turn it into her own style.

Joplin knew her limitations, knew what people were saying about her style, not to mention the political ramifications of a white woman singing like a black woman. In the recording sessions for the Big Brother album *Cheap Thrills*, Joplin was criticized by producer John Simon for being too studied because she planned where to place a moan, a wail, or a shriek and was thus not spontaneous. Other producers thought her approach was shrewd because she thoughtfully laid out her interpretation of a song to its most powerful emotional impact.

Joplin is not typically identified as a songwriter—indeed, she is more known for her performances and the imprimatur she has placed on every song she covered—but one song she did write while in Port Arthur was the autobiographical "Turtle Blues," which first appears on *Cheap Thrills* in which she sings about acting tough but knowing she's not. Another song she wrote early in her life, "What Good Can Drinkin' Do," also contains autobiographical elements—it shows how fruitless it is to drink away your problems. This song appears on the boxed set *Janis* and is believed to be the first time her singing was recorded.

Prior to her making it with Big Brother and the Holding Company and then on her own, Joplin spent much of her time denying her own ambition. In many ways, it is easy to see how her difficult childhood in a conservative town, her intelligence that she generally hid, and her insecurities dovetailed to create a troubled young woman, but such an assessment oversimplifies her life. Joplin's desire for attention was something that drove her into many liaisons—men and women, sexual and platonic—and fueled her toward periods of addiction to drugs, although alcohol was almost always a presence in her social life. But such a cursory judgment discounts the real artistic impact she has made on the world of rock and roll. It also does not account for her understanding of social equality, her beliefs about racial injustice, and her unusual affinity for the material that makes up the blues. Joplin's honesty in her music has been one of her greatest assets; she was not afraid to experience life and show her feelings. She said that she was not trying to be the next Bessie Smith: Her feeling was that culturally speaking, African American people were permitted to and indeed needed to express their hardships through singing and that white people generally did not permit themselves such honesty, because, racial issues aside, it is difficult and painful.

*She had an unshakable commitment to her own truth, no matter how destructive, how weird or how bad. This was a full-blown one-of-a-kind woman—no stylist, no publicist, no image-maker. It was just Janis.*

—Rosanne Cash

## LEGACY AND OTHER INTERESTS

Joplin's legacy lives on through the countless female musicians she inspired, and in the stories, books, films, and theater works about her life and her music. For example, the 1979 film *The Rose* starring Bette Midler is a loose adaptation of her life story but is true to her on-stage presence, its power, and her subsequent off-stage weaknesses.

What is perhaps most consistently examined by scholars, critics, and fans is the fact that Joplin's music became so much more immensely popular after her death; her story took on the form of a myth. She is one of many artists from that era who died before the age of thirty, along with Jim Morrison and Jimi Hendrix, other musicians from the 1960s whose lives were a heady mix of addiction, rock and roll, fame, and emotional fragility. Joplin's career eerily reflects that of one of her idols, Bessie Smith, whose career was also marred by alcohol and drugs. Joplin was compared to Elvis Presley, James Dean, and Sylvia Plath. Some critics believe that Joplin was rock and roll's first martyr. Such thinking tends to reduce her to a cautionary tale and overlook her contributions; Joplin was, however, the first significant female musician of the rock and roll era to meet such a tragic end

But if Joplin was the first martyr among female rock musicians, she may also have been the first truly significant and willing female sex symbol. Despite any perceived weaknesses or shortcomings or inability to look like a stereotypical, mainstream beauty of the late 1960s, the type of a woman whose shoes and purses almost certainly matched and whose hair was certainly not wild and unkempt, Joplin became an unlikely and new kind of sex symbol. Her personality—strong and uncompromising—and her attire, wild even by the standards of Haight-Ashbury, somehow made her attractive. In 1967,

*Janis Joplin sings the blues as hard as any black person.*

—B.B. King

San Francisco photographer Bob Seidemann created a poster from his portrait of her clothed only in love beads. It made her an unlikely pin-up in Haight-Ashbury but a pin-up nonetheless. It also upset her family considerably, who by this time in her career could not understand her life. Her onstage persona was probably more responsible for their discomfort than anything she did offstage or on a record. Her performances could create a frenzy: Women would faint, and men would jump onstage to kiss her. Outside that world, Joplin was still considered freakish, but most of mainstream America considered hippies freaks anyway.

Her hometown, though, never forgot her, even if at times the conservative town did not understand her. Her parents often received threatening and obscene phone calls during Joplin's time as a singer, and after her death, they received phone calls of laughter. Still, in 1988, about 5000 residents sang "Me and Bobby McGee" as a bust of Janis Joplin was revealed, which now sits in the Port Arthur Library.

Joplin's life and the Austin, Texas music scene have been the subject of a documentary called *Janis Joplin Slept Here* (1994) by Tara Veneruso. In 2006–2007, a biographical musical was mounted called *Love, Janis*, that combined her music, musings, and life story as inspired by the book her sister Laura Joplin wrote of the same title. The musical, when performed by the Kansas City Repertory Theatre, set box office records in Kansas City. The success of the films *Ray* about Ray Charles and *Walk the Line* about Johnny and June Carter Cash, which were produced in 2004 and 2005, respectively, and each winners of Academy Awards, gave director Penelope Spheeris the idea to do a film about Janis Joplin. The film is in production, tentatively slated for release in 2010, called *The Gospel According to Janis*; initially, the brash singer Pink was signed to play Joplin, but actress and budding singer Zooey Deschanel has replaced her in the title role. Other actresses who were up for the role include Lindsay Lohan, Britney Spears, and Scarlett Johansson. Texas native and actress Renée Zellweger is associated with another film called *Piece of My Heart* that chronicles Joplin's life but the film does not yet have a director.

## SELECTED DISCOGRAPHY

*I Got Dem Ol' Kozmic Blues Again Mama!* Columbia, 1969
*Pearl.* Columbia, 1971
*Joplin in Concert.* Columbia, 1972
*Janis Joplin's Greatest Hits.* Columbia, 1973
*Janis.* Columbia, 1993
*18 Essential Songs.* Columbia, 1995
*Box of Pearls.* Sony/Legacy, 1999

# FURTHER READING

Bangs, Lester. "Janis Joplin: In Concert." *Rolling Stone* 110 (June 8, 1972). Available online at www.rollingstone.com/artists/janisjoplin/albums/album/152830/review/5942155/in_concert.

Burks, John. "I Got Dem Ol' Kozmic Blues Again Mama! Review." *Rolling Stone* 45 (November 1, 1969). Available online at www.rollingstone.com/artists/janisjoplin/albums/album/93275/review/5541359/i_got_dem_ol_kozmic_blues_again_mama.

Cash, Rosanne. "The Immortals: The Fifty Greatest Artists of All Time." *Rolling Stone* 946 (April 15, 2004). Available online at www.rollingstone.com/artists/janisjoplin/articles/story/5939239/46_janis_joplin.

Echols, Alice. *Scars of Sweet Paradise: The Life and Times of Janis Joplin.* New York: Metropolitan Books, 1999.

Evans, Paul and Richard Skanse. "Janis Joplin biography." *Rolling Stone* online; excerpt from The New Rolling Stone Album Guide. New York: Simon and Schuster, 2004. Available online at http://www.rollingstone.com/artists/janisjoplin/biography.

Friedman, Myra. *Buried Alive: The Biography of Janis Joplin.* New York: William Morrow and Company, 1973.

Hardin, John. "Cheap Thrills Review." *Rolling Stone* 17 (September 14, 1968). Available online at www.rollingstone.com/artists/bigbrotherandtheholdingcompany/albums/album/145787/review/6067715/cheap_thrills.

Heckman, Don. "Janis Joplin, 1943–1970." *New York Times* (October 11, 1970).

Jackson, Buzzy. *A Bad Woman Feeling Good: Blues and the Women Who Sing Them.* New York: W.W. Norton, 2005.

Nelson, Paul. "Janis: The Judy Garland of Rock?" *Rolling Stone* 29 (March 15, 1969).

Official Janis Joplin Estate Web site. See www.officialjanis.com.

Ruhlmann, William, and Bruce Eder. "Cheap Thrills review." *All Music Guide.* Available online at wm09.allmusic.com/cg/amg.dll?p=amg&sql=10:3ifrxql5ldfe.

Unterberger, Richie. "I Got Dem Ol' Kozmic Blues Again Mama! Review." *All Music Guide.* Available online at www.allmusic.com/cg/amg.dll?p=amg&sql=10:gzfexqrdldhe.

Walters, Barry. "Pearl." *Rolling Stone* online (June 16, 2005). Available online at www.rollingstone.com/artists/janisjoplin/albums/album/187603/review/7371337/pearl.

Zito, Tom. "The Death of Janis Joplin." *Washington Post* (October 6, 1970).